*Language Learning
by a Chimpanzee*
THE LANA PROJECT

This is the first volume of a series entitled

COMMUNICATION AND BEHAVIOR
AN INTERDISCIPLINARY SERIES

Under the Editorship of Duane M. Rumbaugh,
*Georgia State University and Yerkes Regional
Primate Research Center of Emory University*

Language Learning by a Chimpanzee
THE LANA PROJECT

EDITED BY

Duane M. Rumbaugh

Department of Psychology
Georgia State University
and The Yerkes Regional Primate
Research Center of Emory University
Atlanta, Georgia

ACADEMIC PRESS   New York   San Francisco   London
A Subsidiary of Harcourt Brace Jovanovich, Publishers

ACADEMIC PRESS, INC.
111 Fifth Avenue, New York, New York 10003

United Kingdom Edition published by
ACADEMIC PRESS, INC. (LONDON) LTD.
24/28 Oval Road, London NW1

Library of Congress Cataloging in Publication Data

Main entry under title:

Language learning by a Chimpanzee
(Communication and Behavior series)

    Includes bibliographies.
    1.   Chimpanzees–Psychology.   2.   Animal communication
3.   Language and languages–Origin.   I.   Rumbaugh,
Duane M., Date   II.   Title.
QL737.P96L36   156'.3   76–27451
ISBN 0-12-601850-2

Lana Chimpanzee

Contents

vii

chapter 2
Linguistic Communication:
Theory and Definition   *55*

ERNST VON GLASERSFELD

chapter 3
Cross-Modal Perception:
A Basis for Language?   *73*

RICHARD K. DAVENPORT

PART II
Design of the LANA Project

chapter 4
The LANA Project:
Origin and Tactics   *87*

DUANE M. RUMBAUGH, HAROLD WARNER, AND

ERNST VON GLASERSFELD

PART III
Lana's Mastery of Language-Type Skills

PART IV
Projects for the Future

PART V
Language and Communication: A Perspective

chapter 16
Communication, Language, and Lana: A Perspective

E. SUE SAVAGE AND DUANE M. RUMBAUGH

Chronological Bibliography of LANA Project Publications

List of Contributors

Numbers in parentheses indicate the pages on which the authors' contributions begin.

Charles L. Bell (143, 263), Yerkes Regional Primate Research Center of Emory University, Atlanta, Georgia

Josephine V. Brown (263), Department of Psychology, Georgia State University, Atlanta, Georgia, and Yerkes Regional Primate Research Center of Emory University, Atlanta, Georgia

Richard K. Davenport (73), School of Psychology, Georgia Institute of Technology, Atlanta, Georgia, and Yerkes Regional Primate Research Center of Emory University, Atlanta, Georgia

Gwendolyn B. Dooley (247), Department of Psychology, Georgia State University, Atlanta, Georgia, and Yerkes Regional Primate Research Center of Emory University, Atlanta, Georgia

Susan M. Essock (193, 207), Department of Psychology, Walter S. Hunter Laboratory of Psychology, Brown University, Providence, Rhode Island, and Yerkes Regional Primate Research Center of Emory University, Atlanta, Georgia

Timothy V. Gill (157, 165, 193, 225, 247), Yerkes Regional Primate Research Center of Emory University, Atlanta, Georgia, and Department of Psychology, Georgia State University, Atlanta, Georgia

Gordon Winant Hewes (3), Department of Anthropology, University of Colorado, Boulder, Colorado

Dorothy A. Parkel (273), Research Department, Georgia Retardation Center, Atlanta, Georgia, and Yerkes Regional Primate Research Center of Emory University, Atlanta, Georgia

Pier Paolo Pisani (131), Computer Center, University of Georgia, Athens, Georgia, and Yerkes Regional Primate Research Center of Emory University, Atlanta, Georgia

Duane M. Rumbaugh (87, 157, 165, 193, 287), Department of Psychology, Georgia State University, Atlanta, Georgia, and Yerkes Regional Primate Research Center of Emory University, Atlanta, Georgia

E. Sue Savage (287), Department of Psychology, Georgia State University, Atlanta, Georgia, and Yerkes Regional Primate Research Center of Emory University, Atlanta, Georgia

Ernst von Glasersfeld (55, 87, 91), Department of Psychology, University of Georgia, Athens, Georgia, and Yerkes Regional Primate Research Center of Emory University, Atlanta, Georgia

Harold Warner (87, 143, 263, 273), Yerkes Regional Primate Research Center of Emory University, Atlanta, Georgia

Royce A. White (273), Research Department, Georgia Retardation Center, Atlanta, Georgia, and Yerkes Regional Primate Research Center of Emory University, Atlanta, Georgia

Foreword

The contents of this volume bring joy to those who have been working with nonhuman primates in a quest for an answer to the question: What makes man human? Heschel has pointed out that whereas medieval man searched for the meaning of God, modern man is attempting to define himself. Project LANA goes a long way in pointing the directions from which such definitions might come.

The volume is composed of two sets of data; only one relates to language learning in the chimpanzee. The other, equally interesting, deals with language construction by *Homo sapiens*. Project LANA thus brings together several disciplinary endeavors: primatology, experimental psychology, cognitive psychology, the computer and information sciences and by indirection, the neurosciences, as well. And, of course, the fundamental issue of mind-brain dualism—the difference between man and beast—is the philosophical issue that sparks the entire program.

I found that a great deal can be learned about human language from a careful reading of the early chapters of this volume. The deliberations of von Glasersfeld, Pisani, and their colleagues in constructing *Yerkish* tell us much about "the state of the art" of human communication analyses. Descriptions of information concepts are basic and clearly presented. The definition of communicative language as the symbolic use of lexical signs should be acceptable to even the most ardent adherent to structural linguistics. However, the problem as to how an arbitrary (i.e., context-dependent) symbolic use of lexical (i.e., context-free) signs comes about is not made completely clear. The rules of grammatical construction are invoked—but are they primary or derivative from a more basic mechanism—as suggested by Savage and Rumbaugh in their summary chapter. Whichever, the artful implementation of the lexical multistore parser and of a correlational grammar (with its stated relation to case grammars) attests to the fertility of the human brain in dealing with this basic problem.

But what about language learning in the chimpanzee? A theme recurs throughout the volume and is made explicit in the final chapter by Savage and Rumbaugh: Language is based on distancing a representation from that which is represented. In human language, as noted, this distancing takes the form of an arbitrary use of the representation. What about the communicative behavior of Lana and the other apes? Davenport makes an excellent point in his chapter when he asks whether cross-modal perception is a prerequisite for such distancing. Besides documenting the just recently demonstrated cross-modal ability of nonhuman primates, he raises the question of mechanism. The classical association areas of primates are remarkable for their sensory specificity and are thus poor candidates. However, microelectrode studies have delineated areas that are primarily polysensory. Many of these areas turn out to be motor areas in primates. Perhaps cross-modal "association" and "transfer" occur by way of "doing"—exercising the motor areas of the brain.

Of course the major contribution of Project LANA stems from Lana's performance. Only 5 years ago, at the International Congress of Psychology in Tokyo, comparative psychologists held a symposium on the state of their field. The tone was rather gloomy. They had not heard of the chimpanzee's challenge to the uniqueness of man. Washoe, Sarah, and Lana—and a whole new generation of scientists and apes are attempting to spell the end of Cartesian dualism. At a recent conference at the Yerkes laboratories celebrating the centenary of Robert Yerkes, its founder, Fouts suggested that a good deal of philosophical anguish could have been spared if Descartes could only have observed today's nonhuman primates. Rumbaugh and his colleagues are more cautious. They fully realize that they are providing the context, writing the programs, generating the languages that are being aped.

This perhaps characterizes the major difference between Project LANA and the other nonhuman communication experiments. Computer control adds the precise specification of who is doing what within the communicative matrix. In my own work, devising and using DADTA (Discrimination Apparatus for Discrete Trial Analysis), a computer controlled system for behavioral analysis, I found that, aside from achieving undreamed-of power in testing, a new level of precision was required in my own thinking about problems. This volume attests to the fact that this new level has now also become a requirement in the analysis of language learning by apes. The expressed hope of its authors, a hope I fully share, is that this necessary sophistication will lead to a better understanding of language learning in children—especially in children who for one reason or another do not share our usual fluency. Perhaps by the time the sequel to this volume is written we shall be able to do better than just say "for one reason or another."

KARL H. PRIBRAM

Preface

The evolution of animal life has produced an immense variety of forms adapted for living in just about every conceivable niche on planet Earth. None of these forms has failed to arouse keen interest among scientists, but one form, the Primates, seems particularly relevant to efforts that would describe and define man, since it is within this order that man himself, according to taxonomists, belongs. So far as man's origins are concerned, however, this classification has raised more questions than it has answered. What is the phylogeny of man in relation to that of other primates and particularly the great apes—the chimpanzee, gorilla, and orang-utan? In what ways are we different from the apes? How many of our psychological attributes are basic characteristics of primates in general and are therefore best understood from a comparative perspective?

If any single attribute of man stands out above all others, it is his egocentrism. Humans have long been prone to view themselves as the focal point of nature if not the universe. We have been ready to promote our own immediate welfare to the detriment of nature and of all other species, and even at the risk of our own ultimate survival. Our generalized biological structure coupled with our advanced intelligence has allowed us to examine the basic processes of nature and, consequently, to extend our ability to survive to all quarters of this planet and beyond. In all probability, our refined intelligence more than anything else has spawned our egocentrism. Be that as it may, we have long engaged in intensive studies to determine the ways in which we are unique and distinctive from other forms of animal life, even from the form most closely related to us—the apes. Much less energy has gone into the definition of points of similarity between man and other animals.

Frank declarations that we are so unique that we cannot be understood through behavioral studies of other primates or other animals in general are no longer tenable. Recent studies of the many disciplines that make up the field of primatology have served to underscore the similarities and not the differences between humans and other primates, and we may now reasonably conclude that morphologically and biologically we are no more distinctive than any other species within the primates. Each form is distinctive, and more and more, the dimensions of human distinctiveness appear to be quantitative rather than qualitative. Behaviorally, for example, we are known for certain capabilities which until very recent years have been held as reflections of unique potential. *Homo sapiens*, for example, had been thought to be *the* tool user, but it is now known that the chimpanzee not only uses tools but also modifies natural materials to make the tools he uses. To date, we appear to be the only form that manufactures tools with which to make other tools, but is doing so anything other than a *quantitative* extension of the basic tool-using behaviors? I think not.

At least one behavioral expression, however, does distinguish us, and that is the acquisition of an infinitely *open* system of communication, a system we call *language*. But what are the requisites for the acquisition of language? To what extent can language be understood as an orderly, natural extension of other animals' communication systems? To what extent should it be defined in terms of performance/expressive characteristics? To what extent does human language reflect refinements in the oral–aural channels? To what extent does language reflect the basic operations of the human brain and are these operations shared with other primate species?

The past decade has produced reports which strongly suggest that language in at least rudimentary form can be mastered by apes, although the behaviors which support this conclusion are not vocal. Does that mean that those skills are basically not linguistic? Or does it mean that language should not be viewed solely as use of the voice? In short, should language be defined in exclusively human terms? Or should it be defined in terms of mastery of psychological skills which allow for an open communication system?

And of what significance is it, moreover, if the ape can master language? What would it mean for our definition of *H. sapiens*? We cannot begin to answer these questions definitively, but to begin with, it would surely suggest that man's psychological resemblance to the apes is much closer than we previously conjectured even in recent years. Might apes be used as subjects in research projects in which ethical constraints preclude the use of children? Might our studies of apes with language skills assist us in the definitions of *man*? Of ourselves in relation to other primates? Of language?

This book is addressed to only some of these questions. Its main purpose is to provide a report of what has come to be known as the LANA Project, a project whose aim was to develop a computer-based language-training system for investigation into the possibility that chimpanzees may have the capacity to acquire human-type language. The name LANA is an acronym for the more formal, complete title of the project—the *LAN*guage Analogue Project. It is also the name of the young chimpanzee selected as the subject of the project. In actual fact, the project was named after Lana, rather than vice versa, because we felt that her identity was well worth preserving.

Lana was born at the Yerkes Primate Center on October 7, 1970. Although she came to be well known in many quarters, there is no reason to conclude that she was other than an average laboratory chimpanzee. After 6 weeks with her mother, she was transferred to the Center's nursery where she was maintained in the company of other young apes.

Prior to the commencement of actual training with lexigrams in the computer-controlled environment, Lana (age 1½ years) had training on two different tasks. The first of these involved use of child's "surprise box," a toy consisting of five switches or buttons that when activated resulted in the appearance of a plastic figure of an animal from behind a plastic door. Lana's task was to operate successfully three or four of the latches in any order and then to depress the leftmost button to signal that she was done. After successfully completing a trial, she received a small food reward. The second task was a matching-to-sample task, using hand-drawn lexigrams from the Yerkish vocabulary as the samples. On any given trial Lana had to point to the sample lexigram given (a food name) and then pick the same lexigram out of a row of lexigrams that initially contained two alternatives and eventually four alternatives, only one of which was correct. Initially the two alternative lexigrams were from different classes (i.e., food and verbs), which allowed Lana to match for color only; as more alternatives were introduced, color was no longer a reliable indicator of the correct answer and Lana had to discriminate between the actual lexigrams involved on any one trial.

Lana's formal language training commenced when she was 2¼ years old.

The LANA Project has been made possible through the joint efforts of a number of people. A team of scientists with diverse interests, skills, and backgrounds has worked through countless issues and questions to define the essence of the system. The contributions of each member of the team will be documented in various ways throughout the course of this book. In addition, the project has benefited from the generous encouragement and cooperation of Dr. Geoffrey H. Bourne, Director of the Yerkes Primate Research Center of Emory University, the home institution for the LANA Project. At many junctures the moral support and encouragement extended to us by numerous friends and professionals has been very important to the success of the project.

Financial support for the LANA Project has been provided by a grant from the National Institute of Child Health and Human Development (NICHD–06016) of the National Institutes of Health and, in part by support from the Animal Resources Branch of the National Institutes of Health to the Yerkes Regional Primate Research Center (RR-00155). The cooperation of the administrations of Georgia State University and the University of Georgia has also been vital.

The project described in this book was actually a pilot study conceived to determine whether or not certain approaches to language study might be feasible. Since the results have been far more impressive than what had been anticipated, we concluded that the LANA Project warrants report in book form, despite the fact that it constitutes only a beginning of one type of investigation into the linguistic abilities of primates other than man. (Because the chapters of this book deal with very specific subject or project materials, no comprehensive index is warranted.)

I wish to express my deep appreciation to Judy Sizemore, Linda S. Smith, and Beth Prouty for their very able assistance in the preparation of the manuscripts for the publication of this book.

DUANE M. RUMBAUGH

PART I

Language Theory and Foundations

chapter 1

Language Origin Theories

GORDON WINANT HEWES
University of Colorado

INTRODUCTION

The question of the origins of language has been debated for many centuries and has resulted in a massive literature scattered across many disciplines (Hewes, 1975). Although contributors to the ongoing argument include many of the most familiar figures in Western thought from Herodotus and Plato to Darwin, Wallace, and Wundt, some have held that the search for language origins is futile. Because the birth of language occurred at a remote epoch and left no reliable witnesses, they contend that it is beyond the reach of scientific reconstruction. This is a curious view inasmuch as some wholly respectable scientific thinking is devoted to events that were also unwitnessed and far more remote in time, such as the formation of galaxies or the origin of life on this planet. *Origins of Life,* for example, is an impeccably scientific journal. John Keosian (1974) observes that those who believe life arose suddenly tend to be preoccupied with defining it precisely, whereas those who see life as having emerged gradu-

3

ally from nonliving systems are more interested in mechanisms at various stages of its emergence. For them "it becomes meaningless to draw a line between two levels of organization and to designate all systems below as inanimate and all systems above as living [p. 285]." His observation may contain an instructive parallel for those who venture to consider glottogenesis.

EARLY IDEAS ABOUT LANGUAGE ORIGIN

Alf Sommerfelt divided glottogonic theorizing into two great periods: pre- and post-Darwinian. During the former, most Western thinkers regarded man as the product of special creation endowed with unique and divinely instituted capacities, including the capacity for language. In Darwin's time, prevailing educated opinion placed the Creation about 6000 years earlier, a date that made it difficult to account for the complexities of existing languages in other than a miraculous fashion. Serious and concentrated intellectual concern with glottogenesis has had three peaks, all within the past three centuries. The first was abstract and theoretical, and was constrained by the absurdly brief geochronological framework based on Biblical tradition; it culminated in the Berlin Academy essay competition of 1769–1772. The next surge of interest came in the two decades after 1860; it was stimulated by Darwinism, and reinforced by more than 50 years of comparative philology. It remains to be seen how long the third, present, revival of interest in glottogonic problems will last; I would like to think that this time we may be able to develop a scientific consensus or paradigm.

In the appendix to this chapter (pages 43–50) the main types of glottogonic theories are listed. To arrive at an even simpler typology of language origin theories is more difficult, since the present theories are cross-cut in several dimensions, according to different criteria. Thus, they could be divided into *supernatural,* in which language is considered a divine gift; *metaphysical,* where language is the manifestation of some abstract principle, such as the "need to communicate"; or *scientific,* as the product of natural biological and environmental factors and processes. Another way to characterize glottogonic theories is in terms of the *initial modality* supposedly employed: (a) vocal–auditory utterances, (b) gestural visual signing, or (c) entirely internal cognitive codes, the externalization of which in any particular sensory mode might be regarded with indifference. Language origin theories may be separated into those that insist only *human beings* can create and maintain language, and those that regard language as part of a *behavioral continuum,* in which the effort to determine the precise point at which nonlanguage animal communication becomes "language" is scientifically unproductive. Glottogonic theories could be classified on the basis of the *nature of their signs:* (a) iconic representations of external objects, actions, or attributes, (b) by-products of endogenous motor behavior, or (c) emotional responses somehow later reduced to conventional signs. The reader is invited to develop still other typologies.

The origin of language is a motif in many mythical traditions, although it is a mistake to suppose that the familiar account in Genesis has had no more influence than any other ancient tale. The Chinese, for example, do not seem to have subjected their glottogonic myth to serious exegesis, and the same can be said of the Hindus. Borst (1957–1963) provides an excellent survey of ancient beliefs about language beginnings. The Biblical account left out just enough details to stimulate endless debate. Although we are told how Adam named the animals paraded before him in the Garden, it is not clear whether Adam's language came to him as a ready-made skill, or arose from his built-in intelligence and anatomical structure. The story of the later confusion of tongues at Babel, leaves equally interesting possibilities for different interpretations. While orthodox Jewish tradition held that Adam's language was Hebrew, a position accepted by the majority of ancient and medieval Christian writers on the subject, the Bible itself on this point is silent. It is also significant that the Judaeo–Christian glottogonic myth was prominently placed at the very beginning of the Scriptures, where it could never be overlooked by any Bible scholar. The holy books of the other great world religions, including the scriptures of Islam, do not accord glottogenesis any such prominent billing.

Probably some time prior to the final priestly redaction of the Old Testament, an Egyptian king, Psammetichus, conducted a pioneer psycholinguistic experiment to determine which language was the most ancient. According to Herodotus, who reported it, the king ordered the isolation of two infants, who were not to be exposed to language until they were around 2 years old. When released, they uttered, *"bekos! bekos!"* interpreted to mean "bread" in Phrygian. Thus the monarch was satisfied that that language was even more ancient than Egyptian. It has been pointed out by later commentators that *bek,* the first syllable of the word the infants supposedly uttered minus the Greek masculine nominative case-ending, comes very close to the bleating of goats, on whose milk the isolated infants had been raised.

GREEK, ROMAN, AND EARLY CHRISTIAN VIEWS

Greek thinkers disagreed on the question of whether language was divinely instituted or humanly invented, and on whether the sounds of words were arbitrary conventions or had some significant phonetic relationship to their referents. This issue was the topic of the *Cratylus Dialogue* of Plato, ca. 400 B.C. Cratylus contends that names were attached to referents by divine mandate, but Socrates thinks otherwise. Socrates also observes that if human beings lacked vocal powers, all men would use gestures as do the deaf. Language is likened to a tool; the felicitous metaphor, "the loom of language," stems from this dialogue. Basically, the argument concerned not the origin of language, but the nature of names for things. The Epicureans believed that language was a natural human creation, not a gift of the gods. The Stoics thought that words had originated in onomatopoeia. The Romans were less interested in the origins of language than the Greeks (although the poet Lucretius, first century B.C., did provide a good statement of the Epicurean position). Instead, they were more concerned with rhetoric and the study of grammar for literary and oratorical purposes. A substantial amount of Roman material concerning the use of gestures in oratory and on the stage has come down to us.

Early Christian writers generally followed Jewish tradition on language origins. Gregory of Nyssa was unusual in suggesting that man had been created with a natural capacity to invent language. Augustine did not cope directly with the problem, although he did discuss child language acquisition and the role of ostensive definition therein; he also dealt with signs and referents in a sophisticated manner. Muslim scholars believed in the divine origin of language, substituting Classical Arabic for Hebrew as the primordial tongue and language of Paradise. Grammatical scholarship eventually revived in the Western world and was carried forward beyond the levels attained by the Greeks and Romans, but the question of how man first acquired language was not really debated; those interested were referred to Genesis. Dante assumed that God had transmitted language to Adam, probably in the form of Hebrew. [See Borst's comprehensive *Turmbau von Babel* (1957–1963) for an extensive treatment of medieval and Renaissance ideas about language origins.]

Worldwide voyages of discovery starting in the fifteenth century brought in new information about languages, and it began to be suggested in the sixteenth century that perhaps not all the newly discovered peoples were descended from Adam and Eve or the dispersion following Babel. C.-G. Dubois (1970) provides a survey of sixteenth-century European notions about glottogenesis. The weakening of centralized Roman Catholic orthodoxy led some to suggest that Adam had not spoken Hebrew, but rather one or another European vernacular such as Frisian or Danish, or even Chinese.

SEVENTEENTH-CENTURY EUROPEAN SPECULATIONS

It was not until the seventeenth century, however, that speculations about language were able to break away from the old theological constraints. At the beginning of the century, Francis Bacon discussed signs and their referents, and the uses of gesture to express ideas. In 1620 Louis Crésol asserted that the hands had made language possible, and wrote a lengthy treatise on various aspects of what would now be called "nonverbal communication." In 1661 Dalgarno suggested that gestures had possessed communicative power for a long time before the rise of speech; John Bulwer devoted a book to manual gesture in 1644. On voyages far from Europe, explorers and merchants made considerable use of sign language to communicate with people whose spoken languages they did not know (Hewes, 1974).

The seventeenth century also saw a bitter debate over the extent to which nonhuman animals have reason. This controversy has been studied by George Boas (1933, 1973), and has had some influence on glottogonic speculation to this day. Against the ideas of Montaigne and others, René Descartes (1637) asserted that beasts were mere automata or machines, whereas man alone of all earthly creatures, though his body too was only a machine, possessed feelings and reason. The criterion of man's unique rationality was his possession of language, the "faculty of arranging together different words, and composing a discourse from them." Noam Chomsky revived this notion along with some additions to Cartesian linguistic thought made by the grammarians of the Abbey of Port-Royal later in the seventeenth century (Chomsky, 1966). Pierre Gassendi (1644) wrote a most effective criticism of Descartes' position, but Descartes' *Discours sur le Méthode* (1637), one of the first major philosophical works published in French, seems to have attracted far more readers than Gassendi's ponderously Latin *Disquisitio Metaphysica*.

An extensive modern critical literature deals with the seventeenth-century language debate, which was only a warm-up for the debate over the same topic that followed in the eighteenth century. Different aspects of the earlier debate are discussed by Aarsleff (1971), Chouillet (1972), Chomsky (1966), Formigari (1970), Gunderson (1964), Knowlson (1965), Megill (1974), and Vendler (1972). T. H. Huxley, writing in 1875 (1893), also carefully examined the Cartesian arguments along with their eighteenth-century reflections in connection with the man–animal dichotomy. In the eighteenth century, the problem of the bête–machine attracted the attention of Samuel Butler, Defoe, Addison, Lord Shaftsbury, Berkeley, Pope, Samuel Johnson, Diderot, Rousseau, and especially de la Mettrie (cf. Sugg, 1968).

In 1668 Geraud de Cordemoy, writing from a Cartesian standpoint, dwelt on language as the criterion of man's distinctiveness; unlike Descartes, he believed that thought could occur without language (cf. Ross, B., Ed., 1972:ix). Cordemoy was aware of the logical difference between speech and language (1668). He paid attention to children's language, noting that as children are touched or shown something by the hand, "at length they learn the name of it [p. 26]."

Another offshoot of the thinking about language that took place during the seventeenth century was the notion that perfect, logical languages could be devised artificially, a notion first adumbrated by Francis Bacon in the *Advancement of Learning* (1605), and explicitly formulated both by Bishop John Wilkins in his *An Essay Toward a Real Character* (1668) and very ingeniously by Foigny and Vairasse (E. Pons, 1932) and Tyssot de Patot (Knowlson, 1963) in works of fiction. Leibniz (1768) and Comenius (1910, 1953 editions) (Jan Komenský) were also interested in these projects. Some recent critics of the languages used in experiments with chimpanzees apparently do not realize that Descartes himself would have accepted not only American Sign Language as a valid language system for testing man's supposed uniqueness as a language user, but also "Yerkish" and the plastic token language created by D. Premack (1970, 1974) (see also Chapters 2 and 4 of this volume). Some very incomplete information about Chinese writing as well as an effort to decipher Egyptian hieroglyphs also affected theories about artificial language during this period. Several of the ideas from seventeenth-century linguistic thought were later satirized in Jonathan Swift's *Gulliver's Travels* (1721–1726). Particularly striking was his satire of the man–beast issue.

Locke in *An Essay Concerning Human Understanding* (1690) discussed the semiotic (his term) and the artificial nature of words, but did not come to grips with glottogenesis, although his work deeply influenced much writing on that topic in the next century. The seventeenth century ended with the appearance of Edward Tyson's *Orang-Outang, sive Homo Sylvestris: or, The Anatomy of a Pygmie* (1699), which was actually a report on his dissection of a young chimpanzee. Tyson was struck by the numerous similarities between this specimen and man, notably in the brain and larynx, and he devotes some pages to the question of why such an animal could not speak. Already in 1661 Samuel Pepys had seen in London a live baboon—or just possibly, a chimpanzee—brought from Guinea, and he raised the same question in his diary, adding that if the creature could not learn speech, it might learn to communicate "by signs."

THE EIGHTEENTH-CENTURY ENLIGHTENMENT DEBATE ON LANGUAGE ORIGINS

The linguistic thought of the eighteenth century has provoked a large twentieth century critical analysis which centers particularly on the language origin debate. A. D. Megill's 1974 dissertation deals specifically with eighteenth-century linguistic thought in France and the German lands. Grimsley (1967) has written on the ideas of nature and language in the French Enlightenment; Aarsleff (1972) on the tradition of Condillac and the Berlin Academy competion; Josephs on Diderot's (1969) concern with gesture; Hastings (1936) on the eighteenth-century prolongation of the bête–machine argument; Gunderson (1964) on de la Mettrie; Knowlson (1965) on ideas about gesture as a universal language; Caldwell (1971) on Diderot's letter on the deaf-mutes; Salmon (1968) on Herder's language origin essay; Loi (1971) and Perkins (1967) on Rousseau's essay on the same topic; Rudowski (1974) and Seigel (1969) on the eighteenth-century theory of signs; Merker and Formigari (1973) on Herder and Monboddo; and Formigari (1971, 1974) on Maupertuis, Boindin, Turgot, and Maine de Biran. Much of the primary material is being reissued in critical editions or facsimile form.

Language origin speculation was highly fashionable in the eighteenth century. The four landmark works were Condillac's *Essay on the Origin of Human Understanding* (1746), with its obvious debt to Locke, Maupertuis' *Reflections on the Origin of Languages* (1756), Rousseau's two major essays—on *The Origins of Human Inequality* (1755) and the *Essay on the Origin of Language* (1761, 1772), and Herder's *Essay on the Origin of Speech* (1772), which won the Berlin Academy prize. Megill observes (1974) that the Enlightenment thinkers tended to be interested in the origins of all kinds of institutions, since the beginnings of anything were believed to hold the key to the understanding of their later character. Chouillet asks (1972, p. 41) whether the Cartesian insistence on language as the test of man's separation from the rest of earthly creation was what led to the marked eighteenth-century concern with language and whether the issue of origin was somehow implied by Descartes' position or was in contradiction to it.

Some eighteenth-century writers held that primordial language must have been handicapped by excessive use of metaphor and by an absence of general concepts. Onomatopoeia was seen as a prime example of "figurativeness." Other writers argued that to the contrary Adam's language must have been perfect, having been divinely inspired (cf. Page, 1972, on English ideas about these topics). In France, considerations of the plight of the congenitally deaf and blind were brought into the problem.

Vico

Giambattista Vico, though he wrote in the eighteenth century, had little in common with either French or English writers on language; Chouillet (1972) looks on Vico as a precursor of the Romantic view of language, which came into being several years after his writings were published. Vico imagined that language had begun in mime and then changed to onomatopoeic and interjectional vocal utterances long before it began to serve as a logical, prose vehicle. The earliest speech was monosyllabic and poetic. After the Deluge, Vico thought that perhaps man had to reinvent language, starting with gestures and physical objects (cf. Megill, 1974, Chap. 6). In 1719, the Abbé Jean-Baptise Dubos asserted that visual signs were inherently more communicative than speech-sounds and possibly more primitive (Rudowsky, 1974). In England, Bernard Mandeville (1670–1733) published *The Fable of the Bees* (1728),10 pages of which are devoted to glottogonic speculation. It includes the hypothetical situation of two young children isolated from all society, who might create a language for themselves, beginning with gestures. Guillaume Hyacinthe Bougéant claimed in 1739 that animals had their own language, and—seriously or not, we do not know—that the souls of animals might be the souls of demons.

Condillac

Étienne Bonnot de Condillac (1715–1780), who used to meet regularly for dinner with Rousseau and Diderot in Paris in the mid-1740s, reexamined Mandeville's hypothetical case of the two isolated children who develop language on the basis of their innate rational powers. Though careful to affirm the Biblical account of how language came to Adam in the Garden of Eden, Condillac supposed that man could reinvent it independently if necessary. The first language of these children, he wrote, could be the "language of action"—gestures, facial expression, body movement, and inarticulate vocalizations, which only later on would be transformed into speech. Aarsleff (1972), as already noted, has traced Condillac's influence on other eighteenth-century writers; they were to reappear especially in the thinking of the Idéologues, who wrote around 1800.

The Philosophes and Glottogenesis

Diderot, the editor of the *Encyclopédie,* did not write on glottogenesis as such, but was concerned with the cognitive and communicative problems of the blind (Diderot, 1749) and the deaf (Diderot, 1751), noting that the "natural order of ideas" might be revealed by a study of the sign language of the deaf. He also described how a person deaf from birth might be led to invent signs (Caldwell, 1971, p. 112). In a work that is supposedly a novel, *Le Neveu de Rameau* (belatedly published in incomplete form in 1805), much attention is paid to gesture (Josephs, 1969). In his capacity as editor for the *Encyclopédie,* however, Diderot commissioned many articles that deal with language and that bear on the glottogonic debate.

Pierre-Louis Moreau de Maupertuis (1698–1759) wrote *Réflexions Philosophiques sur l'Origine des Langues et la Signification des Mots* (1752) and *Dissertation sur les Différents Moyens dont les Hommes se Sont Servis Pour Exprimer Leurs Idées* (1756). Regarding language as a completely human invention, he claimed that gestures and emotional cries had evolved into language prior to the advent of articulate speech.

> If one could go back to the time when men did not have any sort of language, they would have sought to express their most pressing needs first, and certain gestures and cries would have sufficed for that. This was the first language of mankind, and it is still the one which all peoples understand, but it cannot render more than a small number of ideas. It was not until a long time afterward that they thought of other ways to express themselves. One could make this first language more extensive by adding to its natural gestures and cries, cries and gestures by convention, which would supplement what the first could not render, and it is that which they apparently first did [1768 ed., pp. 437–438; cf. Politzer, 1963].

Maupertuis observed that articulate speech, when developed, would have provided "a great number of articulations, combinable to infinity," causing the gesture language to decline except when it was needed to express the emotions.

Not everyone at this period insisted on the primacy of gesture language. Thomas Blackwell the younger, writing on Homer's works in 1735, assumed that man's first language was vocal, was composed of emotional cries, and was delivered in sing-song fashion. Supposedly resembling Chinese, it was monosyllabic and full of metaphor and onomatopoeic words taken "wholly from rough nature [Blackwell, 1735, Sect. III, pp. 36–48]."

In 1748 Julien Offray de la Mettrie issued his *L'Homme Machine*, a powerful attack on Cartesianism (critical ed., A. Vartanian (Ed.), 1960). Using the arguments employed by Descartes to show that animals were mere automata, de la Mettrie asserted that men were likewise automata and that the supposed proof of man's uniqueness and rationality could be undermined by teaching an ape to speak. De la Mettrie thought it quite likely that, with a properly qualified teacher such as someone accustomed to working with deaf human pupils, an anthropoid ape *(un grand singe)* could be turned into a "perfect little gentleman" by speech instruction. De la Mettrie may have known of Tyson's study of the chimpanzee. His suggestion of employing a teacher of the deaf strangely anticipates by almost 220 years the Gardners' experiment with the chimpanzee Washoe, except that they sought to develop a competence in the manual sign language of the deaf instead of speech. De la Mettrie did not think the task would be easy.

> Why might not an ape, by dint of great pains, at least imitate after the manner of deaf-mutes, the motions necessary for pronunciation? I do not dare to decide whether the ape's organs of speech, however trained, would be incapable of articulation. But because of the great analogy between ape and man and because there is no known animal whose external and internal organs so strikingly resemble man's, it would surprise me if speech were absolutely impossible for the ape [*L'Homme Machine*, 1912 ed., pp. 29–31, 100–102, cf. also Gunderson, 1964].

In 1779 Pieter Camper, an anatomist and artist, dissected an East Indian orangutan and concluded that speech would be impossible for such an animal—a judgment with which Georges Cuvier, the great comparative anatomist concurred after some acquaintance with a live orangutan and anatomical studies of his own.

Jean-Jacques Rousseau (1712–1778) first dealt with the topic of language origin in his celebrated "Second Discourse," the *Essai sur l'Origine et les Fondements de l'Inegalité parmi les Hommes* (1755). In this treatise, he claimed that orangutans (by which he and his contemporaries meant both orangutan and chimpanzee, the two anthropoid apes then known to Europeans) were true men long lost in the forests who, failing to undergo the environmental influences that had developed "their brothers" into ordinary human beings, had degenerated (*Oeuvres complètes*, 1826 ed., I, p. 367). Rousseau did not consider language really natural for mankind, even though the speech organs themselves are natural. Instead, he claimed, language is merely conventional, although it has enabled man to progress. As for the idea that man developed language deliberately so that he would be able to think, Rousseau said it would have taken fully developed powers of thought to realize that language was worth inventing. In contrast to

Condillac, who viewed even the earliest people as inherently sociable, Rousseau conceived of primordial man as a solitary, nonsociable creature, who rarely encountered other members of his species. In the much less widely known *Essai sur l'Origine des Langues,* which was not published until 1772 (cf. critical ed., C. Porset, 1968), language was said to have arisen from human needs and emotions rather than from a deliberate effort to establish practical communication with others. Simple physical needs could be met through gestures and cries alone without articulate speech. Gesture language supplemented by natural cries came first and was not superseded by speech for a long time. Then, in northern climes, the voice came into its own for the first time because spoken language was required by the more firmly organized societies, which were necessary under harsh environmental conditions (cf. Perkins, 1967, p. 83). In *Émile* (1762), Rousseau regretted the general neglect of the "language of signs" in education, since it speaks more to the imagination than do words (Josephs, 1969, p. 206). Hunting, Rousseau noted, could be carried on without speech. A critic of Rousseau's "Second Discourse," Salvemini di Castiglione, while denying that human beings could have invented language in spoken form, conceded that primitive hunters might have used gestures and onomatopoeia in communicating about the pursuit and killing of game (Megill, 1974, p. 279).

Helvètius, another *philosophe,* remarked in 1758 that man's superiority over creatures was based on his hands, but was troubled that monkeys, similarly equipped, did not appear to equal man (Hastings, 1936, p. 123). Moses Mendelssohn, who translated Rousseau's "Second Discourse" into German in 1756, reported that he and Lessing often discussed the problem of glottogenesis. Mendelssohn believed that language could have emerged by purely human means, and he favored onomatopoeia as the most likely mechanism. Jean Henri Samuel Formey in 1762 recommended a replication of the Psammetichus experiment to settle the question about language origins (Megill, 1974, p. 311). Charles De Brosses (1709–1777) wrote a large work, *Traité de la Formation Méchanique des Langues et des Principes Physiques de l'Étymologie* (1765) in which he not only assumed that man had created language for himself, but discussed what is now called *sound symbolism.* He posited various "roots" and consonantal sounds as indicators of broad semantic domains. Valmont de Bomare (1764) wrote about anthropoid apes and feral children, concluding that only man possesses inherent speech capacity. Charles Bonnet in 1765 defended the apes, acknowledging their inability to speak but stating at the same time that their brains cannot be very different from ours. He recommended more detailed anatomical research on apes comparable to the effort already being devoted to the anatomy of human beings and domestic animals (Hastings, 1936, p. 127). Significantly, T. H. Huxley quotes Bonnet at some length in 1874

(1893 ed., pp. 247–249). Despite these pro-Pongid sentiments, the great naturalist, G. L. LeClerc, Comte de Buffon, denied that apes have any language capacities, basing his argument both on deficiencies in their vocal apparatus and also on the ground that language is a gift vouchsafed only to mankind (cf. Hastings, 1936, p. 125).

Feral children, long a staple of legend, were arousing enormous popular interest at this time; the most notable example being "Wild Peter," who was supposedly discovered running wild in a wood near Hannover and who had been brought to England as a kind of philosophical exhibit. Carl von Linné (Linnaeus), the great taxonomist, created a special place in his Systema Naturae for Homo ferus, human beings who grow up in a state of nature without language or acquaintance with any human society. Such cases represented a kind of natural Psammetichus experiment bearing on the question of man's ability to create language, although in a state of individual isolation such a system of communication would hardly seem to be necessary.

It comes almost as a shock to encounter in the eighteenth century a writer who adheres to the traditional religious view that language was a divine gift, although numerous obscure parsons and abbés continued to voice such opinions all over Western Europe. Johann Peter Süssmilch was a respected intellectual figure in Berlin when in 1766–1767 he wrote Versuch eines Beweises, dass die erste Sprache ihren Ursprung nicht vom Menschen, sondern allein vom Schöpfer erhalten habe. Although Herder in his glottogonic essay virtually ridiculed Süssmilch's views, Megill (1974, Chap. 11) points out that Süssmilch was no simplistic fundamentalist. He had used linguistic evidence, much of which was drawn from the language of the Greenland Eskimo, to show that even the languages of savage peoples exhibited a level of grammatical perfection that he thought could only be explained as an outcome of a divine gift. Süssmilch admitted in a letter to one Jacob Carpov that "Lucretian men" (i.e., the crude, primitive early human beings described in Lucretius De rerum naturā) might have had the capacity to create a language of gestures, although vocal language with its regular word order and intricate grammatical rules could never have developed out of onomatopoeia (Megill, pp. 334–337). An anonymous critic of Süssmilch in 1769, however, rejected this argument, showing that a primitive system of gestures and cries could achieve the complexity of a spoken language, as he himself had observed in the case of a sign-language created by a born-deaf individual (Megill, p. 346).

Voltaire was unusual among the philosophes in his relative lack of interest concerning language origins. He did suggest in his Philosophie de l'Histoire (1765) that when society was still limited to small, familial groups, man, a naturally sociable creature, probably communicated gesturally before he spoke. Later when larger societies arose, speech was required, and it grew out of onomatopoeia and interjections. These were not especially original views.

The Berlin Academy Essay Competition

In 1769, reflecting its indebtedness to the intellectual work of France, the Royal Prussian Academy of Sciences in Berlin announced a prize essay competition on the topic of language origins, which attracted 34 entries from several countries. The problem was carefully framed to avoid theological complications: "Would men left with only their natural faculties be capable of inventing language? And by what means would they attain to that invention? [Megill, 1974, p. 349]." The winning essay by Johann Gottfried Herder (1744–1803) was published in 1772. A few others were eventually published also, but most of the essays survive only in unpublished manuscript form in the archives of the Berlin Academy of Sciences, where they are to this day. Herder saw the beginnings of language in man's rational thought and considered not only gestures but also interjections and onomatopoeia to be the means whereby it emerged. Man, observing a bleating lamb, would realize because of his superior reason, that that distinctive sound was an obvious sign standing for that animal and its species. In any case, Herder repudiated the notion that divine intervention accounted for language (cf. Salmon, 1968; Josephs, 1969; Megill, 1974; Sapir, 1907). The Abbé de Copineau, one of the few other identifiable contestants, argued that isolated children could develop four kinds of language, one of them gestural—like the sign language of the deaf. The attainment of language, however, would have been a long and arduous task (Court de Gebelin, 1816). Another entrant, identified only as a deaf-born Breslau baron, denied that isolated children would develop any sort of speech. Essayist Number 2 contended that language arose in gesture without further elaboration. Dietrich Tiedemann (1748–1803) argued in his published essay (1772) that gesture language appeared first, later as a purely human invention becoming vocal through sound imitation (Fano, 1962, pp. 265, ff.). Court de Gebelin (1725–1774) sought to reconstruct the "primitive language" from roots in which different "letters" embodied distinctive meanings (1816; cf. Fano, 1962). The Russian savant, Mikhail Vassilievich Lomonosov, objected to what he considered the exaggeration of the role of gesture in glottogenesis. Johann Georg Hamann (d. 1789) felt that the assertion of man's ability to create language unaided by God threatened to destroy the barrier between man and beast (Salmon, 1968).

Later Eighteenth Century Glottogonic Controversy

Three successive French writers, Maupertuis (already mentioned), Turgot, and Maine de Biran, as well as a lesser known commentator, Boindin,
carried on a kind of long-range debate, which began with a short critique of
Maupertuis' ideas by Boindin (1750). Turgot also replied about the same
time, but his remarks were not published until after his death. Finally, Maine
de Biran (1766–1824) added his comments around 1815, which remain
unpublished until 1841 (cf. Formigari, 1971, 1974). None was much interested in the details of how the first language might have come into being;
rather they were interested in the nature of the primordial language, which
would supposedly shed important light on the progress of human cognition.
Turgot argued that the connection between words and meanings was purely
empirical, and that it was based on habits established in infancy. Thus he
agreed with Hume and other eighteenth-century empiricists. Turgot also
supposed that the first languages, being less perfect than more recent ones,
would have been more, rather than less complicated (Grimsley, 1967, p.
297).

If the English tended to exhibit less enthusiasm than the French over the
language origin debate during this epoch, the Scots followed the French
arguments more closely. James Burnett, Lord Monboddo, issued the first
volume of his bulky, six volume treatise *The Origin and Progress of Language* in 1773. He reviewed past work on the subject, but reached the
conclusion that language had been vocal from the start. His most remarkable notions were that apes could probably speak and that man had descended from an apelike ancestor. Monboddo accepted travelers' tales of
benighted African tribes lacking speech (a point supported also by Edward
Long, who wrote in 1774). Herder, who translated part of Monboddo's work
into German in 1784 (cf. Frank Manuel, 1968, p. 6), regretted Monboddo's
belief in a close affinity between man and ape and, following Camper's
anatomical research, which contradicted Tyson's views on ape speech
capacity, denied that such animals could have language.

Other contributors to language origin theory in the last quarter of the
eighteenth century were R. Zobel (1773), J. N. Tetens (1772, 1777), J. C.
Adelung (1781, 1782), J. G. Fichte (1795) and Immanuel Kant (1786). In
1783, Johann Georg Heinrich Feder decided that since so much had already
been written about language origins, it was no longer profitable to say
anything further (quoted in Megill, 1974, p. 450).

But the subject was not entirely dead. Adam Smith, the eminent Scottish
economist, advanced a glottogonic theory based on the laws of imitation
and associational psychology, although his chief concern was the natural

sequence in which the various parts of speech had emerged ("Dissertation on the Origin of Language," in *The Theory of the Moral Sentiments,* 10th ed., 1804). Smith's friend and disciple, Dugald Stewart, also wrote on the same topic, describing how a gestural language gradually gave way to a formalized and arbitrary spoken language (1828, 1829).

NINETEENTH-CENTURY GLOTTOGONIC ARGUMENTS

The ideas of Condillac were revived around 1800 by a group known as the *idéologues* (cf. Seigel, 1969). This clique included the Abbé Sicard, a noted teacher of the deaf and successor of the Abbé de l'Epée, Itard, the mentor of the "wild boy of Aveyron." Victor Degérando, who was interested in gesture languages among primitive peoples, and Jauffret, who proposed that the *Société des Observateurs de l'Homme,* organized by the *Idéologues,* should repeat the Psammetichus experiment on a grand scale. Meanwhile, in a very obscure work on vegetarianism written in 1803, Joseph Ritson argued that man had descended from the apes and that language was no more natural for man than for monkeys or parrots (Hastings, 1936, p. 130). In 1806, in an even less well-known work, D. C. Ries, who had some personal experience in the teaching of the deaf, argued not that gesture language was primordial, but that the capacity of the deaf to acquire speech (through lip reading, for example) proved that man's reason unaided by divine intervention could have achieved language, had it not already been a gift of the Deity.

Reaction, Romanticism, and Philology

The dramatic and explosive rise of comparative philology, which had followed rapidly upon the disclosure by William Jones's demonstration of the relationship between Sanskrit, Greek, and Latin (a conclusion that had been reached earlier by some Catholic missionaries in India, but had not aroused the learned world), now moved scholars away from the speculative, philosophical issue of glottogenesis. As a result, from 1810 until about 1850 little was written about language origins, certainly not by scholars of the caliber of those who had addressed themselves to the problem during the eighteenth century. Louis Gabriel Ambroise de Bonald (1754–1840) and Joseph de Maistre (1754–1821), representatives of the reactionary (and pious) supporters of the revival of the Bourbon monarchy, rejecting the dangerous thoughts of the eighteenth-century *philosophes,* restated the orthodox theory that language was a divine institution (Bastier, J., 1974, pp. 543–544).

Nor was the Romantic movement conducive to attempts to find the origins of man's sublime and poetic instrument, language, in animalistic cries and rudimentary gestures. Goethe, whose long life began during the Enlightenment but who lived on into the full-blown Romantic age, expressed his disdain for glottogonic theorizing in his autobiography (1811–1812). Friedrich Schlegel, a prominent figure in comparative philology, argued in 1808 that highly inflected languages like Sanskrit, Greek, and Latin were much too perfect to have been invented by man alone, although the crude languages of primitive folk might have been generated naturally. By 1830 Schlegel changed his mind somewhat, and regarded all languages as man made, but contended that the process of their development had been exceedingly gradual. Melchiore Cesarotti (d. 1808) asserted that language had arisen quite naturally from onomatopoeia. But some decades later, Alessandro Manzoni (d. 1873) rejected the idea that language had been invented by human beings. Manzoni also refused to believe that isolated children could ever have created their own language (Fano, 1962). Alexander Murray (d. 1813), in a book published in 1823, supposed that languages stemmed from only nine original phonetic roots, with which, by means of tonal variations of these sounds and simultaneous gestures, meaning was communicated. Jacob Heinrich Kaltschmidt referred in 1840 to soundsymbolism, noting the diminutive effect of the vowel /i/; for him the first language was onomatopoeic, and all languages arose monogenetically from the first one. In 1831 and again in 1838, Franz Wüllner advanced the notion that the first words resulted from the "enspiritualization of natural sounds." By this time, enough had been worked out with respect to the reconstruction of "roots" of Indo-European languages and some other families to lead some to suspect that primordial man had in fact communicated with such "roots," which mostly consisted of consonant clusters without distinctive vowels, and which, in comparison to individual consonants, seemed to be peculiarly hard to reconstruct. In 1842 a Danish philologist, J. N. Madvig, returned to the gestural origin theory, as did the Austrian playwright Grillparzer, who thought also that the first speech must have been based on onomatopoeia. In 1844 two curious works appeared: Pierquin de Gembloux's treatise on the "language of animals," from which he supposed speech to have emerged, and Jean-François Sudre's creation of a pasigraphy based on seven musical notes, a venture that recalled some of the universal language attempts of the seventeenth century. Such efforts reflect a strong tendency to relate the smallest significant components of speech (which would now be called "phonemes") to specific areas of meaning.

The major work that preceded the vigorous reopening of the more or less dormant glottogonic issue was Ernest Renan's (1823–1892) *De l'Origine du Language*, 1848 and 1858 (cf. critical ed., Henriette Psichari, 1958). However, Renan's work is disappointingly vague about the mechanisms that might have brought language into existence: Language arose on account of an "intuition" or spontaneous communicative urge. Renan dismissed the eighteenth century efforts to answer the question. Words were based on onomatopoeia, which led to a simple, monosyllabic tongue, lacking inflections. Renan seems to have dodged the real questions, and most of his book is couched in the high-flown idealistic rhetoric of the Romantic period (Fano, 1962, pp. 271 ff.; cf. Sommerfelt, 1954, p. 887). Jacob Grimm (1785–1863) wrote one of the many German essays *"Über den Ursprung der Sprache* which are scattered through the nineteenth century. Grimm viewed the problem as essentially insoluble because of the remoteness of the events involved. This opinion did not prevent him from supposing that the earliest language must have been melodious, prolix, and made up of short words containing simple consonants. For Grimm, language was neither innate (this explanation would somehow lower man to the level of the lower animals), nor divine in origin (which would violate the orderliness of Nature). Instead, it was "man's history, his inheritance," the outcome of the human *Geist*. Concerning the later stages of development of language, Grimm envisaged a sequence beginning with languages made up mostly of monosyllables, then progressing to isolating grammatical structures like Chinese, and culminating in languages characterized by inflectional richness (like German, for example).

In 1850 J.-B. J. Barrois, on a different tack, tried to reconstruct the primitive gesture-language of mankind from a study of depictions of gestures on ancient monuments. He further supposed that God had addressed the ancient Jews in manual gesture and that the Phoenician alphabet was based on finger signing. In a much less naive vein, the gifted armchair writer on ethnology, R. G. Latham, in his article on language written for the Eighth Edition of the *Encyclopaedia Britannica* in 1857, arrived at a notion of lexicostatistics as a means of getting at language chronology in the remote past, and advanced a kind of natural-selective theory of linguistic evolution.

The Impact of Darwinism

In his *Origin of Species* (1859), Darwin barely alluded to the possibility of human evolution, much less to the origins of language. Yet his work soon aroused great interest among the linguists of the time. Even in Darwin's *Descent of Man* (1871), which he seems to have written with some reluctance, language is given minimal treatment. Darwin supposed that speech arose simply from imitations of natural sounds and cries of an emotional character. Nor is there anything more on language in Darwin's *The Expression of the Emotions in Man and Animals* (1872), although this book is justifiably regarded as a pioneer work on what is now known as nonverbal communication. Nevertheless, there were clear implications for language theorists in Darwinism. Darwin had skillfully combined evidence from geology and paleontology such that his readers could not help realizing that man, even though among the latest species to evolve, must have existed a great deal longer than Biblical tradition allowed for. The notion of a vast extension of geological time had been brewing for some time, and, since 1844, had been popularized in successive editions of *The Natural History of the Vestiges of Creation,* an evolutionary work now known to have been written by Robert Chambers. In any case, F. Max Müller, Steinthal, Geiger, William Dwight Whitney, and F. W. Farrar were soon engaged with many others in a new debate on glottogenesis, one informed by a rapidly lengthening geochronological framework and the increasingly plausible idea that man had gradually evolved from an apelike ancestor.

As early as 1861 F. Max Müller engaged the Darwinians in debates on the science of language, in which he reasserted the old Cartesian gulf between man and beast. Müller, a noted Sanskrit scholar, believed that language had begun with roots composed of articulate sounds, and that man had once possessed a handy instinct to guide him in his choice of the most appropriate sounds for particular meanings. Müller claimed that Sanskrit and other Indo-European tongues revealed the existence of some 400 to 500 primordial "root-ideas," which could also be traced in other language families. These phonetic types resulted from innate human responsiveness to the nature of different things and actions through a kind of resonance effect. Accordingly Müller's theory came to be known as the "ding-dong theory." The gestural theory was rejected along with the notions that speech had emerged from onomatopoeia or interjectional sounds, the last two theories being designated the "bow-wow" and "pooh-pooh" theories, respectively. Müller stuck to these points in his *The Science of Language* (1877) and *The Science of Thought* (1887). His motto in these works, which appears on the title page of the 1887 volume, was "No language without reason—no reason without language." (See his paper in *Nature* (1887), which bore this motto as a title.)

In 1862, G. P. Marsh, writing on the history of the English language, suggested the possible origin of language in gestures. The English anthropologist, Edward B. Tylor wrote in 1863 on "beast-children," that is, feral children, that hardy theme from the preceding century was now reinforced by the popular accounts of the mysterious Caspar Hauser case of the

1820s. In 1864 Max Müller examined the language which had been reported in such children. August Schleicher was prompted to write an open letter in 1863 to Ernst Haeckel on Darwinism and linguistics, expressing Vico's view that really to understand something, one must know how it came to be. Schleicher proposed that language be traced to its beginnings with a kind of Darwinian method. He thought that speech began with onomatopoeia and "oral gesture" and that at first it had no syntax whatever. Like living organisms, the world's languages were divisible into species, families, and so on, which he felt should permit a kind of evolutionary reconstruction. In 1865, he elaborated these ideas in his *Über die Bedeutung der Sprache für die Naturgeschichte des Menschen,* putting the problem within the framework of evolutionary biology.

Apparently overwhelmed about this time by papers of dubious scholarship, the *Société de Linguistique de Paris* in 1866 simply banned in its bylaws any communications on the subject, as well as any proposals for universal languages.

This rule did not stop Yves-Léonard Rémi Valade, a teacher at the Paris Institute for the Deaf, from presenting his detailed version of the gestural origin of language in which he noted that the communication of the deaf constitutes a "daily instance" of the conditions of the Psammetichus experiment reproducing the language of the earliest human beings (Valade, 1866, p. 8). His paper, which displays considerable knowledge of sign language in a functioning human community, deserves renewed attention.

The American philologist, William Dwight Whitney (1827–1894) first wrote on glottogenesis in 1867, and dealt with it thereafter in at least nine publications, including the article "Philology" in the Ninth Edition of the *Encyclopaedia Britannica* (1885). He reviewed the ideas of Steinthal, Schleicher, and F. Max Müller, and speculated about the possibility of applying Darwinism to the study of languages. Although he saw language as rooted in a human need to communicate, he recognized that apes, too, have such a need, but still have not developed language. He also discussed the advantages of speech over gesture, which he thought had preceded language. Whitney's major writings on language have been reissued (1971). Hensleigh Wedgewood (one of Darwin's cousins?) supported the onomatopoeic theory in 1866 and contributed an article on glottogenesis to the *Etymological Dictionary* in 1872.

Gustav Jäger wrote in 1867–1870 that language began in animal cries, onomatopoeia, gesture, and in what he called "air pictures" (that is, iconic gestures). Starting with *Homo alalus,* a creature wholly without language, the evolutionary line ran to prehistoric man, who used a combined mimetic and phonetic language. Jäger erroneously attributed deictic or pointing gestures to monkeys. Moreover, he asserted that true language arose suddenly when the small-brained apelike ancestor of mankind gave birth to a "macrocephalic offspring" capable of handling language. In the fourth stage of his complex model, air pictures were replaced by sound imitations (cf. Fano, 1962; Rosenkranz, 1961, pp. 32 ff.) Lazarus Geiger, like F. Max Müller, thought early language was mostly a matter of roots, although he held that these had arisen out of emotional cries or simple sound imitations. He also thought that the presence or absence of certain roots could be used to show the existence or nonexistence at a remote period of particular kinds of tools, weapons, or handicrafts. Furthermore, language was mainly the creation of a few gifted individuals, before which all vocal utterances were gestures, which at first had to be used to explicate spoken words. Geiger wrote in 1868 and 1869, and the fullest statement of his glottogonic views can be found in Contributions to the History of the Development of the Human Race, published posthumously in English translation in 1880.

Edward B. Tylor began writing on language origin theories in 1868, and devoted considerable attention to the problem in his books on anthropology, which appeared in 1870, 1871, and 1881. Among other things, he looked for data in schools for the deaf in both England and Germany and became interested in the sign language of the North American Plains Indians. In addition to dealing with gesture, he also examined the glottogonic role of interjections and onomatopoeia. He reached no definite conclusions. In his review of Tylor's book Anthropology (1881) Alfred Russel Wallace, who independently of Darwin had developed the theory of evolution through natural selection, advanced the theory of "mouth–gesture." This theory held that the tongue and other vocal-tract parts act in sympathetic movement with the gesticulating hands. The accompanying and, in a sense, quite incidental sounds produced thereby would then become associated with the meanings of the gestures, and a lexicon of articulate vocal signs or words would be gradually established. Mouth–gesture is not the same thing as onomatopoeia, although it may underlie sound–symbolism. Wallace continued to develop this theory in an 1895 paper and in a volume published in 1900. R. A. S. Paget (1963), to be discussed at greater length later, credits the original idea of mouth–gesture to J. Rae, who had arrived at it during work on Polynesian languages as far back as 1862. Wallace said that he had hit upon the notion while working as field naturalist among the Malays in the East Indies. Tylor himself had noted as a matter of "great philological interest" the frequent correlation of locatives representing different degrees of distance from the speaker with a graduated series of vowels (Wallace, 1895, p. 371).

Frederic William Farrar (1831–1903) first wrote on glottogenesis in 1860, observing that "a gesture cannot become a word or sentence although it might somehow influence either of them [p. 68]." In 1865 he issued a book on language, containing a review of ideas on origins, and in 1870 reviewed Schleicher's work on Darwinism and language.

Hyde Clarke (1815–1895) anticipated some aspects of the mouth–gesture theory in 1852. His later papers on glottogenesis (1881, 1883, 1887) supplied further evidence concerning mouth–gesture, some of it drawn from Garrick Mallery's work on North American Indian sign language. Clarke (1881, p. 381) rejected the idea that all spoken languages go back to a single ancestor.

Heymann Steinthal (1823–1899) also wrote extensively on the subject, starting with a paper in 1851, which he later revised, and in an 1855 work in which he favorably compared Wilhelm von Humboldt's language theories to those of J. G. Herder and J. G. Hamann. He investigated the relation of reconstructed Indo-European roots to primordial speech forms in 1867 and to the emotional cries and calls of animals in 1871. In his treatise *Der Ursprung der Sprache im Zusammenhänge mit den letzten Fragen alles Wissens* (c. 1877) he emphasized the role of onomatopoeia. The ultimate cause of language was an innate *Geist*, which "humanized our consciousness." Attainment of the erect posture also played a role in making speech possible. Originally the "reflex vocalizations" had to be explicated by gestures to be fully intelligible.

In 1877 Ludwig Noiré (1829–1889) proposed that language arose from the vocal concomitants of heavy physical exertion especially those which occurred in cooperative labor where such actions might be rhythmical. The first spoken words were therefore of the "yo-he-ho" variety, hence the trivial name of this theory—the "yo-he-ho theory." Noiré also wrote a thoughtful treatise on the role of tools and toolmaking in human evolution (1880). His work soon came to the notice of socialist writers, who found in the linkage of cooperative labor and language a congenial theory somehow glorifying the workingman. Friedrich Engels had discussed the role of labor in the "hominization" *(Menschwerdung)* of apes in 1876 and had, following Lewis Henry Morgan's *Ancient Society* (1877), placed the origin of articulate speech in the lower status of savagery. Morgan himself thought that the first language had been gestural with a monosyllabic form of articulate speech coming later. Engels wrote in 1876,

> With the domination over Nature beginning with labor. . . with every new advance toward the human horizon. . . the evolving human beings came to the point where they had *something to say* to each other. The necessity created the organ: The undeveloped larynx of the apes transformed itself slowly but surely through modulation by steadily increasing modulation, and the organ of the mouth gradually learned to pronounce one articulated letter [sic] after another [translation by G. W. Hewes].

A. H. Sayce (1846–1933) claimed that the first language was akin to interjection and that a language composed of roots would have been impossible (1880, p. 168). The sounds in early speech were "few and vague." Much of the earliest vocabulary was onomatopoeic, but prior to its development, gestures had accompanied semiarticulate utterances. The "visual onomatopoeia of gesture" was what led to speech.

Jean Pierre Rambosson wrote on glottogenesis between 1853 and 1881, stressing gestural signing. In his *Origine de la Parole et du Langage Parlé* (1881), however, he says that if the Darwinists were right, and man had appeared on Earth in a primitive state, then the first language would have been gestural. But, against this, he notes that even the most backward-living peoples possess highly complex spoken languages, and that furthermore, there is no convincing evidence that primitive forms of mankind ever existed. Here Rambosson followed the authority of Rudolf Virchow, the very influential anatomist and pathologist, who had shown to his own satisfaction that the 1856 Neanderthal fossil was only that of a pathological specimen of modern mankind.

Garrick Mallery, who had practical experience as a military officer on the North American Great Plains, now came forth with some empirical data about the Indian sign-language system (1880, 1881a,b). He saw significant parallels between sign language and pictographs and petroglyphs. He realized that if there had been a primordial sign-language, it would not have closely resembled that of the Plains Indians or any other system in use where spoken language had long been developed. Nor, he said, could there ever have been a time when man lacked the ability to use vocal sounds, even if the sounds did not take the form of articulate speech. Mallery felt that for early man the main burden of meanings and predication had been borne by gesture, and that gesture had left its traces in all spoken languages and survived in greater or lesser vigor as an accompaniment of speech. He reviewed the work on southern Italian gestures by de Jorio (1832), who had found parallels between recent Neapolitan gesticulation and gestures depicted in Greek and Roman art.

Rudolf Kleinpaul, who had written a paper on the origin of language in 1871, brought out a book on gestures and other nonvocal signs, *Sprache ohne Worte,* in 1888. He also wrote on the same topic in the 1890s. Nicolas Joly held that primitive man had used "profuse gesticulation" and spoke in monosyllables (1887, 1897), but that there was never a stage in human evolution when our ancestors could be characterized as *Homo alalus.* Prior to the discovery of the fossil form which Eugene Dubois called *Pithecanthropus erectus,* Ernst Haeckel (1868) had postulated an ancestral transitional or missing-link apeman form which he called *Pithecanthropus alalus* or "speechless apeman." A. H. Keane supposed in 1895 that remnants of the primitive language of gesture survived in strength among living "primitive races," but that it could be seen among some of the "more emotional higher races, too." (He presumably had the Italians and other Mediterranean peoples in mind.) Herbert Spencer, in a short paper on the origins of music (1894) and in the Fourth Edition of his *Principles of Psychology* (1899) referred briefly to the gestural origin theory, as well as to interjections as a source of words.

From Broca to Wundt

Meanwhile, another empirical area was opening up, now called neurolinguistics. In 1861 Paul Broca had demonstrated the first neurologically localizable "speech area," which still bears his name, in the left cerebral cortex. At that time, it was being hotly debated whether the brains of anthropoid apes differed in any structural way from those of man so that the seat of a faculty of language was a critical issue. Carl Wernicke discovered another language-related part of the left cortex in 1874, and, starting about 1873, John Hughlings Jackson began a long series of notable studies on language and the brain, based mostly on cases of aphasia, including one case reported in 1878 of a deaf mute who suffered some impairment of his signing after left hemisphere injury. Although the work of these investigators was adding steadily to substantive knowledge of the ways in which the brain handled language, linguistics, by now in the "neogrammarian" phase of its development, paid little notice.

In 1891 Sigmund Freud produced a well-known study of aphasias, incorporating both Broca's and Wernicke's areas in a "central speech area." By this time surgical technique had reached a point where patients could survive brain operations, and experimental work conducted through surgical exploration and electrical stimulation was beginning on monkey and ape brains.

Richard Lynch Garner, an American who had become interested in captive monkeys and apes, undertook a quixotic expedition into the field in Gabon, West Africa, where, equipped with the latest wax-cylinder phonographic recording instrument and a large steel cage from which to make his observations, he sought to study and record the "life and language of apes and monkeys" (Garner, 1892, 1896, 1900). His results were meager, although his jungle cage was approached by chimpanzees and many monkeys. The project was later satirized by the French science-fiction writer, Jules Verne in one of his last (and little-known) novels, *Le Village Aérien*, 1901, which appeared in English as *The Village in the Tree Tops*.

George John Romanes (1848–1894) was an ardent Darwinist who investigated intelligence in animals, obviously from a non-Cartesian standpoint. In 1887 he attacked F. Max Müller's claim that there could be no thought without language; Romanes insisted on the cognitive powers of many nonhuman higher mammalian species. In his *Origin of Human Faculty* (1889), Romanes set forth his ideas about glottogenesis at some length (Chaps. 5, 16). He believed that the "germ of sign-making [p. 127]" is present in higher animals, which explains why intelligent domestic animals such as dogs understand human speech to a limited extent, and he says that if they were articulate (that is, if they had sufficient control over components of their vocal tracts), "they would employ simple words to express simple ideas." "I do not say," he adds, "that they would form propositions [p. 128]." Romanes claimed that the foundation of the whole mental fabric of mankind had been laid by gesture language (p. 151). Altogether, Romanes provides a coherent formulation of a glottogonic model rooted in the idea that there is a continuum of intelligence from higher nonhuman species to man. In his theory he combined the gestural hypothesis with the idea that vocal tones convey emotional messages.

J. Donovan, in two papers in 1893 and 1899, advanced a very different theory of glottogenesis, which he termed the "festal origin of language." Group celebration, consisting of dance, mime, and song, not a prosaic need for predicative communication, led to the formation of speech. Susanne K. Langer revived Donovan's ideas in 1960, 1962, 1971, and 1972. Jane Goodall, to be sure, has observed "festal" behavior among wild chimpanzees; her moving description of a "rain dance" performed during a thunderstorm is a particularly good example, although her account is without glottogonic implications (Goodall, 1967).

Raoul de la Grasserie (1895) sought to replace the old idea of an onomatopoeic origin of speech by what he termed "subjective onomatopoeia," which refers to what others had called mouth–gesture. However, there was a slight difference, since in de la Grasserie's formulation the organs of speech were synchronized not with manual gestures but with the actions or movement patterns of the objects referred to. He also suggested that languages of existing primitive peoples should greatly elucidate earlier stages of language evolution—an idea which was to fall into great disrepute among later linguists (Fano, 1962, p. 277).

Around 1900, the psychologist Wilhelm Wundt (1832–1920) turned from his experimental laboratory investigations to the broader field of the psychology of peoples *(Völkerpsychologie)* in which the nature and evolution of language seemed to be of immense importance. Language could not have arisen suddenly without preparation; therefore, a gradual transition from nonlanguage to language must have taken place. Language arose from gesture, and, at first, sounds were incidental. Only slowly did they become capable of carrying a message independently. Wundt recognized that the expressive movements or gestures of the kind that formed the earliest language were not observable even in "the most talented apes." In early man connotative gestures were derived from deixis or pointing, which led to "symbolic signing" (1973, p. 130). The earliest form of speech consisted of *Lautgebärden* or sound gestures. Roback (1954, p. 338) notes that part of the reason linguists neglected Wundt's work on language lay in Wundt's own neglect of the by then massive literature on philology, especially Indo-European philology, although it would have been unrealistic to expect that Wundt, who was already 68 in 1900, should have taken the years necessary to master Sanskrit and 90 years or so of linguistic scholarship. Wundt did look into sign languages, and his work on gesture has appeared in English translation (Wundt, 1973). Ironically Leonard Bloomfield, one of the later leaders in American structuralist linguistics and a dedicated opponent of "mentalism," was once a supporter of Wundt's linguistic position; Bloomfield expressed his admiration in his 1914 book on language. By the 1920s, however, Bloomfield had become a thoroughgoing behaviorist, a switch that Roback has described as "Bloomfield's somersault." As a consequence, the generations of American linguists for whom Bloomfield's *Language* (1933) became a kind of Bible got the impression that curiosity about language origins was hardly respectable in so rigorous a science. Wundt's ideas were never rejected by George Herbert Mead, however, even though he described himself as a "social behaviorist." Long after his death in 1931, Mead was hailed as a seminal figure in semiotics. He wrote extensively on the behavioral significance of gestures, and his ideas, in turn, stimulated Charles Morris (author of *Signs, Language and Behavior*, 1946), who, to be sure, had also been influenced by the ideas of C. S. Peirce, a long-neglected semiotic pioneer.

  Hermann Paul (1846–1921) a contemporary of Wundt, was also interested in language origins. He, too, believed that the earliest vocal language rested on an earlier gestural base, from which it only gradually freed itself. Paul emphasized that the earliest human language users lacked the advantages of modern children who acquire their language in the midst of adult speakers. Paul thought that the language-generating prowess of early man must have exceeded that of modern man, a theory that recalls one of Max Müller's notions. Paul considered onomatopoeia to have been predominant in the formation of spoken words, even though these earliest vocal words had to be explicated gesturally (cf. Sommerfelt, 1954, p. 892; Fano, 1962, p. 279).

DECLINE OF INTEREST IN THE EARLY
TWENTIETH CENTURY

The first three decades of the twentieth century seem somewhat sterile with respect to language origin theorizing, despite the work of Wundt and Paul. Three proponents of the gestural-origin theory before 1914 were psychologists Wilhelm Jerusalem (1907), Harald Höffding (1912), and Vladimir Bekhterev (1913). Max Meyer, a psychologist who had come to the United States, suggested a mouth–gesture connection between digital pointing and tongue-tip articulations (1912, p. 332). Carl Franke, a psychiatrist, attempted around 1911 to reconstruct the language of Ice Age man. He claimed that tonality had played an important part in it, a notion he based on the predominance of labials in the early speech of children. The "thicker gums" of Aurignacian man permitted more complex consonants.

The well-known anthropologist, Alfred Louis Kroeber (1876–1960), wrote in 1901 that it was absurd to suppose one could find the origins of words in reconstructed "roots," and, moreover, that all such efforts to discover ultimate origins were futile (pp. 334–335). During a long and very productive career in which he dealt with almost all aspects of anthropology, Kroeber at no time felt that the topic of language origins was worth more than a brief dismissal. Concerning language and apes, he observed that apes probably lacked language because they had nothing to say—a remark in a very different spirit than that of Romanes, for example. On the other hand Edward Sapir, an anthropologist–linguist whose reputation was nearly equivalent to that of Kroeber, having written his masters thesis on J. G. Herder's *Essay on the Origin of Speech,* actually carried out experiments on sound symbolism (Sapir, 1929).

The general thrust of early twentieth-century linguistics was antimentalistic, drawing heavily on some of the more extreme behaviorist positions in psychology and on the British logical positivists. This orientation precluded speculation about the origins of language and also led the linguistically orthodox to be wary of research on such matters as sound symbolism, possible language universals, and even child language. Such caution enabled the structuralists to erect a system for the analysis of languages that was the envy of social scientists of the time, one possessing an elegance that was matched only by higher mathematics and by physics at its most abstruse.

World War I set back research of most kinds, so that the glottogonic model proposed in 1918 by a Norwegian psychiatrist, Paul Winge, was one of the very few items of note. Winge's scheme included reference to the evolution of bipedalism in man, and he advanced the novel idea that prior to the emergence of speech, people had communicated mainly by drawing pictures to each other. Early language was also characteristically "prelogical." Also, some sexual activities were said to be accompanied by imitative gestures and vocalizations (Sommerfelt, 1954, pp. 894–895).

PIONEER WORK ON NONHUMAN PRIMATES AND LANGUAGE

Anthropoid apes were now being kept alive longer in captivity, and William H. Furness III worked for several years to teach a young orang-utan to produce speech sounds. By dint of daily repetition he succeeded only in achieving a few very poorly enunciated approximations of words like "papa" and "cup" (notably composed of plosives). His mediocre results are considered strong negative evidence for speech capacity in pongids (1916). Just about this time (1912), the now notorious Piltdown "fossil" was presented as a genuine hominid ancestor, combining a very apelike mandible (hardly strange, since it was later shown to be a deliberately stained ape's jaw with filed-down molar teeth) and a fully human braincase. This chimera, not exposed as a deliberate fraud until 1951, stood for years as a major obstacle to the idea of an evolutionary continuum from the early pongids to *Homo sapiens,* since the Piltdown skull appeared to prove that a fully modern human brain, presumably capable of handling language had coexisted in a form with decidedly apelike snout. Eugene Dubois, who had discovered the first *Homo erectus* remains (then known as *Pithecanthropus erectus*) decided to reclassify his find as a giant gibbon. On the other hand, debate still continued over the capacity of Neanderthal man for language, with attention being especially devoted to the genioglossal tubercles on the inside of the mandibular symphysis, which probably have nothing to do with speech at all.

Despite the "fossil evidence" of Piltdown, which seemed to place the split between the ancestry of man and the living anthropoid apes very far back in the Cenozoic, significant experimental psychological work involving chimpanzees got underway, led chiefly by Robert M. Yerkes. Yerkes remarked casually in a book published in 1925 that if apes could not learn to talk, they might at least be capable of communicating in the sign language of the deaf. Two major experiments followed, in which chimpanzees were raised for a time in human households. The first was performed by W. N. and L. A. Kellogg around 1933; in it the couple's son was the chimpanzee's companion, and was studied conjointly with it. The second experiment was that of K. and C. Hayes around 1950. In neither experiment, however, was any effort made to teach sign language to the chimpanzee subjects. The Hayes did try very hard to develop speech in their chimpanzee, Viki, despite Furness's earlier failure with an orangutan; it had just about the same limited results (Hayes & Hayes, 1950, 1951, 1952). These experiments seemed to demonstrate, for the time being at least, that apes could not acquire language. Unaware (as far as I know) of Yerkes's 1925 suggestion, I wrote in 1951 to Keith Hayes, wondering why it might not be more profitable to teach Viki sign language, preferably by employing a native deaf signer. Hayes replied (personal communication, 1951) that sign language had been considered for Viki but that the experiment to inculcate speech would have been compromised had Viki had an alternative language system. Unfortunately Viki died soon thereafter. Studies of social communication by wild primates, ape or monkey, were then still in their infancy, although before World War II, C. R. Carpenter had already obtained field data on Howler monkeys in Panama and on gibbons in Thailand.

GLOTTOGONIC SPECULATION FROM MARR TO RÉVÉSZ

After the Russian Revolution, a Soviet linguist, Nikolai Yakovlevich Marr (1865–1934), developed a school of language research that came to enjoy great prestige because of its supposed Marxian foundation until it was demolished by Stalin around 1951. Marr's theories were very elaborate and somewhat bizarre; they included the idea of a primordial language of gesture (ruchnoĭ yazyk), which was followed by the first vocal language, one curiously based on just four syllabic roots. Marr further supposed that the first speech was a monopoly of a few shamans, who kept it secret from the rest of the population for purposes of social control and obfuscation. Later, with the emergence of class-structured societies, a distinctive type of language developed which faithfully reflected the social mode of production. Marr's conception of four primordial word-roots recalls Murray's scheme of nine (in 1823). Marr's so-called "Japhetic" linguistic schema was thoroughly repudiated, but may, in its heyday, have limited the growth of more plausible linguistic studies.

In France, Marcel Jousse also propounded an elaborate and only slightly less bizarre theory of language and language origins (cf. Jousse, 1936), which, however, was more along the lines of the mouth–gesture theory. Jousse based much of his work on Hebrew roots and upon supposed reflections of mouth–gesture in Biblical literature.

Grace de Laguna, not to be confounded with Marr or Jousse, wrote Speech, Its Function and Development in 1927, and it was reprinted in 1963. Her glottogonic speculations seem much more plausible. Although de Laguna based language on a built-in need for human beings to communicate and coordinate their activities, she refers to such matters as man's terrestrial, bipedal adaptations—the importance of cooperative behavior in hunting, and the origins of the sexual division of labor. In other words, the uses of language were not limited strictly to the cognitive realm. The "critical functions of language" were expressed in declarations, commands, and questions—the first two serving to control the primary behavior of others and the last to elicit responsive signals from another. Language is seen by de Laguna as a much more precise and effective instrument for social control than anything developed in lower animals. Although she rejects the theory of gestural language antecedent to speech, she does discuss pointing (pp. 99, 271), noting that apes do not point things out to one another with their hands and arms, or fingers, whereas the game of pointing and eliciting names for things is highly developed in children. (It remains to be determined to what extent this observation can be verified as a cultural universal.) Her contention that pointing cannot "specify" because it cannot change its form according to the nature of the object is contradicted by Trân Duc Thao (1973), as well as by acquaintance with American Sign Language. De Laguna's observation that "transcendental ideas of an impassable gulf between man and animal are of no help" contrasts favorably with recent views expressed on the problem of language origins by Susanne K. Langer.

O. Jespersen (1860–1943) thought that useful insights about man's early language could come both from studies of child language and of the languages of primitive peoples (1924), although many present-day linguists and anthropologists regard notions like the last as arrogant or racist. Jespersen favored the notion that language originated in emotional, songlike behavior, expressing feelings rather than transmitting practical messages about the environment or stating propositions. Speculating about the order in which the parts of speech might have emerged, he thought that proper names might have come first. Meanings could become attached to sounds through either onomatopoeia or interjections.

W. Oehl in *Das Lallwort in der Sprachschöpfung* (1933) concluded that speech began in children's sound-pictures through the formation of a "vocal image" based on visual impressions. This is not the mouth–gesture theory but is more like F. Max Müller's ding-dong theory. Oehl thought that his theory accounted for sound-symbolism universals. G. P. Murdock, an American cultural anthropologist, has discovered surprising uniformities, worldwide, in primary kinship terms, which may fit Oehl's *Lallwort* ideas. Thus, words for "mother" exhibit a strong preference for nasals, whereas oral stops are more common in words for "father" (Murdock, 1959), and since these words are among the earliest to be recognized by adults in the utterances of babies, they belong in the nursery category.

Jacques van Ginneken proposed a highly original theory in 1939 in which pictorial writing precedes speech; therefore, speech is not more than about 5000–6000 years old! He found evidence for this theory in ancient Egyptian hieroglyphs, and in the most ancient form of Chinese writing, on the Shang oracle-bones and bronzes. When speech first emerged, van

Ginneken believed that it consisted of click consonants of the kind found in Bushman, Hottentot, and a few other African languages. Van Ginneken was not the first to suppose that click-consonants are relics of great linguistic antiquity (cf. W. H. I. Bleek, 1868, who had worked on the Hottentot language) nor the last (Roman Stopa has published on this topic quite recently—1968, 1970, 1973). Gradually, the clicks were reduced to more commonplace consonants, and vowels made their belated appearance. For van Ginneken the absence of vowel-signs in ancient Egyptian writing and their similar absence in various Semitic scripts except when indicated by diacritical-like "vowel points" (as in Hebrew) meant not that these scripts were incomplete as phonetic records but that at the time the scripts were invented, vowels were not present. Van Ginneken's theories have not been widely accepted.

If clicks were not widely regarded as archaic, it was still possible for a linguist like Alf Sommerfelt, writing in 1938, to consider the grammar of Arunta, an Australian aboriginal language, as markedly primitive. So too, Aert Kuipers described Kabardian, a surviving language of the Caucasus, as markedly archaic both in phonology and grammar (1960).

Heinz Werner began to develop his notion of "physiognomic language" around 1925, continuing along the same lines until 1955. He contrasted expressive language, which involves the total organism and blends different sensory modes as in synaesthesia, with "logico-technical discourse," used primarily in the exchange of formal messages. Sound symbolism is a characteristic feature of Werner's physiognomic language level, in which words are embedded in a context lacking sharp boundaries. Malinowski saw something of the same thing in his analysis of the language along the Trobriand Islanders (1935).

Revival of the mouth–gesture theory was mainly the work of R. A. S. Paget in England and Alexander Jóhannesson in Iceland. Paget wrote steadily on the topic in books and articles from about 1925 until his death in 1955. He believed that Lower Paleolithic man had not achieved articulate speech but had used a gestural–mimetic language not unlike the sign languages of the deaf. The very slow growth of tool making during the Lower Paleolithic suggested that language development might have been similarly slow (cf. R. J. Pumphrey, 1951). Paget assembled data from many unrelated language families around the world, which showed phonetic and semantic resemblances that he did not think could be explained except by the mouth–gesture theory. Giorgio Fano (1962), after an extensive review of almost all glottogonic theories, found mouth–gesture to be "the only one upon which one can found an acceptable solution of this vexatious problem [p. 290]," MacDonald Critchley, a neurologist who has written much on gesture and on language and the brain, also considers mouth–gesture to have been a significant factor in the evolution of speech (*Silent Language*, 1975). For a long time, unknown to Paget, Jóhannesson was working up data supporting the same hypothesis. In *Origin of Language* (1949), he presented material from both Indo-European and Semitic sources. In Indo-European, he claimed that about 5% of the words could be attributed to interjection, 10% to onomatopoeia, leaving 85% explainable as direct or indirect derivations from mouth–gesture.

The Hungarian–Dutch psychologist, Géza Révész, became interested in glottogenesis around 1939. His major work on the origins and prehistory of language appeared in German in 1946 and was translated into several other languages including English (1956). It drew numerous reviews and offers a good survey of most of the serious theories of language origin, including its author's own ideas. Révész found fault with all previous efforts and instead supported social "contact theory," in which man is seen to have an internal need to communicate such that initial "contact sounds," or cries addressed to others, are gradually refined into speech. For less intelligent animals, emotional contact suffices, but man's highly intelligent status required a system of intelligent communication as well. For someone who considered previous theorists unsound in their reasoning, Révész's "contact theory" is, to say the least, disappointing: He failed to explain how "contact sounds" really became words. He posited three essential functions in language: imperative, indicative, and interrogative, which will be recognized as practically identical to de Laguna's "critical functions": commands, declarations, and questions.

E. H. Sturtevant (1947) did provide examples of how a sign might originate, although his best examples were of gestures and not the more difficult vocal signs. A group of ancient hunters, for example, might use onomatopoeia in the celebration of their kill, imitating the call of the vanquished animal; in another example, a "tired mother" out berry-picking with her child, might indicate with a wave of her hand that the child should continue picking. Kelso de Montigny (1949), in a short article on language origin, relied on the standard onomatopoeia and interjectional arguments. In a lengthy philosophical monograph, Arno Bussenius (1950–1951), advanced a kind of evolutionary schema based on the gradual progressive evolution of cognitive competence, which developed the ability to impose meanings. But articulate speech did not appear until the Upper Paleolithic. An unusual element in Bussenius's presentation was his view that the mastery of fire was an important key to full language capacity, since burning wood promoted a "fantasizing" stimulus (1951, Vol. 5, p. 157). No one else found the roots of language in Paleolithic pyromania.

In several articles between 1941 and 1951, Oddone Assirelli, a follower of Trombetti, wrote on glottogenesis, in reviews of the click theory of van

Ginneken, and the contact theory of Révész. He favored a gestural explanation and supported Tcang Tceng Ming's ideas about the gestural components in early Chinese writing. For Assirelli, gesture–language had coexisted
for a long period with speech, during which time speech changed from click
sounds to more common kinds of sounds. Truly articulate speech appeared
at the same time as the first *Homo sapiens*.

William Entwhistle (1949) suggested that early language was not
grammatical, observing that in everyday modern speech a great deal of the
meaning in any verbal message is really supplied by the environmental or
social context. He gave an example of English sentence: *What's his name is
bringing in the thingummybob!* He supposed that in very small groups of
people having limited interests, language could function well at such a
vague level. "The determining factor in language is the hearer's acceptance
of conventional symbols as standing intelligibly for meanings [p. 121]."
Meanings, of course, were just what official linguistic science had striven to
eliminate from consideration, and their omission explains why the early
efforts at making computers into acceptable translators were such fiascos.

LANGUAGE ORIGIN IDEAS: 1950 TO THE
PONGID BREAKTHROUGH

The 1950s were not rich in new glottogonic ideas. Felice Bruni (1951)
fell back on onomatopoeia, although he was aware that reconstructed roots
did not support this explanation. Gertrud Pätsch (1955) advocated a work-
related theory based more or less on Engels and perhaps indirectly on Noiré.
Karl Ammer (1958) placed the beginning of articulate speech in the Upper
Paleolithic, a theory that was no longer very novel. A. Roback (1954, Chap.
4) supported the mouth–gesture idea, which he called the "voco-sensory
origin theory." He also saw onomatopoeia as the incipient reproduction of
perceived sounds in the form of vocomotor images. Roback's glottogonic
model actually incorporates the three main acoustic explanations: sound
imitation, mouth–gesture, and a third explanation resembling F. Max Müller's ding-dong hypothesis. Interjections, if one were to add them, can be
considered a subset of onomatopoeia, since they can be thought of as
imitations of the emotional cries or calls of others. Friedrich Kainz, a
psychologist of language, wrote on language origins in 1937 and later
devoted several chapters to the topic in his comprehensive *Psychologie der
Sprache* (3rd ed., 1962–1965). In 1961, he also wrote on the topic of
"animal language," shwing that it is not really language in any useful sense
of the term, and that it does not shed any light on man's language capacity.

J. M. Briceño-Guerrero, a Venezuelan who had been a student of Kainz in Vienna, issued in 1970 a small book on glottogenesis that is worth mentioning as one of the few books on that topic published in Spanish in modern times. Both Kainz and his former student manage to avoid commitment to any particular glottogonic theory.

Chomsky versus Skinner

In 1957 the well-known American psychologist B. F. Skinner issued his *Verbal Behavior,* which he intended to be the definitive explanation of language phenomena from the standpoint of operant behavioral theory. Surprisingly, the book contains some remarks about language origins (see pp. 464, 461, and 467), including a reference to Paget's mouth–gesture theory. It was not for this reason, however, that Skinner's work soon became the target of a very powerful attack in *Language* by Noam Chomsky (1959), whose own *Syntactic Structures* (1957) was already causing consternation in more traditional linguistic circles. Chomsky's views about the innate basis for human language competence, his revival of what he called "Cartesian linguistics" (1966), and his repudiation of the long-cherished tenets of behaviorism in linguistics, marked a kind of paradigm shift. But on the question of how language had come into existence (to which the structuralists had certainly been indifferent), Chomsky offered only the unsatisfactory notion of "mutation." The reports of the experimental inculcation of modest language competence in chimpanzees did not shake Chomsky's Cartesianism, and his remarks at the 1975 New York Academy of Sciences Conference indicated that he did not take much stock in the announced subject-matter of that affair.

The philosopher of language, F. Waisman, following one of Wittgenstein's leads, suggested in his discussion of gesture (1965, p. 65) that an entire language could originate from deictic or ostensive definitions. Such a language could have negatives and numerals.

Hockett and the Design Features of Language

In several papers, Charles F. Hockett drew attention to what he called the "design features of language," some of which he found in the social communication systems of honey bees and birds, but which were most fully represented in the spoken language of man. In a joint paper with Robert Ascher (1964), which presented a general scenario on hominization, it was proposed that language arose from the "opening up of the primate call system," so that it became productive and semantic. In this process, calls, which before had been distinctively emotional, blended into new wordlike compounds usable as labels for particular kinds of objects or actions. Hockett modified his list of design features in successive publications, but in its original form it served to stimulate glottogonic thinking (cf. R. A. Hinde, Ed., 1972). Hockett's feature of "duality of patterning," which is what the French call "double articulation," may have received too much emphasis as a criterion of true language and may, in fact, have arisen rather late in the evolution of speech. Although William Stokoe, Jr. has described something analogous to duality of patterning in American Sign Language (1960), it is possible that a sign language lacking thoroughgoing duality could exist (perhaps at the price of severe restrictions on the size of its lexicon), and that the emergence of duality is one of the very few available solutions for the formation of a large lexicon, given the peculiar constraints that may characterize the memory capacities of higher mammals.

Revival of Glottogonic Speculation in the 1960s

Thomas A. Sebeok began to investigate animal communication in the early 1960s, and in his work defined the subfield of zoosemiotics. In 1969 came his annotated bibliography on zoosemiotics, and in 1970 a large volume that he had edited appeared, dealing with the same subject. Although Sebeok has never espoused any particular glottogonic model, his work in animal communication has stimulated research and theory in this area. He has remained rather dubious of the true status of the linguistic accomplishments of chimpanzees, invoking the ghost of the performing horse, Clever Hans.

Morris Swadesh (1909–1967) came to the problem of glottogenesis from a properly orthodox linguistic background, having been trained both by Leonard Bloomfield and Edward Sapir and having done extensive work on American Indian languages. In the 1950s, however, he began to develop, in the face of much criticism, a lexicostatistical method which was at first applied to questions of language chronology. Eventually he was led by his data to the highly unconventional view that all existing languages in the New and Old Worlds could be traced back to a single ancestral stock, which was spoken about 40,000 to 50,000 years ago. This theory sounded more like Trombetti than Bloomfield, although Swadesh's other teacher, Sapir, had not only drastically reduced the number of New World linguistic phyla but had offered the unsupported suggestion that Na-Dene (a North American language stock which includes Athabaskan) might be related to Sino-Tibetan. In an article in a Mexican journal in 1965 and in a posthumously published volume, *The Origin and Diversification of Language* (1971)

Swadesh marshaled the evidence for a monogenetic model of the evolution of spoken languages, presenting data which, without precisely saying so, suggested the mouth–gesture theory developed by Paget and Jóhannesson.

Work along these lines is being continued by Mary LeCron Foster (1969, 1970, in press), who also places the advent of articulate spoken language about 40,000 years ago. It was approximately at this time, of course, that the Upper Paleolithic Era dawned, and from this time also come the earliest skeletal remains of *Homo sapiens sapiens,* along with evidence of a rich and rapidly diversifying technology. Berkeley anthropologists with great expertise in hominid evolution and African prehistory appear to agree with Foster's model, which is not very different from that of Swadesh, and which, as we have seen, had been advanced previously on more subjective grounds. Alexander Marshack's work on what appears to be evidence for Upper Paleolithic notation or tally marking (1975), also supports the notion that a striking expansion of human cognitive powers took place during that period, especially in Europe.

The resurgence of interest in glottogenesis in the early 1970s can be partly explained by the convergence of ideas and data from several previously compartmentalized disciplines, not all of which were "officially" concerned with language phenomena. The study of animal communication, including birdsong and insect sounds, had had a long and separate career. The stimulating effects of Hockett's "design features" approach apparently helped to bring this body of research to the attention of linguists and anthropologists, as did Sebeok's development of zoosemiotics. Field studies of nonhuman primates had greatly expanded, starting in the early 1950s in Japan and Africa, and by the 1960s they included some extremely important long-term work on chimpanzees in the wild, along with less extensive work on the gorilla and the orangutan. Human paleontology underwent an explosive expansion at this time stimulated by unexpectedly rich discoveries of new fossil material, mostly specimens of Australopithecine grade, in southern and eastern Africa. Since 1950, advances in knowledge of the earliest phases of hominization have been phenomenal. Interest in the existence or extent of language capacity in the early hominids no longer seems absurd, given the kinds of information about their locomotor behavior, tool-making proclivities, ecological relationships, and cranial anatomy that have become available during the past 35 years. The Piltdown fake was exposed at the beginning of the 1950s, and thereby a serious barrier to viewing the evolution of the hominid brain as a continuum from comparatively late common latest pongid-hominid ancestors was removed (Jerison, 1973). Neurologists had been deeply concerned with the brain in relation to language for over a century, studying the many varieties of aphasia, for example, but until the 1960s they generally worked in isolation from linguists. Most linguists and psychologists working on "verbal behavior" managed until then to regard the brain as a black box so that with a few honorable exceptions, including Roman Jakobson (1956, 1964), most of them virtually ignored the massive literature accumulated over the years by neurosurgeons and clinical neurologists. Even the study of child language had been relatively neglected by linguists until the 1960s, which seems surprising in light of its current popularity.

Within the main body of psychology, the changes of the past two decades seem to amount to a paradigm shift (in Kuhn's, 1970, sense), one marked by the emergence of a sturdy interest in cognitive psychology, and a belated discovery of the importance of the work of Jean Piaget. The explosion of interdisciplinary information also saw the founding of new journals, like *Brain and Language* and of explicitly interdisciplinary scholarly aids such as *LLBA (Language and Language Behavior Abstracts)* and *DSH (Deafness, Speech and Hearing Abstracts)*, whose clienteles are obviously very diversified in terms of their academic specializations.

Trained investigators in these many fields were probably shocked when their researches led them to wonder what the "experts" knew about the origins and evolution of human language and speech. They must have found that cupboard embarrassingly bare, or at best stocked only with ideas and data hardly more advanced than those of the 1860s and 1870s.

THE CHIMPANZEE ERA OF GLOTTOGONIC RESEARCH

Appropriately enough in the present context, we may designate the decade prior to the date of this volume the Chimpanzee Era of glottogonic research. We do so not because everyone working on the language-origin problem accepts the evidence presented so far on the language capabilities of anthropoid apes, nor because of the particular language medium of some of the experiments (manual gesture happens to fit one of the standard glottogonic theories), but rather because this brief period from about 1966 to 1976 has produced at last some empirical data that permits us to circumvent the Cartesian barrier between man and beast. Until the Gardners and Premack in their somewhat different experiments had begun to demonstrate a degree of language-handling capacity in nonhuman primates, discussion of the origins of language always presupposed that language is uniquely human. Once this basic tenet was shaken, the question took on the dimensions of a soluble biological problem instead of a metaphysical exercise. As already noted, there are many well-read and intelligent scholars, like

Susanne K. Langer, who, though fully aware of the chimpanzee studies, still insist on a fundamental dichotomy between man and beast (Langer, 1972, Vol. 2; Powers, 1974, 1975; Dance, 1975). In Langer's case this position is the more surprising, since she is one of the few people outside anthropology to have recognized the bearing of the Australopithecine evidence on language origins (Langer, 1972, Vol. 2, p. 298). On the other hand, biochemical work ably summarized by Mary-Claire King and A. C. Wilson (1975) indicates that if language-like behavior could be elicited in a nonhuman species, it would most probably be in *Pan troglodytes* (chimpanzee), the organism closest to mankind. Indeed, they suggest that man and chimpanzee are close enough to be considered sibling species.

The Australopithecine evidence also influenced the thinking of the Hanoi philosopher, Trân Duc Thao. In several articles, and then in a book, *Recherches sur l'Origine du Langage et de la Conscience* (1973), he addressed the topics of glottogenesis and the origins of human consciousness in a Marxian framework, but did not simplistically assume either development to be the outcome of communal labor as had Engels. Trân's model is based on the progressive elaboration of the pointing gesture, which is still observable in the ontogeny of language in the human preverbal infant. His account of the growth of a lexicon and grammar from ostension is much more complete than Wittgenstein's (1958) brief allusion to the matter or Waisman's discussion (1965) already mentioned. Trân discloses no personal acquaintance with the sign language of the deaf, an understanding that might have enriched his presentation. When it comes to explaining how gesture language was transformed into speech, Trân is considerably less successful.

Other recent contributions to the gestural theory include papers by this writer (Hewes, 1973a, 1974, in press), William Stokoe, Jr. (1974a, b, in press), A. Kendon (ms.), B. K. Sladen (1974), D. Kimura (1974), and several others. Although R. J. Duffy and K. L. Duffy (1975) do not tie their comment to a language-origin theory, they observe that "there is a common symbolic competence underlying gestural and verbal communication, and . . . aphasia is an impairment in this competence, which is reflected in impaired visual and gestural performance [p. 127]." They add that the voluminous research on aphasia has been focused too narrowly on speech and written language deficits. Nelson Goodman (1967) asked a related question, "Don't you think . . . that before anyone acquires language, he has an abundance of practice in 'developing and using rudimentary prelinguistic symbolic systems in which gestures and sensory and perceptual occurrences of all sorts function as signs? [p. 25]."

The origin of language in song has also acquired a recent supporter in Frank B. Livingstone (1973). In connection with this theory, Earl Count's

(1974) criticism should be consulted. A. E. Mourant (1973) discussed glottogenesis on the supposition that its mastery in early man came at a much later age in the life span that it does now, when children usually learn to speak only a few years after infancy. Studies of very young chimpanzees by the Gardners and others do not support this notion: Sign language begins to be acquired well within the first year of life, and prior to the age at which human infants start to produce speechlike vocalizations.

J. N. Hattiangadi (1973) has proposed that language arose in early hominids through the play-imitation of adult calls, but like so many other efforts to derive speech directly from nonhuman vocal behavior, his theory does not seem to take into account the extensive neural restructuring that would have been required to bring vocal calls under voluntary cortical control, lateralizing them to one cerebral hemisphere in the process. James Hamilton's (1975) argument is more neurologically oriented. He says that predatory mammals exhibit better performance on delayed reward tests than nonpredators, and that the evolution of the hunter hominid entailed selection for memory capacity, an attribute that seems to have been an important element in language emergence. Laughlin and d'Aquili (1974) suggest that the hominids, perhaps beginning with the Australopithecines, possessed "cognitive extension of prehension," by which they mean understanding of causal relationships beyond the immediate sensory field, and which they see in man's advanced tool-using abilities and also in language. They reject Hockett's blending of formerly discrete primate vocal calls as a plausible part of a glottogonic model, but in its place they offer no replacement, such as the gestural hypothesis, despite the promise of their chapter headed "Structuralism and Language Acquisition."

Philip Lieberman and Edmund Crelin and others collaborated in an elaborate laboratory project to reconstruct the vocal tracts and vocal output capacities of certain hominid fossil forms (cf. Lieberman, 1975). If their findings are valid, spoken language of a fully modern kind would not have been possible until the time of the pre-Neanderthal Steinheim and Rhodesian populations, and the Neanderthalers might have been limited in their speech to slower delivery and a more limited phonetic range compared to modern man. As for the Australopithecines (based on casts of the Sterkfontein individual formerly called "Plesianthropus") no articulate language would have been possible for them, although a full range of vocal cries would presumably have been present. If speech with its several special features was impossible or limited for earlier hominids until two or three hundred thousand years ago, a lengthy period of gesture-language (or else, no language of any sort) seems to be indicated, although this is not a matter discussed by Lieberman et al. (cf. Lieberman, 1975). This project has drawn heavy fire centered chiefly on the question of the speech-aptitude of Neanderthal man, to which Lieberman has prepared rejoinders.

On the topic of Neanderthal man's language, James Hamilton (1974) offers the notion that the somewhat larger average brain size of Neanderthal man compared to *Homo sapiens sapiens* may have been due in part to "the need to store efficiently potentially ambiguous verbal data," with the implication that with further language evolution, such ambiguity was markedly reduced. If language handling, which takes up about 20% of the total cortical volume, has really become easier during the past 40,000 to 50,000 years as a result of lexical and grammatical advances, a moderate reduction in brain volume might have been selectively advantageous, given the immense circulatory and metabolic demands of a big brain. It is tempting to point to the far more striking reduction over the past 30 years in the size of computers. To be sure, hominid neurons have not been progressively miniaturized; instead, the language programs may have become much more efficient.

In 1973, R. J. Alexander argued that the need for enhanced communication with others explains language emergence despite the evidence on the importance of private thinking. I would assume that "private thinking" was rendered more effective as soon as predicative or propositional communication in whatever modality came into being. Chimpanzee studies indicate that among subjects trained to use some kind of language system, learning to name or label objects leads to some improvement in the ability to solve problems.

R. M. Allott (1973) reexamined sound symbolism, using data from many different languages around the world, and found evidence for sound symbolism even in color-terms, where it might not have been expected. If his findings can be supported, Allott has seriously undermined the dictum of de Saussure on the "arbitrariness of the linguistic sign." If there really is a tendency for words that sound similar to have similar meanings in languages not known to be historically related, it would be hard to maintain that word-signs are truly arbitrary.

In a short article published in 1967, Roger W. Wescott reopened the closed subject of language evolution. Eric H. Lenneberg's *Biological Foundations of Language* came out the same year, and soon afterward came the first publications about the chimpanzee experiments performed by the Gardners and by David Premack. In 1970, in quick response, a Neurosciences Research Symposium assembled 13 specialists from various fields to discuss the question of whether apes are capable of language (Ploog & Melnechuk, Eds., 1972). Ambitious as the symposium was, it may have been held too soon after the initial research appeared to permit any kind of scientific consensus, as the Gardners' concluding remarks in the resulting volume indicate. Since then, there have been several smallish conferences on language and apes, most of them in the United States, and a few in Western Europe, although their focus has not necessarily been upon the wider question of language origins. In 1972 a symposium with 13 participants was held in Toronto, the proceedings of which were issued as a book, *Language Origins*, edited by R. W. Wescott (1974). Articles on glottogenesis began to crop up in such publications as *American Anthropologist, Current Anthropology,* and *Man,* testimony that the topic is once more respectable.

In September 1975 over 900 people attended a 4-day conference on the origins and evolution of language and speech sponsored by the New York Academy of Sciences. This conference had over 80 participants. Not since the Berlin Academy essay competition over 200 years earlier had a distinguished academy recognized that the origins and evolution of language and speech constitute topics worthy of serious investigation. A thorough review of the 1975 conference would be out of place here. Still a few points can be made. First, although linguistics was represented in the program, the emphasis was on biology, a reflection, perhaps, of the orientations of the organizers, S. Harnad, H. Steklis, and Jane Lancaster. The concluding remarks were presented by Robin Fox, a cultural anthropologist; David Premack, psychologist; Sherwood Washburn, a human paleontologist-anthropologist; and Oscar Marin, a neurologist. Conspicuously absent was a representative from linguistic science. Reports of work on the development of language in apes constituted an important part of the proceedings, along with papers on work in neurolinguistics and psycholinguistics, animal communication, and on cognitive evidence from prehistoric archaeology. Only one special glottogonic theory, the gestural theory, was the subject of an entire session, although this same theory also appeared in other discussions, in Lamendella's glottogonic model, and in papers by Steklis and Harnad, and by Marshack. Comprehensive glottogonic scenarios were limited to the models of J. Lamendella and Julian Jaynes; both models incorporated a version of the gestural hypothesis.

CONCLUDING OBSERVATIONS

This survey of the history of language origin theories must end in inconclusive fashion, primarily because it has been compiled at a time when the literature relating to the topic has reached the proportions of a flood of new and only slowly digestible information. It seems clear to me that the work on language capabilities in apes has been one of the important developments triggering the reopening of the problem. The work with apes and language has made it possible, for the first time, to manipulate factors in the learning of a first language, in a way that would be quite unethical if the subjects were human children. The profoundly deaf are a population in which language can be investigated without necessarily equating language with speech, but deaf children's acquisition of language cannot be endlessly tampered with, in a manner acceptable with chimpanzee subjects. There are many possible practical educational and therapeutic spin-offs from the language work with chimpanzees. More important in the long run may be the increased understanding of that area of behavior which has had so much to do with making us "human": the institution of language.

An appendix follows which lists with brief annotations the principal language origin theories, to which reference has been made in the foregoing historically organized account.

APPENDIX: THE GLOTTOGONIC THEORIES

Divine Origin

The Biblical account (Gen. 2:19–20, 11:1–9), followed by many centuries of exegesis, had more influence on language origin theories than other supernatural explanations. Hinduism assumed that the language of the gods and of the Cosmos was Sanskrit. In Islamic thought the primordial language was held to be Arabic. The Jews and Christians tended to argue in favor of Hebrew.) For the Chinese the problem centered mainly on the origin of the Chinese writing system, devised by a Sage Emperor in the remote past rather than on the beginnings of speech. *Language Origins: A Bibliography* by the writer (Hewes, 1975, 2nd rev. ed., pp. 835–836) lists over 200 works on the divine or supernatural origin of language. Until the eighteenth century, few European writers offered any other explanation.

Single Mutation

Hardly more scientific than the divine theory, this view holds that one or a few mutant genes suddenly equipped some ancient hominid with the power of language. N. Chomsky (1967) has attributed man's innate language acquisition competence to such a mutation. Alexander (1973) points out the absurdity of the idea of a "language gene."

Innate Propensity

This theory can be regarded as an even less precise version of the mutation theory since the "innateness" is usually offered without any biological explanation. It may satisfy those who reject supernaturalism but do not wish to explore the problems beyond saying that the phenomenon is a natural given. Some or all of man's propensity for language may well be innate, but that does not mean that "innateness" constitutes an explanation.

Social Pressure or Need

The same objections apply here, except that the proffered explanation is one remove more distant. Social necessity, presumably acting upon an existent innate capacity, causes language to emerge or become manifest. Gregory of Nyssa (fourth century A.D.) found this explanation more plausible than direct divine creation of language. The idea can be found in a great many other writers, especially since the close of the seventeenth century. See John Locke, Adam Smith, W. D. Whitney, and G. Révész.

Contact Theory

This theory, a special version of the one immediately above, was proposed by G. Révész (1946, 1956). Man supposedly has inherent communicational needs comparable in some respects to those of lower animals, for whom simple emotional calls suffice. For man with his far more developed intellect, however, contact and communication must have intellectual content, ergo: language.

Social· Control or Coöperation

Grace de Laguna (1927, 1963 2nd ed.), regarded language as a response to a need for more effective social control. She emphasized "decontextualization" as an important ingredient in the emergence of propositional or predicative language. Edmund Critchley has wondered why social control or cooperation, if they sufficed for man, did not likewise lead to language in apes.

Conventionalist Theory

Men at some time in the distant past decided to establish language by assigning socially agreed upon (vocal) signs to referents. This theory was one of the positions debated in Plato's *Cratylus Dialogue*. Words are therefore purely arbitrary inventions. Critics have wondered how, in the absence of an existing language, the participants in such a conference could have carried on their deliberations as they determined which sounds to assign to different meanings. Some have suggested that they could have done so in gestures, an explanation that assumes a preexistent gesture language, requiring, in turn, still another explanation.

Vocalic Theories

These do not constitute a single theory but a category of glottogonic explanations that contain the assumption that language has always been vocal–auditory, and hence grew out of nonhuman animal calls and cries. Linguistic scientists, for the most part, adhere to this general view, which may be called "vocalist." Various advantages have been cited for sound-based language, although sometimes only to explain why a gestural system would have eventually given way to speech.

Interjectional, Emotional Cry, or "Pooh-Pooh" Theory

This theory may be subsumed under the above; however, it stresses not just any kind of vocalizing but calls or cries triggered by strong emotions, emotions aroused by such stimuli as environmental dangers, pain, sexual drives, or even satisfaction and delight. F. Max Müller (1877) designated this explanation the "pooh-pooh" theory. In modern man, such "animal" calls or cries, including laughter, shrieks, and sighs, seem to be mediated in a very different part of the brain than speech, and furthermore, are bilaterally represented. Nonhuman calls or cries appear to have very limited descriptive, predicative, or propositional content; at the most, perhaps they differentiate between terrestrial and airborne predators and the like.

Onomatopoeia, Sound Imitation, or the Echoic Theory (the "Bow-Wow" Theory)

This theory assumes that speech results not simply from innate emotional reflexes but arose when early man began to imitate, with varying degrees of accuracy, diverse natural sounds. Modern man clearly possesses such a capacity for imitation, and it can be trained to the point where manmade imitations of certain animal calls may produce responses in the animals imitated comparable to the responses they make to their conspecifics. Numerous bird species exhibit similar sound-imitative capabilities. Critics of onomatopoeia as a language-origin theory note that in known spoken languages, words of onomatopoeic origin, while present, comprise only a small percentage of the lexicon, and some seemingly onomatopoeic words are derived from nonimitative root-forms. In a composite language-origin model, onomatopoeia may be allotted a significant but not central role in word-formation.

Work-Chant or Yo-He-Ho Theory

Vocal sounds may be uttered during strenuous effort, and in joint or communal labor their rhythmic production may help coordinate the actions of individuals. L. Noiré (1877) saw this type of utterance as the main factor in glottogenesis, and his idea was attractive to socialist writers. A variant but still labor-related theory holds that the noises made in working with particular kinds of implements were vocally imitated (i.e., onomatopoeically) and eventually turned into words standing for tools or processes. A. S. Diamond (1960, p. 265) observes that such theories posit much too much elaboration of joint labor among primordial men.

Ding-Dong Theory

This theory was the contribution of F. Max Müller, who held that man had an innate propensity for associating certain sounds with certain kinds of objects and actions, responding to them in a manner analogous to the way an object resonates when struck. This manner of word-formation is to be distinguished from onomatopoeia. Müller held that the primitive, reconstructed Indo-European "roots" were the outgrowth of this ding-dong effect. Diamond (1959) comments that such a view "depends on a mysterious law of harmony, which takes us nowhere [p. 265]."

Festal Origin

J. Donovan in 1893 and 1895 saw the beginnings of language in dance, song, and related expressive soundmaking. Otto Jespersen (1924) likewise thought that early language must have been "musical and passionate." Similar views were expressed by Suzanne K. Langer in 1962; in 1972 she deemphasized this approach.

Vocal Play

Similar to the above except that the play or expressiveness was held to have occurred in infants and young children, beginning with cooing and babbling.

Babbleluck Theory

E. L. Thorndike (1943) proposed that the selective reinforcement of initially random babbling leads to standardized vocalizations, which eventually became words. He saw such reinforcement as a process that not only serves to teach every human infant the speech of its community, but also as one that could have operated to develop a primordial spoken language. He did not explain how the parents of the earliest babblers were able to shape infant vocalizations. Révész (1959, p. 219) explicitly rejected this idea.

Sing-Song Theory

A theory similar to the two immediately above, this notion was revived by Frank B. Livingstone (1973), who attributed singing to the Australopithecines. He did not implicate organized festal occasions in his theory or place the singing behavior at an infantile or child level. Commentators on Livingstone's theory were generally unpersuaded by it.

Language and the Brain

Properly speaking, this is not a "theory" of language origin but simply the view that much or all of language emerged as a result of cerebral evolution and specialization, involving such developments as lateralization of functions, enhanced memory storage, and the evolution of sound-decoding neural mechanisms. Some investigators interested in this approach have looked for language-related features that might have left traces on the inside of the braincase. Others have thought in terms of a "cerebral Rubicon" or threshold, usually related to brain size, above which language in hominids was possible. These views can be contrasted to those in which the emergence of language is seen chiefly in terms of the evolutionary changes in the vocal tract.

Language and the Vocal Tract

These views also reflect a focus of interest rather than a clear-cut theory. They hold that the main seat of language origin is related to the vocal tract in its anatomical and physiological aspects. Simplistic formulations suggest that man developed language when his tongue achieved the shape, size, and flexibility found in modern man, or when the larynx moved to a relatively lower position than it occupies in other mammals. Theorists focusing on the vocal tract tend to equate language with speech.

Gestural Theory

Obviously this theory is not capable of accounting for the whole of glottogenesis, since the existing languages of mankind are spoken rather than gestural. Gestural formulations do show, however, how naming could have arisen out of simple pointing, and are able to relate primordial language to the already highly developed visual and manipulatory capabilities of the primates. The gestural approach also gains credibility in the light of the marked incapacity of nonhuman primates, including the pongids, to acquire even rudimentary speech sound production, or control, although recent experiments have shown that chimpanzees and other apes may be taught simple language-like communication systems, or, if one wishes, rudimentary language. This writer is only one of a great many proponents of this theory, which still, of course, requires further hypotheses, if it is to explain how a gestural language might have been transformed into a vocal one (cf. Hewes, 1973, 1974, 1975; Stokoe, in press; Kendon, ms.; Wescott, 1974; Steklis & Harnad, in press; Lamendella, in press).

Mouth–Gesture

This is one of the theories that could explain how a gestural language might have been transformed into a spoken one. First suggested in 1962 by J. Rae, and elaborated by A. R. Wallace, to some extent by W. Wundt, and then by R. A. S. Paget and A. Jóhannesson, it has attracted support from several others (G. Fano, 1962, E. Rossi, 1962, and this writer). It asserts that the tongue, lips, and other vocal organs tend to act in unison or "sympathy" with the hand and arm movements when the latter are employed in sign language and probably also when the hands and arms engage in tool using. If such movements in the vocal organs are accompanied by vocalization, the resulting sounds would resemble articulate speech, which might eventually acquire the same meanings as the already used gestural signs. Grace de Laguna, A. S. Diamond (1959, pp. 269–270), who considered it "dangerous," and G. Révész, are among those who have rejected this theory. Sound-symbolism may be explicable on the basis of mouth–gesture (cf. R. M. Allott, 1975).

Tools and Language

The notion that words arose as sound-imitations of the actions of various tools has been mentioned. A broader theory proposed by many language-origin theorists proposes that tool making, tool using, and language possess very similar neural program patterns of a syntactic character.

That tools resemble words is a much older idea found in Plato's *Cratylus*. I have suggested (Hewes, in press) that the task of butchering the carcasses of large game animals entails similar programming sequences, and therefore if the evolution of language were connected with implemental activity, it was probably also linked to skilled dissection procedures. Finally, as specialized plant-food processing also came to involve complex action-programs including fire maintenance, fire making, and cookery, these too may have had a glottogonic influence or feedback effect.

Polygenesis versus Monogenesis

Once more, both theories represent views about language evolution rather than explanatory models. Linguists as divergent in their views as Alfredo Trombetti and Morris Swadesh have inclined toward a single ancestor for all spoken language systems, and some others are disposed to accept such a view (M. L. Foster, in press). Few linguists are prepared to accept the evidence in favor of monogenesis; if language, on the other hand, had multiple origins, they would hardly have been simultaneous, and polygenic origin models therefore present the possibility that some human groups might have existed without language (or at least without spoken language) for a longer time than others. Such theories are hardly in keeping with egalitarian principles. South African click languages are a kind of test case for these conflicting views. Edmund Critchley (1967) suggested that language may have been invented and lost more than once in the long course of human evolution. Monogenism, in accordance with Occam's Razor, possesses the virtue of elegance. Current interest in language universals need not commit one to either side of this dispute, since the observable similarities could have arisen in a common, ancestral language or could have been generated independently on the basis of pan-human psycholinguistic unity of some sort.

"Primitive Languages" and Glottogenesis

Primitive languages do not provide an explanation of glottogenesis, but are a possible source of information about the early stages of language evolution. The theory was quite popular in the nineteenth century, when some held that the languages of technologically backward, isolated peoples must be primitive. On the other hand, even in the eighteenth century, some writers (e.g., Süssmilch, 1766–1767) rejected this notion. In recent times, linguistic scientists have been nearly unanimous in proclaiming as dogma the cognitive equivalence of all languages. If one language is "less advanced" than any other, it is so only because its lexicon is smaller—a condition that presumably can change in short order should the speakers of such a language need to engage in modern science, philosophy, or politics. It may be that the doctrine of the evolutionary equivalence of languages deserves reexamination, particularly in connection with efforts to understand the evolution of language systems in the past 10,000 or so years, when enormous technological, social, and other changes engulfed some language areas leaving others much closer to conditions of 8000 B.C.

Combination Theories

With such a range of glottogonic theories to draw from as I have just outlined (and I have not begun to consider all of the variants which have been suggested under most of the preceding rubrics), theorists can obviously construct complex glottogonic models by combining any two or more of them. Some, indeed, cannot stand alone, as I observed is the case with gestural theory, which has to be supplemented by another theory to account for the prevalence of spoken languages. No scientific law compels us to build theories on a single, unitary basis, especially if the phenomenon we may be interested in seems to be highly complex (certainly the case with language!). Perhaps a plausible glottogonic model might incorporate a fair number of the foregoing theories, except for the miraculous ones. Some lexical domains (such as bird names, which are known to exhibit a high incidence of onomatopoeia) may have originated quite differently than others. Counting systems, worldwide, seem to have been quite transparently based on fingers, toes, hands, and feet, an unlikely source for plant or animal names, and so on.

REFERENCES

N.B.   Reference has been made in this chapter to over 300 titles. In order to keep the length of the following bibliography within reasonable bounds, all items listed in G. W. Hewes, *Language origins: A bibliography* (2 vols.), 1975, The Hague: Mouton & Co., have been omitted with a few exceptions.

Aarsleff, H. The history of language-origins theory. *Annals, New York Academy of Sciences,* in press.
Alexander, R. J. Towards a multidisciplinary view of language: Some biolinguistic reflections. *Linguistische Berichte,* 1973, No. 25, 1–21.
Allott, R. *The physical foundation of language,* 2 vols. Seaford, Sussex: ELB Printers, 1973.
Bastier, J. Linguistique et politique dans la pensée de Louis de Bonald. *Revue des Sciences Philosophiques et Théologiques,* 1974, *58,* 537–560.
Blackwell, T. *Enquiry in the life and writings of Homer.* Menston, England: Scolar Press, 1972.

Boas, G. *The happy beast in French thought of the seventeenth century.* New York: Octagon Books, 1966.

Boas, G. Theriophily. In *Dictionary of the history of ideas* (Vol. 4). New York: Charles Scribner's Sons, 1973.

Boindin, N. Remarques sur le livre intitulé reflexions philosophiques sur l'origine des langues et la signification des mots. *Oeuvres* (2 vols.). Parfait l'aimé, (Ed.), Paris: Prault fils, 1753. Italian translation, in L. Formigari (Ed.), *Maupertuis, Turgot, Maine de Biran: Origine e funzione de linguaggio,* pp. 91–93. Bari: Editori Laterza, 1971.

Bonnet, C. *Oeuvres d'histoire naturelle et de la philosophie* (Vol. 4). Neuchâtel: S. Fauche, 1764–65.

Borst, A. *Der Turmbau von Babel: Geschichte der Meinungen ueber Ursprung und Vielfalt der Sprache und Voelker* (4 vols.). Stuttgart: A. Hiersemann, 1957–63.

Briceño-Guerrero, J. M. El origen del lenguaje. Caracas: Monte Avila Editores, Colección Estudios, 1970.

Caldwell, R. L. Structure de la lettre sur les sourds et muets. *Studies on Voltaire and the 18th century,* 1971, *84,* 109–122.

Chouillet, J. Descartes et le problème de l'origine des langues au 18e siècle. *Dix-huitième siècle,* 1972, 39–60.

Count, E. B. On the phylogenesis of the speech function. *Current Anthropology,* 1974, *15,* 81–90.

Dance, F. E. X. Speech communication: The sign of mankind. In M. J. Adler (Ed.), *A symposium on language and communication.* Chicago: The Encyclopaedia Britannica, 1975.

Diamond, A. S. *The history and origin of language.* London: Methuen and Co., 1960.

Diderot, Denis. *Rameau's nephew and other works.* (J. Barzun & R. H. Bowen, trans.), Indianapolis: Bobbs-Merrill, 1964.

Duffy, R. J., Duffy, J. R., & Pearson, K. L. Pantomime recognition in aphasics. *Journal of Speech and Hearing Research,* 1975, *18,* 115–132.

Fano, G. Saggio sulle origini del linguaggio. Con una storia critica della dottrine glottogoniche. Torino: Guilio Einaudi Editore, 1962.

Formigari, L. *Linguistica ed empirismo nel seicento inglese.* Bari: Editori Laterza, 1970.

Formigari, L. *Maupertuis, Turgot, Maine de Biran: Origine e funzione del linguaggio.* Bari: Editori Laterza, 1971.

Formigari, L. Language and society in the late eighteenth century. *Journal of the History of Ideas,* 1974, *35,* 275–292.

Foster, M. L. The symbolic structure of primordial language. In S. L. Washburn & E. R. McCown (Eds.), *Perspectives in human evolution* (Vol. 4). Menlo Park, California: Benjamin, Inc., in press.

Gardner, B. T. *Signs of language in child and chimpanzee.* Paper presented at the annual convention of the American Psychological Association, Chicago, 1975.

Gardner, B. T., & Gardner, R. A. Evidence for sentence construction in the early utterances of child and chimpanzee. *Journal of Experimental Psychology,* 1975, *104,* 244–267.

Goethe, J. W. Dichtung und Wahrheit. In Eduard von der Hellen (Ed.), *Werke* (Vol. 10). Stuttgart: Cotta, 1911–1912.

Grimsley, R. Some aspects of 'nature' and 'language' in the French Enlightenment. *Studies on Voltaire and the 18th Century,* 1967, 66, 659–677.

Gunderson, K. Descartes, La Mettrie, language and machines. *Philosophy: The Journal of the Royal Institute of Philosophy,* 1964, *39,* 193–222.

Hamilton, J. Hominid divergence and speech evolution. *Journal of Human Evolution,* 1974, *3,* 417–424.

Hastings, H. Man and beast in French thought of the Eighteenth Century. *Johns Hopkins Studies in Romance Literature and Language,* 1936, *27.*

Hattiangadi, J. N. Mind and the origin of language. *Philosophy Forum*, 1973, *14*, 81–98.

Hewes, G. W. Primate communication and the gestural origin of language. *Current Anthropology*, 1973, *14*, 5–24. (a)

Hewes, G. W. An explicit formulation of the relationship between tool-using, tool-making, and the emergence of language. *Visible Language*, 1973, *72*, 101–127. (b)

Hewes, G. W. Gesture language in culture contact. *Sign Language Studies*, 1974, *4*, 1–34.

Hewes, G. W. *Language origins: A bibliography* (2 vols.). The Hague: Mouton and Co., 1975.

Hewes, G. W. Current status of the gestural theory of language origin. *Annals, New York Academy of Sciences*, in press.

Huxley, T. H. On the hypothesis that animals are automata, and its history. In *Methods and results: Essays*. London: Macmillan and Co., [1874], 1893.

Jauffret, L. Introduction aux mémoires [1803]. In G. Hervé (Ed.), *Le premier programme de l'anthropologie. Société d'Anthropologie de Paris, Bulletin et Mémoires*, 1909, *10*, 473–487.

Jerison, H. *Evolution of the brain and intelligence*. New York: Academic Press, 1973.

Jerison, H. A current anthropology book review: Evolution of the brain and intelligence. *Current Anthropology*, 1975, *16*, 403–426.

Josephs, H. *Diderot's dialogue of language and gesture: Le Neveu de Rameau*. Columbus: Ohio State University Press, 1969.

Kainz, F. *Psychologie der Sprache* (5 vols.). Stuttgart: F. Enke, 1962–65.

Kendon, A. Gesticulation, speech and the gesture theory of language origins. Unpublished manuscript.

Keosian, J. Life's beginnings—origin or evolution? *Origins of Life*, 1974, *5*, 285–293.

Kimura, D. *The neural basis of language and gesture* (Research Bulletin No. 292). Department of Psychology, The University of Western Ontario, London, Ontario, 1974.

Kimura, D., & Archibald, Y. Motor functions of the left hemisphere. *Brain*, 1974, *97*, 337–350.

King, M., & Wilson, A. C. Evolution at two levels in humans and chimpanzees. *Science*, 1975, *188*, 107–116.

Knowlson, J. R. The idea of gesture as a universal language in the XVIIth and XVIIIth centuries. *Journal of the History of Ideas*, 1965, *26*, 495–508.

Kuhn, T. *The structure of scientific revolutions* (2nd ed., rev). Chicago: University of Chicago Press, 1970.

Kuipers, A. *Phoneme and morpheme in Kabardian (Eastern Adyghe)*. The Hague: Mouton and Co., 1960.

Lamendella, J. T. Relations between ontogeny and phylogeny of language. *Annals, New York Academy of Sciences*, in press.

Laughlin, C. D., & d'Aquili, E. G. *Biogenetic structuralism*. New York: Columbia University Press, 1974.

Lieberman, P. *On the origins of language: An introduction to the evolution of human speech*. New York: Macmillan Publishing Co., 1975.

Livingstone, F. B. Did the Australopithecines sign? *Current Anthropology*, 1973, *14*, 25–29.

Livingstone, F. B. On Hewes and early vs. late Pleistocene dating. In R. W. Wescott (Ed.), *Language origins*. Silver Spring, Md.: Linstok Press, 1974.

Loi, I. Note all'*Essai sur l'origine des langues* di J. J. Rousseau. *Lingua e Stile*, 1971, *6*, 479–486.

Marshack, A. Some implications of the Paleolithic symbolic evidence for the origin of language. *Annals, New York Academy of Sciences*, 1976.

Megill, A. D. The Enlightenment debate on the origin of language. (Doctoral dissertation, Columbia University, 1974). *Dissertation Abstracts International*, 1975, *36*, 1728A-1729A. (University Microfilms No. 75–18, 418)

Merker, N., & Formigari, L. *Herder—Monboddo: Linguagio e societá*. Bari: Editori, Laterza, 1973.

Meyer, M. F. *Psychology of the other-one, An introductory textbook of psychology*. Columbia: Missouri: The Missouri Book Co., 1921.

Page, A. The origin of language and eighteenth-century English criticism. *Journal of English and Germanic Philology*, 1972, *71*, 12–21.

Perkins, M. L. Rousseau on history, liberty and national survival. *Studies on Voltaire and the 18th Century*, 1967, *53*, 79–169.

Politzer, R. L. On the linguistic philosophy of Maupertuis and its relation to the history of linguistic relativism. *Symposium*, 1963, *17*, 5–16.

Pons, E. Les langues imaginaires dan le voyage utopique: Les deux grammairiens: Vairasse et Foigny. *Revue de Littérature Comparée*, 1932, *12*, 500–532.

Powers, J. H. *From communication to speech communication: The accomplishments of Sarah, Viki, and Washoe.* M. A. Thesis, Denver University, 1974.

Premack, D. La langage et sa construction logique chez l'homme et chez le chimpanzé. In E. Morin & M. Piatelli-Palmerini (Eds.), *L'unité de l'homme*. Paris: Éditions du Seuil, 1974.

Premack, D., & Premack, A. J. Teaching visual language to apes and language deficient persons. In R. Schiefelbusch and L. L. Lloyd (Eds.), *Language perspectives—acquisition, retardation and intervention*. Baltimore: University Park Press, 1974.

Ries, D. C. *Versuchte Vereinigung zweyer entgegensetzten Meinungen, ueber den Ursprung der Sprache, auf Erfahrungen und Beobachtungen an Taubstummen gegruendet*. Frankfurt am Main: Andreá, 1806.

Ritson, J. *An essay on abstinence from animal food as a moral duty*. London: R. Phillips, 1802.

Roback, A. A. Destiny and motivation in language. Cambridge, Mass.: Sci-Art Publishers, 1954.

Rosenkranz, B. *Der Ursprung der Sprache: Ein linguististisch-anthropologischer Versuch.* Heidelberg: Carl Winter, Universitaets-Verlag, 1961.

Rossi, E. *Die Entstehung der Sprache und des menschliches Geistes.* Munich: Ernst Reinhardt Verlag, 1962.

Rudowski, V. A. The theory of signs in the eighteenth century. *Journal of the History of Ideas*, 1974, *35*, 683–690.

Salmon, P. Herder's essay on the origin of language, and the place of man in the animal kingdom. *German Life and Letters*, 1968, *22*, 59–70.

Seigel, J. P. The Enlightenment and the evolution of a language of signs in France and England. *Journal of the History of Ideas*, 1969, *30*, 96–115.

Sladen, B. K. The evolution of the human capacity for language. *Bulletin of the Orton Society*, 1975, *24*, 37–47.

Steklis, H. D., & Harrad, S. From hand to mouth: Some critical stages in the evolution of language. *Annals, New York Academy of Sciences*, in press.

Stokoe, W. C., Jr. Motor signs as the first form of language. In R. W. Wescott (Ed.), *Language origins*. Silver Spring, Md.: Linstok Press, 1974. (a)

Stokoe, W. C., Jr. Appearances, words and signs. In R. W. Wescott (Ed.), *Language origins*. Silver Spring, Md.: Linstok Press, 1974. (b)

Stokoe, W. C., Jr. Sign language autonomy. *Annals, New York Academy of Sciences*, in press.

Vendler, Z. *Res cogitans: An essay in rational psychology*. Ithaca: Cornell University Press, 1972.

Verne, J. *Le village Aérien*, 1901 (English translation: *The Village in the Treetops*). I. O. Evans (Trans.) London: Arco Publications, 1964.

Waisman, F. *The principles of linguistic philosophy*. London: Macmillan, 1965.

Washburn, S. L. CA comment on H. T. Jerison, "Evolution of the brain and intelligence." *Current Anthropology*, 1975, *16*, 412.

Wescott, R. W. The origin of speech. In R. W. Wescott (Ed.), *Language origins*. Silver Spring, Md.: Linstok Press, 1974.

Wescott, R. W. Protolinguistics: The study of protolanguage as an aid to glossogonic research. *Annals, New York Academy of Sciences*, in press.

chapter 2

Linguistic Communication: Theory and Definition

ERNST VON GLASERSFELD

University of Georgia and Yerkes Regional Primate Research Center

INTRODUCTION

Until about 20 years ago, there seemed to be no urgent need to specify very rigorously what we meant when we used the word "language." It was an accepted fact that language belonged exclusively to humans and that there could be no serious contender for that monopoly. Then, in the 1950s, came the "information explosion" and with it the sudden interest in computing machines. Would these machines ever be able to "think" and to handle human language? The suggestion caused a good deal of indignation, and debates tended to become fierce among both laymen and scientists (Taube, 1961; Armer, 1963; Minsky, 1963). The debate may still flare up today, but the fury has diminished. The kinds of task that computers have been celebrated for doing during the intervening years are not likely to threaten man's monopoly of "thinking."

However, a different contender has appeared on the scene. The publication of work with chimpanzees by the Gardners (1971), Premack (1971),

Fouts (1973), and ourselves (Rumbaugh, von Glasersfeld, Warner, Pisani, Gill, Brown, & Bell, 1973) once more called into question the assumption that *Homo sapiens* is the only organism that can handle language. Oddly enough, these publications have not stirred up indignation among laymen. On the contrary, there is a great deal of rather benevolent interest in just how well the various chimpanzees are doing. Only among scientists have there been some signs of alarm. But in contrast to the debate about "thinking," this time attempts are made to define what the contested term means. That is just as well, for if we do not state what it is we are arguing about, we could go on arguing forever. Thus it is important to provide an acceptable definition of "language," and to outline some criteria by which we can recognize language when we find it.

In what follows I shall try to formulate criterial characteristics of the phenomenon we have in mind when we use the term "language," and then to suggest how those criteria might be applied to determine whether or not a given organism is using a linguistic system of communication. I would like to point out that, although language also plays an important role in the cognitive development and functioning of individual organisms, we shall be concerned here only with its communicatory function.

LANGUAGE AND SPEECH

The fact that "language" has always implied *human* language has led to a confusion of two terms, "speech" and "language," which, although certainly related, are not at all the same. Because human language is presumed to have existed as speech long before the development of other channels such as gesture, hieroglyphs, or ideograms, it was taken for granted that *all* language had to be spoken. Many linguists thus came to consider "speech" and "language" as quasi-synonyms, and consequently felt justified in studying language by investigating the acoustic, physical manifestations of speech. I am not suggesting that phonology is not an interesting area of study, but the isolation and classification of speech sounds will not get us very far in an attempt to define language. Sapir, one of the fathers of American linguistics stated this point quite clearly in 1921:

> A speech-sound localized in the brain, even when associated with the particular movements of the "speech organs" that are required to produce it, is very far from being an element of language. It must be further associated with some element or group of elements of experience, say a visual image or a class of visual images or a feeling of relation, before it has even rudimentary linguistic significance [p. 10].

Yet, in the four decades that followed, linguistics focused mainly on speech sounds and disregarded linguistic function and meaning (see, e.g., Bloomfield, 1933; Greenberg, 1954; Hockett, 1954). This approach was rather like attempting to study computational operations by analyzing transistors and all the electronic devices that flip and flop in a computer, while disregarding the programming. The program in this analogy corresponds to what we call "language," and the mechanisms that implement it (transistors, etc.) correspond to "speech." Computational operations can typically be carried out by very different sorts of machines, electric, mechanical, or hydraulic. Electronic machines are preferred mainly because they are faster and because it is much easier to solder wires than to make gears and hydraulic valves. Similarly, the acoustic channel of speech is perhaps the most efficient and practical way to implement a linguistic system for living organisms as we know them, but this does not mean that language *must* be implemented through speech.

The emphasis on phonology and the concomitant lack of interest in semantics (the very aspect without which a system *cannot* have communicatory function) sprang from Bloomfield, whose theoretical stance was close to Watson's stark "behaviorism," and who held that a science of semantics could begin only when it was reduced to a "mechanistic psychology," which, in turn, must be reduced to physiology (Ullman, 1959, p. 7; Wells, 1961, p. 274). Clearly, very rigid behaviorists could have nothing to do with what Sapir had called "elements of experience," "visual images," or "feelings of relation." Yet, if language *does* function as a means of communication, an analysis of it will have to take the direction pointed out by Sapir (1921):

> The mere sounds of speech are not the essential fact of language, which lies rather in the classification, in the formal patterning, and in the relating of concepts. Once more, language, as a structure, is on its inner face the mold of thought. It is this abstracted language, rather more than the physical facts of speech, that is to concern us in our inquiry [p. 22].

WHAT IS COMMUNICATION?

So long as we speak as ordinary people to other people, we are fairly sure that we know what the word "communication" means. Even when we hear of "communication gaps," we have a good idea of what is involved. This feeling of confidence evaporates, however, when we begin to read what psychologists, especially animal psychologists, have to say about communication. In their usage, the term "communication" is, as Thomas Sebeok (1975) has said, "an undefined prime." It is not that attempts at definition have not been made; on the contrary, there have been quite a few. But the trouble is that, to date, these attempts have not helped us to separate what we know is *not* communication from the manifestations that we feel *are* communication. When we read, for instance: "Communication can be said to occur whenever the activities of one animal influence the activities of another animal [Alexander, 1960, p. 38]," we do not have to think long to conjure up examples that meet this criterion and are still far from anything we would normally call communication. Alexander's definition may apply to "interaction," but it is far too general to isolate events of communication. Under this definition, pushing, pulling, fighting, wounding, and even eating another animal would all qualify as "communication." Its only useful feature is its implicit stipulation that there must be at least *two* animals for the kind of transaction we are interested in. That point must be made, as there exists a legitimate use of the term "communication" to describe the interaction within *one* organism, say, between the eye and the brain, or the brain and the muscle.[1]

The very insufficiency of any attempt to define "communication" in terms of action and reaction draws attention to some of the aspects of the phenomenon that need to be specified. First, as has been clear for a long time (cf. Rosenblueth, Wiener, & Bigelow, 1943; Haldane, 1955) communication is not a *mechanical* phenomenon, in that the amount of energy involved in the sender's transmission does not determine what the receiver does. In other words, in communication there is no thermodynamically calculable relationship between the energy change that constitutes the signal and the energy expended as a result of receiving the signal. Instead, in communication there is always an exchange of "information," and it is the informational character of all communication processes that sets them apart from mechanical or chemical interaction. Of course, the information aspect has to do with *meaning*, but the connection is not as simple as it may seem to the ordinary language user.

In the more than three decades that have passed since the publication of the pioneering paper by Rosenblueth *et al.* (1943), the differences between mechanical and informational processes have been made very clear. We now have two complementary theories that allow us to define "communication" unequivocally. On the one hand there is the *mathematical theory of communication* (Shannon, 1948; Wiener, 1948a,b), which deals with the transmission of signals, their recognition by a receiver, and the code by means of which they are translated into messages. On the other hand, there is *information theory* (MacKay, 1954, 1969), which deals with the

---

[1] Norbert Wiener (1948b) made this distinction by speaking of "intercommunication" when sender and receiver were two separate organisms, and of "communication" when sender and receiver were two parts of one organism. Since this usage is not likely to become general, I use the term "communication" in the context of this chapter to refer to communication between *two* organisms.

sending and interpreting of messages. In the first, "information" is a purely quantitative concept; in the second, a qualitative aspect is added. Strictly speaking, therefore, what we ordinarily call "meaning" plays a part only in the second theory. The first theory contains only a weak counterpart to "meaning" in the processes of *encoding* and *decoding*. Wiener (1948a) gives an admirably clear example of those processes:

> If I send one of those elaborate Christmas or birthday messages favored by our telegraph companies, containing a large amount of sentimental verbiage coded in terms of a number from one to one hundred, then the amount of information which I am sending is to be measured by the choice among the hundred alternatives, and has nothing to do with the length of the transcribed "message" [p. 202].

The "encoding" takes place when the telegraph employee gives me the list of one hundred messages, and instead of spelling out my choice, I merely say, "Number 55." Since there is a fixed, conventional connection between each of the messages listed and some number between one and one hundred, another employee, one say in Honolulu, who receives the code number 55 can at once "decode" it by selecting the printed form number 55 that carries the message I have chosen. Note that there is, of course, a second coding and decoding involved in this transaction, namely the transformation (according to Morse code) of the number 55 into the corresponding electric impulses that do the actual traveling to Honolulu and which, in technical terms, constitute the *signal*. This second transformation is analogous to the first, since it, too, is done according to a preestablished fixed coding system. In both these transformations the code, i.e., the total set of fixed correspondences, must be known to both the transmitter and the receiver, and it must be the same code at both ends of the channel. The code lists the conventionally established significations of "artificial signs" sometimes referred to as "meaning" (e.g., a certain sequential pattern of impulses *means* "55," or the number 55 *means* "Many happy returns!") To use the term in this sense is confusing, however, because this sort of "meaning" is always fixed; that is, it must have been agreed on by the code users. Used in this sense, "meaning" would refer in speech, for example, to the rules that govern the conversion of a word or sentence into speech sounds according to the phonetic conventions of the language being used. These rules have nothing to do with what we ordinarily call the "meaning" of a word or sentence. Thus I may have satisfactorily decoded someone's speech sounds and be quite sure of what he has *said* to me, yet, at the same time, I may be quite unsure as to what he *meant* by it.

Thus, decoding a signal and interpreting a message are alike in one respect: In both cases one makes a selection. In decoding, one selects the item (i.e., the message) that has been conventionally linked to the signal at hand. In interpreting, one selects the meaning of the message. The difference is that in interpreting, the possible meanings are not preestablished in a conventionally fixed list. There are several reasons—logical, epistemological, and psychological[2]—why this is so, and they all substantiate the general observation that a message cannot be treated as a detached, independent item the way a signal can. In order to interpret a message, the receiver must take into account a "context," i.e., aspects of his own present state, aspects of the sender's state, and above all an implicit or explicit hypothesis as to *why* the message was sent. Information theory has provided a model by means of which we can approach this very complex process of interpretation (MacKay, 1954, 1969, 1972).

The messages in information theory as well as the signals in the theory of communication are goal directed, in that the source sends them in order to achieve a certain result. This is not to say that there must always be an individual addressee; "to whom it may concern" messages are just as purposive as addressed messages. Finally, it is important to realize that information theory is the more comprehensive of the two models, since it covers not only information conveyed via artificial signs in *communicatory* messages, but also information obtained via the perception of natural signs that enable the perceiver to make inductive inferences.

The distinction between "natural" and "artificial" signs was made by Susanne Langer (1948, p. 59) on the basis of her logical analyses and independently of the technical theories. I have shown elsewhere (von Glasersfeld, 1974) how closely her ideas match those of the cyberneticist and how necessary her distinction is if we want to define "communication." Charles Hockett, in his description of human language by means of design features, approaches the characteristic of artificiality by his conditions of "arbitrariness" and "traditional transmission" (Hockett, 1960a,b, 1963; Hockett & Altmann, 1969). An "arbitrary" sign, in Hockett's definition, is one that has no "iconic" relation (perceptual analogy) to what it signifies, and therefore anyone who does not yet know such an arbitrary sign cannot derive its meaning from the physical characteristics of the sign itself. It can be acquired only by learning, either through "traditional transmission" from the older generation, or, if it happens to be a newly created sign, by agreement with the other users. So far as communication is concerned, however, it is not the arbitrariness of a sign that makes it communicatory but

---

[2] Logical and epistemological, because if signs are used as symbols, their definition has to be an intensional one, i.e., a more or less subjective construct for both sender and receiver. Since there is no way for one user to match another user's constructs directly with his own, his interpretation of a message frequently has to take into account inferences drawn from prior communication experience with the particular sender. The "psychological" indeterminacy springs from the fact that one and the same linguistic message can be sent for widely varying purposes.

its artificiality. The well-known road sign that consists of a capital Z is certainly "iconic," in that it is a stylized picture of the curve to which it refers, but it is communicatory because it is artificial (since it is not part of an actual curve) and because it was put there for the specific purpose of warning approaching motorists.

The concept of "purpose" is essential for the definition of communication, and the purpose has to be on the side of the source or sender (Burghardt, 1970; Thorpe, 1972, pp. 46–47). If someone whom I do not want to offend has cornered me and is telling me an interminable story, I may reach the point where I can no longer suppress a yawn. If he notices it, he may, in spite of my efforts to look interested, infer that I am bored. This interpretation, I maintain, must not be called "communication." It is no different from the inductive inferences we draw from practically everything we perceive; to make such inferences simply requires experience with the phenomena in question. If we see smoke, we infer that there is a fire; if we see a flash of lightning, we infer that there will be thunder (and vice versa); and if someone yawns, we infer that he is either tired, bored, or both. Returning to the example, if the person telling me the boring story happens to be someone whom I do not need to indulge, I may react differently. I may simply say, "That's the third time you've told me that story," or "Let's talk about something else." In either case I would be *communicating* to him that I would like him to stop boring me. There could be no doubt on my side about the purposiveness of my communication.

THE RESTORATION OF PURPOSE

For a long time, any mention of "purpose" was considered taboo by many scientists. The reason for this lay in the fact that the concept of purposive action or goal directedness had been tied up with final causes and what was considered to be Aristotelian teleology. It was believed that talk of purpose inevitably entailed the belief that something in the future could determine what was taking place now or had happened in the past. Ayala (1970) has questioned whether such an inversion of the cause–effect sequence was, in fact, what Aristotle had in mind. However that may be, there can be no doubt that the authorities who, in this century, proscribed the use of "purpose" in scientific explanation firmly believed that it involved some such unscientific conception. Ralph Barton Perry (1921), perhaps the most astute *behaviorist* philosopher, expressed it very clearly:

> That a reference to the future as in some sense governing the act, is an essential feature of the traditional conception of purpose appears from the commonest terms of the teleological vocabulary, such as "for the sake of," "in order to," "with a view to," "in fear of," "in the hope of," "lest," etc. [p. 103].

Perry's attempts to avoid "reference to the future" in his theory of behavior are remarkable because with his formulation of "determining tendencies" (which are based on past experience) he comes so very close to the cyberneticist's definition of "purpose." The fact that he did not quite get there was probably due to the lack of a functional model that could demonstrate how an experientially acquired condition or set of conditions could take over the very function that the traditional teleologists ascribed to the future.

Twenty years later, when Hofstadter (1941) published his brilliant analysis, the lack of a functioning model was certainly the reason why he was careful to ascribe descriptive but not explanatory power to his definition of "objective teleology." It is worth looking at his summary of that definition because it foreshadows with remarkable precision the cybernetic model that was built in the years that followed.

> Thus *the unitary attribute of the teleological actor is not the possession of end alone, or sensitivity alone, or technique alone, but of all three in inseparable combination.* However, it is also true that although they can not be separated in the unitary attribute they may nevertheless be analyzed out independently by the use of a plurality of acts of the same agent [italics in original, pp. 34–35].[3]

If we substitute the modern cyberneticist's terms (e.g., Powers, 1973) for the three components, we have *reference value* (for "end"), *sensory function* (for "sensitivity"), and *effector function* (for "technique"). We know that in an actual feedback-control system these three components can never be separated because the operation of the system is dependent on their circular arrangement. This arrangement is such that no one point can be isolated as initial "cause" and no one point can be isolated as terminal "effect." The system operates as a unit and, to use the fashionable term of general systems theory, as "a whole." Nevertheless, as Hofstadter accurately foresaw, the observer can assess the characteristics of the three components by considering the system's behavior over time and with regard to different *disturbances*.

It is surely one of the most intriguing aspects of the intellectual history of Western civilization that whereas functioning implementations of the principle of "negative feedback" had been designed and built since the third century B.C. (Mayr, 1970), the principle itself with all its implications for the behavior of living organisms and the nervous system was formulated only about three decades ago (Rosenblueth et al., 1943). Since then, we have seen the proliferation of "goal-seeking" devices that incorporate purposes in no uncertain terms; but at the same time, we still have influential people who consider "purpose" one of the fictitious "perquisites of autonomous

---

[3] I am indebted to Thomas Sebeok for having drawn my attention to Hofstadter's essay.

man" a creature whose "abolition has long been overdue" (Skinner, 1971, pp. 13, 191). To rant against the concept of goal-directed or purposive behavior at a time when automatic pilots can keep an aircraft on a preestablished course and missiles can home in on a moving target is hardly a sign of objectivity. With the advent of cybernetics and control systems, the concept of purpose has been given not only scientific but also practical technological validity, in that we can use it to construct functioning mechanisms. That, to my knowledge, is the best validation of a scientific principle we can ask for.

I do not intend to suggest that *all* the behavior of living organisms must necessarily be purposive. Reflexive behavior, for instance, cannot be classified as purposive because it is, by definition, a linear cause–effect chain not under the control of a closed feedback loop. Hinde and Stevenson (1970) have suggested that behavior must be analyzed extremely carefully and, above all, with regard to how the consequences of an activity affect that activity. This is a crucial question for the observer who wants to decide whether or not an organism's behavior is goal directed. But the question is not quite as simple as it seems. In an organism of a certain complexity, no one feedback loop is an independent entity with a constant reference value or "goal." As MacKay (1966, 1967), Powers (1973), and in an elementary way Miller, Galanter, and Pribram (1960) have indicated, an organism must be viewed as an hierarchical system of control loops, in which the reference value of one unit is itself controlled by another.

The consequences of a communicatory act are important for the sender. It is on the basis of the consequences that he assesses whether or not his message has achieved the desired effect. But that is not the essential criterion for the observer who wants to decide whether or not a sign is to be considered purposive. A general purposiveness is inherent in the artificiality of the sign or signs used, and does not depend on the effect the sign may or may not have on a single receiver. The warning Z sign alongside the highway is a purposive communicatory sign regardless of how many motorists pass it without reducing their speed.

FROM SIGN TO SYMBOL

If we accept the basic idea that, in order to be communicatory rather than inferential, signs have to be in some sense artificial,[4] we can at once state the first of three criteria for the characterization and recognition of

[4] I deliberately say "in some sense artificial," because in nonhuman species signs are clearly not invented and agreed on as they are among humans. Nevertheless there are communicatory signs and they are artificial; for an analysis of this artificiality derived from Tinbergen's (1952) concept of "incipient movement," see von Glasersfeld, 1974, 1975.

"language." Although communicatory signs taken alone cannot be considered a *linguistic* system, they do constitute a prerequisite for such a means of communication. Thus we can say that before there can be "language" there must be a set or *lexicon* of communicatory signs. The size of the lexicon, i.e., the number of signs it contains, is theoretically irrelevant, provided there are enough discrete and individually differentiated signs to allow for the combinatorial patterning required by my third criterion, which will be explained later.

The second criterion is that these signs be used *symbolically*. This characteristic was approached by Hockett's concept of "displacement," in an attempt to reconcile the manifest freedom of topic provided by human language with the psychological dogma according to which he was trying to explain behavior, including "verbal behavior," as response to a stimulus. By "displacement" Hockett meant that: "We can talk about things that are remote in time, space, or both from the site of the communicative transaction [Hockett & Altmann, 1969, p. 63]."

We can hardly deny that this is so. But as a criterial condition this kind of displacement is not quite enough. The reason for the insufficiency is clearly delineated in Hockett's original explanation: "Any delay between the reception of a stimulus and the appearance of the response means that the former has been coded into a stable spatial array, which endures at least until it is read off in the response [Hockett, 1960a, p. 417]."

This describes what goes on in signaling which, we may say, is always bound to a more or less immediate experiential context, i.e., to things that have happened or are happening. But language allows us to talk not only about things that are spatially or temporally remote, but also about things that have no location in space and never happen at all. The very fact that we can make *understandable* linguistic statements about space and time, right and wrong, Humpty-dumpty, and the square root of minus one demonstrates rather incontrovertibly that language can deal with items that have nothing to do with "observable stimuli" or with the "referents" of the traditional theory of reference in linguistic philosophy.

In order to become a *symbol,* the sign has to be detached from *input.* What the sign signifies, i.e., its meaning, has to be available, regardless of the contextual situation.[5] In other words, symbolic meaning has to be conceptual and "inside" the system. That is precisely what Ogden and Richards (1923) illustrated by means of their famous triangle in which the word is directly tied to a conception only, and such links as it may have to

---

[5] Georges Mounin in a recent book review states that the condition of "displacement" is "not well formulated; one should perhaps speak of messages *outside a situation* [Mounin, 1974, p. 205, my translation]."

things (i.e., items of perceptual experience) are imputed. In other words, these links are indirect and arise through epistemic connections between the concepts and perceptual experience. Susanne Langer (1948) clearly differentiated the use of symbols from that of signs:

> Symbols are not proxy for their objects, but are vehicles for the conception of objects. To conceive a thing or a situation is not the same as to "react toward it" overtly, or to be aware of its presence. In talking about things we have conceptions of them, not the things themselves; and *it is the conceptions, not the things, that symbols directly "mean"* [italics in original, p. 61].

The role of symbolicity in the characterization of *linguistic* communication can be illustrated taking as an example the famous "language of the bees." There no longer is any doubt that the bees' "dance" constitutes an elaborate system of communication (von Frisch, 1974; Gould, 1975). It has a lexicon of artificial signs,[6] and it certainly has combinatorial patterning and "displacement," since the messages are made up of distance indication and directional indication, and always refer to items that are themselves remote from the dance site. But precisely because these messages are always produced with reference to a specific target location from which the sender has just returned and to which the recruits are to go, they cannot be said to have symbolicity. To qualify as language, the bees' dance would have to be used also *without* this one-to-one relation to a behavioral response (e.g., in comments, proposals, or questions concerning a foraging location), and this has never been observed. In short, a communication system that allows for *imperatives* only—no matter how sophisticated and accurate they might be—should not be called a language.

THE SEMANTIC ASPECT OF SYNTAX

The third criterion for the application of the term "language" is *combinatorial patterning*. This is equivalent to Hockett's "openness" (Hockett & Altmann, 1969) or "productivity" (Hockett, 1960a,b), which Hockett (1960a) describes as follows:

> The language also provides certain patterns by which these elementary significant units (morphemes) can be combined into larger sequences, and conventions governing what sorts of meanings emerge from the arrangements. These patterns and conventions are the *grammar* of the language [p. 418].

---

[6] That the signs are produced by *dancing* and thus cannot be part of the flight they designate makes them artificial, and the fact that they are also somewhat iconic (because direction relative to the sun is indicated by direction relative to gravity or an artificial light) does not affect that artificiality.

Hockett's conception of openness or productivity is, of course, closely connected with what linguists call "syntax," i.e., the conventional rules of the language that govern the sequencing of words. From the communication point of view, however, the crucial aspect as Hockett pointed out is that from the sequences or sentences taken as wholes, meanings emerge that are on a level above the meanings of the individual signs or words that compose the sequence. It is, indeed, this conventional, rule-governed combinatorial meaning that makes possible the theoretically infinite openness of language. Whereas in English sequential order is the main device for the expression of combinatorial meaning, in other languages, such as Latin or German, case-endings or case-specific articles are equivalent devices. The important point is that language has *some* way to express certain relations between the items designated by single signs or words. This may be achieved by different means in different languages: by rules of sequential order; by prefixes, infixes, or suffixes; or by specific words, such as prepositions, which have relational meaning only. But language as a system of communication is characterized by the fact that such relations are expressed by word combinations.[7]

To sum up this brief description of language as a communicatory system, we can say that it has three indispensable characteristics.

1. There must be a set, or *lexicon,* of artificial signs.
2. These signs can be and are used as *symbols;* in other words, they are used on the conceptual level and without reference to a particular perceptual or behavioral instance of the item they signify.
3. There must be a *grammar,* that is, a set of conventional rules that govern the formation of sign combinations that have semantic content in addition to the meanings of the individual signs.

THE RECOGNITION OF LANGUAGE

Given the three characteristics described in the preceding sections of this chapter, we can now ask how we can discriminate communicatory

[7] Note that *relations* are always the result of some conceptual operation on the part of the perceiver; they are not inherent in what is perceived but in the way of perceiving. That this is so even with the simplest spatial relations expressed by prepositions was shown by Spencer Brown (1969). One could say, therefore, that any communication system that provides for the expression of conceptual relations (which as such are never *perceptually* present) must have "symbolicity." But since this way of arguing involves basic epistemological considerations, I have here chosen the simpler approach to "symbolicity" via the perceptual and behavioral absence of referents.

behavior from simple interaction, and linguistic communication from non-linguistic signaling. Clearly it is one thing to set up criteria for language on the basis of theoretical considerations and quite another to specify observable behavioral manifestations that would indicate that these criteria are satisfied. Among the criteria I have discussed, there are two that seem particularly elusive from an observational point of view: the artificiality of signs and their use as symbols.

If we are observing organisms with whom we have not established a system of communication, it will at times be difficult or even impossible to decide whether a particular behavior is being carried out for its own sake (i.e., to reduce an internal or environmental disturbance) or for the purpose of communication (i.e., to reduce a disturbance by the attempt to modify in a nonmechanical way the behavior of another organism that is creating the disturbance). There is, obviously, no neat demarcation line between the two. Any threat gesture, posture, or vocalization that constitutes part of a larger aggressive or agonistic activity chain cannot be said to be a communicatory sign, so long as it has been observed only in conjunction with the other parts of the chain. But when it occurs without the other parts and functionally replaces them, we should give it communicatory status (cf. Tinbergen, 1952). A single observation or even a few isolated sporadic observations will hardly ever be sufficient to decide whether or not it occurs in isolation. Familiarity with the organism, its whole behavioral repertoire, and above all with the kinds of disturbance that bring it into action will be indispensable.

In the laboratory setting, on the other hand, when a chimpanzee spontaneously makes a conventional gestural sign, picks up pieces of plastic and places them on a magnetic board, or presses specific keys in a keyboard for *specific* rewards there can be no doubt about the *artificiality* of the signs used or about their communicatory function. Even if, as some suggest, this signing or pressing of keys were due to some form of conditioning by means of reinforcement, there would still remain the fact that the chimpanzee discriminates between different reinforcers and communicates by his choice of a particular sign which one it wants at the moment. If it can be observed that a request, say for a slice of banana, is coupled with an expectation of a slice of banana and therefore will not be satisfied by the window being opened, then the communicatory function of these signs is established. In this connection it should be remembered that several years before the various communication studies with chimpanzees began, Mason and Hollis (1962) demonstrated that nonhuman primates can not only communicate but also create artificial communicatory signs for the cooperative solution of a problem.

To *prove* that an organism in the wild is using signs symbolically may be very difficult indeed unless the observer can communicate with the organism. A sign is turned into a symbol and thus acquires "symbolicity" when it is used without any connection to a perceptual or behavioral instance of its signification. Delay in time and distance of location are not sufficient. When witnessing a sign for the first time, the observer can never be sure that the sign was not the response to an instance of its referent in the remote past, or that it will not lead to a behavioral response on the part of the receiver in some distant future. On the other hand, the experienced observer *who is aware of the theoretical distinctions* between the symbolic use of signs and signaling should be able to decide that question at least tentatively on pragmatic grounds. I have no doubt that an observer studying the communicatory dance of the bees, for example (which in its symbolic nature seems to come closer to "language" than anything that has been observed in the great apes), could decide before long whether or not bees display situation-detached, and, therefore, symbolic dancing. It would be necessary only to look for the existence of dance events that are neither directly tied to foraging behavior nor given as imperatives to the recruits. Among nonhuman primates, *play* has frequently been observed together with specific signs that indicate to the partner that a given act is not to be taken seriously. "The messages or signals exchanged in play are in a certain sense untrue or not meant, [and] that which is denoted by these signals is nonexistent [Bateson, 1972, p. 183]." This definition comes very close to symbolicity. In fact, Piaget has always maintained that play and imitation are crucial elements in the development of symbolic capabilities (see, e.g., Piaget, 1967).

In a laboratory or experimental environment, the issue can be decided much more easily. Once some communication has been established so that the organism can be asked questions, we can test whether or not the subject has a representational conception of a given item. Any *novel* question concerning the character or use of an item that is not perceptually present at the moment can be answered correctly only if the subject has a sufficiently clear and detailed representation of the item named. That, after all, is what we mean when we speak of conception.[8]

Finally, there is the question of combinatorial rules, or grammar. Once we know at least some of the signs by means of which a given species communicates, it should not be impossible to find out whether combining two or more signs adds something to their meaning and whether these combinations are recurrent and rule governed. The issue, however, has been thoroughly befogged by the general confusion concerning descriptive rules and rules of action. It is one thing to acquire a rule-governed behavior and

[8] This point was recently made also by Premack (1975) with regard to his work with the chimpanzee Sarah.

quite another to isolate and specify the rules that govern it. In early infancy, for example, we all acquire the skill of crawling. As Piaget has shown, up to the age of 5 to 6 years, children invariably give erroneous descriptions of the sequence of arm and leg motions involved in crawling, even when they have just performed it. Only about a third of children aged 8–10 can specify the rules correctly; and even in a test of adults, by no means all subjects gave the correct description (Piaget, 1974, pp. 14–15). So it is with our use of language. Unless we happen to be linguists, "we always operate *within* a framework of *living* rules [italics in original, Sellars 1967, p. 315]." That is to say, we operate according to rules to which we have adapted without having formulated them. In this sense we are said to "know" the rules when our performance conforms to them. This is the only way we should speak of rules in the linguistic attempts of nonhuman primates. If they produce a substantial number of novel sign-combinations that conform to the grammar of the language they are using, then they must be credited with rule-governed productivity and "knowledge" of the grammar.

To conclude these notes on how to recognize manifestations of language, I repeat that this recognition will be more difficult and will require a much subtler approach with organisms in their natural habitat than in an experimental situation. The artificiality of signs and thus their communicatory status, may be established only after prolonged observation in the wild. In the laboratory it is a foregone conclusion that the signs are artificial since they are manmade and, as such, not part of the subject's original behavioral repertoire. The use of signs as symbols by free-living organisms could be established only after a minute examination of their sign repertoire and the activities preceding and following the occurrence of specific signs. In the experimental situation, on the other hand, how the signs are being used can be discovered by certain questions, i.e., by means of the very system of communication to which the subject is being introduced. The question of conformity to grammatical rules of sign combination is a good deal easier to decide. Provided there is a preestablished grammar, there will be no problem in determining whether the subject's novel combinations are grammatical. With a free-living species, of course, the grammar would first have to be discovered by the observer. That discovery may be difficult since the human observer is necessarily anthropocentric and will always tend to look for a grammar that resembles the grammar of his human language.

REFERENCES

Alexander, R. D. Sound communication in orthoptera and cicadidae. In W. E. Lanyon & W. N. Tavolga (Eds.), *Animal sounds and communication*. Washington, D. C.: American Institute of Biological Sciences, 1960.

Armer, P. Attitudes toward intelligent machines. In E. A. Feigenbaum & J. Feldman (Eds.), *Computers and thought*. New York: McGraw-Hill, 1963.

Ayala, F. J. Teleological explanations in evolutionary biology. *Philosophy of Science*, 1970, *37*(1), 1–15.

Bateson, G. *Steps to an ecology of mind*. New York: Ballantine, 1972.

Bloomfield, L. *Language*. New York: Henry Holt, 1933.

Brown, G. S. *Laws of form*. London, England: Allen & Unwin, 1969.

Burghardt, G. M. Defining "communication." In J. W. Johnston, D. G. Moulton, & A. Turk (Eds.), *Communication by chemical signals*. New York: Appleton, 1970.

Fouts, R. Acquisition and testing of gestural signs in four young chimpanzees. *Science*, 1973, *180*, 978–980.

Gardner, B. T., & Gardner, R. A. Two-way communication with an infant chimpanzee. In A. M. Schrier & F. Stollnitz (Eds.), *Behavior of nonhuman primates*, Vol. 4. New York: Academic Press, 1971.

Gould, J. L. Honey bee recruitment: The dance-language controversy. *Science*, 1975, *189*, 685–693.

Greenberg, J. H. Concerning inferences from linguistic to nonlinguistic data. In H. Hoijer (Ed.), *Language in culture*. Chicago: Univ. of Chicago Press, 1954.

Haldane, J. B. S. Animal communication and the origin of human language. *Science Progress*, 1955, *43*, 383–401.

Hinde, R. A., & Stevenson, J. G. Goals and response control. In L. R. Aronson, E. Tobach, D. S. Lehrman, & J. S. Rosenblatt (Eds.), *Development and evolution of behavior: Essays in memory of T. C. Schneirla*. San Francisco: Freeman, 1970.

Hockett, C. F. Chinese versus English: An exploration of the Whorfian hypothesis. In H. Hoijer (Ed.), *Language in culture*. Chicago: Univ. of Chicago Press, 1954.

Hockett, C. F. Logical consideration in the study of animal communication. In W. E. Lanyon & W. N. Tavolga (Eds.), *Animal sounds and communication*. Washington, D. C.: American Institute of Biological Sciences, 1960. (a)

Hockett, C. F. The origin of speech. *Scientific American*, 1960, *203*(3), 88–96.(b)

Hockett, C. F. The problem of universals in language. In J. H. Greenberg (Ed.), *Universals of language*. Cambridge, Massachusetts: M. I. T. Press, 1963.

Hockett, C. F. & Altmann, S. A. A note on design features. In T. A. Sebeok (Ed.), *Animal communication*. Bloomington: Indiana University Press, 1969.

Hofstadter, A. Objective teleology. *Journal of Philosophy*, 1941, *38*(2), 29–39.

Langer, S. K. *Philosophy in a new key*. Cambridge, Massachusetts: Harvard University Press, 1942. (Mentor paperback, 1948.)

MacKay, D. M. Operational aspects of some fundamental concepts of human communication. *Synthese*, 1954, 9(3–5), 182–198.

MacKay, D. M. Cerebral organization and the conscious control of action. In J. C. Eccles (Ed.), *Brain and conscious experience*. New York: Springer, 1966.

MacKay, D. M. Ways of looking at perception. In W. Wathen-Dunn (Ed.), *Models for the perception of speech and visual form*. Cambridge, Massachusetts: M. I. T. Press, 1967.

MacKay, D. M. *Information, mechanism, and meaning*. Cambridge, Massachusetts: M. I. T. Press, 1969.

MacKay, D. M. Formal analysis of communicative processes. In R. A. Hinde (Ed.), *Non-verbal communication*. Cambridge, England: Cambridge Univ. Press, 1972.

Mason, W. A. & Hollis, J. H. Communication between young Rhesus monkeys. *Animal Behavior*, 1962, *10*(3–4), 211–221.

Mayr, O. *The origin of feedback control*. Cambridge, Massachusetts: M. I. T. Press, 1970.

Miller, G. A., Gallanter, E., & Pribram, K. H. *Plans and the structure of behavior*. New York: Holt, 1960.

Minsky, M. Steps toward artificial intelligence. In E. A. Feigenbaum & J. Feldman (Eds.), *Computers and thought*. New York: McGraw-Hill, 1963.

Mounin, G. Review of R. A. Hinde's "Non-verbal communication." *Journal of Linguistics*, 1974, *10*, 201–206.

Ogden, C. K. & Richards, I. A. *The meaning of meaning*. New York: Harcourt, 1923. (Harvest paperback, 1946).

Perry, R. B. A behavioristic view of purpose. *Journal of Philosophy*, 1921, *28*(4), 85–105.

Piaget, J. *Six psychological studies*. New York: Random House, Vintage, 1967.

Piaget, J. *La prise de conscience*. Paris: Presses Universitaires de France, 1974.

Powers, W. T. *Behavior: The control of perception*. Chicago: Aldine, 1973.

Premack, D. On the assessment of language competence in the chimpanzee. In A. M. Schrier & F. Stollnitz (Eds.), *Behavior of nonhuman primates*, Vol. 4. New York: Academic Press, 1971.

Premack, D. Overview. *Conference on origins and evolution of language and speech*. New York: New York Academy of Sciences, 1975.

Rosenblueth, A., Wiener, N., & Bigelow, J. Behavior, purpose, and teleology. *Journal of Philosophy of Science*, 1943, *10*, 18–24.

Rumbaugh, D. M., von Glasersfeld, E., Warner, H., Pisani, P. P., Gill, T. V., Brown, J. V., & Bell, C. L. A computer-controlled language training system for investigating the language skills of young apes. *Behavioral Research Methods and Instrumentation*, 1973, *5*(5), 385–392.

Sapir, E. *Language*. New York: Harcourt, 1921. (Harvest paperback, 1965.)

Sebeok, T. A. Semiotics: A survey of the state of the art. In T. A. Sebeok (Ed.), *Current trends in linguistics*, Vol. 12. The Hague: Mouton, 1974.

Sebeok, T. A. The semiotic web: A chronicle of prejudices. *Semiotica* (in press).

Sellars, W. Language, rules, and behavior. In S. Hook (Ed.), *John Dewey: Philosopher of science and freedom*. New York: Barnes & Noble, 1967.

Shannon, C. E. The mathematical theory of communication. *Bell System Technical Journal*, 1948, *27*, 379–423, 623–656.

Skinner, B. F. *Beyond freedom and dignity*. New York: Bantam/Vintage, 1971.

Taube, M. *Computers and common sense—the myth of thinking machines*. New York: Columbia Univ. Press, 1961.

Thorpe, W. H. The comparison of vocal communication in animals and man. In R. A. Hinde (Ed.), *Non-verbal communication*. Cambridge, England: Cambridge University Press, 1972.

Tinbergen, N. 'Derived' activities: Their causation, biological significance, origin, and emancipation during evolution. *Quarterly Review of Biology*, 1952, *27*(1), 1–32.

Ullman, S. *The principles of semantics*. Oxford: Blackwell, 1951 (2nd edition, 1959).

von Frisch, K. Decoding the language of the bee. *Science*, 1974, *185*, 663–668.

von Glasersfeld, E. Signs, communication, and language. *Journal of Human Evolution*, 1974, *3*, 465–474.

von Glasersfeld, E. The development of language as purposive behavior. *Annals of the New York Academy of Sciences* (in press).

Wells, R. Meaning and use. In S. Saporta (Ed.), *Psycholinguistics*. New York: Holt, 1961.

Wiener, N. Time, communication, and the nervous system. *Annals of the New York Academy of Sciences*, 1948, *50*, 197–219. (a)

Wiener, N. *Cybernetics*. Cambridge, Massachusetts: M. I. T. Press, 1948. (b)

chapter 3

Cross-Modal Perception: A Basis for Language?

RICHARD K. DAVENPORT

Georgia Institute of Technology and Yerkes Regional Primate Research Center

Throughout its history, American comparative psychology has had two opposing trends. One is the attempt to account for learning in all animals by reference to the same common principles. Although different scholars have proposed different constructs, they were believed to apply equally to all organisms, and any differences among individuals or taxa were considered quantitative. At the same time, a persistent, if not vigorous line of investigation has sought to discover tasks on which taxa differ qualitatively, presumably reflecting different processes. The former approach, initiated after Darwin's publications and bolstered by its own successes, has clearly been very influential for many years. Unfortunately, however, it has led to a constriction of research in learning. Only a few species have been studied; these few have been treated interchangeably, and the tasks required of individual subjects in the studies have been limited and simple. As a consequence, many interesting issues, some involving the differential capabilities of various taxa, have been relatively unstudied.

Within the second tradition, the search for characteristics differentiating *Homo sapiens* from other creatures has been a persistent interest, one found in many other disciplines as well as psychology. The use of tools, cultural transmission, and the use of language, for example, have long been regarded as preeminently human. Recently, however, the extent to which these abilities are shared with nonhuman primates (and other animals) has come under scrutiny. Cultural transmission has been found in monkeys, tool use has been observed in apes and other species, and now it appears that a human-like language may also be possible in apes (Fouts, 1974; Gardner & Gardner, 1969; Premack, 1971; Rumbaugh, Gill, & von Glasersfeld, 1973). All of these discoveries still need detailed study. This chapter is specifically concerned with a psychobiological capacity that we believe is essential to the development of linguistic abilities in the chimpanzee: cross-modal perception.

In most human adults the sensory modalities are known to operate in concert. Information received by one modality is coordinated with information from other modalities, and adaptive behavior presumably depends to a large extent on this integration. The extent to which intersensory integration is shared with psychologically unusual and neurologically damaged humans, with infants, and with other animals, however, has not as yet been clearly established.

BACKGROUND

The concept of the interrelatedness of the senses, variously termed intermodal transfer, cross-modal transfer, intermodal integration, intermodal generalization, and cross-modal perception, has had a long philosophical history extending at least as far back as Locke and Berkeley; yet the clinical and experimental investigations into this concept are relatively recent in origin. Neurological case studies in the late 1800s provided some interesting data on the topic, but von Senden's observations of people blinded at an early age whose sight was restored in adulthood, published in 1932, were more directly relevant. Experimental cross-modal work with humans, including very young children, normal adults, and the blind, deaf, and neurologically damaged, has grown in the past few years (see the review by Freides, 1974). Experimental investigations aimed directly at cross-modal perception and using other animals as subjects are likewise recent and as of yet few in number.

Prior to 1970 two assumptions about cross-modal integration prevailed. One held that cross-modal perception is uniquely human, and the other that it is dependent on language. These assumptions came from several sources. First, until recently, attempts to demonstrate clear cross-modal perception in nonhuman primates met with repeated failures or at least with great difficulties (Ettlinger, 1967; Ettlinger & Blakemore, 1967, 1969; Wegener, 1965; Wilson & Shaffer, 1963), whereas the same phenomenon has frequently been shown in normal human adults. Second, neuroanatomical differences between man and nonhuman primates are known to exist in areas of the brain that may be related to cross-modal perception. In the brain of nonhuman primates as compared with the human brain, the auditory, visual, and somesthetic association areas are relatively independent (Geschwind, 1965; Hewes, 1973; Jensen, 1971; Lancaster, 1968), and there is a paucity of cortical–cortical connections among projection areas. Such connections are presumed to be essential to cross-modal functioning (Myers, 1967). In addition, evidence supporting a relationship between cross-modal perception and language comes from the apparent ontogenetic improvement in cross-modal perception accompanying the development of language in human children (e.g., Blank & Bridger, 1964).

A half dozen experiments performed since 1970, however, have drastically altered these assumptions about cross-modal perception (at least with touch and vision). Our own research (Davenport & Rogers, 1970, 1971; Davenport, Rogers, & Russell, 1973, 1975) has clearly shown that apes have the capacity for visual–tactual cross-modal perception of multidimensional objects or representations thereof, even when they have had no previous experience with those objects. Monkeys have been shown to have similar abilities (Cowey & Weiskrantz, 1975). Preverbal human infants (below 1 year of age) have also been found to have visual–tactual cross-modal perception without specific training (Bryant, Jones, Claxton, & Perkins, 1972). Thus, the speculation that neuroanatomical differences explain the incapacity of nonhumans for intermodal integration requires reassessment. Moreover, the verbal mediation hypothesis has been clearly disproved, insofar as it proposed that language is essential to cross-modal perception. (Language obviously may be facilitative.)

CROSS-MODAL METHODS

Several procedures exist for assessing the cross-modal perception of similarities and differences. The one most frequently used is the transfer of training method, which requires the subject to learn a discrimination in one modality and then perform (or learn) the discrimination in another modality. For example, the subject learns to discriminate between a cube and a sphere first visually and then tactually. If learning occurs more rapidly in the second modality than in the first, cross-modal transfer of the learned discrimination is said to have occurred, and cross-modal perception is presumed. The effects are usually measured by savings-in-learning scores in the second testing over a large number of trials and problems. A limitation of this design is that a test-sophisticated subject need not operate on a principle of perceptual equivalence in order to show a good saving score on the second assessment. Since subjects are exposed to multiple trials and problems, good performance in the second modality may be attributable to rapid learning unrelated to experience in the first modality. In addition, with this procedure, the subject may treat the problems in the separate modalities as unrelated tasks with the result that no positive transfer (or perhaps even negative transfer) may occur.

The second approach, the matching-to-sample procedure, permits immediate or delayed comparison of the objects/stimuli/percepts in two modalities. Cross-modal matching requires the subject to match an object presented in one modality with an identical object (usually one of several) presented in another modality. Trials are repeated with a given set of discriminanda until subjects reach a clear criterion of matching. As in the transfer design, when trials with a given set of discriminanda are repeated, the subject may learn the association by rote and correctly match without having learned a principle of equivalence. Whether association by rote has in fact occurred can be determined after training by testing the subjects on a series of single matching-to-sample problems each presented once using *new* discriminanda (objects never seen or felt before).

The same end may be achieved in the transfer design if analysis is limited to the first trial in the second modality. If the subject performs correctly on the first exposures, then the subject must be operating on the principle of perceptual equivalence.

In both procedures, failure in cross-modal matching and transfer can be caused by difficulty in cross-modal perception or trouble in *intramodal* discrimination (Bryant, 1968). Using Bryant's suggested controls, assessment of intramodality matching-to-sample, Milner and Bryant (1970) showed that some reported cross-modal deficiencies might be explained as failures of intramodal discrimination. Another problem is that a failure of cross-modal perception may be attributable to the failure of the subject to "understand" the requirements of the task. In the majority of cross-modal studies with children, for example, the task is described by verbal instruction, demonstration, or both. When a child then fails to perform correctly, the experimenter cannot determine the basis for the failure: Was the subject incapable of performing the task, or could he not understand or remember what he was supposed to do because the instructions and test devices were inappropriate. Over the years psychologists have become painfully aware that sometimes the inability of their animal subjects to behave in a "desirable" manner results from the experimenters' failure to arrange an appropriate experimental situation or to give the proper "instructions" to the animals.

EXPERIMENTS WITH APES AND MONKEYS

My collaborators and I have been continuously engaged in cross-modal research with chimpanzees since 1969 and with monkeys since 1973. During this period we have investigated a number of cross-modal phenomena and have demonstrated the following cross-modal abilities in apes. (Henceforth, the term *haptic* will be used in place of *tactual*, in order to underscore the active, palpating, information-seeking characteristics of the hand.)

1. Visual to haptic cross-modal perception with complex stereometric objects using a matching-to-sample procedure (Davenport & Rogers, 1970).

The phrasing *visual to haptic* means that the sample was presented visually, and the subject selected its match on the basis of haptic cues. (*Haptic to visual* means the reverse.) This first experiment was to demonstrate unequivocally the presence of visual–haptic cross-modal perception of equivalence in nonhuman primates; it laid to rest the contentions that language is a necessary mediator (Ettlinger, 1967) and that only humans are neurologically equipped for the process (Lancaster, 1968; Myers, 1967). The basic paradigm for this study and those following is sketched here. On any one trial, the subject was presented with three multidimensional objects. One, the sample, could be seen but not touched, and two others, one a match for the sample and one different, could be touched but not seen. A tug on the matching object was rewarded; a tug on the nonmatch went unrewarded. Repeated trials were given on this set of objects with the sample randomly changed for each trial until the subject chose correctly on a reasonable number of trials. Other sets were similarly presented for training until we were sure that the subject was either: (a) matching on the basis of cross-modal stimulus equivalence or (b) performing a rapidly learned conditional discrimination. To test these alternatives, subjects were given 40–60 "unique" matching-to-sample problems composed of new objects never seen or felt before. In order to eliminate specific learning or transfer, we gave only one trial on each problem. Subjects did match significantly often on these tests, and such matching could only have been done on the basis of the perception of cross-modal *equivalence*. A second experiment was done to study the bidirectionality of the phenomenon (Davenport et al., 1973). Here the complex stereometric sample was presented for haptic exploration, and the choices for visual examination and selection were presented behind windows. To indicate a choice, the subject simply touched the covering window. Within the limits of our experiment—a small number of subjects, objects of unknown discriminability, and a relatively few unique problems—the task proved equally easy in both directions; however, this matter needs further investigation.

    2. Visual to haptic cross-modal perceptual equivalence with life-sized photographs and some variations in the representational characteristics (stimulus properties) of the visual stimuli (Davenport & Rogers, 1971; Davenport et al., 1975).

A number of somewhat informal experiments and observations, for example, Köhler (1925) and Hayes (1951), have suggested that chimpanzees do recognize photographs, but in these reports, it has not been clear that recognition occurred on first exposure and was not based on specific associational training. Using a matching-to-sample design, life-size photographs were substituted for the visual stimuli, and the experiment confirmed that a chimpanzee could respond to photographs of an object as well as to the object itself. A second experiment with these photographs (Davenport et al., 1975) confirmed the bidirectionality of the phenomenon. These experiments laid the foundation for futher study of the chimpanzee's ability to respond on the basis of a "representation" of an object.

Some anthropological field reports have suggested that primitive (photographically naive) people may be unable to recognize the representational characteristics of photographs without specific learning (Deregowski, 1972; Segal, Campbell, & Herskovitz, 1966). Our chimpanzees were, so far as we know, photographically naive.

We replicated the haptic to visual matching-to-sample experiment in every way, except that the choice objects were half-size photographs of the haptic samples (Davenport et al., 1975). The results showed clearly that chimpanzees were able to recognize the representational characteristics of a small photograph without specific learning. In another experiment we continued to explore the representational characteristics (stimulus properties) of the visual discriminanda by using high-contrast photographs as choice objects. In high-contrast photographs, all textural and depth cues are completely eliminated from the original photograph so that only a solid black figure on a homogeneous white background remains. Chimpanzees were also successful in matching sample objects to these photographs (Davenport et al., 1975). In the next experiment the visual properties of the objects were further degraded by their representation in the form of rather poor quality line drawings; however, the chimpanzees were still able to match the line drawings with the haptically presented samples (Davenport et al., 1975).

    3. Haptic to visual cross-modal perceptual equivalence with a delay imposed between sample and response.

This was the first experiment in the series explicitly designed to study memory in cross-modal perception (Davenport et al., 1975). In this initial experiment the delay interval was only 15–30 seconds and we did not explore intramodal memory. Unexpectedly the matching-to-sample accuracy with the delay was not significantly different from the simultaneous procedure previously used, even when testing was with the "unique" discriminanda.

4. Haptic to visual transfer of training.

In this experiment, after discrimination tasks had been learned haptically, the same discriminanda were presented visually for one trial only. Chimpanzees successfully demonstrated haptic to visual perceptual equivalence with this method.

5. Haptic–visual matching-to-sample in monkeys.

Using essentially the same apparatus with which we had demonstrated cross-modal perception in apes, we were completely unsuccessful in demonstrating cross-modal perception in Old World monkeys, despite prolonged and intensive training. We believe that the apparatus and procedure were not appropriate for these animals. A number of different factors seemed to contribute to the monkeys' failure: their general inattention, their lack of care in palpating the objects, and their tendency to develop position habits and other strategies which interfered with the cross-modal requirements. We abandoned this experiment upon the publication of the Cowey and Weiskrantz (1975) report of successful haptic–visual cross-modal perception in monkeys demonstrated in an experiment using radically different and more appropriate procedures.

6. Auditory–visual matching-to-sample in chimpanzees and monkeys.

The aim of the experiment was to present pulse patterns similar to Morse Code either auditorially or visually; these patterns were to be matched to an identical pulse train in the other modality. Even after extraordinary training, monkeys showed no improvement whatsoever. At this writing six chimpanzees who have demonstrated visual–haptic cross-modal perception are being trained but have shown little improvement so far.

Significant auditory–visual cross-modal transfer of an intensity or pulse pattern discrimination has been found in a prosimian (Ward, Yehle, & Dorflein, 1970), in rabbits (Yehle & Ward, 1969), and in rats (Over & Mackintosh, 1969), but no studies of visual–haptic equivalence have been reported in nonprimates. To make sensible comparisons of taxa, methods, modalities, and stimulus properties, much more research is clearly needed.

Intuitively, cross-modal transfer of intensity and pulse pattern seems a simpler, if not fundamentally different, phenomenon than the perception of cross-modal equivalence with more complex discriminanda. Cross-modal integration of these elementary stimuli may well be handled by common neuromechanisms (Sutherland, 1959) including multimodal cells (Bentel, Dafny, & Feldman, 1968; Horn, 1965; Spinelli, Starr, & Barrett, 1968). Bentel et al. conclude that, "the theory about modality specificity cannot be upheld . . . [p. 350]" and that "there exists an interaction between the auditory and visual pathways giving rise to convergence of flash and sound stimuli at the single-cell level in the primary visual cortex [p. 350]." Such a process could lay the foundation for cross-modal function where elementary visual and auditory stimulations are involved. Ettlinger (1973) has theorized that in apes and man (and presumably some monkeys) higher-order cortical systems enable cross-modal perception, whereas in prosimians and nonprimates cross-modal integration may be mediated through a lower subcortical system.

SIGNIFICANCE

The importance of further research to the understanding of cross-modal functioning seems clear. A number of fundamental issues regarding cross-modal perception still require clarification:

1. What roles do maturation and experience play in its expression?
2. What are the neurological requisites for the phenomena, and in what manner do neuroanatomical characteristics facilitate cross-modal perception?
3. What is the nature of the information processing that permits integration of information among the several modalities?
4. To what extent do other behavioral capacities, such as language, mediate or facilitate perceptual integration?
5. To what extent do cross-modal capabilities contribute to adaptive behavior in general and to cognitive processes and language in particular?
6. In what manner and to what extent do intramodality characteristics in and of themselves affect cross-modal functioning?

An increased knowledge of cross-modal perception could provide a powerful tool to study the historically important and difficult question of central information processing in animals. For example, Le Gros Clark (1971), among others, has given a prominent place in hominid evolution to the increasing complexity of the brain, which permits a functionally higher and more complete analysis and synthesis of stimuli to which the end organs are receptive and a lesser role to alterations in morphology of the receptors per se.

What evolutionary occurrences could have accounted for this central elaboration are not yet known. One suggestion (Geschwind, 1965; Lancaster, 1968) is that in man, the angular gyrus is the neurological elaboration which is critical for the attachment of a "name" to the cross-modal percept. On the basis of his extensive neurological and theoretical work, Geshwind (1965) has stated that, *"it cannot be argued that the ability to form cross-modal associations depends on already having speech,* rather we must say *that the ability to acquire speech has as a prerequisite the ability to form cross-modal associations* . . . [italics in original, p. 175]" and further (Geschwind, 1970), "the ability to form cross-modal linkages was a necessary (although not sufficient) condition for the acquisition of language [p. 1249]."

In our view, cross-modal perception of equivalence requires the derivation of a modality-independent "representation," cognition, or concept of a stimulus or event. Animals that can have the same or similar "representation," regardless of the means of peripheral reception, possess a great advantage in coping with the complex demands of living, especially in unusual circumstances in which one modality may be operating suboptimally, when precise and accurate response is necessary on the basis of limited information, or when cognitive manipulation is required. To the extent that an animal also may have a "name" for the representation, be it sound, gesture, or posture, the processes of perception, memory, problem solving, and other cognitive processes would seem to be greatly enhanced, thus laying a foundation for interanimal communication.

ACKNOWLEDGMENT

Our research was supported in part by a grant from The National Science Foundation and by Grant RR-00165 from The National Institutes of Health. The author wishes to recognize research collaborators C. M. Rogers, I. S. Russell, and K. J. Pralinsky.

REFERENCES

Bental, E., Dafny, N., & Feldman, S. Convergence of auditory and visual stimuli on single cells in the primary visual cortex of unanesthetized, unrestrained cats. *Experimental Neurology,* 1968, *20,* 341–351.

Blank, M., & Bridger, W. H. Cross-modal transfer in nursery-school children. *Journal of Comparative Physiology and Psychology,* 1964, *58,* 277–282.

Bryant, P. E. Comments on the design of developmental studies of cross-modal matching and cross-modal transfer. *Cortex*, 1968, *4*, 127–137.

Bryant, P. E., Jones, P., Claxton, V., & Perkins, G. M. Recognition of shapes across modalities by infants. *Nature*, 1972, *240*, 303–304.

Clark, W. Le Gros. *The antecedents of man*, 3rd ed. Chicago, Illinois: Quadrangle Books, 1971.

Cowey, A., & Weiskrantz, L. Demonstration of cross-modal matching in rhesus monkeys, *Macaca mulatta*. *Neuropsychologia*, 1975, *13*, 117–120.

Davenport, R. K., & Rogers, C. M. Intermodal equivalence of stimuli in apes. *Science*, 1970, *168*, 279–280.

Davenport, R. K., & Rogers, C. M. Perception of photographs by apes. *Behaviour*, 1971, *39*, 2–4.

Davenport, R. K., Rogers, C. M., & Russell, I. S. Cross-modal perception in apes. *Neuropsychologia*, 1973, *11*, 21–28.

Davenport, R. K., Rogers, C. M., & Russell, I. S. Cross-modal perception in apes: Altered visual cues and delay. *Neuropsychologia*, 1975, *13*, 229–235.

Deregowski, J. B. Pictorial perception and culture. *Scientific American*, 1972, *227*(5), 82–88.

Ettlinger, G. Analysis of cross-modal effects and their relationship to language. In C. G. Millikan, & F. L. Dailey (Eds.), *Brain mechanisms underlying speech and language*. New York: Grune and Stratton, 1967.

Ettlinger, G. The transfer of information between sense-modalities: A neuropsychological review. In H. P. Zippel (Ed.), *Memory and transfer of information*. New York: Plenum, 1973.

Ettlinger, G., & Blakemore, C. B. Cross-modal matching in the monkey. *Neuropsychologia*, 1967, *5*, 147–154.

Ettlinger, G., & Blakemore, C. B. Cross-modal transfer set in the monkey. *Neuropsychologia*, 1969, *7*, 41–47.

Fouts, R. Language: Origins, definitions and chimpanzees. *Journal of Human Evolution*, 1974, *3*, 475–482.

Freides, D. Human information processing in sensory modality: Cross-modal functions, information complexity, memory, and deficit. *Psychological Bulletin*, 1974, *81*, 284–310.

Gardner, R. A., & Gardner, B. T. Teaching sign language to a chimpanzee. *Science*, 1969, *165*, 664–672.

Geschwind, N. Disconnection syndromes in animals and man. *Brain*, 1965, *88*, 237–294, 585–644.

Geschwind, N. Intermodal equivalence of stimuli in apes. *Science*, 1970, *168*, 1249.

Hayes, C. *The ape in our house*. New York: Harper, 1951.

Hewes, G. W. Primate communication and the gestural origin of language. *Current Anthropology*, 1973, *14*, 5–24.

Horn, G. The effect of somaesthetic and photic stimuli on the activity of units in the striate cortex of unanesthetized, unrestrained cats. *Journal of Physiology*, 1965, *179*, 263–277.

Jensen, A. R. The role of verbal mediation in mental development. *Journal of Genetic Psychology*, 1971, *118*, 39–70.

Köhler, W. *The mentality of apes* (translated from the 2nd Revised Edition by E. Winter). London: Harcourt, 1925.

Lancaster, J. B. Primate communication systems and the emergence of human language. In P. C. Jay (Ed.), *Primates: Studies in adaptation and variability*. New York: Holt, 1968.

Milner, A. D., & Bryant, P. E. Cross-modal matching by young children. *Journal of Comparative Physiology and Psychology*, 1970, *71*, 453–458.

Myers, R. E. Cerebral connectionism and brain function. In C. G. Millikan and F. L. Dailey (Eds.), *Brain mechanisms underlying speech and language*. New York: Grune and Stratton, 1967.

Over, R., & Mackintosh, N. J. Cross-modal transfer of intensity discrimination by rats. *Nature (London)*, 1969, *224*, 918–919.

Premack, D. Language in chimpanzee? *Science*, 1971, *172*, 808–822.

Rumbaugh, D. M., Gill, T. V., & von Glasersfeld, E. L. Reading and sentence completion by a chimpanzee. *Science*, 1973, *182*, 731–733.

Segal, M., Campbell, D. T., & Herskovits, M. J. *The influence of culture on visual perception.* Indianapolis: Bobbs-Merrill, 1966.

Spinelli, D. N., Starr, A., & Barrett, T. W. Auditory specificity recordings from cats' visual cortex. *Experimental Neurology*, 1968, *22*, 75–84.

Sutherland, N. S. Stimulus analyzing mechanisms. *Proceedings of a Symposium on Mechanization of Thought Processes*, 1959, *2*, 575–609.

von Senden, M. *Raum-und Gestaltauffassung bei operierten Blindgeborenen vor und nach der Operation.* Leipzig: J. A. Barth, 1932.

Ward, J. P., Yehle, A. L., & Doerflein, R. S. Cross-modal transfer of a specific discrimination in the bushbaby (*Galago senegalensis*). *Journal of Comparative Physiology and Psychology*, 1970, *73*, 74–77.

Wegener, J. G. Cross modal transfer in monkeys. *Journal of Comparative Physiology and Psychology*, 1965, *59*, 450–452.

Wilson, W. A., & Shaffer, O. C. Intermodality transfer of specific discrimination in the monkey. *Nature (London)*, 1963, *197*, 107.

Yehle, A. L., & Ward, J. P. Cross-modal transfer of a specific discrimination in the rabbit. *Psychonomic Science*, 1969, *16*, 269–270.

PART II

Design of the LANA Project

chapter 4

The LANA Project: Origin and Tactics

DUANE M. RUMBAUGH, HAROLD WARNER, AND ERNST VON GLASERSFELD

Georgia State University
Yerkes Regional Primate Research Center, and
University of Georgia

The germinal idea for the LANA Project was formulated by Duane Rumbaugh in the fall of 1970 after considerable reflection on the chimpanzee language project reports of Beatrice T. and R. Allen Gardner, David Premack, and Roger Fouts. To one who had spent the past 12 years studying nonhuman primate behavior, the prospects that the chimpanzee and possibly the other great apes as well might be able to master the rudiments of language were most intriguing. As impressive and as tantalizing as those reports were, the one-on-one aspect of the training situations seemed painfully time consuming. Only with a great investment of human time would such situations allow for the systematic variations of training procedures that would differentially influence the course of acquiring and using linguistic skills. Without such variations it would be impossible to accumulate the type of research data that would help us fully understand these skills by defining their antecedents and parameters.

At the time, Rumbaugh was working full time at the Yerkes Regional Primate Research Center as its Associate Director and Chief of Behavior. There he was able to consider research projects that might well not have been feasible in any other setting, for the Yerkes Center is replete with a variety of specialists in primatology. One of those specialists is Harold Warner, Chief of the Biomedical Engineering Laboratory. The germinal idea of the LANA Project concerned the possibility of devising an electronic system that would enhance in several ways the efficiency and objectivity of research into the acquisition of language-type skills by ape subjects. Such a system contained the potential for automating certain aspects of training so that the subject would be in the training situation 24 hours a day 7 days a week. Equally important, an automated system would allow for a more economical use of manpower, for greater objectivity in defining the training conditions and in recording responses executed by the subjects, and for a technology that might extend research efforts to various settings.

Rumbaugh and Warner held a number of conferences to assess the feasibility of implementing the idea. They considered various means whereby the system might detect a response on the part of the subject and might allow for the exchange of messages between ape and human. From these deliberations, they concluded that a computer-based system would probably be feasible and that the effort should include a linguist.

The late Clarence R. Carpenter, Professor of Psychology at the University of Georgia, was at the time serving with the Scientific Advisory Board for the Yerkes Primate Center. Since Rumbaugh knew him well as a professional colleague, he asked Professor Carpenter to recommend a linguist who might be interested in joining the project. Professor Carpenter recommended Ernst von Glasersfeld, of the University of Georgia Psychology Department, as one who was both qualified and who would probably be interested in pursuing the application of computer science to language training. Professor von Glasersfeld was contacted and expressed interest. He, in turn, recommended that his long-term computer-skilled colleague, Pier Pisani, also join the effort. Thus it was that the project of designing a computer-based system adequate to the complex task of working with anthropoid ape subjects became a team venture.

Further conferences among the four team members led to submitting a proposal to the National Institutes of Health in early winter, 1970, requesting funds for a 4-year period to support efforts to design and construct the projected system. We applied to this organization because, although initial work would be limited to ape subjects, we were confident that ultimately the project would lead to a better understanding of human language and some of its cognitive prerequisites. The grant was awarded.

A series of working conferences took place which dealt with the many problems that arose as we began designing and building the system. These conferences also included, in addition to those already mentioned, Timothy V. Gill, who at the time was a behavioral technician; Charles Bell, an electronics technician; and Josephine V. Brown of the Psychology Department of Georgia State University, an infancy specialist with strong interests in comparative-developmental studies with apes and human children.

The possibility of teaching an ape to communicate by means of a keyboard dated back to some of the earliest deliberations. Both in the American Sign Language used by the Gardners and in Premack's plastic sign language, word-concepts are the smallest units of expression. Since this is also true of man's earliest writing systems, which were made up of ideograms, we saw no reason why the keys of the planned keyboard should not represent whole words. Such a system would eliminate the task of composing words out of letter-like elements which, we felt, might well overtax the ape's capabilities. Basically, we wanted a system in which complex motor requirements for linguistic expressions would be minimal. The selection and depression of keys on a board seemed simple enough—and it was.

The keys, of course, had to be differentiated from one another. This was accomplished by embossing on their surfaces distinctive lexigrams composed through combinations of nine stimulus elements and three primary colors. (See Chapters 5, 6, and 7 of this volume, for details regarding the lexigrams, keys, keyboards, and the entire system.) The keys and the console within which they were mounted were designed to permit their ready relocation in order to prevent their positions from serving as cues to their functions. The subject was to discriminate and to select the word-keys on the basis of the lexigrams alone.

Ernst von Glasersfeld developed the language for the project. It was agreed that it would be labeled *Yerkish,* in honor of Robert M. Yerkes, the founder of the laboratory within which the LANA Project was conceived and conducted. Yerkes was a very insightful, pioneering psychobiologist and among others had anticipated the possibility that the chimpanzee might master the rudiments of a language if it were not a spoken language (Yerkes, 1927). The rules of sentence structure for Yerkish had to be straightforward enough to be managed by an analyzer that could be implemented in a small computer (PDP8E). Since the LANA Project was a pilot study, moreover, there was no need for its language system to incorporate all of the nuances and ambiguities of ordinary English.

Language learning and usage was to be the behavioral medium whereby our ape subject would interact with its environment. Initial training would be simple, fundamental operant conditioning whereby the subject, Lana, would come to master the basic discriminations and responses necessary to address the computerized system. Subsequent training would gradually be escalated to demand the mastery of a working vocabulary and of "stock" sentences whereby Lana could obtain incentives including food and entertainment by linguistic-type requests. She was to receive little "for free."

Through the course of continuous training, we anticipated that Lana would come to learn the power of linguistic-type expressions and that she would bring to bear upon the formulation of those expressions enough creativity so that she would eventually formulate new and appropriate sentences. She might use those sentences for a variety of purposes such as solving unforeseen problems, commenting on her environment, and, we hoped, engaging in conversation with man.

It was our hope that this study would shed light not just on the linguistic abilities of the chimpanzee but on the language itself. We reasoned that to the degree that we might succeed in developing refined language skills in the chimpanzee, an animal which in nature does not develop public linguistic communication skills, certain fundamentals of language would be revealed. The requisites and basic parameters of language would no longer be just the subject of philosophy, learned or idle. Rather through the course of systematic, scientific inquiry, its basic structure and dynamics might be clarified. And to the degree that the basic operations of language would become known, we believed (and still believe) that new and efficient tactics would emerge for both the study and the language training of the thousands of mentally retarded children in the world who for various reasons fail to develop expressive linguistic skills during their early years.

In brief, through the contributions of modern technology and through pooling the skills of psychologists, engineers, linguists, and others, we proposed to explore a new approach to man's language and the cognitive operations on which it rests, an approach which would begin with the tutelage of a chimpanzee named Lana.

During the 4-year span of the initial phase of the LANA Project, we have seen a number of developments, which have been very gratifying to our concerns as educators. Timothy V. Gill, initially a behavioral technician, exercised impressive initiative in devising crucial training strategies and despite the demands of the LANA Project, he is currently a doctoral student in developmental-comparative psychology at Georgia State University in Atlanta. Charles Bell has developed significant competencies in designing and building the system, having wrestled its development from the very beginning. A number of students—Shelley Johnson, Barbara Tilford, Gwendolyn Dooley, Michael Haberman, Beverly Wilkerson, Susan Essock, Tom Smith, Elizabeth Riopelle, and others—have had the opportunity to work on the project. The results of the project have served as educational materials in institutions across the country from kindergartens to universities. In short, the LANA Project has already touched the lives of millions of people, and because of that, we as scientists and educators, are most gratified.

chapter 5

The Yerkish Language and Its Automatic Parser

ERNST VON GLASERSFELD

University of Georgia and Yerkes Regional Primate Research Center

PRELIMINARY REMARKS

It might seem reasonable to divide the description of the language Lana is using into three sections so that each would reflect one of the three criteria for the recognition of language set out in Chapter 2 of this book; but only two of the criteria will serve that purpose. The division implied by the first and the third criteria (a set or a *lexicon* of artificial signs and a *grammar* that governs the combinatorial patterning of signs) is a division traditionally made by linguists in their description of languages, and I shall adhere to it, even though my classification of the lexicon and the "correlational" grammar I am using do not conform to traditional linguistics. The second criterion, however, concerns the *symbolic use* of signs and not the signs themselves (von Glasersfeld, 1974b). As I explained in Chapter 2, any artificial sign can be used symbolically, since this use in no way depends on the physical characteristics of the sign or on its meaning.[1] The

---

[1] There is not a single word in our natural languages that could not be used symbolically. Even demonstrative adjectives and other expressions that would seem to be irrevocably tied to perceptually present items by their "pointing" function are severed from the perceptually present (and thus become symbols) when they are used in hypothetical or fictional contexts.

description of a language, therefore, need not and indeed cannot include anything concerning "symbolicity" (that is, character and function of symbols).

Yerkish is an artificial language that was designed for the specific purpose of exploring the linguistic potential of nonhuman primates. It was designed under a number of constraints, both theoretical and practical. In what follows I shall try to show which aspects of the language were determined by these initial practical constraints and which by the theory underlying its design. Since the language was created at the same time as the computer system that monitors all the communication events for which it is used, there will inevitably be some overlap in the description of the language and that of the automatic sentence analyzer, or parser. Also, since the grammar we are using is a correlational grammar, i.e., one that takes into account the *semantic* aspects of combinatorial patterns (unlike traditional systems of grammar, which tend to consider *syntactic structures* quite apart from semantics), the description of the lexicon and that of the grammar will have to merge at several points. Nevertheless, this chapter will be articulated into relatively independent sections dealing with the word signs (lexigrams), the meaning and grammatical classification of word signs, combinatorial patterns, the parsing system, and, finally, a brief application of the concept of grammaticality to a sample of Lana's output.

DESIGN OF THE LEXIGRAMS

At the very inception of the project it had been decided that, in view of the success the Gardners had with American Sign Language (Gardner & Gardner, 1969, 1971, Fouts, 1974) and Premack had with word signs made of plastic shapes (Premack, 1971), the language would be visual. Moreover, the visual word signs were to be fixed units, so that each one could be placed on a separate key of a keyboard, which would serve as an input device to a computer. After these decisions had been made, but before the actual work on the project had begun, I spent my spare time trying to devise a feasible graphic system in which word signs could be composed out of design elements in such a way that each design element would have a constant semantic value. Apart from its theoretical attractiveness, the idea was tempting because a language in which all word signs were made up of meaningful design elements (corresponding to *morphemes* in natural languages) would open up innumerable possibilities for testing our subject's conceptual development. Since the vocabulary of the subjects was not

Table 1
SEMANTIC COLOR-CODING OF LEXIGRAMS

Color	General type	Lexigram classes
Violet	Autonomous actor	AP, AV, AO, AM.
Orange	Spatial objects, Spatial concepts	FA, FP, TF, CT, WR.
Red	Ingestibles	EU, EM, ED.
Green	Parts of body	PB.
Blue-gray	States and conditions	ST, LS, CD.
Blue	Activities	VA, VB, VC, VD, VE, VG, VL, VM, VP, VS, VT, VW.
Black	Prepositions, determiners, particles	DC, DD, DQ, DP, LP, IF, NF, PP, XA.
White[a]	Affirmation	"YES."
Yellow[a]	Sentential modifiers	Query, Please, Negation, Period.

[a] White and yellow are available for sentential modifiers only. They must be placed at the beginning of a message.

expected ever to exceed a few hundred items, the design of such a graphic system seemed quite possible.[2]

Once work on the mechanical and electronic machinery that was to constitute the interface with the computer had begun, it became clear that, for reasons of technical construction and budget, the design elements would have to be limited to 12 (see Chapter 7 of this volume). This limitation posed a new problem since with a dozen elements there is no possibility of semantic constancy even in a universe of discourse as limited as the one that was foreseen for a chimpanzee. To avoid having design elements that were sometimes semantically indicative and sometimes not, I gave them no semantic significance at all. Thus they became theoretically equivalent to phonemes in spoken language (or "cenemes" in Hockett's terminology; cf. Hockett, 1961, p. 47). There was, however, a big difference. While the user of a natural human language composes his utterances from the fixed set of preestablished vocal elements that linguists call "phonemes," the user of our artificial language (at least for the time being) would not be concerned with the composition of word signs out of design elements because the word signs would appear as fixed lexigrams on the keys of the keyboard.

The first task, then, was to choose design elements that were readily discriminable from each other, could be superimposed on one another, and

[2] The American Indian language, Yuchi, for instance, has phonemes that are constant semantic markers in the formation of nouns; and the Arabic language, especially in its classical form, conveys a great deal of abstract categorial information by the insertion of semantically constant vowels into consonant verb roots.

Table 2

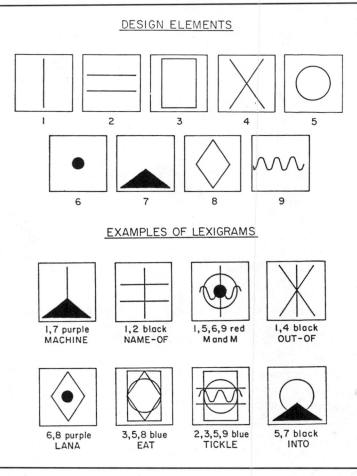

once superimposed would yield combinations that were still discriminable. Since the total number of lexigrams was to remain within the range of a few hundred, it was clear that we would be able to manage with something less than a dozen design elements. Nine elements used singly and in combinations of two, three, and four would yield 255 individually different lexigrams, and that was considered more than sufficient. In addition to the nine design elements, we decided to use three colors, selecting them so that superimposing one on another gave rise to three intermediary colors.[3] Since

[3] Since the limitation on design elements was imposed by the structure of the "feedback projectors" (see Chapter 7 of this volume) the mixing of the three basic colors takes place in

the colors would modify the background and not the graphic designs, which would always appear in white, the absence of a color element would produce a black background. For the combinatorial design of lexigrams, therefore, we had nine graphic elements and a total of seven background colors. To characterize a few additional items that are not subject to the same rules as ordinary lexigrams (because they function as "sentence markers"; see page 102), two special elements were used: a blank white field and a yellow background.

Having thus regained a certain amount of flexibility, I decided to use the seven background colors for a gross semantic classification and assigned each color to serve as the background for one class of items only. Such a limited classification would necessarily be crude, but would still permit some tests of our subject's conceptual categorization. (For the color code, see Table 1.)

As design elements, seven line-figures were chosen that satisfied a theoretical criterion of discriminability: If placed on a 30 × 45-point grid, none of them shared more than 50% of its grid points with another figure. Two filled-in figures, a small circle and a flat isosceles triangle, completed the set of nine graphic elements (see Table 2).

THE LEXICON

One of the first considerations in the choice of lexical items concerned the interactive character of the communication facility. Because the computer that monitors all linguistic transactions is programmed to respond to certain correctly formulated requests by activating the mechanical devices that fulfill the requests, the lexicon had to contain all the items that could possibly be put under automatic management. Besides food and drink, the possibilities included the playing of taped music or sounds, the projection of movies and slides, the opening and shutting of a window, and, though these have not yet been implemented, the switching on and off of lights and raising and lowering the room temperature. Altogether these possible requests involved some 30 lexical items.

In providing for requests addressed not to the computer but to a human agent (i.e., one of the technicians), we attempted to create lexigrams for as many activities, objects, states, and relational concepts that might conceivably play a part in linguistic exchanges with a captive chimpanzee.

projection. The graphic elements appear in white and their background is either colored or black, according to what color elements are combined with them. The addition of 7 colors to the design elements raised the total of possible combinations of 2, 3, and 4 elements to 1785.

After I had gathered all the information I could from the primatologists and behavior specialists of the team, I devised a preliminary vocabulary of some 150 words supposed to reflect items and activities that might be of interest both to experimenters and chimpanzee in the kind of environment the Yerkes Center was providing for our communication study. The result was inevitably an anthropocentric vocabulary. There is some evidence, it is true, that the great apes organize their perceptual world in a manner compatible with our own, but we know little about what—if anything—might motivate a lone captive chimpanzee to communicate with a machine or a human technician. Since our subject was and still is years away from sexual maturity, food and drink were the only safe bets. Thus it was gratifying to observe that Lana showed a very constant interest in two additional incentives we devised, the projection of a movie and of slides, and that she also came to use a window-opening phrase whenever some noise from the outside led her to suspect that there might be something worth seeing out there.

Another consideration in the compilation of the lexicon was the need to avoid ambiguity. If a language is to be used as a means of communication and not as the raw material for the composition of poetry or emotionally suggestive prose, words that have more than one meaning should be avoided because they inevitably complicate the process of interpretation. Although it can be said that all natural languages contain words with more than one meaning, this feature is in no way a requirement for their communicatory function. Insofar as possible, therefore, lexigrams were chosen to designate only one type of item. Thereby we eliminated a gratuitous difficulty for the subject and also made it possible to design the automatic parser in a much more compact way because it did not need complex disambiguation procedures.

The Yerkish lexigrams, thus, have one meaning each, and this one meaning in most cases corresponds to one meaning of an English word. Since most items in the English lexicon have more than one meaning, there is no one-to-one relation between English words and lexigrams. For instance, the English words "back," "ear," "eye," "foot," and "head," can all, depending on the context, designate objects, activities, or attributes. Although the different usages of a word may all derive from a single, underlying concept (e.g., "my back," "to back my car," and "the back seat") some of these words can, in addition, designate several items which conceptually have little or nothing to do with one another (e.g., an ear of a rabbit and an ear of corn). The Yerkish lexigrams that correspond to the English words listed above, however, designate parts of the body exclusively. In a few exceptional cases, the meaning of a lexigram is somewhat larger than that of a single English word and has to be translated by means of a word combination (e.g., *name-of, which-is, out-of*).

In a traditional lexicon, it is customary to divide the lexical items (words) into nouns, verbs, adjectives, etc. This grammatical classification derives from the roles (parts of speech) words play in sentences. In a language such as Latin, this type of classification is a rather obvious descriptive device, since Latin words in most cases change their form according to the role they play, and are morphologically marked for specific parts of speech (e.g., *amor*, noun; *amare*, infinitive verb; *amo*, finite first person present indicative.) In English the morphological marking of parts of speech has all but disappeared, and hence there is no obvious reason why the word *love*, for example, when taken by itself and *not* as part of a specific string of words, should be considered a noun rather than an infinitive or a finite verb form. What is more important is the fact that this grammatical classification, both in Latin and in English, is based predominantly on the linguistic characteristics of lexical items and their use and not on the conceptual characteristics of the items they designate. A linguist faced with the two sentences *I love Mary a lot* and *I have a lot of love for Mary* must classify *love* as verb in the first and as noun in the second. Because verbs are supposed to designate activities or processes, and nouns things or static items, this classification inevitably produces the misleading impression that *love* expresses an activity in the one sentence but not in the other. Yet on the conceptual level *love* in both sentences designates neither an activity nor a thing but a relationship. Traditional grammars relegate such considerations of meaning, or underlying concepts, to the realm of semantics and continue to formulate their rules in terms of the old grammatical word-classes. This is one point where correlational grammar departs from the tradition (Ceccato, 1949; Ceccato, Beltrame, von Glasersfeld, Perschke, Maretti, Zonta, & Albani, 1960, 1963; von Glasersfeld, 1961, 1969). The lexicon with which a correlational grammar operates is divided into classes that are defined not in terms of the morphological characteristics of words, but in terms of the functional characteristics of concepts. These functional characteristics are derived from the role or roles the concept plays in the cognitive representation of experiential situations. In the case of "things," for instance, these characteristics include the kinds of activity the thing can perform as actor and the kinds of activity in which it can play the part of direct object; in the case of "activities" the characteristics include the kinds of change the activity can bring about, the kinds of material it requires, etc.

Though the Yerkish universe of discourse—the set of things about which one can communicate in Yerkish—is at present only a small fraction of that of English or any other natural language, it could be considerably expanded without increasing or altering the grammar currently in use. As it is, the system allows for 46 lexigram-classes of which 37 are in use at the moment. Thus nine more classes can be added, and this addition would expand the system by 25%. A much larger expansion, however, could be achieved by simply increasing the number of lexigrams in those classes that do not contain special function words. In the present arrangement, 25 of the 37 operative classes fall into that category. By filling them with new items, we could at once reach the system's ceiling of 250 lexigrams and greatly increase the possibilities of expression. This has not been done because it seemed far more interesting to explore our subject's capabilities with regard to sentence structure rather than her retention of ever larger numbers of lexical items.

THE CONCEPTUAL LEXIGRAM CLASSES

In the following section, I shall briefly describe the lexigram classes that are in operation at present and list the items in each class that have been used by Lana already or are now ready for insertion into the system. Items from this latter category will appear in parentheses.

Items that can eat, drink, groom, tickle, bite, and/or give things or make things happen in the environment, are called "Autonomous Actors." They are subdivided into four groups and thus gave rise to four lexigram classes:

Familiar Primates (AP), i.e., human and nonhuman primates that can be addressed by name: *Beverly, Billy, Lana, Tim*.

The personal pronouns *you* and *me*, since they are reciprocally applied to the same kind of item, have been added to this class. In Yerkish, however, personal pronouns do not mark a case. Hence, the sentences *You tickle me* and *Me tickle you* are both grammatically correct.

Unfamiliar Primates (AV), i.e., human and nonhuman primates that cannot be addressed by name because no name has been assigned to them. At present the lexigram *visitor* is the only member of this class.

At some future date we may introduce lexigrams for *man, woman*, and *ape*. When that is done, we shall have to decide whether or not a sentence such as *Please man move into room* should be accepted in Yerkish. I believe it would be more interesting to allow only *you* and proper names as vocatives.

Nonprimates (AO), i.e., other animate organisms. At present this class contains only the lexigram for *roach*.

Since our subjects are expected to get access to an outdoor compound, more animal names will eventually be inserted into this class.

Inanimate Actor (AM), i.e., the "machine," which comprises the computer, the keyboards, and all the computer-activated mechanisms. The single lexigram in this class is *machine*.

The differences between these four classes spring from the fact that some of the items can perform activities that the others cannot. The primates and the machine, for example, can respond to requests for "giving" things and for "making" certain changes in the environment; a nonprimate such as a roach cannot respond to that kind of request. Similarly, primates and nonprimates can eat and drink, whereas the machine cannot.

Those objects which we often refer to as "physical objects," i.e., items that are tangible and have a location in space, are divided into several classes according to their mobility and/or their function.

Absolute Fixtures (FA), i.e., items that can neither move nor be moved: *cage, piano, room, (keyboard)*.

(Note: the "piano" is a small second keyboard used to test the subject's musical abilities.)

Relative Fixtures (FP), i.e., items that cannot change their location but can change their configuration by "stationary" motion: *door, window*.

Although the window can be opened automatically by a suitable request addressed to the machine, the door can be opened only by a request addressed to a technician.

Transferables (TF), i.e., items that can change place and hands, that can be "given" by one actor to another: *ball, blanket, bowl, box, can, cup, feces, shoe*.

Some of these items are sometimes placed into a computer-activated hopper, and then they can be obtained by a request addressed to the machine. Otherwise requests for them have to be addressed to a technician.

Parts of Body (PB), these are items that can change their location but cannot change hands: *ear, eye, foot, hand, mouth, nose*.

Solid and liquid food items are divided into three classes because the solids are divided into "units" and "materials." This second division was made for two reasons. The automatic dispensers were too small to handle whole bananas and apples, and it also makes for a better training situation if the subject receives small pieces and thus has to formulate the request all the more frequently. This arrangement makes it possible to differentiate requests for a whole item from requests for a piece of an item by means of two different sentence structures.

Edible Units (EU), i.e., food items that are dispensed as wholes: *M&M, (nut, raisin)*.

Edible Materials (EM), i.e., food items that are dispensed in pieces: *apple, banana, bread, cabbage, chow*.

Drinks (ED), i.e., ingestible liquids: *coffee, coke, juice, milk, water*.

A special class of conceptual categories is represented by lexigrams which serve to indicate conceptual parts of spatially extended items. They have one grammatical feature in common: They are used with the preposition "of."

Conceptual Categories (CT), applicable to spatial items: *color, piece, (beginning, bottom, end, side, top)*.

One more class that would fall into the traditional category of nouns is formed by lexigrams that designate perceptual items of a special kind: states of the environment that are caused by an agent.

Ambiental Conditions (CD), i.e., percepts considered the result of an agent's activity: *movie, music, slide, TV, (cold, heat, light)*.

In the category traditionally called adjectives, there are at present a set of color terms and two lexigrams designating "open" and "shut."

States (ST), i.e., properties that can be predicated of other items: *black, blue, green, open, orange, purple, red, shut, white, yellow, (clean, cold, dirty, hard, hot, soft)*.

Spatial indications are divided into three classes. The first of these contains spatial adverbs that can be used in predicative constructions. The other two correspond to prepositions.

Locational States (LS), i.e., spatial indications that can be predicated of other items: *away, down, here, up*.

Locational Prepositions (LP), i.e., items that function as markers for relational concepts and specify the spatial location of the item that precedes them (i.e., where it is) relative to the location of the item that follows: *in, on, outside, under*.

Directional Prepositions (DP), i.e., items that function as markers for relational concepts and specify the direction of the item that precedes them (i.e., where it is going) relative to the location of the item that follows: *behind, into, out-of, to*.

As Yerkish has at present no tenses or other indications of time, it also contains no prepositions for temporal relations. Once lexigrams designating temporal or sequential concepts are introduced, it will be interesting to see if our subjects extend the use of *in* and *on* to the temporal domain. It should not surprise us if they do, since on the conceptual level inclusion and other spatial relations arise from an attentional pattern that is neither spatial nor temporal in itself.

Several other lexigrams also designate relational concepts. One of them is translated as *of* and corresponds to the partitive function of the English preposition; that is, it expresses the part–whole relation. It does not, however, express the possessive relationship or any of the other possible meanings of the English word "of." Thus, in Yerkish one can say *color of banana*, *piece of apple*, or *top of box*, but not *friend of Tim*, *sign of fear*, or *house of cards*.

Partitive Preposition (PP), i.e., indication of part–whole relation: *of*.

Recently a lexigram for "and" was created, but it corresponds to a small part of the range of uses of the English conjunction. It can be used to link two actors or two direct objects of one and the same activity but not to link two phrases or sentences.

Additive Conjunction (XA), i.e., indication of dual agent or dual object: *and*.

Three lexigrams designate relations for which there is no one-word expression in English. One of them indicates the semantic connection between a lexigram and the item it designates; the other two, the relations of sameness and difference.

Semantic Indicator (NF), i.e., indication of semantic nexus: *name-of*.

Similarity–Difference Marker (IF): *same-as*, *different-from*.

The last of the "two-word" lexigrams designates the relations of attribution or specification that connect an item and a property, either when that property is attributed to it (in English by an attributive adjective) or when the item is characterized by means of the property (in English by a relative clause; see page 116).

Attributive Marker (WR): *which-is*.

At the time of writing, nine classes of activity lexigrams as listed below have been used, and three more (listed in parentheses) are ready for insertion. Some of the activities necessarily involve a direct object (transitive = t.); some of them cannot involve a direct object (intransitive = i.), and some of them may function either way (i. & t.).

Ingestion of Solids (VE) i. & t.: *eat*.

Ingestion of Liquids (VD) i. & t.: *drink*.

Relational Motor Act (VA) i. & t.: *groom, tickle*.

Transferring (VB) t. (locomotion causing object's change of place): *carry*.

Locomotion (VL) i. (change of place): *move, swing*.

Change of Place and State (VT) t.: *put*.

Change of Hands (VG) t.: *give*.

Conative Activity (VW) t.: *want*.

Causing or Creating Change (VM) t.: *make*.

Application of Force (VC) t.: (*pull, push.*)

Maintaining Position (VS) i.: (*lie, sleep, stand.*)

Perceptual Activities (VP) t.: (*feel, hear, see.*)

Finally Yerkish contains three classes of particles, which correspond to "determiners." As in English, they are used in the place of articles, but since Yerkish has no articles, some of these lexigrams have a wider range than their English translations.

Demonstrative (DD): *this, what*.

Quantitative (DQ): (*all, many*), *no*, (*one*).

Comparative (DC): *less, more*.

There are five other graphic signs that differ from ordinary lexigrams in that their position in a string (i.e., a sequence of lexigrams) is fixed. Four of them can be used only as the first item at the beginning of a phrase or sentence, and they modify the mood of the whole utterance that follows; i.e., they are "sentential markers." The fifth is the equivalent of a "period" and is placed at the end of every utterance.

Request Sign (imperative): *please*

Query (interrogative): "?"

Negation: *not*

Affirmation: *yes*

End-of-message Sign: "."

AN INTERPRETIVE CORRELATIONAL GRAMMAR[4]

The grammar of Yerkish was derived from the "correlational" grammar implemented some years ago in the *Multistore parser* for English sentences (von Glasersfeld, 1964, 1965, 1970; von Glasersfeld & Pisani, 1968, 1970). It is an *interpretive* grammar and lays no claim to being "generative" or "transformational" in the Chomskian sense of these terms.

Although the theoretical bases of the correlational approach to grammar were published 15 years ago (Ceccato et al., 1960), the revolutionary idea contained in this approach has been slow to spread. Put very simply, the idea is the realization that no language can be satisfactorily analyzed and described unless one has a viable analysis and classification of the nonlinguistic conceptual structures that find expression in language. Ideally, a correlational grammar should contain a complete mapping of the semantic connections between the elements and structures of a given language, on the one hand, and the elements and structures of conceptual representation, on the other. The amount of work required to produce such a mapping for any natural language is, of course, vast. Fillmore's (1968) "case grammar" sprang from a similar relational approach. The work of Charniak (1972) and the painstaking analyses of conceptual dependency by Schank (1972, 1973, 1975) represent substantial advances in this line of research. It will take a good deal more time and effort to map the conceptual semantics of the average language user's universe of discourse, but it should not really surprise anyone that language turns out to be an enormously complex system. What matters is that enough progress has been made to encourage the hope that the task can, indeed, be completed.

In this context it must be said that Chomsky's introduction of the terms "surface structure" and "deep structure" (Chomsky, 1956, 1965) seemed a step in the right direction, but his interpretation of deep structures has remained wholly dependent on linguistic concepts. This limitation prevented him and his followers from getting down to the truly characteristic features of the underlying structures, namely, the cognitive operations and routines by means of which these structures are put together. Thus, since Chomsky does not attempt to specify deep structures in their own cognitive terms, he can specify them only insofar as they differ in their surface expression (i.e., on the linguistic level); he cavalierly leaves all the really interesting cognitive part to the intuition of the native speaker and to

---

[4] Parts of this description of the grammar of Yerkish have appeared in the *American Journal of Computational Linguistics* (Vol. 1, 1974, microfiche 12) and are reprinted here by courtesy of the publisher.

mysterious innate processes. Indeed, as Chomsky (1956) was careful to state
and as he reiterated (1965), his generative–transformational grammar was
intended as a linguist's description of language and *not* as a model of the
language-user.

Correlational grammar, on the other hand, is an interpretive device and
aims at providing a model of the language-user in the receiving role. (Note
that "model" in this context means a mechanism that, given the same input
as the thing to be modeled, will yield the same output, although it may
employ quite different means to do so.) Correlational grammar, therefore, is
not primarily concerned with demonstrating in an axiomatic way that every
grammatically correct phrase or sentence is a case under a formalized rule
or set of rules, but rather with transforming the *content* of a given piece of
language into a canonical form of preestablished conceptual–semantic elements or modules. An interpretive system of this kind presupposes the
grammaticality of its input. But since it is designed to interpret all grammatical pieces of language, it can be used to define operationally as "grammatical" any input that it can interpret, and as "ungrammatical" any input that it
cannot.

When designing a correlational grammar for a *natural* language, the
task of bringing the interpretive capability of the grammar to a level anywhere near the interpretive capability of the native user of the language is
truly enormous. In the case of an artificial language, however, this problem
is altogether eliminated because the lexicon, the rules of concatenation, and
the interpretive grammar can all be designed at the same time. Since there is
no native user who already has a universe of experiential content and
well-established semantic connections (by means of which this content is
linked to linguistic expressions), the designer is free to tailor the lexicon as
well as the syntax of his language to the universe of discourse he envisages.

That is to a large extent how Yerkish was designed, especially with
regard to the rules of grammar. The result is that the user of Yerkish can
communicate in grammatically correct lexigram strings no more than the
correlational grammar of Yerkish can interpret.

In creating an artificial language, the semantic connections between the
signs (words, gestural signs, or lexigrams) and their meanings can be made
as univocal (unambiguous) as desired. Moreover, because Yerkish is based
on English and because the output of subjects in the experimental environment is evaluated by speakers of English, the lexical semantics of Yerkish
(i.e., the meaning of single lexigrams) could be left implicit to a certain
extent. For example, the Yerkish parser does not have to contain an exhaustive semantic analysis of lexigrams such as *ball* or *banana* because it can be
taken for granted that the reader of the parser's output will be quite familiar
with the concepts designated by these two words. What the parser must

contain, however, is a mapping of those specific characteristics of concepts that determine their potential for entering into structural relations with other items.

In any correlational grammar, the relational characteristics of conceptual items determine the classification of lexical items. Thus, if the language is to contain items that can be eaten and items that can be drunk, the lexigrams designating these items will be divided into *edibles* (classes EM and EU, i.e., direct objects suitable for the activity designated by *eat*) and *drinkables* (class ED, i.e., direct objects suitable for the activity designated by *drink*).

In short, Yerkish grammar requires a lexicon in which classes of lexical items are exhaustively characterized with regard to the specific relations into which their members can enter with members of other classes. This exhaustive characterization of each lexigram is supplied not by listing all the other classes with whose members it can potentially form connections but by a string of indices each of which specifies a connective relation and the place in it a member of that class can occupy. Thus we come to the relational concepts, or *correlators*, which are instrumental in the building up of complex structures both on the conceptual and on the linguistic level. Strictly speaking, a correlator is a connective function that links conceptual items on the cognitive, representational level. Natural languages indicate these connective functions by a variety of means: prepositions, verbs, nouns, and other types of words that incorporate a preposition (e.g., *enter, entry, invade,* and *income,* incorporate the relation designated by the preposition *in*), conjunctions and other particles, syntactic markers, and frequently word-order. Since these linguistic elements indicate correlators, we should call them "correlator expressions." However, once it has been made clear that correlators function on the conceptual level, connecting concepts with other concepts or combinations of concepts, we can in most cases use the term "correlator" for both the relational concepts and the linguistic devices that express them.[5]

In designing an artificial language, the classification of lexical items and the definition or explication of relational concepts must go hand in hand since the first is done in terms of the second. The relational concepts have to be explicitly listed and explicated by some sort of paraphrase. In principle, that is what a "case grammar" does. Its cases, basically, are relational concepts (see, for example, Fillmore, 1968). Correlational grammar, however, attempts to cover not only the generic relational concepts underlying

---

[5] One area where the distinction has to be maintained is the semantic analysis of natural languages, because correlator expressions such as prepositions rarely have a one-to-one correspondence to relational concepts. Instead, they mark the presence of one of a set of relational concepts.

the "syntactic" functions of traditional grammar but also as much as possible of those relational concepts that traditionally have been considered "semantic." Its list of correlators, therefore, is very much longer and more specific than the lists of "cases" that have been suggested by the proponents of case grammars.

CORRELATORS: THE CONNECTIVE FUNCTIONS OF YERKISH

In its present form,[6] the Yerkish grammar operates with some 30 correlators. The first 10 of these correspond to what, in traditional grammars, is subsumed under the generic subject–verb relation. Here they are subdivided according to the type of actor and the type of activity. There are five actor/activity correlators that require an "autonomous animate actor" (AP, AV, or AO):

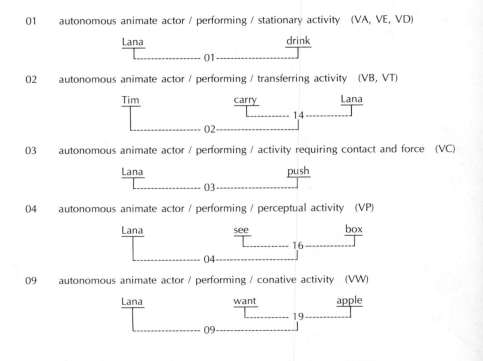

01   autonomous animate actor / performing / stationary activity   (VA, VE, VD)

    Lana   drink
    └──────────── 01 ────────────┘

02   autonomous animate actor / performing / transferring activity   (VB, VT)

    Tim   carry   Lana
                           └────── 14 ──────┘
    └──────────── 02 ────────────┘

03   autonomous animate actor / performing / activity requiring contact and force   (VC)

    Lana   push
    └──────────── 03 ────────────┘

04   autonomous animate actor / performing / perceptual activity   (VP)

    Lana   see   box
                           └────── 16 ──────┘
    └──────────── 04 ────────────┘

09   autonomous animate actor / performing / conative activity   (VW)

    Lana   want   apple
                           └────── 19 ──────┘
    └──────────── 09 ────────────┘

[6] Note that in this and the three following sections I am describing the Yerkish grammar and not Lana's performance. The examples given here were chosen to demonstrate the grammar, and many of them *have never been used by Lana*.

Two actor/activity correlators require an "intentional causative agent–actor," i.e., a primate or the machine (AP, AV, AM):

05   causative agent / causing / item's change of hands   (VG)

```
   Machine              give                    M&M
   ┬                    └---------- 17 ----------┘
   └--------------- 05---------------------┘
```

06   causative agent / causing / item's or ambiental change of state   (VM)

```
   Machine              make                    movie
   ┬                    └---------- 18 ----------┘
   └--------------- 06---------------------┘
```

Two further actor/activity correlators can have as actor any item that is capable of changing its spatial location:

07   movable actor / performing / locomotion, i.e., changing its own place   (VL)

```
   Tim                                   move
   ┬-------------------- 07-----------------------┘
```

08   movable actor / performing / stative activity without change of place   (VS)

```
   Shelley                               stand
   ┬-------------------- 08----------------------┘
```

The last correlator that corresponds to the traditional subject–verb class but does *not* involve an activity is that of the simple predicative relation. In English this relation is expressed by the so-called auxiliary verb *to be*. Yerkish, however, contains no auxiliaries, and the predicative relation is designated by the mere juxtaposition of an item and the property (ST) or locational state (LS) that is predicated of it:

10   item / described by / predicated state

```
   banana                              black
   ┬----------------- 10-----------------------┘
```

Next there is a group of ten correlators which correspond to what in traditional grammars is subsumed under the generic "verb-object" relation. In Yerkish they are again subdivided according to the type of activity and the type of item that serves as patient:

11   ingestion of liquids / involving as patient / solid food   (EU or *piece-of* EM)

```
   eat                                 M&M
   ┬----------------- 11-----------------------┘
```

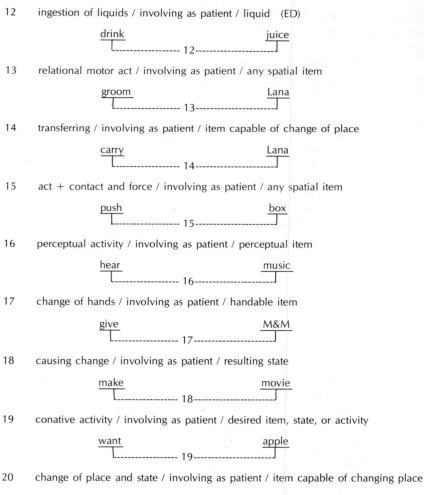

12   ingestion of liquids / involving as patient / liquid   (ED)

drink   juice
└----------------- 12----------------------┘

13   relational motor act / involving as patient / any spatial item

groom   Lana
└----------------- 13----------------------┘

14   transferring / involving as patient / item capable of change of place

carry   Lana
└----------------- 14----------------------┘

15   act + contact and force / involving as patient / any spatial item

push   box
└----------------- 15----------------------┘

16   perceptual activity / involving as patient / perceptual item

hear   music
└----------------- 16----------------------┘

17   change of hands / involving as patient / handable item

give   M&M
└----------------- 17----------------------┘

18   causing change / involving as patient / resulting state

make   movie
└----------------- 18----------------------┘

19   conative activity / involving as patient / desired item, state, or activity

want   apple
└----------------- 19----------------------┘

20   change of place and state / involving as patient / item capable of changing place

put   cup
└----------------- 20----------------------┘

Several correlators concern spatial relations. There are two basic types, one involving a *directional* indication, the other a *locational* one. In each case, the specific direction or location can be indicated by one of the locative lexigrams (LS) or by a prepositional phrase. By "prepositional phrase" we mean an already made combination consisting of a preposition and some other item that specifies the location. For technical reasons these prepositional phrases are correlated separately in the present system and form a preliminary step toward the correlation of the spatial relation proper.

Hence the constructions involving a preposition (DP or LP) as indicator of a spatial relation requires two correlators to be applied in succession:

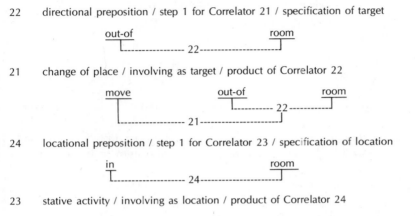

22   directional preposition / step 1 for Correlator 21 / specification of target

21   change of place / involving as target / product of Correlator 22

24   locational preposition / step 1 for Correlator 23 / specification of location

23   stative activity / involving as location / product of Correlator 24

The second step of this construction can also be formed with the activity lexigram *put*. It then expresses the complex relations "change of place" and subsequent "state in place" of the direct object. (For example, *to put a ball on the table* means to move the ball from where it is onto the table and to make it stay there.)

29   change of place and state / involving as target / product of correlator 22 or 24

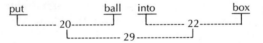

Two further correlators that function in the same way as those of the spatial relations are expressed by the "partitive" preposition *of* and the "additive" conjunction *and*. For both there is again a two-step construction:

25   item considered "part" / step 1 for Correlator 26 / partitive preposition

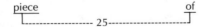

26   product of Correlator 25 / part–whole relation / item considered "whole"

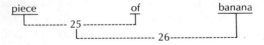

34   additive conjunction (XA) / step 1 for Correlator 35 / second item of couple

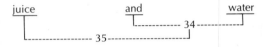

35   first item of couple / conjunctive relation / product of Correlator 34

The relation between an item and the lexigram that has been chosen as its name is expressed by the lexigram *name-of*, which is also constructed in two steps, the first of which usually involves the demonstrative *this* accompanied by some form of ostensive indication of the item to be named.

27   semantic indicator (NF) / step 1 for Correlator 28 / item to be named

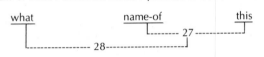

28   new lexigram or *what* / semantic nexus / product of Correlator 27

Of the many varied relations of specification which in natural languages are expressed by articles, quantifiers, demonstratives, interrogatory adjectives etc., Yerkish contains only two at present. There is one correlator for the relations indicated by demonstrative, quantifying, and interrogative lexigrams (DD and DQ) and another for the relation indicated by the comparative lexigrams *more* and *less* and the item to which they are applied.

30   determiner / applied to / item to be specified

32   comparative quantifier / applied to / item to be specified

Another correlator functions as specification in the sense of a restrictive relative clause in natural language. It is expressed by the compound lexigram *which-is* (WR) first correlated to the specification by means of the predicative Correlator 10 and then by Correlator 31 to the item to be specified.

31   item to be specified / attribution / restriction marker   (WH)

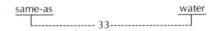

```
apple                    which-is              red
 T                         L-------- 10-------------J
 L----------------- 31----------------------J
```

Finally, Yerkish has a correlator expression for one more relation: similarity or difference, i.e., the relation resulting from the specific comparison of two items that may be perceptually present or purely representational.

33   sameness–difference marker / applied to / term of comparison

```
same-as                          water
 L----------------- 33----------------------J
```

As is the case with the lexigram classes, we have not yet reached the maximum number of correlators foreseen in the present system. The computer program is designed for a maximum of 46 correlators. At present the system is operating with the 35 just listed (of which Lana's messages have so far involved 26) and with 3 more functions that handle the "sentential markers" for request, query, and negation. Thus we have eight more correlator slots that can be successively filled with new relational concepts as the progress of our subject and the requirements of future experimentation dictate.

YERKISH SENTENCE STRUCTURE

Given a basic list of correlators and their linguistic expression, the classification of lexical terms can be carried out by listing for each item the correlators that *potentially* can link it to other items. To give an example, there is a relational concept (Correlator 11) paraphrased as "active ingestion of solids, involving solid food as direct object"; on the linguistic level, this relation is expressed by the juxtaposition of two lexical items in a certain order. If we have the lexigram *eat*, which designates "active ingestion of solids," and another lexigram *raisin*, which designates a subcategory of "solid food," we can form a combination, or *correlation*, with the two lexigrams that can be represented as the structure:

```
        (LH)                    (RH)
(a)     eat                     raisin
         T                       T
         L----------------- 11----------------------J
```

Because the order of succession of the two items in the linear linguistic expression is obligatory and cannot be reversed, it is not enough for the grammar merely to supply the information that the lexigrams *eat* and *raisin* can be linked by Correlator 11. The grammar must also specify that in this correlation, *eat* has to be the left-hand piece (LH) and *raisin* the right-hand piece (RH). This information is part of the permanent lexicon of the system. It is recorded there by means of "correlation indices" (I_c's), which consist of the number of the potential correlator plus an indication which specifies whether the items to which this I_c is assigned can function as LH-piece or as RH-piece. Thus in Example (a) both *eat* and *raisin* can be assigned to Correlator 11, but *eat* would be assigned the correlation index I_c : 11-LH, whereas *raisin* would be assigned the correlation index I_c : 11-RH. Thus when either of these two words appear in any two-word phrase describing the concept defined by Correlation 11, *eat* will always have to be the left-hand member and *raisin* will always have to occupy the right-hand position.

In many cases, of course, several lexical items, all members of the same lexigram class, can function in the same place. Therefore, I_c's are actually assigned to lexigram classes, not to single lexical items. On the one hand, this indexing of classes rather than individual items is more economical with regard to storage space; on the other, it permits the addition of new lexigrams to the existing classes without in any way disturbing the operative part of the lexicon.

Let us add another correlation and expand Example (a). The relational concept paraphrased as "autonomous animate actor performing stationary activity" is Correlator 01. The paraphrase "autonomous animate actor" comprises three lexigram classes of the present lexicon, namely "familiar primates" (AP), "unfamiliar primates" (AC), and "nonprimates" (AO); it excludes the fourth "actor" class, i.e., "inanimate actor" (AM), or the machine. The paraphrase "stationary activity" comprises three lexigram classes, namely "ingestion of solids" (VE), "ingestion of liquids" (VD), and "relational motor activity" (VA). Given the lexigram sequence *Lana eat* the interpretive grammar finds that *Lana*, belonging to class AP, bears the I_c : 01-LH; whereas *eat*, belonging to class VE, bears the I_c : 01-RH; on the strength of these complementary indices the grammar will allow the correlation:

(b)

The grammar, it must be remembered, is an interpretive one, and its rules have been formulated in such a way that the automatic parser can apply them. Allowing a correlation, therefore, means that the parser in its progress from left to right along the input string of lexigrams records that correlation as a possible part-interpretation. It is recorded as a "product" in order to be tested for its potential correlation with other parts of the input string.

Correlations that link single lexigrams, such as Examples (a) and (b), can be made and checked on the basis of the I_c's assigned to each lexigram in the lexicon. In order to discover whether or not such a product can be correlated with other lexigrams of the input, each product must be assigned a string of I_c's that represents its individual potential for functioning as LH-piece or RH-piece in larger correlations that link it with other lexical items or products. The procedure that assigns I_c's to a given product is the dynamic part of the grammar. It is governed by *operational* rules that are rather complicated, since the correlability of a given product often depends on more than one of its constituents. An example will help to make this clear. Correlator 30 is paraphrased as "determiner applied to an item to be specified," and among the products it creates are phrases such as:

With regard to Correlator 30, *raisin* and *ball* are identical pieces. But as potential RH-pieces of a larger correlation, one formed, say, by Correlator 11 (paraphrased as "ingestion of solids, involving as direct object a solid food"), they are not at all equivalent. The correlation:

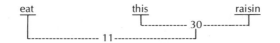

would be acceptable, whereas the correlation:

would *not* be acceptable because *ball* does not belong to the lexigram class EU (defined as "solid food") and therefore is not a potential RH-piece of Correlation 11. For this reason if the string *eat this ball* occurs as input to the interpretive grammar, it must be rejected as incorrect. To implement this discrimination, the phrase *this raisin* must be assigned I_c : 11-RH, but the phrase *this ball* must not. In other words, before any product made by Correlator 30 can be assigned the I_c : 11-RH, it must contain as its right-hand piece an item that belongs to the lexigram class "solid food."

In the implementation of the parser, as the preceding example demonstrates, the assignation of I_c's to products has to be determined not only by the specific correlator responsible for the product to be classified but also by the pieces that the product contains. The conditions these assignation rules express vary for each correlator, and many products require the application of more than one rule. This, indeed, is the reason why an interpretive correlational grammar cannot be represented by means of a small set of powerful, generalized rules. Thus it might seem that correlational grammar would be a much less economical approach to the analysis of language than the relatively concise formalizations of some other modern grammars. Closer examination, however, shows that this is not so. Generative–transformational grammar, for instance, when used for the purpose of interpretation requires a vast number of selection rules in order to deal with the very same *semantic* information that is involved in our assignation rules. Applied to the preceding example, a generative grammar would allow the string *eat this ball* on the basis of the syntactic classification of the words it contains, but would subsequently eliminate it as incorrect on the basis of specific selection rules. Since the rules governing syntactic connections and the rules governing semantic selection operate in different ways and with altogether different classifications, an automatic parser using that kind of grammar must continually shift back and forth between the syntactic and the semantic ways of operating. The difference is simply this: In correlational grammar these rules are incorporated in one homogeneous correlation procedure, whereas in all syntax-based grammars they constitute an unwieldy adjunct of functionally different accessory procedures that tend to consume more and more space and time as their operational implementation is improved and completed.

PECULIARITIES OF THE YERKISH GRAMMAR

The grammar of Yerkish had to be kept as simple as possible for several reasons. Most importantly, the rules of the language to which the linguistic behavior of our subject would have to conform had to be few and consistent from the learner's point of view; nevertheless the Yerkish structures built upon them had to be translatable easily and without major structural changes into comprehensible English. As a result, Yerkish grammar may seem somewhat unusual. In the following paragraphs, the more salient deviations from English grammar will be explained.

Yerkish at present has only one voice, the active, and three moods:

indicative, interrogative, and imperative. Both the interrogative and the imperative are formed not by specific verb forms or word order as in many natural languages but by sentential prefixes, or markers. The prefix of the interrogative is the conventional question mark "?"; that for imperatives (requests) is an arrow translated into English as "please." The keys representing these lexigrams must be pressed at the beginning of a string. The lexigram string following them always has the form of an indicative statement even when it constitutes a command or a question. If the string is actually to be interpreted as an indicative statement, it must not be preceded by either "?" or *please*. Hence we have:

Tim move into room.	=	indicative statement
? Tim move into room.	=	interrogative (query)
Please Tim move into room.	=	imperative (request)

A third lexigram that functions as a sentential prefix is *no*, which corresponds to an overall negation of the statement.

No Tim move into room. = negation

This last sentence corresponds to the English "It is not the case that Tim moves into the room." However, since Lana has spontaneously come to use the lexigram *no* to mean what, given the situational context, can only be interpreted as "don't", this *no* is now allowed to function also as the negative imperative.

As yet, there are no tenses in Yerkish except the present. A simple past and future are foreseen, and when in use they will be designated by particles preceding the activity lexigram in the string. These particles will function as auxiliaries, which at present Yerkish does not possess. The English linking verb "to be" is taken over by Correlator 10, which is expressed by the juxtaposition of a lexigram belonging to one of the classes of items that are modifiable and a lexigram designating a specific state or property. For example

Ball red.	=	'The ball is red.'
Tim here.	=	'Tim is here.'

The absence of an explicit linking verb is noticeable also in conjunction with the "naming function," an important instrument in Lana's acquisition of new lexical items. It is used together with the ostensive definition of new lexigrams, which are placed at the beginning of a string of the form:

X name-of this. = 'X is the name of this,'

where X is the new lexigram. The same sentence structure can be turned into a question:

> *? What name-of this.* = 'What is the name of this?'
> *? What name-of visitor.* = 'What is the name of the visitor?'

The lexigrams *this* and *visitor* are the only ones that are permissible in this question because any other lexigram would preempt what is being asked for. Strings such as: *? What name-of Tim* already contain the lexigram for which the question asks and therefore make no sense.

Two English constructions that have a specificative and restrictive function, "the red ball" and "the ball which is red," are one and the same in Yerkish. The specificative relation is expressed by a lexigram which is translated into English as the compound *which-is* (Correlator 31). Example:

> *Ball which-is red.* = 'the red ball' or 'the ball which is red.'

Spatial prepositions in Yerkish were originally strictly divided into locational and directional categories (lexigram classes LP and DP). However, since Lana has spontaneously used *behind* and *outside* (both classified as "locational") to indicate the target of a directional activity and since this usage is also allowable in English and other natural languages, we have removed the restriction with regard to these two prepositions.

Until recently there were no conjunctions in Yerkish, but a somewhat restricted form of "and" is now ready to be introduced into the system. Two actors of one and the same activity can be linked by the Yerkish *and*, and so can two direct objects. Thus, we now have sentences such as:

> *Tim and Lana eat.*
> *Lana drink juice and water.*
> *Please Tim give ball and M&M.*

But the parser will reject sentences such as:

> **Lana drink juice and banana.*
> **Please Tim give ball and machine.*

Owing to the restricted workspace in the computer, we have not attempted to design control routines for phrase and sentence conjunction. The system, therefore, cannot as yet handle expressions such as, *Tim drink coffee and Lana eat piece of chow.*

This last example brings to mind a deliberate peculiarity of Yerkish grammar. The classification of lexigrams makes a distinction between "edible units" and "edible materials," a distinction that makes little sense to an English-speaking person (see the explanation on page 99). However, it results in the use of two rather different sentence structures according to the type of "solid food" that is mentioned. The items designated by lexigrams of class EU, for instance, can be asked for as wholes whereas items designated by lexigrams of the class EM can only be obtained one piece at a time. Thus, the computer will honor the requests:

>   *Please machine give M&M.*

and

>   *Please machine give piece of chow.*

But not

>   **Please machine give piece of M&M.*

or

>   **Please machine give chow.*

This distinction is a rigid rule for the computer, since the automatic dispensers can handle only pieces of chow, apple, banana, etc. In requests addressed to Tim or other human companions Lana can of course request:

>   *Please Tim give apple.*

Yerkish also contains some minor peculiarities that an English-speaking person must keep in mind. A Yerkish structure involving Correlator No. 17 (change of hands, involving as direct object a handable item) implies that the speaker is the receiver of the item that changes hands unless another receiver is explicitly indicated by a prepositional phrase. Thus, if Lana produces the string:

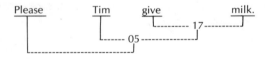

it must be understood that the milk is to be given to Lana. But a receiver can be explicitly specified by adding a prepositional phrase, which yields the correlational structure:

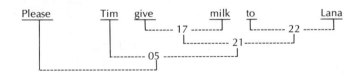

English "resultative" verbs (e.g. "to open" and "to clean") are broken up in Yerkish. The causative element is rendered by *make*, and the effect by a lexigram designating the resulting state or property. Also, in Yerkish these constructions require that the agent be specified. Thus, *Please (Tim) open the window* becomes:

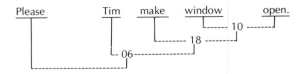

Translated literally into English, this string should read 'Please, Tim, make (the) window be open,' since the correlator that links *window* and *open* is Correlator 10, i.e., the *predicative* relation equivalent to what is expressed by the English "to be." In this case as in most occurrences of Correlator 10, the Yerkish string is easily understood without the explicit linking verb.

The Yerkish *make* is not limited to causing a change of state of specific items but can be used also to indicate a number of perceptual conditions or events in the environment. Specific sensory events such as *movie, music, slide, heat, cold*, and *light* are considered the result of activities subsumed by *make*. In Lana's wholly technological environment this use of *make* is quite reasonable. It obviously makes sense for her to request, for example:

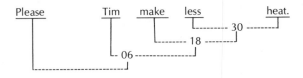

It is, indeed, the machine that causes the projector to start running. Similarly, in Yerkish one can correctly say:

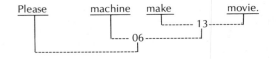

In Lana's experience, it is in fact Tim who causes less heat by turning down the thermostat. This kind of request, however, has not yet been made by Lana.

Make and *want* open the way to "embedded" constructions, since they can govern clauses. A simple example of embedding is:

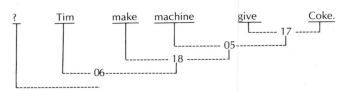

Once lexigrams of class VP ("perceptual activities") have been introduced, there will be embeddings of the kind:

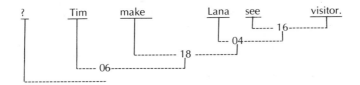

and even double embeddings such as:

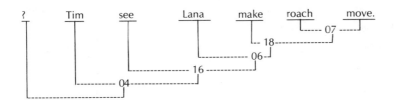

At this time, however, the lexigrams for "to see" or "to hear" have yet to be introduced and therefore Lana cannot produce sentences that contain this type of embedding.

Lest these correlational diagrams create the impression that Yerkish structures are invariably right-branching, here are two examples that contain left-branchings:

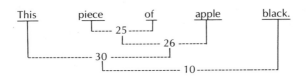

which in English would read: "This piece of apple is black," and likewise:

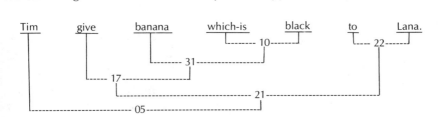

Though the examples of Yerkish sentence structure given in these pages are few, they should convey some idea of the versatility and flexibility of this wholly automated grammar, especially if they are considered in conjunction with the lists of lexigram classes and of correlators discussed earlier. Lana has made spectacular progress in her mastery of the linguistic communication facility. Nevertheless, Yerkish grammar as it stands allows many constructions that are still far beyond Lana's reach. The area of "embedded" phrases has only been touched upon, and Lana has not yet been introduced to the lexigrams designating perceptual activities (class VP), which would at once lead to a variety of complex sentence structures. The operational lexicon at this moment is approaching 100 items, or 40% of the system's capacity. Nine more lexigram classes and eight more correlators could be added at a moment's notice without any alteration of the procedures and programs that constitute the automatic parser. In short, although Lana has proven to be an extremely quick and responsive pupil, the teaching system is still a good bit ahead of her.

THE MULTISTORE PARSER

There are two reasons why an automatic parser capable of monitoring all linguistic transactions was included in the Yerkes communication facility. The first was our wish to create a training environment that would be operative at least partially for 24 hours a day without the need of permanent human attendance. Therefore, the system had to be able to respond to certain requests automatically. In order to do so, the system had to be able to understand these requests at least to the degree that it could discriminate those to which it was supposed to respond from those to which it was not. The second reason was that the system would need to provide an objective grammatical analysis of all the linguistic input produced by the experimental subjects. The first of these objectives could have been attained by a crude and relatively simple system of tags or code signals that would have had nothing whatever to do with *language*. But since the second objective in any case required the installation of a comprehensive parser of Yerkish lexigram strings, the obvious solution was to make the system's automatic responses dependent upon the sentence analyses provided by the parser. The sophisticated electromechanical interface between the computer and the various devices it can command in response to certain linguistic requests is discussed elsewhere in this volume (see Chapter 7). In this section, therefore, I shall try to give a brief outline of the parsing *procedure*; the computer program that implements this procedure is described in the next chapter by Piero Pisani, who collaborated in developing the Multistore parser since its first implementation 13 years ago in Italy and without whom it would never have become an operational system.

The parser of the Yerkes facility is a direct but drastically reduced derivative of the Multistore parser for English sentences (von Glasersfeld & Pisani, 1968, 1970). The rate of reduction can be illustrated by two comparative indications: The parser for English operated with some 500 correlators, whereas the grammar of Yerkish operates with 46. The original Multistore system occupied over 200,000 machine words in the largest computer that was available in 1968; the automatic parser of Yerkish is implemented in a central core area of about 2500 machine words in what can almost be called a minicomputer.

Input to the system is provided by means of a keyboard containing at most 125 lexigram keys arranged in panels of 25 each. Four such panels are in use at present, making a total of 100 keys and lexical items. The parser, however, can handle a lexicon of 250 items. Since the keyboard panels are readily exchangeable, the operational lexicon could be extended to the parser's full capacity of 250 by preparing 10 keyboard panels and using different subsets of five on different days or during different sessions.

When a key in the keyboard is pressed, it activates the corresponding lexical item in the machine's permanent lexicon, provided the system has been switched on. It is switched on by means of a horizontal bar mounted above the keyboard which has to be pulled down and held down throughout the input of a message. A message is composed by pressing several keys in succession and is ended by pressing the "period" key. This end-signal is essential for the computer because the grammaticality of a string can be established only when the string is considered complete by the sender. Many strings contain parts which, if they were taken as wholes, would not be grammatically correct messages. For instance *Please machine give* is not an acceptable statement in Yerkish because *give* is a transitive activity word that requires specification of what is given, but *please machine give juice*, where *juice* specifies the direct object of the activity, is a grammatical utterance.

In the machine's lexicon, the lexigram entries are ordered according to the conceptual classification of the items the lexigrams designate. If a lexigram key is pressed, a code signal travels to the machine's lexicon and "activates" the corresponding entry. Let us assume that this entry is *Tim*. Activation of a lexicon entry has several immediate effects. First, the lexigram code is passed on to the output printer which types out the corresponding English word, in this case the name "Tim." Second, a new code signal emanates from the particular lexicon area in which the activated entry is located and which represents the *lexigram class* to which it belongs. This new signal activates the particular line in the central Multistore area, i.e., the workspace of the machine, where the I_c string that characterizes that lexigram class is recorded. A diagram showing how I_c strings are recorded in the

Multistore area may be helpful in visualizing how the procedure functions. The Multistore area can best be imagined as a rectangular arrangement with 46 horizontal lines, one for each of the 46 lexigram classes, and 46 columns, one for each of the 46 correlators foreseen in this implementation of the system (see Figure 1). Since the I_c's assigned to lexigram classes indicate not only the numbers of the correlators by means of which items of that class can be linked to other items but also the place (LH or RH) the items take in the particular correlation, the I_c columns in the Multistore area are all subdivided into an LH-column and an RH-column. The lexigram *Tim*, for example, belonging to class AP, activates a total of 13 LH-markers and 10 RH-markers in the Multistore area. In Figure 1, in which only six correlators are specifically indicated, the lexigram *Tim* is represented by the LH-markers of Correlators 01, 02, and 03.

If the key for *drink* is pressed after the key for *Tim*, the result will be the activation of those markers that represent the I_c string assigned to the lexigram class VD on the line of that class in the Multistore area. In the diagram, these would be the RH-marker in the column of Correlator 01 and the LH-marker in the column of Correlator 12.

If now the "period" key is pressed, the machine will scan the Multistore area and will discover that in column 01 there is an LH-marker on line AP and an RH-marker on line VD. The mere presence of LH- and RH-markers in a correlator column, however, is not yet sufficient for the machine to produce a correlation. It must also check whether these two markers were entered in the proper sequence, i.e., whether the LH-marker originated from a lexigram that actually came first and the RH-marker from a lexigram that followed immediately after that first one. The order of input is, of course,

Lexigram class	Correlators											
	01		02		03		⋯	12		⋯	16		⋯	46	
	LH	RH	LH	RH	LH	RH		LH	RH		LH	RH		LH	RH
AP (L_1)	×		×		×							×			
⋮															
VD (L_2)		×						×							
⋮															
Class 46															

Figure 1. Diagram of the Multistore lexicon. For each I_c in the I_c string characterizing a lexigram class, there is a marker in the Multistore cell that is the intersection of the line representing the lexigram class and the column representing the correlator indicated by that I_c. The marker further indicates whether members of the particular class can function as LH- or RH-pieces in correlations represented by that column.

recorded at the same time as the activation of the markers, and I have indicated it in parentheses at the beginning of the individual lines of the diagram (L_1 = lexigram 1, etc.).

The most general rule of a correlational parser is very simple: Whenever successive entries result in the activation of first an LH-marker and then an RH-marker in *one* I_c column, the two input items represented by these markers can be correlated by the correlator indicated on top of the column in which the markers are found. Thus, if the lexigrams *Tim* and *drink* were followed by the "period" sign, the machine would accept these two words as a grammatical utterance and would assign to it the structure:

If instead the input continued after the lexigram *drink* with the lexigram *water* and only then the "period" key were pressed, there would be combinable markers also in column 12. Since the scanning procedure follows the order of input, the machine would first discover the possibility of making a correlation in column 01, just as it did in the preceding case. It would, indeed, "make" this correlation, and it would record it as a "product," indicating that the product consists of lexigram L_1 and lexigram L_2 and is linked by Correlator 01. At this point it would interrupt its scanning of the Multistore columns and would switch to the "reclassification routine," i.e., the procedure by means of which I_c's are assigned to products (see page 113).[7] This reclassification routine always consists of one or several of three basic types of rules, each one of which determines whether or not a specific I_c of a set that is preestablished for each correlator is to be assigned to the product in hand. The first type simply assigns a given I_c unconditionally to the product. The second type assigns a given I_c if the LH-piece (or in other cases the RH-piece) of the product had that same I_c in its string. The third type assigns a given I_c only if two conditions are satisfied. At present only one Yerkish construction requires this rule: the conjunctive relation implemented by Correlator 35. The dual condition for the assignation of a given I_c in this case is that both the LH-piece of the product and the RH-piece of the product's RH-piece have that I_c in their strings.

The reclassification routine, in fact, inserts the product that is being reclassified into the Multistore area as though it were an input item and activates LH- and RH-markers in the line on which the product is recorded.

---

[7] In different implementations of the Multistore parser the point in the operational flow at which products are reclassified has not always been the same. One version of the Yerkish parser, for example, scans for and records all products arising after input of a new lexigram and only then begins the reclassification of these products.

When the reclassification of a product has come to its end, its line has exactly the same form and function as the line of an input lexigram; the only difference is that at the beginning of the line instead of the input-number of a lexigram, there is the indication that it is a product and a record of the lexigrams or products it consists of.

In our example, then, after the key for the lexigram *water* and the "period" key have been pressed, the part of the Multistore area that is operative in the analysis of the input lexigram sequence would appear as shown in Figure 2.

The reclassification of Product 1 is such that no correlation can link it to lexigram L_3, once that has appeared in input. Lexigram L_3, however, produces a correlation with L_2 in the column of Correlator 12, and the reclassification of this product (Product 2) activates an RH-marker in column 01. This gives rise to Product 3, which, since the "period" key has now been pressed, constitutes the final product that comprises all the lexigrams of the input. This product has the structure:

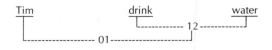

The procedural description of this example should make it clear that the Multistore parser embodies a system of *analysis by synthesis*. Whenever a lexigram is added to those that have already been put in, the machine searches for and actually makes all the "products" that are permissible according to the grammar at that point. Some of these products will be dead ends in that they cannot be incorporated into larger ones when the subsequent lexigrams of the input are considered. They constitute side branches of the path that seeks a correlational structure linking *all* the lexigrams of the given input sequence.[8] When such a comprehensive structure is found at the point when the period key has indicated that the input sequence is finished, this structure is a "final product," and the fact that it *could* be found demonstrates that the input was a *grammatical* sequence.

Since both the Yerkish lexigrams and the Yerkish grammar were specifically designed to avoid ambiguity, we have at present no cases in which

---

[8] This exhaustive construction of all *possible* grammatical part-structures within an input sequence differentiates computer interpretation from human interpretation. Whereas the human interpreter proceeds on the basis of situation-bound expectations, computers have so far always had to proceed on the basis of theoretical rules that do not take into account the pragmatic context of an utterance. Analysis and classification of the living-experience from which our expectations arise has begun only recently (e.g., Schank, 1972, 1973, 1975), and the procedures and data base such analysis would require is, in any case, far beyond the capacity of a small computer.

Lexigram class	Correlators													
	01		02		03		···	12		···	16		···	46	
	LH	RH	LH	RH	LH	RH		LH	RH		LH	RH		LH	RH
AP (L₁)	×		×		×							×			
⋮															
VD (L₂)		×						×							
⋮															
Product 1 L₁-01-L₂												×			
⋮															
ED (L₃)									×			×			
⋮															
Product 2 L₂-12-L₃		×													
⋮															
Product 3 L₁-01-P₂												×			

Figure 2. Diagram of Multistore area after input. The diagram shows all markers activated by the input lexigrams *Tim, drink*, and *water*, and by the products that arise from these lexigrams. The dotted lines connect the complementary markers in the correlator columns that give rise to products.

the parser could possibly come up with more than one final product for a grammatical input sequence. It is unlikely that this univocality will be preserved when more correlators and conceptual lexigram classes are added. By then, however, we anticipate that Lana will have a firm enough grasp of the principles of communication (e.g., the principle that any communication requires a context for its interpretation) to resolve such ambiguities as may crop up in Yerkish by reference to the situational context in which they occur. For the present, the absence of ambiguities in Lana's messages is an enormous advantage: Because of it the question of appropriateness can almost always be decided definitively by the observer. If her utterances could be correct and at the same time interpretable in more than one way, it would often be quite impossible to determine which interpretation was really the one she intended.

It is important to emphasize that the parser's verdict of correctness is based exclusively on the grammar. The parser, that is, establishes the grammaticality of an utterance, not its appropriateness in a given situation. Appropriateness can be assessed only on the basis of situational context, motivation of the communicator, and effects of the communication on the receiver—none of which, in view of the present state of computer science, can be perceived by a computer.

To conclude this brief and necessarily superficial description of the parsing procedure, I would like to stress that many of the present restrictions of Yerkish grammar do not result from the nature of correlational grammar, nor from limitations inherent in the multistore system, but exclusively from the fact that we are working with a very small computer, and, therefore, have space only for the most elementary interpretive algorithms. At the outset of the project, we decided that the automatic parser, including the operative lexicon of 250 lexigrams, should be contained in a central core area of no more than 5000 machine words. To anyone familiar with computers it will be clear that this limit necessitated a quite extraordinary compression of data. In fact, we were able to succeed only by exploiting every single "bit" of that core and by using the method of "significant address," which had been developed during our work on the Multistore parser for English sentences. Figures 1 and 2 illustrate, at least in a superficial way, how the data compression was achieved: The formal similarity between the lexicon area and the operational Multistore area in which correlations are produced indicates that the two are, in fact, located in the same area of the computer's central core. The two data structures are superimposed one on the other in that area. This layering of data structures and functions will be described in greater detail in the next chapter; here I have presented only an outline of the procedure that enables the computer to decide whether or not a given input sequence of lexigrams is grammatical.

THE GRAMMATICALITY OF LANA'S SENTENCE PRODUCTION

The automatic parser is one of the features that make the Yerkish communication project different from other efforts at communication with nonhuman primates. Because the computer records every linguistic transaction while the Multistore system assesses every input sequence to determine whether or not it conforms to the preestablished grammar, a data base is created, which can be analyzed in many ways. To illustrate one of these possibilities, I shall here summarize some of the results that emerged from a study of Lana's sentence production during the month of September 1974.

The only aspect with which I was concerned in that study was grammaticality. Specifically, how many of the lexigram sequences produced by Lana showed a correct correlational structure and how many did not. This way of looking at the performance of a language user is what linguists call "assessing syntactic competence." From the point of view of the ordinary human language-user (who uses language as a means of communication in order to achieve certain results in or through the receiver) it is, of course, quite absurd to single out syntactic competence as the all-important criterion of linguistic proficiency. A great deal of our daily linguistic production is syntactically faulty or incomplete, but nevertheless it generally achieves our communicatory purposes, and even when it does not, the failure is only very rarely due to *syntactic* deficiency. I emphasize this fact so that the results derived from this survey of Lana's production record will not be construed as evidence of her *communicatory* competence. These results are derived from the automatic records of Lana's messages and therefore do not take into account whether or not the individual messages were appropriate to the contexts in which Lana composed them on her keyboard. All they show is that Lana has in some way acquired the capability of producing lexigram sequences that conform to the grammar of Yerkish much oftener than they would if they were assembled randomly.

The terms "type" and "token" are indispensable in such an analysis of sentence production. "Types" are defined as individually different lexigram sequences, and "tokens" are defined as the occurrences of one and the same "type." Consider the following list of sample sentences: *Lana drink milk, Lana drink juice, Tim drink milk, Machine give juice, Machine give juice to Lana*. In this list there are five "types" each represented by one "token" (i.e., one occurrence of a type). The list *Please machine give juice, Please machine give juice, Please machine give juice*, on the other hand, contains but one "type" represented by three "tokens."

Discriminating between types and tokens is of the utmost importance if we want to discuss whether Lana's production of grammatical lexigram strings can be explained by the conventional theories of conditioning or requires the assumption of some kind of rule-learning.

All theories of conditioning by reinforcement are based on the principle that a behavior "response" is more likely to recur if it is reinforced. In order to be reinforced, however, a behavior must occur at least once, for it is obvious that nothing can reinforce an organism for "emitting" a behavior which that organism has not yet emitted. Applied to verbal or key-pressing behavior this principle means that, though we can condition our subject to produce more and more tokens of the types we reinforce, we cannot condition her spontaneously to produce *types that are both novel and grammatical*. (Even training for the production of novel behaviors alone is difficult and requires a great deal of time and patience both on the part of trainer and trainee; cf. Bateson, 1972, p. 276.)

Table 3 shows a breakdown of Lana's production of four-, five-, and

Table 3
LANA'S SENTENCE PRODUCTION DURING SEPTEMBER 1974

| Length of string | Errors | | Grammatical strings | | | | | |
| | | | | | Computer reinforced | | Other strings | |
	Types	Tokens	Total types	Total tokens	Types	Tokens	Types	Tokens
4 lexigrams	80	98	76	2756	4	2664	72	92
5 lexigrams	91	101	152	738	3	315	149	423
6 lexigrams	71	84	125	1577	4	1288	121	289

six-lexigram strings during the 1-month period. They are divided into grammatical and ungrammatical strings, and in each group the number of types is given as well as the number of tokens.

In September 1974 Lana's keyboard consisted of 3 panels of 25 lexigram keys each. Thus the keyboard contained 74 lexigrams plus the "period" key. Since we have no computer program that can generate all possible grammatical strings of, for example, 4 lexigrams from a lexicon of 74, I cannot say precisely what percentage of the 30×10^6 random combinations Lana's keyboard could theoretically generate from four lexigrams would be grammatical. (The strings we are talking about, regardless of whether they are grammatical or not, are, of course, types, not tokens.) On the basis of a manual compilation of the grammatical 2-, 3-, and 4-lexigram strings that can be made from a lexicon of 49 lexigrams using the same grammar, I know that the grammatical strings would amount to approximately 15%, 1.7%, and .2%, respectively of all possible combinations. Without knowing the actual figures, therefore, we can say that the percentage of grammatical strings decreases quite drastically with the length of the string. At the 6-lexigram level it is safe to assume that no more than one out of 10,000 randomly combined strings will be grammatical.

Since the proportions of ungrammatical to grammatical strings in Lana's record are 80:76, 91:152, and 71:125 for 4-, 5-, and 6-lexigram strings, respectively, Lana clearly demonstrates a strong tendency toward grammaticality. This should not surprise anyone, because the reinforcement she received was always contingent upon the grammaticality of the strings she produced. Thus, on the face of it, her performance is just one more confirmation of reinforcement theory.

If we look at the actual strings she produced, however, we get a very different picture. As an example, let us take the 6-lexigram strings. (The figures are roughly the same for all three groups.) Of the 125 grammatical types in this group, 4 are requests for food to which the computer automatically responds (e.g., *Please machine give piece of chow*). These four types account for 1288 tokens. Lana was deliberately trained to produce them, and she has consistently used them to nourish herself. Of the remaining 289 tokens, 61 are answers to questions which were part of an experiment testing Lana's proficiency in the use of color terms, and they represent 45 types. Since some of these answer types were produced as a result of task-specific training, I shall disregard this group even though many of these types were spontaneously produced novel strings. We are now left with 76 other types of which Lana produced 228 tokens. Nearly all of these types are sentences Lana used to ask for something or someone to move or be moved in or out of her room, or to ask that food or drink be moved *behind room* (by which phrase she came to indicate the automatic dispensers). None of these types were produced as the result of training; they were all spontaneously formulated by Lana. Once they *had* been formulated, they were no doubt reinforced by being answered, and that accounts for their repetition (e.g., 36 tokens of *? You carry Lana out-of room* and 34 tokens of *? You move chow behind room*). Their first occurrence, however, was not only a spontaneous production each time but also in some cases a rather imaginative transference of a meaning acquired in a very specific context to a context that was substantially different.

To conclude this survey of Lana's production, we must ask two questions. First, how can we explain the fact that Lana composed on her keyboard 76 strings of 6 lexigrams that were grammatical sentences and that did not figure in any training program, whereas during the same period she produced only 71 6-lexigram strings that were ungrammatical? Second, how can we explain the fact that Lana's error rate showed no increase as the lexigram strings she produced got longer? Both phenomena could be interpreted as the result of Lana's acquisition of a small number of rules. But the mere assumption of rule-learning does not really explain anything; it only introduces a new term for an unobservable process. The important factor, I believe, is this: The Yerkish language and its grammar were deliberately based on conceptual lexigram classification and conceptual connectives. Therefore, the rules that have to be learned to produce grammatical structures in Yerkish are not purely linguistic rules, but rules that are relatively close to the rules that govern conceptual representation. The chimpanzees at Reno, at Santa Barbara, and in Oklahoma, as well as Lana, have all shown that they can operate on the symbolic-representational level. If they indeed can, the grammaticality of Lana's Yerkish production, her creation of novel strings, and the constancy of her error rate (her errors were caused by distraction and "typing errors" rather than incapacity) are not really surprising. Once she had acquired the "names" for objects and for certain relations, the grammatical structure of sentences in most cases was merely a reflection of the structure of her representations.

REFERENCES

Bateson, G. *Steps to an ecology of mind*. New York: Ballantine, 1972.

Ceccato, S. Il linguaggio. *Methodos*, 1949, *1*, 229–258.

Ceccato, S., Beltrame, R., von Glasersfeld, E., Perschke, S., Maretti, E., Zonta, B., & Albani, E. *Linguistic analysis and programming for mechanical translation*. Milan, Italy: Feltrinelli, 1960 and New York: Gordon & Breach, 1962.

Ceccato, S. (Ed.). *Mechanical translation: The correlational solution*. Milan, Italy: Center for Cybernetics, University of Milan, 1963.

Charniak, E. *Toward a model of children's story comprehension*. Artificial Intelligence Lab. Report AI TR-266. Cambridge, Massachusetts: M.I.T., 1972.

Chomsky, N. *Syntactic structures*. The Hague: Mouton, 1956.

Chomsky, N. *Aspects of the theory of syntax*. Cambridge, Massachusetts: M.I.T. Press, 1965.

Fillmore, J. The case for case. In E. Bach and R. Harms (Eds.), *Universals in linguistic theory*. New York: Holt, 1968.

Fouts, R. Language: Origins, definitions, and chimpanzees. *Journal of Human Evolution*, 1974, *3*, 475–482.

Gardner, R. A. & Gardner B. T. Teaching sign language to a chimpanzee. *Science*, 1969, *165*, 664–672.

Gardner, B. T. & Gardner R. A. Two-way communication with an infant chimpanzee. In A. M. Schrier & F. Stollnitz (Eds.), *Behavior of nonhuman primates*, Vol. 4. New York: Academic Press, 1971.

Hockett, C. Linguistic elements and their relations. *Language*, 1961, *37*, 29–53.

Premack, D. On the assessment of language competence in the chimpanzee. In A. M. Schrier & F. Stollnitz (Eds.), *Behavior of nonhuman primates*, Vol. 4. New York: Academic Press, 1971.

Schank, R. C. Conceptual dependency: A theory of natural language understanding. *Cognitive Psychology*, 1972, *3*, 552–631.

Schank, R. C. *Causality and reasoning*. Castagnola, Switzerland: Fondazione Dalle Molle, 1973.

Schank, R. C. *Conceptual information processing*. New York: North Holland-Elsevier, 1975.

von Glasersfeld, E. Translation and the structure of meaning. *International Conference on Machine Translation of Languages and Applied Language Analysis*. London, England: H.M. Stationery Office, 1961.

von Glasersfeld, E. A project for automatic sentence analysis. *Beiträge zur Sprachkunde und Informationsverarbeitung*, 1964, No. 4, 38–46.

von Glasersfeld, E. Multistore: A procedure for correlational analysis. *Automazione e Automatismi*, 1965, *9*(2), 5–28.

von Glasersfeld, E. Semantics and the syntactic classification of words. Paper presented at the Third International Conference on Computational Linguistics, Sanga Säby, Sweden, 1969.

von Glasersfeld, E. The correlational approach to language. *Pensiero e Linguaggio*, 1970, *1*, 391–398.

von Glasersfeld, E. The Yerkish language for non-human primates. *American Journal of Computational Linguistics*, 1974, *1*, microfiche 12. (a)

von Glasersfeld, E. Signs, communication, and language. *Journal of Human Evolution*, 1974, *3*, 465–474. (b)

von Glasersfeld, E. & Pisani, P. P. *The Multistore system MP-2*. Scientific Progress Report. Athens, Georgia: Georgia Institute for Research, 1968.

von Glasersfeld, E. & Pisani, P. P. The Multistore parser for hierarchical syntactic structures. *Communications of the Association for Computing Machinery*, 1970, *13*, 74–82.

chapter 6

Computer Programs

PIER PAOLO PISANI

University of Georgia and Yerkes Regional Primate Research Center

THE MULTISTORE

An important function of the computer in the Lana project was to perform an objective grammatical analysis of the subject's linguistic input. In performing this task, a fully automatic grammatical parser was needed. In the years between 1962 and 1969, as part of a research project on the automatic analysis of natural language, E. von Glasersfeld and I had already developed such a system for the English language (von Glasersfeld, Pisani, Burns, & Notarmarco, 1965–1966). Known as the Multistore Parser, its purpose was to recognize and explain structural patterns in sequences of words, i.e., sentences. The recognition of these structural patterns is made by means of a system of rules that operate on a sequence of words whose individual characteristics are preestablished. The individual characteristics are a collection of connectives that represent the possibilities a word has to form a syntactic combination (correlation) with another item. Each word has a preestablished sequence of correlational indices (I_c's), which represent its string of potential links (see Chapter 5).

131

Each I_c is identified by the code number of the relation it establishes between two items, and by an indication of whether the items to which the I_c is assigned can be an LH-piece (Correlator Function 1, or CF1) or an RH-piece (Correlator Function 2, or CF2), because the order in which two items can form a linguistic relation is fixed. In the following relation,

the Correlator 11 is the link, but the item *Eat* must have the I_c 11 CF1 and the item *Banana* the I_c 11 CF2. When two adjacent words have complementary functions of the same I_c as seen in *Eat* 11 CF1 and *Banana* CF2, a "product" is made and recorded in the form:

This product is considered as one item and can now become a left-hand (LH) or a right-hand (RH) piece in a wider correlation. It is therefore treated as a single word, i.e., it is assigned strings of I_c's which indicate its correlational possibilities both with adjacent words and with adjacent products already made.

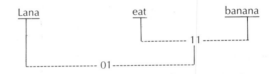

The product *Eat* 11 *Banana* is made first, and once made, is assigned the I_c that enables it to become an RH-piece in the correlation with *Lana*. Single words, however, because they are vocabulary items, are assigned their strings of I_c's a priori; products, since they arise during the procedure, are assigned their I_c-strings dynamically. The assignment of specific I_c's to a product depends on (a) the correlator responsible for the particular correlation, and (b) the characteristics (I_c's) of the item (word or product) which constitutes the first (LH) or the second (RH) correlatum. The operational cycle that assigns the I_c's to a product is the "reclassification" which will be discussed later.

THE COMBINATORIAL PROBLEM

The amount of data involved in an analysis of this kind is enormous. Let us consider a sentence consisting of x words, each of which has an average of y l_c's. In order to check the correlational compatibility between only two adjacent words, every l_c of the first word must be tested for a match with every l_c of the second word. This operation yields a total of y^2 matching operations. Because this process must be repeated for all possible word pairs, within the input sentence, $y^2(x - 1)$ matching operations are necessary to match all the words in the sentence. This figure refers only to the matching of single words. If we now consider that the preceding operations (y^2) result in x_1 products and that each of these products is assigned a string of y_1 correlational indices that represent its possibilities for correlating with another adjacent piece—either a word or a product—we obtain a new level of matching operations. The procedure for matching these products with the $x - 2$ words of the sentence will involve $y_1y(x_1/x)(x - 2)$ matching operations. If to this figure we add the number of operations necessary to match all the products with the words and all the products made in the immediately preceding level—$2y_1^2(x_1 - x_1/x)$—the total of matching operations would come to

$$y^2(x - 1) + y_1y(x_1/x)(x - 2) + 2y_1^2(x_1 - x_1/x)$$

The reclassification routine also involves a great number of operations of this kind. About half of the correlational indices assigned to a product depend on the correlator responsible for that correlation; the other half depend on the string of indices that the two pieces of the product have. According to the presence or absence of specific indices in the strings of the first or second correlation, preestablished sets of indices are assigned to the product. The reclassification of x_1 products would then add $(y_1^2/2)x_1$ matching operations to the previous total.

The amount of work involved in a procedure of this kind seemed forbidding, and we were forced to look for an economical way of handling correlational indices; as a result, the Multistore system was developed (von Glasersfeld & Pisani, 1968, 1970).

THE MULTISTORE APPROACH

The basic idea of the Multistore consists of preestablishing in a given area of the machine's central core as many separate positions as there are correlators in the system. The arrangement of these positions represents the sequence of the correlators. Thus, at any point in the procedure, a given l_c cannot be used several times in several different ways, according to the diverse data it contains, but only as one single item, which, by its possible coordinates, implies its various significations. Moreover, the l_c's do not have to be compared one by one with the I_c's of other adjacent words or products, but are simply addressed to one and only one preestablished position. Thus the majority of the comparisons that would otherwise be necessary are avoided. Also, it is not necessary after every successful match to identify which items the matched I_c's represent, because the very position of the matched I_c's immediately implies what they stand for. To establish whether two I_c's are complementary and represent a correlation thus becomes a simple task of checking already-present information according to the rules of sequence of correlational function implicit in the location of the markers being handled. This arrangement results in two major advantages.

1. Identifying the type of match is now binary, i.e., it is simply a question of the presence or absence of a single bit of information rather than a comparison of numeric codes. In fact, the identification can be done by binary switches rather than through coded elements.

2. The number of matches decreases to

$T + y(x - 1)$ matching the individual I_c's of word pairs,

$T + y_1 x_1$ matching the individual I_c's of word and products,

$T + y(x_1/x)(x - 2)$ matching the individual I_c's of products and words,

$T + y(x_1/x)x_1$ matching the individual I_c's of products and products,

where T is the number of I_c's in the system that are no longer individual inputs, but have been permanently represented in the Multistore area and define all possible correlations.

The advantage of this arrangement is that as the system grows, the increase of I_c's affects only the simple factor T, whereas, in an ordinary combinatorial procedure, it would affect all the elements that have to be multiplied with one another to calculate the total combinations.

DESCRIPTION OF PROCEDURE

The Multistore can be represented as a rectangular area divided into lines and columns. Every column represents one of the I_c's in the system. The lines divide the area into "levels." The levels are not preestablished; they are determined by the succession of words in input. Thus each level bears the identity of the word it represents. For each I_c in its I_c string, every input word causes the insertion of a marker into the Multistore column corresponding to that I_c, and the level of that marker in the I_c column corresponds to the input number and the position of that word in the sentence. Thus all the markers inserted for one word represent the correlational possibilities of that word. If, in a line of level x, an I_c from the I_c string of the first word, representing CF1 of correlator y of the first word, has caused the insertion of a marker into the column corresponding to that I_c, and if an I_c y of the second word has caused the insertion into the line of level $x + 1$ of a marker representing CF2 of the same I_c, a correlation containing the first and the second word is made. The product number x_1, consisting of the word x and word $x + 1$, is the product of correlator y. This product belongs to level $x + 1$, and when it is assigned a string of I_c's by the appropriate rules of reclassification, it is inserted into the Multistore on the level $x + 1$. This placement means that it can enter into combinations only with those words that belong to the immediately preceding level $(x - 1)$, or with products that contain the word of the immediately preceding level $x - 1$. Any correlation made in this cycle of operation would still belong to the level of product x_1. In our specific case, product x_1 could correlate only with an item of level zero, which does not exist, because product x_1 is on Level 2 and already contains the first word. Hence, we can formulate a restrictive rule to the effect that a product can be a potential second correlatum in a correlation only if its lower level is larger than 1. The Multistore system lends itself to the introduction of many such restrictive rules.

When, on a given level, all products that have sprung from the insertion of markers corresponding to the word of that level have been reclassified and the products originating from that reclassification have, in turn, been reclassified and have inserted their markers and there are no more products to be reclassified, the procedure inserts the next word and thus begins the next level. This means that once any given word in a sentence has been inserted, all preceding words and products become "inactive" pieces. At that point they have exhausted every possible attempt at correlating with "active" pieces and from then on merely represent latent correlational possibilities with subsequent items. When all correlational possibilities of the last word of the sentence have been exhausted, the fact that there is no new word to enter determines the end of the analysis. At this point the product that contains all words of the sentence represents the correct structure of the sentence.

The first complete program MP1 (see Figure 1) was written in 1964 for use on a GE425 computer. Its primary purpose was to show the applicability of the Multistore system to correlational grammar. It was then used as a research tool during the course of the research project on automatic English sentence analysis. A second version, MP2, was written in 1967 for use on an IBM 360/67 computer, and was intended for the same research project. It was an enlarged and more sophisticated version of MP1 using all machine central core (250K) available at the time. The present program, Multistore parser for Yerkish (MPY), is a reduced and suitably adapted version of the previous Multistore parser. It is reduced in that instead of the 400–500 correlators possible in the English parser, it allows for a maximum of 46; instead of six correlator types (allowing for different types of inversion), it has only one in it; the sentence length is 7 lexigrams rather than 16 words, and whereas the words of the English vocabulary had up to six or eight individual meanings, the lexigrams are grammatically univocal. Finally, the English parser had a special program to recognize and deal with idiomatic phrases, but no such program is necessary in Yerkish.

Several solutions as well as several restrictions result from the fact that in many respects the Yerkish program is a machine-oriented one. It is structured in an area of the central core divided into lines and columns, the size of which is about 2K. Each line consists of 50 machine words and is divided into two sections, A and B (see Figure 1). Section A contains all the data necessary to define a line; Section B consists of 46 words, of as many words, that is, as there are correlators in the system. Each line specifies as permanent data (a) the reclassification rules to be applied to a product made with an I_c, the number of which corresponds to the line number and, (b) the string of I_c's assigned to a lexigram class (see Chapter 5). Each word of Section B is divided into 12 bits as illustrated below.

0   marker of CF1 of a lexigram

1   marker of CF2 of a lexigram

2   marker of CF1 of a product

3   marker of CF2 of a product

4

5   marker for reclassification rule of CF1

6

7

8   marker for reclassification rule of CF2

9

10

11

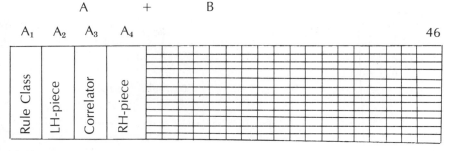

Figure 1

Bits 0 to 3 are used therefore in the matching procedure, whereas bits 4 to 9 are used in the reclassification routine.

PROCEDURE

Each lexigram entering as part of an input sentence is written in one line of the Multistore area, and its specifications are recorded in Section A. The code number of the lexigram class to which it belongs is written into Section A_2 of the Multistore line. For each I_c contained in the string of the lexigram class, a marker is permanently stored according to the correlational function in bit 0 or 1 of the corresponding position of the line, that is, in the position bearing that I_c as label. According to its correlational function, a marker can be either an LH piece or an RH piece. If the marker is an RH-piece, its column is searched immediately after it has been read for a complementary and contiguous left-hand piece. If one is found, an indication of product is recorded in the first free line of the Multistore. This address consists of three pieces of data

1. The address of the line of Section B to which the LH-piece that has been found belongs. This address is recorded in area A_2
2. The address of the line of Section B to which the RH-piece that has been inserted belongs. This address is recorded in area A_4
3. The relative address of the column that characterizes both LH- and RH-pieces, which is recorded in the area "correlator" A_3

After the characteristics of the product are recorded, and if there are no other LH-pieces with which the RH-piece at hand can combine, the routine for the scanning of I_c's is resumed. If the insertion of the next I_c of that lexigram causes a new product to be made, the procedure is repeated and the product is recorded on the next free line of the Multistore area. Only after all the I_c's

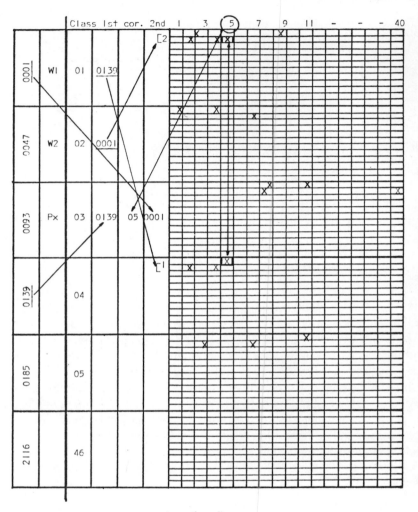

Insertion diagram

of the piece that caused the production have been scanned can the re-classification routine take place, starting from the first newly recorded product.

RECLASSIFICATION ROUTINE

The information contained in the area "correlator" of the line containing the record of the product gives the address of the Multistore line dedicated to the correlator responsible for that product. The line is then searched from left to right for a bit 6 or 9 set ON. If a bit 6 is found ON this implies that a marker *CF1* of the product—bit 2 in the corresponding column of the product's line—must be set ON. This is done without further control if bits 4 and 5 of the same word are OFF, indicating that the assignation is unconditional (see Chapter 5). If bit 4 is ON, however, the LH-piece of the product has to be examined for the presence of a CF1 in the same I_c column. A marker CF1 of the product (bit 2) can be set ON only when in the same column on the line addressed by LH-piece of the product bit 0 is ON if this LH-piece is a lexigram, or bit 2 is ON if it is a product. If bit 5 is ON, the RH-piece of the product has to be examined for the presence of a CF1 in the same column. Except for the line that is addressed by the RH-piece, the procedure in both cases is identical. If bit 9 is found ON, a marker *CF2* of the product—bit 3 in the corresponding column of the product line—must be set ON. This is done without further control if bits 7 and 8 of the same word are OFF, indicating that the assignation is unconditional. However, if bit 7 is ON, the LH-piece of the product has to be examined for the presence of a CF2 in the same I_c column. A marker CF2 of the product (bit 3) must be set ON only if in the same column on the line addressed by the LH-piece of the product, bit 1 is ON if this LH-piece is a lexigram, or bit 3 is ON if it is a product. If, however, bit 8 is ON, the RH-piece of the product has to be examined for the presence of a CF2 in the same I_c column. Except for the line that is addressed by the RH-piece, the procedure again is identical in both cases. Each time a marker CF2 of a product (bit 3) has been inserted, the reclassification routine is suspended, and a cycle of the production routine is performed for the CF2, the RH-piece just assigned. Only when there are no further products to be reclassified or recycled can a new lexigram be admitted into the analysis procedure.

There are five special lexigrams in input (see Chapter 5) that are treated by the system as signals, and are therefore not candidates for the production routine. The "end-of-message" sign signals to the system the beginning of the complete sentence routine. This routine handles three successive controls to determine:

1. Whether the sequence of lexigrams has generated a complete product, that is, a product that contains all the lexigrams of the input sentence. If such a product is not present, the system switches to an error routine indicating and recording that the input sentence is ungrammatical.
2. Whether the sentence is a request, that is, whether a lexigram *Please* is used as first item in the sequence of lexigrams. If another lexigram (*No, Yes,* or *?*) was used as first item, the system bypasses the next control.

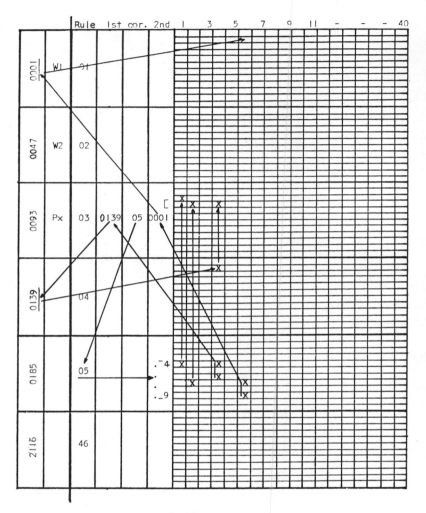

Reclassification diagram

3. The nature of a request. This must be determined in order to activate
   the appropriate mechanism in the experimental room, for example,
   a food dispenser, the film projector, or the mechanism that opens
   the window shutter.

At this point the output routine starts recording in printed form the
entire input from the keyboards, the system's responses, and the time of day.

This is a general outline of the procedure of combination, production,
and output. In addition to this procedure, there are several routines that

serve to meet special requirements, such as decoding the input lexigram into design elements and colors for the projectors or activating delay tasks to control-timed responses, e.g., film projection. The whole program, including the Multistore area and a vocabulary of 250 lexigrams, is contained in approximately 4000 machine words of the PDP8ECA central core. The system presently handles sentences containing up to six lexigrams not counting the "sentential marker" prefix or the period signal. Processing times for six-word sentences are about 200 msec.

REFERENCES

von Glasersfeld, E., Pisani, P. P., Burns, J., and Notarmarco, B. *Automatic English sentence analysis, ILRS T-11 and ILRS T-14.* Language Research Section, Milan, Italy, 1965–1966.
von Glasersfeld, E., and Pisani, P. P. *The Multistore system MP-2.* Georgia Institute for Research, Athens, Ga., 1968.
von Glasersfeld, E., and Pisani, P. P. The Multistore Parser for Hierarchical Syntactic Structures. *Communications of the ACM,* 1970, 13(2), 74–82.

chapter 7

The System: Design and Operation

HAROLD WARNER AND CHARLES L. BELL

Yerkes Regional Primate Research Center

INTRODUCTION: AN AUTOMATED SYSTEM

Early in the conceptual discussions between Duane Rumbaugh and Harold Warner, when the basic performance requirements of the system were outlined, it became clear that control of the teaching instrumentation would have to be highly automated to meet the complex demands that would be made of it. Such a system would be called upon to assure 24-hour attendance to the animal's needs (sustenance, entertainment, etc.); to record accurately for later analysis all interchanges between the animal and the instrumentation and the experimenter; and to perform immediate objective analysis for correct syntax of all linguistic outputs from the animal, followed by prompt dispensing of the requested service. Finally, it should provide reasonably flexible means for eventual extension of the vocabulary, grammar, syntax structure, and services offered.

As we proceeded to examine the design feasibility of automating the system employing computer-type logic circuitry to meet our requirements,

143

simple logic and solid-state memory gave way to complex processor-type logic, large capacity memory, and complex patch-cord programming. Very shortly, we realized that we were engaged in the design of a computer, and a very cumbersome one at that. Some relatively simple calculations taking into consideration engineering design and development time, construction time, and equipment and material costs, indicated that it would be cheaper to purchase an off-the-shelf minicomputer. Such a machine, with its magnetic core memory, would offer great flexibility in operation and programming, thus readily permitting expansion of vocabulary, grammar, and syntax extension and analysis. We therefore decided to purchase a PDP8E/CA minicomputer from the Digital Equipment Corporation along with any plug-in modules and peripheral equipment necessary for our input–output requirements. We planned to add our own in-house-designed equipment such as keyboards, visual displays, diode matrices, and interfaces required to translate Yerkish words into binary code words (the language of the computer) and back into Yerkish words for presentation on Lana's and the experimeter's visual displays. Purchasing the computer, its plug-in modules and peripherals proved to be a wise decision.

THE INSTRUMENTATION SYSTEM

The Computer

The basic computer package came equipped with the central processor, a programmer's console, the console teletype control, the power supply, and a magnetic core memory consisting of 4000 words. All were mounted in a 19-inch-wide vertical standing cabinet with space for additional plug-in modules, company options and our in-house-designed visual-display interfaces. We supplemented this basic computer package with 8000 words of additional magnetic core memory to contain our expected program; a magnetic tape unit for rapidly loading the program into the computer, making additional copies of the program, and storing the experimental data; a programmable clock to time the various computer functions and vending devices; and two input–output buffers for interfacing the keyboards and vending devices with the computer. Finally, we added a teletype and paper-tape reader/punch for communicating with the computer during programming and to enable the computer to print binary words onto a punched paper tape and simultaneously translate them into mnemonic English (four-letter abbreviations of English words printed by the teleprinter) on a printed hard copy.

Although we were thoroughly familiar with logic circuitry and its use in instrument design as well as with the general philosophy of computers, we were not familiar with interfacing a computer in real time, on-line, with the complex instrumentation expected to be employed in this research. Accordingly, very early in the first year of the research, after all the computer hardware had been ordered, Harold Warner attended a 1-week crash course in computer interfacing given at the Georgia Institute of Technology, which consisted of five 8-hour days, four 3-hour evenings, and an 8-hour weekend. Our successful interfacing of the computer attests to the value of the course.

Technical information regarding the interfacing, and operation of the computer with the keyboards, visual displays, and vending devices has been given elsewhere (Warner et al., 1976). A machine language called SABR was employed to program the computer. The philosophy of this form of programming and details of the program manuscript, as well as application of the programming technique to a project of this nature, are covered in Chapters 5 and 6.

The Keyboards

Recognizing that the keyboards would be exposed to Lana 24 hours a day usually without supervision and would have to withstand such severe abuse as powerful blows by Lana's hands and feet, the impact of objects thrown at them, damage by food, liquids, and bodily excrements, and the wear and tear of normal use, we designed them very conservatively. In particular, the lexigrams (geometric figures denoting words) embossed on the faces of the keys would have to be protected from damage by Lana's fingernails and teeth.

To provide sufficient strength in the keyboards that would be exposed to Lana, we used a baseplate made of $\frac{5}{8}$-inch silicon alloy aluminum with 25 holes in it for keys. The keys were made of solid acrylic plastic, and the lexigrams on their faces were protected against damage by a sheet of 10-mil clear vinyl plastic. This sheet of plastic was sandwiched between a $\frac{3}{32}$-inch silicon alloy aluminum inner plate and a $\frac{3}{8}$-inch silicon alloy aluminum outer plate. The inner plate prevents the vinyl plastic from exerting pressure on the key while the outer plate prevents Lana from pinching or biting the plastic. Figure 1 shows the sandwich assembly of the base plate, inner plate, vinyl plastic, and outer plate of the keyboards.

Another requirement was special lighting for the keyboard. All keys in use during a particular experiment would have to be dimly lighted throughout the experiment and would have to brighten when pressed, thereby cueing Lana that successful depression had occurred. To meet these speci-

Figure 1. Assembly of keyboards showing sandwich arrangement of base plate, inner plate, vinyl plastic and outer guard plate.

fications, we used a miniature, long-life electric lamp bulb and a locking relay for each key. The relay serves both to effect the brightening of the lexigram and to deliver the information at the output of the keyboard that a key has been depressed. The bulb for both dim and bright illumination is recessed into the base plate, as shown in Figure 2, so that the keys can be edge lighted.

Corresponding to the 25 keys are 25 microswitches contained on a backing plate that is fastened to and supported by the keyboard base plate. Each microswitch can be individually adjusted for activation by its particular key. The closure of a microswitch, in turn, activates the locking relay, thereby both brightening the corresponding key and generating a signal to the diode-coding matrix, the function of which is to translate this signal into a binary code word. Five aluminum pivot-bars ensure that limited depression of a key will activate the corresponding microswitch.

Four of these keyboards are now in use, and several of them have been used throughout the past 4 years. Rugged and waterproof, they have been remarkably free of maintenance. Not one of the microswitches, lamp bulbs, or relays has failed. Rearranging the lexigram keys in the keyboards to prevent Lana from learning to select lexigrams on the basis of location alone (location-cuing) is laborious, but fortunately, except during the first 6 months of the study, such rearrangements were infrequent.

Figure 2. Edge lighting of keys and construction of a single key.

The Visual Displays

Fourteen multiple-image projectors, arranged seven each in two rows, were made available to Lana directly above her keyboards. We dubbed the bottom row her "send" projectors and the top row her "receive" projectors. When Lana keys a sentence on her keyboards, her send projectors display the lexigrams to her from left to right in the sequence in which she keyed them. In the same manner, replies from an experimenter are displayed to Lana on her receive projectors. An identical set of projectors was installed above the experimenter's keyboard. Since every sentence sent by Lana is received by the experimenter, and vice versa, Lana's send projectors are in parallel with the experimenter's receive projectors, and her receive projectors are in parallel with the experimenter's send projectors. The experimenter's keyboard consists simply of several rows of electrical push-buttons labeled with the English equivalents of the Yerkish lexigrams. This keyboard transmits switch-closure information to the same diode-coding matrix as does Lana's keyboard; however, an additional diode line indicates to the computer that the sentence originated from the experimenter's keyboard.

We procured the multiple-image projectors from Industrial Electronic Engineers, Inc., in Van Nuys, California. Each projector consists of 12 projector lamps, a film reticle containing the elements to be displayed, and a

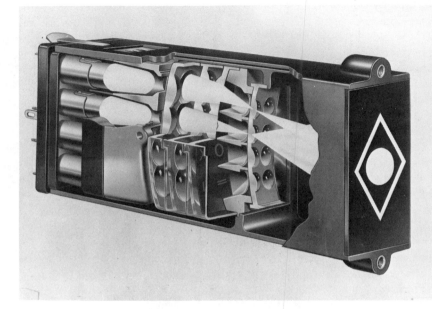

Figure 3. Cutaway drawing of IEE projector.

lens system that focuses the element in front of any one or more of the projection lamps onto a common, focal-plane screen. Figure 3 is a cutaway drawing of one of these projectors. To construct a lexigram on the screen of the projector, it is only necessary to turn on simultaneously the projection lamps behind the elements that make up that particular lexigram. In our system the computer, via a 12-bit code word, one bit applied to each projection lamp, determines which lamps will light. The reticle contains the nine simple geometric elements of the lexigrams plus three primary colors. These colors are projected separately and in combination to produce the six colors that form the backgrounds of the lexigrams.

From the beginning Duane Rumbaugh reasoned that we should be able to make use of the IEE projectors to implement the visual display. Charles Bell conceived of the idea, as detailed above, of forming various lexigrams by projecting combinations of the basic geometric elements onto the common screen. Harold Warner then devised the visual-display control interfaces that made possible gated sequence-control of each projector.

Visual-Display Control Interfaces

How do the visual displays order the lexigrams from left to right in the sequence in which they are depressed on the keyboards? This function is performed by our in-house-designed visual-display control interfaces. One interface operates between the computer and Lana's send projectors and the other operates between the computer and Lana's receive projectors. Two binary-code words, an instruction word and a lexigram-element data word, are necessary from the computer to these interfaces in order to enter properly the data word into the correct projector in the proper row (send or receive). The instruction word addresses the proper interface for send or receive and also instructs the interface to sequence the projectors by arming them individually according to the order of reception of each data word (translation of a Yerkish word). The data word is then entered only into the armed projector to form the lexigram. From the content of this same instruction word the interface knows when to clear the projectors of all lexigram information. Lana's keyboard signal causes addressing of the send interface; the experimenter's keyboard addresses the receive interface. It should be remembered here that while the send interface drives Lana's send projectors, it also drives the experimenter's receive projectors, since they are connected in parallel with Lana's send projectors; likewise the receive interface drives both Lana's receive projectors and the experimenter's send projectors.

The Vending Devices

Devices to vend food, candy, liquids, and services are activated by the computer via a 12-bit binary code word, which is impressed on its input–output registers after a correct request by Lana. The services Lana is able to request include motion picture films, slides, music, and a window view. Whenever, for example, Lana requests the window view by producing the sentence *Please machine make window open,* the computer's input–output register through a single "on" bit of the 12-bit binary code word activates a motor which lowers a blind, giving Lana her window view. After a predetermined interval the blind is raised again, closing off the view. An object hopper which previously vended objects such as a blanket, toys, etc., is no longer employed.

THE EXPERIMENTAL CHAMBER

After the design of the language and the instrumentation system was set and well underway, we proceeded to look seriously into the design of the experimental chamber that would house Lana, and within and about which would reside the various components of the instrumentation system. Here again, as with the keyboards, the inside surfaces of the room had to be strong enough to withstand the strength and ravages of a chimpanzee up to 6 or 7 years of age. In addition, the following were important specifications:

1. There had to be minimal difficulty in keeping the chamber clean in the face of bodily excrements and discarded foods and liquids.
2. It had to be easily adaptable to the installation of our planned instrumentation units.
3. There had to be prompt and simple access to the animal by the experimenters.
4. The room had to be bright and easily accessible for photography.
5. The chamber needed to be well ventilated.

After several meetings, and consultation with various construction groups, an experimental chamber was constructed. Three walls, the ceiling and the floor were constructed of 1-cubic-foot units made of $\frac{1}{4}$-inch acrylic plastic and the fourth wall was constructed with a $\frac{1}{2}$-inch stationary leaded glass panel and a leaded glass sliding door. The room's interior dimensions were 7 feet × 7 feet × 7 feet and thus, the stationary glass panel and sliding glass panel were each $3\frac{1}{2}$-feet wide. A floor drain in the plastic acrylic floor, positioned directly over the existing drain in the original room's concrete floor, functioned reasonably well when wet-mopping the chamber. The corners of the room, where possible, were coved to minimize the accumulation of soil. Ventilation was accomplished by tapping the air-conditioning of the main building and ducting cooled air to a perforated section in the ceiling of the chamber; return air escaped easily from many small openings around the various instrumentation units. Figure 4 shows photographs of the experimental chamber and computer area: Figure 4a illustrates the construction used in the chamber walls; Figure 4b shows the keyboards, visual displays, and vending devices; and Figure 4c is a view of the computer, auxiliary instrumentation rack and the experimenter's keyboard. See Figure 6 for the proper orientation of these photographs.

The keyboards, visual displays, vending devices, etc., were easily mounted through the walls and about the room. The transparent acrylic construction rendered Lana and all instrumentation readily observable for photography.

THE INSTRUMENTATION SYSTEM OPERATION

In this section we will follow a signal through the entire system from the depression of a key at the keyboard to the presentation of the displays and the activation of the vending devices. Two cycles will be described to ensure that all major system components are placed in their proper context in the

(a)

Figure 4. Experimental chamber and computer area. (a): the construction used in chamber walls; (b): the keyboards, visual display, and vending devices; (c): a view of the computer, auxiliary instrumentation rack and the experimenter's keyboard. (See Figure 6 for orientation of these photographs.)

(b)

(c)

overall system operation. This operation can best be understood by referring to the system block diagram in Figure 5 and also making reference to the experimental chamber diagram in Figure 6. In these figures, the major components in the system block diagram are keyed by letter to their positioning within and about the experimental chamber diagram.

When Lana depresses a dimly lighted lexigram key on the keyboards (A), a microswitch actuates a locking relay which brightens the lexigram and causes a diode-coding matrix (D) to generate a binary code word. The patch panel (B) between Lana's keyboards and the diode-coding matrix permits relocation of the word-keys at selected time intervals to rule out location-cuing of the lexigrams. The experimenter's keyboard (C) is connected directly to the diode-coding matrix and allows identical inputs into the system by the experimenter when conversing with Lana; however, a special code is generated and recognized by the computer (F) when the experimenter makes use of his keyboard.

When the binary code word for the first Yerkish word of a potential sentence exists at the input/output computer register (E), the following sequence of events takes place: The computer examines the word, withdraws from core memory the proper combination of basic lexigram elements and background color elements, and generates an instruction word and a data word, both in binary code. These two words are then routed to the computer's positive input/output bus, labeled Output Signal Bus (W) in the diagram. They are then impressed upon the visual-display control interfaces, labeled Control interface (G) in the diagram. There, as already described (see page 148), they permit the correctly addressed interface to cause the Yerkish word, originally depressed by Lana on the keyboard, to appear on the screen of the first of seven send projectors (L) via lampdrivers (J). The computer stores this first word in its memory. In like manner, depression of another lexigram key will cause the second depressed lexigram to appear on the second send projector, while allowing the first lexigram to remain displayed on the first projector. Each Yerkish word is also printed-out in mnemonic English on the teletype. The entire process is repeated until the desired sentence has been composed.

When Lana has finished a sentence, she depresses the period key, and the following events take place: Again, through the above-described signal-flow path, a binary code word appears on the input/output interface of the computer. This indicates to the computer that a sentence has been completed, and at this point the computer, using the parser, evaluates the sentence for correct syntax. The manner in which the parser performs this analysis is described in detail in Chapters 5 and 6. The computer reads the input/output interface (H) on which the real-time binary clock (Y) has impressed a binary code word indicating the time of day and prints-out this

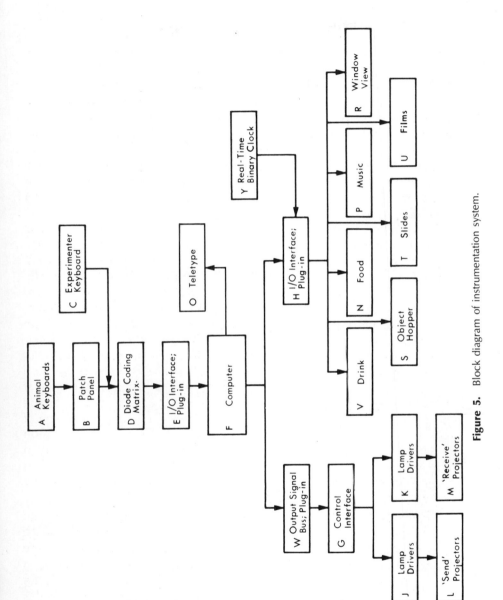

Figure 5. Block diagram of instrumentation system.

153

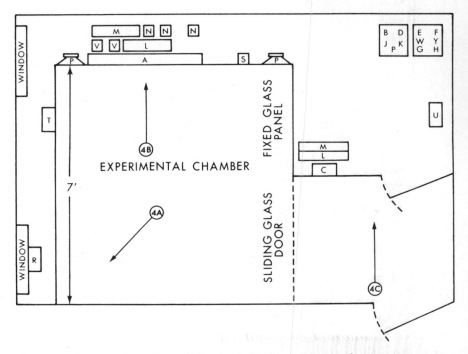

Figure 6. Diagram of experimental chamber indicating positioning of various instrumentation components (Letter-keyed to Figure 5) (the encircled 4A, 4B, and 4C, together with the directional arrows, refer to Figure 4).

time at the end of the sentence on the computer teletype. If the sentence syntax is correct, the computer simultaneously impresses a binary code word on the input/output interface (H), which in turn selects the proper vending device (V, N, etc.), and actuates it by means of a power relay.

The preceding description has depicted the sequence of events when Lana makes requests of the computer. During any exchange between Lana and the computer, or between Lana and one of the experimenters mediated by the computer, essentially the same signal-flow paths are employed, with the exception that the action of the parser and the vending machines may be ignored. All exchanges among Lana, the computer, and an experimenter, whether correct or incorrect, are encoded on the punched paper tape and printed on the computer's teletype. The time of day is always printed-out following depression of the period key.

The entire instrumentation system has performed amazingly well, considering how innovative this study is. At the outset of the project, we considered there was a good probability that perhaps two or even three new starts would be necessary in the overall training concept, which could lead to major redesign of the instrumentation. None of this proved to be necessary. The instrumentation system operated as it had been conceived, and considering the size and complexity of the instrumentation even the normal debugging was minimal.

REFERENCE

Warner, H., Bell, C. L., Rumbaugh, D. M., & Gill, T. V. Computer-controlled teaching instrumentation for linguistic studies with the great apes. *IEEE Transactions on Computers,* *C-25*(1), January 1976.

chapter **8**

Training Strategy and Tactics

TIMOTHY V. GILL AND DUANE M. RUMBAUGH

Yerkes Regional Primate Research Center, and
Georgia State University

The broad framework of the language-training program as described in detail elsewhere in this volume was established at the very beginning of the language project. The training situation would be computer-controlled (see Chapter 4), and, as Lana mastered Yerkish, the artificial language developed specifically for the program (see Chapter 5), she would acquire ever greater control over her environment. The specific tactics of the training program were designed to implement these general principles and also grew out of the following questions and considerations:

(1) How intensive should the training program be? More specifically, how should training be distributed over the course of each day? Before training began we had no way to estimate how rapidly Lana would progress. We could not predict from the Gardners' experiences with Washoe or from Premack's with Sarah what we would encounter using a computer-controlled system, which differed substantially from both the American Sign Language used by the Gardners and the plastic sign language developed by Premack. In addition, our approach would employ a novel setting for

chimpanzee training. The Gardners kept Washoe in a rich social milieu and worked with her throughout each day. Premack, in contrast, utilized a more conventional laboratory environment and worked with Sarah for a limited number of hours each day. Although both achieved remarkable results, their research provided few guidelines for developing the optimal training regimen within a computer-based system.

(2) Exactly how should language training be initiated? Should it be aimed at building sentences from individual words or at breaking complete sentences apart?

(3) What incentives would Lana find rewarding? To ensure that Lana would work steadily within the system, the values of the incentives would have to be high and would have to include a wide variety of foods, drinks, events such as movies and music, and social incentives.

(4) We would have to engage and maintain Lana's attention throughout training. Fundamentally, it was anticipated that as Lana attained control over the events of her day and gained access to various incentives through use of correct Yerkish, sustained attention would emerge. Prompt and reliable feedback through both evaluation and reward would be essential for maintaining her attention, although such feedback would be fully available to Lana only after she had learned to attend to the cues telling her which keys had been pressed and to the lexigrams projected above her keyboard with each key depression.

(5) How much and what kind of social contact should she be given? Should her social contact be provided by human attendants or by another ape?

(6) Ways would have to be found to eliminate undesirable behaviors in Lana through extinction or at most mild punishment. What forms of punishment would be effective?

SPECIFIC TRAINING STRATEGIES

Intensity of Training

The considerations just listed resulted in some basic decisions regarding Lana's new linguistically contingent lifestyle. With regard to the intensity of training, it was decided that Lana would live in the language environment 24 hours a day. There, her linguistic expressions would provide repeated, reinforcing engagement with the system, since she would have to obtain all of her necessities and social interactions by making appropriate requests of it.

Initiation of Training

Lana's early training consisted of teaching her to use the keyboard and to use certain "stock" sentences to obtain foods and drinks. First she was taught to request various incentives by pulling down the "go-bar" (thereby activating the system) and pressing single keys. She was then required to precede each request with *Please* (thereby signaling an impending request to the computer) and to follow each one with a *Period* (which signals to the computer that an expression has been completed). The next stage entailed the introduction of a modified form of holophrastic (whole phrase) training suggested by Ernst von Glasersfeld. The keys for a correct request—for example, *Machine Give M&M*—were placed in a row in correct order and were connected electrically so that the depression of any one key activated all of them. Lana was still required to pull down the go-bar and to press the *Please* key before depressing a key from the holophrase and to press the *Period* key afterward. After Lana had mastered this phase of training, the object to be requested was separated from the holophrase. Now Lana had to depress four keys to make a request—the *Please* key, one key from the holophrase in addition to the key for the object requested, the key for the object requested, and the *Period* key. During the following phase of training Lana was required to press each lexigram key separately, the keys still being arranged in correct order on a single row of the keyboard. After she had mastered this phase, the keys were scrambled randomly first within a single 5-key row (the remainder of the keys being inactive) and then within the entire 25-key matrix. Initially they were rearranged at least once a day. (Through use of duplicate keys, a limited amount of functional rearrangement was possible through the selective activation and deactivation of redundant keys.) Gradually the keys were relocated less often, as it became apparent that relocation had a negligible effect on Lana's accuracy and only served to increase her response time. Whenever a new lexigram was introduced, however, the new key was frequently repositioned to ensure that Lana learned the lexigram rather than its position.

During this early training period, several instructional techniques were also employed in the training sessions to encourage Lana to communicate through her keyboard. Since Lana seemed to thrive on social contact, the behavioral technicians maintained close contact with her and frequently entered her room to "model" the correct behavior, taking her finger and pressing the correct key with it or pointing to the appropriate key or set of keys. They would also verbally admonish her for pressing the wrong key. After helping Lana in these ways, the technicians would leave her to work on her own. Although these supportive techniques were used in the training sessions (i.e., sessions during which new skills were being taught to Lana), the experimenters gave no such assistance during the *test* phases in which proficiency levels on various skills were assessed. During tests every precaution was taken to preclude the possibility that any extraneous cues might aid Lana's performance. Blinds were installed to deny her visual access to the experimenter; the sequence of trials for different tasks was randomized; her responses were automatically recorded by the teleprinter; and, when possible, experimenters not involved in training were used to test Lana. Finally, whenever possible, Lana's performance on the first trial only of novel tasks was assessed to preclude the possibility that practice effects might enhance her accuracy.

Incentives

The incentives chosen to facilitate communication with Lana were those foods and drinks which she particularly liked and which she never seemed to tire of, such as apples, bananas, Coke, coffee, milk, juice, M&Ms, and bread; entertainment such as movies, slides, music, and a view of the outdoors; and social events such as tickling, swinging, and grooming. To sharpen Lana's attention still further, food and drink items central to a particular task were visible to her through the plexiglass wall behind which the vending machines were located. So that she would work steadily, Lana received only small amounts of the incentive requested per request, but within limits she could ask repeatedly for additional amounts. Lana attended closely to what was loaded into the vending machines and eventually learned to ask for the items she saw by specific names (see Chapter 9).

Promotion of Attention

A number of decisions were made to promote Lana's attention and to cope with what we believed to be her very limited short-term memory. "Active" keys (those which if depressed would be sensed by the computer) were made distinguishable from inactive ones by back-lighting. Active keys were made to brighten still further when depressed (see Chapter 7) so that Lana would be able to refer back to any part of an expression still in progress. (Keys that have been depressed remain differentially illuminated until the depression of the period key terminates the expression.) To enhance attention further and to position Lana with some consistency at the keyboard, a go-bar which Lana had to pull down to activate her keyboard was installed.

Social Contact

To provide social contact, it was first decided that an orang-utan, Biji, would live in the language-training situation with Lana. Since they had lived together for many months prior to the beginning of the study, they were close companions, and we hoped that they both might benefit from language training. Within the first few weeks of the study, however, it became apparent that the orang-utan was a much slower subject than Lana. As a result, she was both interfering with Lana's work on the keyboard and restricting Lana's linguistic expressions to requests for the barest necessities of life—food and drink. Consequently Biji was removed. Up to that point, Lana had shown no interest in the movies, music, slides, or the opportunity to view the out-of-doors by asking that the window be "opened." Shortly after Biji's removal, however, Lana began requesting all of these events. Biji had apparently been a distraction rather than an aid to Lana as she learned the language. Quite possibly the various incentives such as movies had held little reward value for Lana as long as she had the companionship of another ape. Thereafter, Lana's contact with other apes occurred only during hours of play outdoors.

During early training we maintained that Lana should have little interaction with the experimenter so that her strict training schedule would not be disrupted. We soon found, however, that the social aspect of language training was of great importance. Accordingly we modified our initial decision and began allowing increased social contact between Lana and the experimenters. Lana did much better in an informal social setting with the training procedures modified as needed. We believed that this alteration of procedure was consonant with the goals of our program, which was essentially a *pilot* study to determine the feasibility of a computer-based approach to language training. It also allowed us to capitalize upon the relationship that Tim Gill had already developed with Lana. After this decision was made, the several behavioral technicians were allowed upon specific and appropriate request to enter Lana's room and tickle, swing, or groom her, or take her for an outing. They would also allow her to groom them if her formulation of the request was correct (*Please Lana groom Tim/Shelly*) and if they elected to answer *Yes*.

Punishment

We devised several methods for disciplining Lana, but we also employed a number of preventive measures to reduce the likelihood that discipline would be needed. For example, the sessions were initially very short. Lana never received an incentive unless she completed at least part of a task correctly, and she never received any "free" food even in the morning—she started her day by asking for her milk. If Lana would not work despite these measures, the experimenter left the room or as a more drastic step temporarily deactivated her keyboard. The latter move brought forth plaintive cries from Lana and proved increasingly effective in disciplining her. With her keyboard deactivated, she had no access to the world, no control over its events. Lana was physically punished only when she damaged part of her training equipment in a "deliberate" manner.

Conclusions

We tried to maintain an optimal amount of pressure on Lana to learn and to improve; at all times, however, we adhered to a fundamental principle of learning—Lana was not to be challenged or otherwise pressed to do anything which at the time was too difficult for her. It was always evident when Lana approached the point of frustration; she would become tense and would tend to whimper and balk. Those signs told us to decrease the pressure, which was always done. As Köhler noted 50 years ago, in training chimpanzees, tasks must be of graduated complexity, or the subject will lose interest in them.

Lana has now received 3 years of training and is in good health. By any standard she is a well-adjusted chimpanzee, particularly for a chimpanzee that was born and raised in captivity. She is gentle with the technicians who work with her routinely. They can and do take her out for walks and she plays very gently with them. Although technicians are not chimpanzees, they can fulfill the social roles which chimpanzees serve for one another remarkably well. Recently Lana has been introduced to four young chimpanzees who are also entering language training. She is compatible with them, and has reassured everyone that she is a socially competent chimpanzee.

Interestingly, Lana is relatively quiet, although members of her species are known for being vociferous. Normally their screams are frequent, piercing, and readily triggered by vocalizations of another chimpanzee. Might it be that because Lana's vocalizations had relatively little communication value during her formative years, she has not cultivated her vocal skills as she otherwise might have? And is it premature to conclude that modern technology has given her another tool—language—that is much more powerful than her normal vocal skills could ever have been?

PART III

Lana's Mastery of Language-Type Skills

chapter 9

Lana's Acquisition of Language Skills

DUANE M. RUMBAUGH AND TIMOTHY V. GILL

Georgia State University, and
Yerkes Regional Primate Research Center

From the first day of her introduction to the language training program, Lana was basically a cooperative subject. Problems we encountered in training her seemed to reflect specific methods we were using rather than any lack of cooperation on her part. Methods that appeared to be counterproductive were changed, and, consequently, Lana progressed rapidly in her training and mastered the system more readily than had been anticipated.

Within the first 2 weeks of training she mastered the two stock sentences which she could use to obtain a variety of foods and drinks. These were: *Please machine give* (item name, e.g., *juice*) and *Please machine give piece of* (item name, e.g., *banana*). She then mastered the stock sentence she needed to request a variety of events—music, slides, a movie, and the opening of a window to permit a view of the outdoors. This sentence took the form *Please machine make* (event name, e.g., *movie*). Only small portions of food or drink were given her after each request in order to promote frequent contact between her and the system, and likewise she received only 30 seconds at a time of her movie (*Primate Growth and Development—A*

165

Gorilla's First Year!) and other events. Of course, she could repeatedly ask for more and usually did. Records of her activity during the evening hours revealed that she tended to watch her movie more or less continuously until it was finished. She also learned to ask for tickling, grooming, and swinging first from Tim and then from the other technicians working on the project.

Evidence suggests that after Lana had learned to request a variety of items, she apparently took note of that portion of her requests which consisted of the stock formulation *Please machine give* and which, perhaps unnecessarily from her point of view, had to be repeated each time. On one occasion, for example, when she was asking more or less randomly for "chow" (a commercial monkey food preparation) and for water, she came forth with *Please machine give chow water*. We do not know whether she intentionally asked for both chow and water, whether she made a frank mistake, or whether she "changed her mind" and altered the item of request. Nevertheless, we believe that it was through her discernment of the repeated lexigrams in her stock sentences of request that she began to differentiate the lexical units which served as words for specific items. As we will describe later in this chapter, she was eventually trained to go beyond learning the names of things and to master the concept that things have names.

Our greatest concern was that Lana might never attend to the lexigrams on the projectors or be sensitive to their order, for without attending to their order, she would never master the Yerkish syntax or grammar. In fact, however, she attended well to the projectors from the first. As described in greater detail elsewhere (see Chapter 7), whenever Lana depressed a key, there resulted both a flash of light at the keyboard and the production of a lexigram on one of the projectors. Undoubtedly, these features of the training system greatly encouraged Lana to cultivate her basic "reading" skills.

But we believe that still another feature of the system contributed unexpectedly to engaging Lana's attention. In an earlier chapter (Chapter 8) it was noted that a "go-bar," a switch that Lana had to pull in order to activate her keyboard, was installed to encourage Lana to be consistent in how she addressed the keyboard. The installation of this bar proved to be fortunate in many ways we had not anticipated. Most importantly, it appears that certain events brought about by Lana's climbing on the bar first stimulated her interest in the lexigrams which appeared on the projector row whenever she depressed keys. Lana frequently climbed upon the go-bar and swung from it, and from time to time one of her hands or feet would accidentally hit and depress one or more keys as she did so. (Initially the surfaces of the keys protruded about $\frac{1}{8}$ inch beyond the plate of the console.) More and more when she returned to the keyboard to generate a sentence of request, she tended to take heed of whatever lexigrams might be there already. At that time only the word *Please* could constitute the beginning of a sentence, and if some other word was on the projector, Lana became more and more likely to erase that beginning by depressing the *period* key thereby resetting the keyboard for the next expression. (We had not intended for the *period* key to serve as an electronic eraser for Lana, but she came to use it as one anyway.) If the *Please* key had been the one accidentally depressed, however, Lana appeared to take special note both of its greater brightness (depressed keys gained additional brilliance to differentiate them from the others) and of the lexigram for *Please* on the first projector. Rather than erasing it, she tended simply to build upon it to complete a sentence that might be correct and gain some desired incentive. Lana acquired this skill spontaneously and it became highly refined during the first 4 months of formal training. Our detection of it gave rise to the four experiments to be described, which served to quantify her primitive reading and sentence completion skills.

"READING AND WRITING"

The experiments (Rumbaugh, Gill, and von Glasersfeld, 1973) employed a technique whereby certain three-word-long sentence beginnings were fed into Lana's projector system. Two of these beginnings were valid and could be built upon to formulate syntactically correct statements of request which the system would honor automatically. These were: *Please machine give* and *Please machine make*. To the former beginning Lana could add item names such as *juice, milk, piece of chow,* or *piece of bread,* and to the latter she could add, for example, *window open, music,* and *movie.* The other sentence beginnings were invalid, since they could in no way be completed to formulate correct sentences. These invalid beginnings were either inversions of otherwise valid beginnings (e.g., *Please make machine; Please give machine*) or they contained a second or third word that had been selected at random (e.g., *Please window Tim; Please make of*). With about 90% accuracy Lana erased the invalid sentence beginnings, appropriately rejecting any attempt to complete them, through prompt depression of the *period* key. With a similar level of accuracy, she attempted to complete the sentences validly started for her by requesting whatever specific items she wanted.

In these experiments we also demonstrated that we could stop any one of the nine stock sentences, which by this time Lana had mastered, at every possible word position and she would finish it. Again her accuracy was about 90%. We concluded from these studies that Lana had mastered the basics of reading as called for in her training situation and that if the skillful selection of the appropriate lexigrams and the depression of them in accordance with the grammar of Yerkish constituted writing, she was on her way to literacy. Lana could read and she could write! After only 6 months of formal training, she was further ahead in the acquisition of language-relevant skills than we had originally thought she might ever be.

ELIMINATION OF ERRORS: FIRST TEN MONTHS

Riopelle (1974) made a number of detailed analyses in an attempt to discern the patterns whereby Lana eliminated various types of errors during the first 10 months of her training. Lana's use of *give* and *make* was remarkably accurate, the error rate ranging from .004% to .02% with thousands of usages per month. In sentences in which Lana used both activity words incorrectly by combining them into *give make* (*Please machine give make* . . .), 48% were terminated promptly, an indication that she sensed her error; 37% were followed with a request appropriate to the second word, *make* (e.g., *music, window open*); and 15% were finished with a request appropriate to *give* (e.g., *M&M, juice*). This observation suggests that when Lana used *give* and *make* in the same sentence in that order, she perhaps "changed her mind" about the nature of her request in midsentence. Of the sentences in error because Lana keyed *make give,* 67% were terminated promptly; only 11% were followed by an incentive appropriate to the second word, *give*; and 22% were followed by one appropriate to *make*. Apparently the same interpretation cannot be applied to both types of error.

Another type of error resulted when Lana used all the right words to form a correct sentence but made a mistake in word order. In making this type of error, she most often inverted the order of two words appropriately adjacent to each other and very rarely put a word or words out of order by two or more positions (an error of permutation). Of the inversions, 64% included placing the addressee after the activity, e.g., *Please give machine juice*. Another 27% included the preposition *of*; with half of the errors of this type, she placed *of* at the very end of the sentence instead of just before the type of food dispensed (e.g., *piece banana of, piece chow of*) and with the other half *of* was placed before *piece* (e.g., *give of piece banana*). The remaining 9% of the inversions showed no consistent pattern.

Of the errors of permutation, 75% occurred when the activity word was placed before the addressee, e.g., *Please give milk machine*. The remaining 25% entailed the use of *of*, e.g., *Please machine give of apple piece*.

Both errors of inversion and errors of permutation occurred primarily between the second and fourth months of the project. Clearly the first 6 months of the project were highly productive in eliminating the majority of the errors of inversion and permutation from the stock sentences Lana used to obtain basic rations, entertainment, and socialization.

Another type of error occurred when Lana used two words of the same class in one sentence, a violation of Yerkish grammar. Usually (57% of the time) the repetition involved two incentives (e.g., *water* and *juice*). In 23% of such errors, the repetition involved two addressees (e.g., *Please machine Tim give milk*), and in 20% the repetition was of two activity words (e.g., *groom make*). During the first 2 months when Lana asked for more than one incentive in a single sentence, she usually asked for both water and chow, e.g., *Please machine give water chow*. Only rarely did she request three items in a sentence, and some of these errors may have resulted from her making a mistake in trying to select the *period* key to terminate the sentence. When two addressees were used and the sentence continued, the request more often than not was appropriate to the second addressee, e.g., *Please machine Shelley tickle Lana*. We cannot know the degree to which this type of error was due to Lana's having been conditioned to use *machine* after *Please,* but we believe it to have been very high. The fact that in sentences containing double addressee errors *machine* was the first of the two addressees 93% of the time supports this conclusion. In 64% of such cases Lana terminated the sentence immediately after depressing the lexigram for the second addressee.

The specific patterns according to which Lana eliminated these errors surely reflect the placement of the keys, the sequencing of training, and a host of other factors; consequently, the reader should not draw any conclusions about the nature of language acquisition from this section. Nonetheless, the general observation that Lana did increasingly sense and eliminate her errors in sentence composition through prompt use of the *period* key is significant.

YES AND NO

The use of *Yes* and *No* was initially taught to Lana in reference to the door and window to her room. She would be asked, for example, *? Window open* or *?Door shut*, and in order to obtain reinforcements she would have to respond correctly with *Yes* or *No*.

It is noteworthy that once Lana had mastered the use of *No* in this context as a negation ("it is not true that . . ."), she spontaneously began to use it as a protest. This use of *No* occurred for the first time when she saw a technician drinking a Coke outside her room. When she determined that none was available to her through the machine, she stamped her foot and then vigorously hit the *No* key. From that point on, Lana frequently responded with *No* when technicians either ate or drank something she did not have available or when they took preferred foods from reservoirs of her vending devices.

Lana also used the word *No* to declare that despite Tim's statements to the contrary a certain type of incentive was not in the machine, e.g., *No chow in machine.* (See Chapter 12.)

Lana's extended use of *No* (her redefinition of it) suggests that she had learned something about the arbitrary meanings of words and perhaps more importantly that concepts occur in clusters that are rather closely mapped or related in cognition. In examples just given, the concepts "no it is not," "don't do that," and "there is none" have a common vector of meaning in addition to their individual meanings.

NAMING TRAINING

Lancaster (1968) and others have noted the importance of names in language. Names permit ready reference to things and events regardless of past, present, or future. Despite the importance of names, however, little systematic research has been done on the acquisition of naming skills.

In the context of her stock sentences, Lana used the names of things such as *milk, water, juice,* and *chow,* from the onset of training, but these sentences were all acquired through basic operant conditioning procedures, and provided her with little opportunity to learn that certain lexigrams were names of objects and that others were names of addressees, activities, relationships, states, and so on.

Accordingly, we set about to teach her certain discriminations that we believed would help her learn the names of the incentives she obtained through using her stock sentences and more importantly would teach her the concept that things in general have names.

Training to this end (Gill & Rumbaugh, 1974) began with two of her most valued incentives—banana slices and M&M candies. One of these was presented to her on a small plastic tray as the question was posed to her through use of the experimenter's keyboard, *? What name-of this.* If M&Ms were on the tray, the correct answer was *M&M name-of this*; likewise if a banana slice was on the tray, the correct answer was *Banana name-of this.* This phase of the project began in the summer of 1973 when Lana was 2.75 years old and had 6 months of formal language training. Correct responses were rewarded according to Lana's option: Tim would press the *Please* key (which had been deactivated on Lana's keyboard), and Lana could ask for anything from an M&M to being groomed or tickled.

Lana required 1600 trials and 2 weeks work to learn the names of these two incentives. Lana was then given two transfer of training tests. In the first, she was presented with five incentives in the manner just described. All five—pieces of apple, pieces of Monkey Chow, pieces of bread, a glass of juice, and a soccer ball—were incentives that she was particularly fond of and that she had repeatedly obtained through the use of stock sentences. The question was whether she would be able to learn their specific names. Interestingly, she succeeded in naming *ball* on its first presentation. She rapidly mastered all the other names over the course of 10 randomly sequenced trials. The second test exhausted the supply of items available at that time—a glass of milk and Lana's blanket. The fact that Lana correctly named both of these items on their first and all following presentations is evidence, we believe, that she had gone beyond learning the names of the previous seven incentives and had mastered the abstract concept that things have names.

From this point on, the mastery of new names has not been particularly difficult, and on occasion, in fact, Lana has apparently inferred some names herself. In one instance, Tim had set up the system to teach her the name *slide*. He typed *Please machine make slide* into his keyboard, and Lana then saw a few slides. She in turn went to her keyboard without any instigation from Tim and used the key for *slide* for the first time in the sentence, *Slide name-of this period*. Also, she has at times commented on the names of things while in the process of experiencing them. While watching her movie, for example, she has frequently commented *Movie name-of this period*. She has spontaneously named all of her foods *prior to* and through the course of requests to obtain them.

Through the course of her training in learning names, Lana apparently tried many new formulations during the evening hours when she was left to herself. *Please machine give piece of this period* and *Please machine name this period* are examples of such expressions.

It was also during the course of this training that Lana spontaneously diversified her use of the interrogative marker ?. So far as the computer program was concerned, ? was the functional equivalent of *Please*, and hence the two lexigrams coupled together were redundant. Eventually when making requests of people, Lana came to use it by itself (e.g., *? Tim move into room period*). On occasions, however, when her motion picture was exhausted and repeated requests of *Please machine make movie period* were to no avail, she began using it to ask a question, e.g., *? Machine make movie period*.

USE OF "STOCK" SENTENCES FOR OTHER THAN THE ORIGINALLY INTENDED PURPOSE

Each of the stock sentences had been taught Lana to enable her to attain a specific incentive. Whenever she formed the sentence *Please* (technician's name) *move behind room period,* for example, the technician named would move behind her room. The technician would always tap on the walls as he or she went, and Lana appeared to enjoy matching the maneuver. Once the technician was behind the room, he or she would then tap on the window curtain, enticing Lana to use another stock sentence, *Please machine make window open period.* Once the window blind was lowered, Lana could see the technician and watch him blowing smoke rings or bubbles, and performing other antics.

On February 21, 1974, after slightly more than 1 year of formal training, Lana first used the sentence *Please* (technician's name) *move behind room period* for a purpose different from the one originally intended. She apparently did so because the system was not delivering bread as it should. The technician, Beverly Wilkerson, was about to leave for the day and had just loaded pieces of bread into one of Lana's vending devices. Lana repeatedly asked, *Please machine give piece of bread period,* but no bread was forthcoming. Within the span of 1 minute she then made the requests, *Please machine move into room period, Please Shelley period, Please Tim period,* and then quite appropriately *Beverly move behind room period.* Noting these sentences and requests, Beverly obligingly said *Yes,* went behind the room to the general area of the dispenser, and noted that it had not been properly activated. Once the problem was corrected, Lana returned to repeatedly forming the sentence *Please machine give piece of bread.*

Among the possible interpretations of the behavior just described, we must include the possibility that Lana made the appropriate request to Beverly by chance. Even if this was the case, Lana was able to capitalize on the success of her chance request, for in subsequent formal tests where equipment failures were intentionally staged, Lana reliably came forth with the request that the technician move behind the room. Of all the sentences that Lana might have generated, however, the one she did seemed the most appropriate to a novel problem. We believe that Lana had some general sense of the equipment malfunction. For one thing, she knew the components of the system quite well. One had only to point to the tape deck, for example, and she would ask *Please machine make music period.* In like manner, she demonstrated that she understood the function of the slide projector, the motion picture projector, and so forth. These observations support the conclusion that Lana knew the problem lay "behind the room," the only phrase she had to refer to the source of the problem. This incident is but one example of Lana's appropriately transferring a stock sentence to use in a situation other than the one for which it was originally designed. As Lana progressed in linguistic compentency and mastery of the conceptual foundations of language use, she began initiating conversations first with Tim and eventually the other technicians that contained still other novel usages. (See Chapter 12 of this volume.)

CONVERSATIONS

One of our initial goals was to engage a chimpanzee in conversation (Chapter 4). We had considered various ways of enticing Lana into conversations, but these all proved unnecessary. It was Lana, on her own initiative, who instituted conversation with us, composing an appropriate request through use of components of stock sentences. She did so on March 6, 1974, in the late afternoon.

The Coca-Cola Company is headquartered in Atlanta, and somehow it seems providential that Lana's first conversation had to do with "Coke." (We do not really believe that, but we would like to.) Tim was drinking a Coke about 4:00 p.m., standing just outside of Lana's room and in her full view. Lana knew the word for Coke and could ask for it when it was in one of her liquid dispensers. Lana looked at Tim and either by a highly improbable sequence of chance events or with comprehension asked, *? Lana drink this out-of room period.* She had come to use the word *this* primarily in reference to things for which she had no formal name, an unplanned development which grew out of the name-learning studies discussed above. Tim responded *Yes*, opened the door, and shared his "this" with Lana "out-of room." The scenario was repeated twice; if chance was originally the causal agent, it had been supplanted by learning. We talked about the significance of the exchange and decided that we should conduct continued observations to determine whether Lana knew that "this" was really "Coke." Another 15 cents was invested in the Coca-Cola Company, and at 4:41 Tim presented himself outside Lana's room with another Coke. Lana's first response was the stock sentence *Please machine give Coke period,* which was correct but not appropriate since the machine had no Coke to vend. Next she said *Please Lana drink Coke this room period.* Perhaps she intended to say *out-of room* instead of *this room,* but she did not. Tim said *No.* Lana came back with the original composition, *? Lana drink this out-of room period* to which Tim responded with a question for clarification, *? Drink what period.* Lana answered, *? Lana drink Coke out-of room period.* Tim said *Yes*, the door was opened, the Coke was shared; and Lana's first conversation, one she had both initiated and successfully negotiated, had been recorded.

From this conversation emerged our working definition of the term *conversation*. The definition has three criteria:

(1) A conversation must be a linguistic-type of exchange between two beings.
(2) At least one of the communications transmitted by each of the two beings must contain novelty.
(3) The topic of the exchange must remain relatively constant across time (Rumbaugh & Gill, 1976a,b).

Without specific training to do so Lana had become a conversationalist. As with the definition of *No*, she had expanded the definition of *drink* on her own initiative to include not just an ingestible fluid (our definition) but also an activity (drinking). Her sentence *? Lana drink this out-of room period* came from two additional sources. She had learned to use *this* in the name-learning sessions but only as part of her answers (e.g., *M&M name-of this period*). The phrase *out-of room* came from one of the two stock sentences Lana used whenever she wanted to be taken outdoors: *Lana move out-of room period* and *? (technician's name) carry Lana out-of room period*. From these sources Lana composed a perfectly reasonable and adaptive statement, *? Lana drink this out-of room period*. And when asked to specify the referent for *this*, she did so—*Coke*. (Subsequently, as we will recount later on in this chapter and in Chapter 12, many of Lana's most active conversations have been directed toward solving problems, either those which occurred fortuitously or those which we contrived for specific purposes.)

MOVE IT TO THE VENDING DEVICE

On April 30, 1974, Lana asked that milk be moved behind the room as a requisite to its being loaded into the machine's vending device. On this morning Lana was particularly hungry; since she had been very obstreperous the afternoon before, her rations had been cut to enhance her motivation for the following day's work. Tim entered the anteroom with a large pitcher of cold milk in one hand, his cup of coffee in the other. The coffee was irrelevant so far as Tim was concerned, but from Lana's point of view, it was not. Lana knew the name for coffee and relished it black with no sugar. Seeing Tim with his coffee, Lana initiated the following conversation:

LANA: *Milk name-of this.*   [8:54 a.m.]
  TIM: *Yes.*

LANA:	*Milk name-of this.*	[8:55 a.m.]
TIM:	*Yes.*	
LANA:	*Milk this.*	[8:56 a.m.]
	? Tim give Lana coffee.	[8:57 a.m.]
TIM:	*No.* (Although at times he has honored this request, this time he elected not to, for milk, not coffee, was the incentive appropriate to her state of heightened food-motivation.)	
LANA:	*? Tim move milk coffee.* (This was the first suggestion that she was going to ask Tim to move something from one point to another in space. She had not received specific training to ask that this be done.)	[8:58 a.m.]
TIM:	(No response.)	
LANA:	*? Tim move behind room.*	[8:58 a.m.]
TIM:	*Yes.* (Thereupon Tim set down the pitcher of milk and moved behind the room to the general area of the vending devices where the milk would ordinarily be loaded into the machine. Lana's response was to hoot with apparent agitation; she also displayed piloerection and a furrowed brow. In a few seconds, Tim returned to the anteroom, picked up the milk, and stood once again in Lana's full view.)	
LANA:	*Milk of this coffee.*	[8:59 a.m.]
	? Tim give milk name-of.	[9:00 a.m.]
	? Tim move milk behind . . . (The sentence was not completed; however, Tim interpreted it to mean that Lana did not know how to finish what promised to be a novel question and one that was quite appropriate to the context.)	
TIM:	*? Behind what.*	
LANA:	*? Tim move milk behind room.* (With this statement Lana had asked for the first time that a person move something other than his own body from one point to another in space.)	[9:01 a.m.]
TIM:	*Yes.* (He then loaded the vending device with milk, and Lana began to work for it by requesting it repeatedly.)	

Although she had not been asked to do anything, Lana first named that which was in the pitcher—*milk*. Eventually she stopped asking Tim to move behind the room and began asking that he move the milk behind the room, a

requisite to its being loaded into the machine. Again, when asked by Tim
? Behind what, Lana specified that the milk be moved behind the *room.*
Without specific training, Lana had begun to ask that people move things
other than their own bodies through space. From this episode emerged a
routine whereby Lana asks that milk or chow be moved behind the room,
and then asks the machine for portions thereof once the machines have been
appropriately loaded.

GIVE NAME-OF THIS

On Monday, May 6, 1974, Tim started to teach Lana the name of *box.*
He had taught her *bowl* and *can* on previous days by baiting each object
with M&M candies and giving them to her whenever she requested either
? Tim give Lana this bowl period or *? Tim give Lana this can period.* Likewise
he initiated training with the box by baiting it with M&M candies and
holding it in Lana's view. The key for *box* had been on Lana's board from the
beginning, but she had never been taught its function.

LANA: *? Tim give Lana this can.* (Apparently she was   [11:36 a.m.]
          calling the "box" a "can.")

TIM: *Yes.* (And he gave her the empty can used in the
          initial sessions, though it seemed clear that she
          wanted the box with the M&M's.)

LANA: *? Tim give Lana this can.*   [11:42 a.m.]

TIM: *No can.* (This reply meant that Tim did not now
          have the can to give her, since he had just given it
          to her.)

LANA: *? Tim give Lana this bowl.*   [11:43 a.m.]
          (In this instance, it seemed that Lana was calling
          the "box" by a name appropriate to the second
          of the two previously used objects in name-
          training.)

TIM: *Yes.* (And he gave her the empty bowl used in the
          previous sessions which she promptly discarded.)

LANA: *? Shelley* (The sentence was not finished.)   [11:43 a.m.]

TIM: *No Shelley.* (This response was a way of saying
          that Shelley was not present.)

LANA: *? Tim give Lana this bowl.* (Before Tim could   [11:44 a.m.]
          answer, she continued the conversation.) *? Tim*
          give Lana name-of this.   [11:45 a.m.]

TIM: *Box name-of this.* (Thereupon he gave her the

name of the vessel which she apparently wanted.)

LANA: *Yes.* (Interestingly, this is the response which technicians give when Lana does something correct.) [11:46 a.m.]

LANA: *? Tim give Lana this box.* [11:47 a.m.]

TIM: *Yes.* (Thereupon he gave it to her. She immediately ripped it open and extracted the M&M candies.)

Without being specifically trained to do so, Lana had asked for the name of something that she presumably wanted and had forthwith used the information to ask that the object be given to her. Although we had asked her hundreds of times to name things she already knew, we had not taught her to ask us for the names of things. She had apparently abstracted from the former experience the fact that she might ask us for names of things if need be.

At 1:01 p.m. on the same day, Tim presented Lana with a cup baited with M&M candies. At the time she did not know the name *cup*. As she had done with the box, she asked for the name of the receptacle and then used that name to request that the cup be given to her.

Noteworthy also was Lana's use of *yes* after Tim gave her the name for *box*. When Lana performs correctly the technicians always respond initially with *yes* through the computer. That Lana too responded with *yes* when Tim "performed correctly," suggests that this response might have been the best way she knew to say, "That's what I wanted to know!"

USE OF "TO"

The linguist on our team insisted that if Lana were to use her name as the indirect object, it would have to be preceded by the word "to." Training to accomplish that end began on May 9, 1974, with the following session.

TIM: *? Tim give can to Lana.*

LANA: *Yes.* (Tim gave the can to her.)

? Tim give bowl to Lana.

TIM: *Yes.* (Tim gave the bowl to her.)

Other short training sessions in the use of "to" occurred on May 11 and 12. On May 13, Lana spontaneously used the word "to" correctly in the request, *? Tim give ball to Lana.* Not more than 30 minutes of training in all were needed to teach her to use the word "to" before using her name.

A REQUEST FOR A NONPRESENT OBJECT

On May 20, 1974, just a few minutes before 9 o'clock, Lana asked Tim to *move the milk behind the room*, although the milk had not yet been brought to the room. Tim was running a bit late in cleaning Lana's room, a task which always preceded giving her her morning's milk. He was sitting on a stool just outside Lana's room when she asked:

LANA:	*? Tim move into room.*	[8:58 a.m.]
TIM:	*No.*	
LANA:	*? Tim give.*	[8:59 a.m.]
	? Tim give milk behind room.	
TIM:	*No give.* (Incorrect use of "give.")	
LANA:	*? Tim move milk behind room.*	[9:00 a.m.]
TIM:	*Yes.*	

Tim then went to the kitchen, returned with the milk, and loaded it into the machine. Thereupon Lana asked repeatedly that the machine "give" it. Lana's morning milk is a tradition, and asking for it when it was not there was something she came to do on her own quite probably in part as a function of temporal conditioning; time of day was one cue which elicited the request that the milk be moved behind the room.

ORANGE (FRUIT) = THE APPLE WHICH-IS ORANGE (COLORED)

On May 28, 1974, Lana generated for the first time a name for something she apparently wanted but for which she had no formal name—an orange. She therefore coined a descriptive name to ask for the orange which Tim held outside her room.

TIM:	*? What color of this.*	[10:10 a.m.]
LANA:	*Color of this orange.*	[10:11 a.m.]
TIM:	*Yes.*	
LANA:	*? Tim give cup which-is red.* (This was probably an attempt to request the orange however, be-	[10:13 a.m.]

	cause a red cup was part of her object/color naming materials, Tim responded with the latter object.)	
TIM:	Yes. (Thereupon he gave her the cup, which she discarded.)	[10:14 a.m.]
LANA:	? Tim give which-is shut.	[10:16 a.m.]
	? Shelley give.	
TIM:	No Shelley.	[10:16 a.m.]
LANA:	Eye. (A frank error, probably.)	[10:16 a.m.]
	? Tim give which-is orange.	[10:21 a.m.]
TIM:	What which-is orange.	[10:21 a.m.]
LANA:	? Tim give apple which-is green. (At this point, Lana frequently confused the keys for the colors orange and green.)	[10:22 a.m.]
TIM:	No apple which-is green. (In other words, "I have no green apple to give.")	
LANA:	? Tim give apple which-is orange. (Thereupon she bounded with apparent enthusiasm to the door to receive "the orange-colored apple.")	[10:23 a.m.]
TIM:	Yes. (And he gave it to her.)	[10:23 a.m.]

In coping with this problem, Lana brought to bear her color-naming skills (Chapter 11) in conjunction with her word *apple* to achieve a descriptive label. She has done something similar on several occasions with an overly ripe banana, by terming it *banana which-is black*. Likewise she called a cucumber *banana which-is green*, and referred to a Fanta orange drink as the *Coke which-is orange*. (Providentially the Coca-Cola Company manufactures Fanta. The name Lana coined does not involve her in copyright problems.)

But when the orange-colored apple is in an orange bowl, how does Lana ask for it?

LANA:	Lana want eat ball which-is black. (The use of black as a color was a frank error.)	[4:34 p.m.]
TIM:	? This ball which-is black. (And he held up a black ball from the object/color training set.)	[4:35 p.m.]
LANA:	Lana want ball which-is orange.	[4:36 p.m.]
TIM:	(Tim then held up an orange ball from the object/color training set.)	
LANA:	Lana want eat ball which-is orange.	[4:40 p.m.]
TIM:	No eat ball which-is orange. (In other words, he told her that ball is not to be eaten.)	
LANA:	Lana want eat this (pause) in bowl.	[4:43 p.m.]

Thus Lana specified the *ball* both by what she would do with it (eat it) and by where it was located.

On November 18, 1974, Lana asked for the first time that the *bowl of chow* be moved behind the room. Once again no specific training led to this step. On this occasion, asking only that the bowl be moved would not have sufficed, for there were two bowls, an orange one which was empty and a green one full of monkey chow. This being the case, Tim refused to honor the simple request he would normally have complied with. Instead he required that she come up with some new expression appropriate to the context.

LANA:	*? You move chow behind room.*	[3:08 p.m.]
TIM:	*No.*	
LANA:	*? You move into room.*	[3:08 p.m.]
TIM:	*No.*	
LANA:	*? You move chow behind room.*	[3:09 p.m.]
TIM:	*No.*	
LANA:	*? You move chow into room.*	[3:09 p.m.]
TIM:	*No.*	
LANA:	*? You move chow out-of room.*	[3:10 p.m.]
TIM:	*No.*	
LANA:	*? You move into room.*	[3:11 p.m.]
TIM:	*No.*	
LANA:	*? You move behind room.*	[3:12 p.m.]
TIM:	*No.*	
LANA:	*Bowl name-of.*	[3:13 p.m.]
	Bowl name-of.	[3:14 p.m.]
	Bowl name-of this green.	[3:15 p.m.]
	Bowl name-of this green.	[3:16 p.m.]
	? You move behind room.	[3:16 p.m.]
TIM:	*No.*	
LANA:	*Bowl name-of.*	[3:17 p.m.]
	Bowl of in.	[3:17 p.m.]
	Bowl of this green.	[3:18 p.m.]
	? You move into room.	[3:19 p.m.]
TIM:	*No.*	
LANA:	*? You move——.* (She depressed the wrong key and erased).	[3:20 p.m.]
	Bowl name-of this.	[3:20 p.m.]
TIM:	*Yes.*	
LANA:	*? You move bowl behind room.*	[3:21 p.m.]
TIM:	*? What bowl.*	

LANA:	*Bowl name-of this which-is orange.*	[3:22 p.m.]
	Bowl name-of this which-is orange.	[3:22 p.m.]
TIM:	Yes. (An orange bowl was present, but it did not contain chow.)	
LANA:	*? You move bowl which-is green.*	[3:23 p.m.]
TIM:	No.	
LANA:	*Bowl name-of this which-is green.*	[3:24 p.m.]
TIM:	Yes.	
LANA:	*? You move bowl of orange.*	[3:25 p.m.]
	? You move bowl of chow.	[3:26 p.m.]
TIM:	Yes. (Thereupon Tim moved the bowl of chow behind the room and put the chow into the vending device.)	
LANA:	*Please machine give piece of chow.* (Repeatedly)	[3:28 p.m.]

On November 22, 1974, a related conversation occurred, one influenced by the fact that generally whenever Lana asked for chow to be moved behind the room, Tim delivered *one* piece to the vending device.

LANA:	*? You move chow behind room.*	[5:20 p.m.]
TIM:	No.	
LANA:	*? You move chow behind room.*	[5:20 p.m.]
TIM:	No.	
LANA:	*? You move behind room.*	[5:21 p.m.]
TIM:	No.	
LANA:	*? You. move chow behind.*	[5:22 p.m.]
TIM:	(No response)	
LANA:	*? You move of.*	[5:22 p.m.]
	? You move bowl which-is orange.	[5:23 p.m.]
TIM:	Yes. (And Tim moved an orange bowl behind the room, but it was not the bowl that contained the chow.)	
LANA:	*? You move chow behind room.*	[5:25 p.m.]
TIM:	No.	
LANA:	*? You move chow behind room.*	[5:25 p.m.]
TIM:	Yes. (And he carried one piece of chow and put it into the appropriate vending device.)	
LANA:	*Please machine give piece of chow.* (Thereupon she obtained the one piece.)	[5:26 p.m.]
	? You move chow behind room.	[5:26 p.m.]
TIM:	Yes. (Again he delivered one piece to the vending device.)	

LANA: *? You move chow behind room.*   [5:27 p.m.]
  TIM: Yes. (Again he delivered one piece to the vend-
          ing device.)
          ? What name-of this. (Pointing to the bowl).
LANA: *Bowl name-of this.*   [5:29 p.m.]
          ? You move bowl of chow.   [5:29 p.m.]
  TIM: Yes. (And he loaded several pieces into the de-
          vice.)
LANA: *Please machine give piece of chow.* (Re-   [5:30 p.m.]
          peatedly.)

Lana eventually was rewarded for asking that a *bowl of chow* rather than just *chow* or a *bowl* be moved. On November 25, 1974, it was noted that Lana had carried forward her new skill of asking that a *bowl of chow* be moved behind the room.

LANA: *? You move bowl of chow.*   [4:04 p.m.]
  TIM: Yes. (And the vending device was loaded.)
LANA: *Please machine give piece of chow.* (Repeatedly.)   [4:05 p.m.]

The foregoing exchange also suggests, as do many other observations, that Lana had become aware that there were *constraints* upon the lengths of sentences that might be formulated. When *? You move chow behind room* did not work as it had in the past, Lana introduced the phrase *bowl of chow*. The addition of that phrase no longer allowed for the addition of *behind room*, for that would have made for a seven-word sentence not including the *please* and *period* keys; hence, the phrase *behind room* was deleted.

In the following conversation, we again see that Lana was versatile in specifying the object of her request. She was first asked whether she wanted an apple. She then asked for it as *this which-is red*, but when Tim offered her a piece of red plastic, to which *this* might have referred, she chose to reject it.

  TIM: *? Lana want apple.*
LANA: Yes. (Thereupon Tim went to the kitchen and got   [12:41 p.m.]
          one.)
          You give this to Lana.   [12:41 p.m.]
  TIM: *? Give what to Lana.*
LANA: *? You give this which-is red.*   [12:41 p.m.]
  TIM: *? This.* (Tim held up a red piece of plastic as he
          responded.)
LANA: *? You give this apple to Lana.*   [12:43 p.m.]
  TIM: Yes. (And gave her the apple.)

Lana might have said *yes* when offered the piece of plastic. She did not, but instead requested that the *apple* be given to her.

DRINK MILK; EAT BREAD

In late 1974 and early 1975, Lana learned to answer when Tim posed the questions, *? Lana want drink* and *? Lana want eat* with an appropriate liquid or food. On January 9, 1975, Lana, seemingly on her own initiative, improved upon an expression.

LANA:	*? You move milk behind room.*	[9:11 a.m.]
TIM:	*? Lana want drink.*	
LANA:	Yes.	[9:11 a.m.]
TIM:	*? What Lana want drink.*	
LANA:	*Lana want drink milk eat.*	[9:12 a.m.]
	.	[9:12 a.m.]
	? .	[9:12 a.m.]
	Lana want drink milk bread.	[9:13 a.m.]
	Lana want drink milk eat bread.	[9:13 a.m.]

To the sentence *Lana want drink milk*, Lana added the word *eat*, then substituted for it the object *bread*, and then put everything together as she formulated *Lana want drink milk eat bread*. On the next day when Tim asked *? Lana want drink period*, Lana responded as she had on January 9 with *Lana want drink milk eat bread period*.

SENSITIVITY TO THE LIMITS OF SENTENCE LENGTH

At the time of these experiments, as already stated, Lana could unite no more than six words in a sentence in addition to one of four lexigrams *Please, ?, Yes*, and *No* plus the *period*. (Lana's new system will have a 10-word capacity.) On many occasions Lana's behavior strongly suggested that she was sensitive to that constraint. For example, on January 15, 1975, Lana asked of Tim, who was drinking coffee, *? You give*. She then pushed the key for *coffee*, but when it did not work, she finished the sentence with *this which-is black period*. Tim replied *Yes*, but not wanting her to drink from his cup, poured some coffee on her plastic bench. Lana did not particularly seem to relish this method of receiving coffee, but she licked it up anyway and then asked, *? You give cup of*. She then pointed alternately to the key for *coffee*, which was not working, and the key for *this* and finally pressed the latter key to end the sentence with *this period*. This time Tim did let her drink from his cup in accordance with her revised, more specific request. Since the *coffee* key was not working, it was impossible for Lana to ask for a *cup of this which-is black* within a six-word sentence. To overcome this difficulty, she pointed alternately to the *this* and *coffee* keys, perhaps to equate the two, and then asked that the *this* be from a *cup*.

PUT THE MILK IN THE MACHINE

On January 24, 1975, Lana was quite hungry because her morning's milk was extraordinarily late. Tim was still cleaning. It was then that the following conversation, which shows an impressive extension of linguistic skills, took place. In it she did not just ask that the milk be moved "behind the room," but that it be put into the machine. (The origins of *put* and *in* are discussed later.)

LANA: *Tim put milk in* . . . (At this point Lana stopped for about 10 minutes and looked at her various keys, pausing occasionally at *cup, bowl, behind,* and *room.* It was as though she did not know what the next word, properly *machine,* should be.)

TIM: *? What give milk.* (He used her keyboard.)   [10:26 a.m.]

LANA: (no response).

TIM: *? What give milk.* (To that question Lana again gave no response, an indication that she simply did not "know" the appropriate response. At this time Tim pointed to the key for *machine,* which Lana depressed, and then finished the sentence with the two words *give* and *milk,* so that the jointly produced sentence read *Machine give milk.* At this point Tim left Lana's room to answer an outside call. Upon his return he read the following request:)

LANA: *Tim put milk in machine.*   [10:27 a.m.]

TIM: *Yes.* (He did so, whereupon Lana asked repeatedly for the machine to vend milk).   [10:27 a.m.]

Lana had been trained to use *put* and *in* during the several days which preceded the above conversation. During this training, either Tim or Lana would put a ball in, on, or under a bowl or a box. Lana's task was to recount who had done what, e.g., *Lana put ball under box, Tim put ball in bowl*, and so forth. At this task Lana became very accurate, performing without error on 10 successive trials. From her mastery of it, furthermore, she was apparently able to extend the use of *put* and *in* quite appropriately to ask not only that Tim *move* the milk behind the room, her traditional request, but also that he *put* the milk in the machine.

Prevarication?

Perhaps Lana does not lie, but she can be obstinate. On January 16, 1975, for example, she refused to give the name of a *very* familiar object, an orange box, which came from her basic set of training materials. She had named it hundreds of times on prior occasions.

TIM:	*? What name-of this which-is orange.*	
LANA:	*Can.*	[10:20 a.m.]
TIM:	*? What name-of this which-is orange.*	
LANA:	*Color.*	[10:21 a.m.]
TIM:	*? What name-of this which-is orange.*	
LANA:	*Cup.*	[10:24 a.m.]
TIM:	*No.* (At this point Tim was exasperated and took a break. He returned 5 minutes later with the same question.)	
TIM:	*? What name-of this which-is orange.*	[10:29 a.m.]
LANA:	*No name-of this bowl.*	[10:31 a.m.]
	No name-of.	[10:31 a.m.]
	No name-of this which-is orange.	[10:33 a.m.]
TIM:	*No.*	
	Box name-of this which-is orange.	[10:33 a.m.]

LEARNING THE USE OF "MORE"

The word *more* was introduced to Lana on several occasions after she had consumed the first ration of some food or drink; in this context, "more" referred to an additional amount. Lana's training in the use of this word is presented in its entirety to demonstrate how rapidly Lana incorporated new words into familiar expressions and appropriately generalized their usage.

LANA:	*? You put juice in cup.*	[3:29 p.m.]

TIM: *Yes Tim put juice in cup.* (But he did not hand the
        cup to Lana.)

LANA: *? You give juice to Lana.* (A request that the juice   [3:30 p.m.]
        be given to her.)

TIM: *Yes.* (He gave it to her, and Lana drank all of it;
        Tim retained possession of the cup.)

TIM: *? Lana want more juice.* (The first introduction of   [3:31 p.m.]
        the word *more*.)
        ? Lana want more juice.

LANA: *Yes Lana want more juice in . . .* (Did not finish
        sentence.)

TIM: *? More juice in what.*

LANA: *Lana want more juice in cup.*   [3:33 p.m.]

TIM: *Tim put more juice in cup.* (He complied, but the
        cup of juice was not given to her.)

LANA: *Yes you give juice to Lana.*   [3:35 p.m.]
        ? You give Lana.   [3:36 p.m.]
        ? You put more juice in cup.   [3:37 p.m.]

TIM: *Yes Tim put more juice in cup.* (And did so.)

LANA: *? You give cup of juice.*   [3:38 p.m.]

TIM: *Yes.* (And Lana drank all of the juice.)

LANA: *? You put more juice Lana.*   [3:39 p.m.]

TIM: (ignored this statement; syntax incorrect.)

LANA: *? You put more juice in cup.*   [3:40 p.m.]

TIM: *Yes.* (And he put more juice in the cup.)

LANA: *? You give juice more cup.*   [3:40 p.m.]

TIM: *No.* (The syntax was incorrect.)

LANA: *? You give juice to Lana.*   [3:41 p.m.]

TIM: *Yes.* (And he gave it to her.)

LANA: *? You put juice more cup.*   [3:42 p.m.]

TIM: *No juice more cup.* (That is not the correct formu-
        lation.)

LANA: *? You put more juice in cup.*   [3:42 p.m.]

TIM: *Yes Tim put more juice in cup.* (He put more
        juice in the cup, but the cup was not given to
        her.)

LANA: *? You give more juice to . . .*   [3:43 p.m.]
        ? You give juice more.   [3:43 p.m.]
        ? You give juice more.   [3:44 p.m.]
        ? You put juice in machine.   [3:44 p.m.]

TIM: *No.*

LANA: *? You put juice in cup.*   [3:44 p.m.]

TIM: *Juice in cup.* (The cup was full, since more juice

	had been put in the cup as a result of a prior request.)	
LANA:	*? You give more juice to.*	[3:45 p.m.]
	? You give juice to Lana.	[3:46 p.m.]
TIM:	*Yes.* (And it was given to her to drink.)	

On February 3, 1975, Lana had her next session with the word "more."

LANA:	*Please you give cup of juice.*	[5:00 p.m.]
TIM:	*Yes.* (And gave her a cup of juice, which she emptied.)	
LANA:	*? You put Coke in cup.* (No Coke was present.)	[5:00 p.m.]
TIM:	*No Coke.*	
LANA:	*? You put more juice in cup.*	[5:01 p.m.]
TIM:	*Yes.*	
LANA:	*? You put juice of.*	[5:02 p.m.]
	? You put.	
	? You give juice to Lana.	[5:02 p.m.]
TIM:	*Yes.* (Thereupon he gave her the juice to drink, though he kept possession of the cup.)	
LANA:	*? You give cup.*	[5:03 p.m.]
	? You give cup of juice.	[5:03 p.m.]
TIM:	*Yes.* (And he gave her the cup of juice to drink.)	
LANA:	*? You put more of.*	[5:04 p.m.]
	? You put more juice in cup.	[5:05 p.m.]
TIM:	*Yes.* (The cup being empty, Tim put more juice into it as specifically requested by Lana.)	

On February 4, 1975, for the first time Lana asked for "more" of something to be put into the machine, another instance of her generalizing word usage appropriately. The time was in the morning, and she had had her first ration of milk and one piece of bread through the machine. It is important to note that during the following episode a pitcher of milk and a piece of bread were in clear view near the vending devices "behind the room."

LANA:	*? You put bread in.*	[9:31 a.m.]
	Please machine give milk. (Lana probably got a few drops of milk although the device was essentially empty.)	[9:31 a.m.]
	Please machine give milk.	[9:32 a.m.]
	? You put more bread in machine.	[9:33 a.m.]
TIM:	*Yes.* (And he did so.)	

LANA:	*Please machine give piece of bread.*	[9:34 a.m.]
	Please machine give piece of bread.	
LANA:	*? You move into room.*	[9:37 a.m.]
TIM:	*No.*	
	? Lana want drink.	
LANA:	*Yes Lana want drink.*	[9:38 a.m.]
	? You move more bread in machine.	[9:38 a.m.]
TIM:	*No move more bread in machine.* (Her syntax was incorrect; also, there was no bread readily available to honor her request.)	
TIM:	*? You want drink.*	
LANA:	*Yes Lana want drink milk.*	[9:39 a.m.]
	? You move milk behind room.	
TIM:	*Milk behind room.* (Note that the pitcher of milk had been there all this time.)	
LANA:	*Yes.* (Apparently acknowledging that it was.)	[9:39 a.m.]
	? You move. (Erased)	[9:39 a.m.]
	? You put more milk in machine.	[9:40 a.m.]
TIM:	*Yes.* (Thereupon he put "more" milk into the machine. Lana then asked for it repeatedly from the machine.)	

From this point on, Lana quite reliably asked for "more" once the first ration had been consumed. We do not claim that by this time Lana had a generalized meaning for the word "more," which would apply to all situations involving increments to a base amount, but observations do support the conclusion that when Lana used "more" she was referring to our addition to the initial ration.

CROSS-MODAL TASKS

The topic of cross-modal perception is discussed at length by Richard K. Davenport in Chapter 3 of this volume. In it, he examines the ape's capacity for cross-modal perception and the relationship presumed to exist between this type of perception and language. The question we wish to consider here is whether Lana's language skills facilitated cross-modal perception.

To answer this question, we designed an experiment in which Lana was first taught to respond *same* or *no-same* to pairs of visually presented stimuli, half of which comprised identical members and half of nonidentical members. (Originally we attempted to teach her to respond *same* and *different*, but gave up when she, interestingly enough, opted to use *no-same* in lieu of *different*.)

Lana was next asked whether she could give the names of the six objects—ball, box, can, cup, shoe, and bowl—which comprised one set of her training materials. She was taught to reach through a portal and to identify each one by touch (haptic sensing), then to give the name in response to the question posed through the computer, *? What name-of this period.* Within the span of only 29 trials, Lana could name the objects in this way without error. She named the ball correctly on the first presentation; probably its homogeneous character made it easy to identify. (With the cup the handle appeared to be the major cue, for she would stop sensing when she felt it and give the name.)

In the first cross-modal test of *same* and *no same* (different), we presented all possible combinations of the six training objects to form heterogeneous pairs along with trials on which the pairs were homogeneous. On each trial, one member of the pair was presented visually, the other haptically and out of her view. Over the course of all 60 trials presented in this way, she was 92% correct, significantly more often than Davenport's and Rogers' apes (see Chapter 3, this volume) had been after months of training. But the training materials used in this first cross-modal task were both familiar to her and were objects she was able to name. What were the relative contributions of familiarity and of ability to name in Lana's performance?

We obtained 60 stimulus pairs of objects which to Lana were initially both novel and without names. Half of these we held in reserve so that they would be novel at the time of cross-modal testing. The remaining half were mounted on a board so that she could see them at any time of the day and so that twice a day for a half-hour at a time she could manipulate them as well. Her opportunity to become familiar with these objects spanned 2 weeks; she was not rewarded for any of her explorations of them.

For cross-modal testing, half of the pairs consisted of identical members and half of nonidentical members. Within each half equal numbers of pairs were composed of familiar and unfamiliar items. Lana was significantly better (80% correct) when judging familiar objects for *same* and *no same* than when she was judging unfamiliar objects (57% correct). Familiarity facilitated her cross-modal perceptions.

Next we wanted to determine whether names *qua* names, apart from familiarity, contributed to the accuracy of cross-modal perceptions. Does having a name for an object contribute anything beyond the more basic dimension of familiarity? In this study we used five foods for which Lana had names and for which she had worked through use of stock sentences: M&M candies, bread, banana, apple, and Monkey Chow biscuits. She had asked for each of these foods thousands of times over the course of the previous 18 months. Although Lana got the bread, banana, and apple in "pieces" from the machine, we used whole slices of bread, whole bananas, and whole apples in the experiment. She had certainly seen these whole objects many times. All possible combinations of these five foods were used for half the trials in this study; on half of those trials the pairs were identical and on the other half the pairs were composed of different materials, e.g., an M&M and a slice of bread.

The other materials were also foods, but Lana had no formal names for them and she had never received them through the machine. (Months after this phase of training was concluded some of the materials were thus delivered and named for her.) These foods were cabbage, carrot, cucumber, sweet potato, and orange. They had been given to her by hand to supplement her diet in whole or at least in relatively large units rather than in small slices. During the experiment, although she did not get these foods through the machine as she had the others mentioned above, she did get them in portions of approximately the same size as those vended through the machine.

As before, on each trial one member of the stimulus pair was presented visually and the other haptically out of Lana's view. With pairs composed of the familiar and *named* foods, Lana was significantly better (88% correct) in judging for *same* and *no-same* than she was on the other trials where familiar but *unnamed* food comprised the pairs (63% correct). Still other tests indicated that there was some advantage (84% versus 72% correct, although not statistically reliable) if the member sensed haptically was the named one of the two and the member sensed visually the unnamed one. These data support the contention that naming does provide support for accurate cross-modal perceptions apart from the familiarity *qua* familiarity which inherently accrues to objects as the names for them are learned.

DISCUSSION

An important development in the experiments reported here was Lana's acquisition of many critical linguistic-type skills for which she had received no specific training. Unquestionably she would never have acquired these skills spontaneously had she not received prior, very specific training in certain language fundamentals; nevertheless, having received such training, she showed a readiness to expand her ability to use linguistic-type communication in a number of significant, and, to her, novel directions.

All of these spontaneous innovations reveal a considerable degree of abstracting and generalizing ability; as the data show, Lana's performances on occasion involved transferring information learned in one situation to another, and generalizing skills learned in limited contexts to deal with broader problems.

The first instance of Lana's spontaneous acquisition of linguistic-type skills was the most crucial—her learning to read lexigrams. We could and did provide specific training to teach her to read the lexigrams embossed on the surfaces of keys, but we had not implemented methods to train her to equate these lexigrams with the lexigram-facsimilies which her projectors produced. Our greatest concern was that she might never attend to what was shown on her projectors or grasp the significance of the order in which the lexigrams were projected. Without these skills, the type of communication we planned would be impossible. Our fears were groundless. Without specific training, Lana did learn how to read the projected lexigrams, and she also grasped the importance of their serial order to the point that she could complete valid sentences begun for her or erase invalid sentence beginnings presented to her by the experimenter.

A second example of the spontaneous acquisition of skills on Lana's part was her use of names. Her initial training in this skill was specific and arduous. Once she had grasped the basic concepts involved in using names, however, Lana took off on her own. Not only did she prove facile at learning new names, but she also began spontaneously requesting the names of objects for which she had no name. Alternatively, she has "invented" her own names for objects by combining lexigrams already in her vocabulary in novel ways. In addition, she spontaneously began to use "this" as a pronoun to refer to objects whose names she had not learned.

Lana's use of No is a particularly interesting example of her generalizing ability. Having learned this word in the context of simple negation, she expanded it with no particular training to use as a form of protest.

Lana's novel use of stock sentences reflects in a different way her mastery of the abstract concepts which underlie language use. In response to a problem situation, she spontaneously began using stock sentences for purposes different from those she had originally been taught were appropriate, and yet her novel uses of these sentences were completely suitable to the situations at hand. Subsequently, Lana moved beyond the "stock-sentence" phase and began composing entirely novel and appropriate sentences on her own. Finally, it was Lana herself who initiated the practice of conversation with us.

We believe that the success Lana has had so far in acquiring linguistic-type skills supports our view of language—that the foundations of language are to be found in the processes of intelligence. Man's outstanding ability to use language is, in part, a function of his high intelligence. We suggest that chimpanzees do not use public language in the field because they lack sufficient intelligence to agree upon the meanings of things that might serve as words and otherwise to develop language-type communication systems.

The data presented here, however, suggest that they have covert language processes and that they can acquire and use certain appropriately designed public language-type systems instituted by man. There is no reason to suppose that a public language-type ability is present in chimpanzees as a specific genetic trait; rather, we believe that intelligence includes the specific functions needed for language use—the ability to order and catalogue and ultimately to interrelate objects and events found in the environment of the individual and to encode these events and objects in a symbolic form. In chimpanzees the level of intelligence permits the development of only rudimentary public language-type skills; intelligence of the level found in humans clearly does permit its use. The present project and other chimpanzee language-training projects have succeeded because man and ape were able to agree on the symbolic referents of various stimuli, e.g., lexigrams. The similarities of their intellects allowed them to do so even though the respective levels and surely even many parameters of their intelligence differ profoundly.

Of course, we may never understand the nature of Lana's achievement precisely. We cannot assume that Lana "understands" the meaning of every word she uses as we do, but the consistent appropriateness of her novel sentence constructions as found in the data presented here support the conclusion that she has conceptual meanings for many of them and also for their relationships. It is our belief, then, that Lana has acquired skills involved in at least the rudiments of linguistic communication.

For the forseeable future the question of the limits of Lana or any chimpanzee should remain open. Certainly she has already surpassed several times over the level of competence we initially held for her. At this time it would be premature to conclude that the ape is or is not capable of mastering a given aspect of language skill.

REFERENCES

Gill, T. V., & Rumbaugh, D. M. Mastery of naming skills by a chimpanzee. *Journal of Human Evolution*, 1974, *3*, 483–492.

Riopelle, E. T. *Acquisition of language-relevant skills by a chimpanzee (Pan)*. Unpublished master's thesis, Georgia State University, 1975.

Rumbaugh, D. M., Gill, T. V., & von Glasersfeld, E. C. Reading and sentence completion by a chimpanzee *(Pan)*. *Science*, 1973, *182*, 731–733.

Rumbaugh, D. M., & Gill, T. V. Language and the acquisition of language-type skills by a chimpanzee *(Pan)*. In K. Salzinger (Ed.), *Psychology in progress*. Vol. 270. New York: Annals of the New York Academy of Sciences, 1976a.

Rumbaugh, D. M., & Gill, T. V. Lana's mastery of language skills. In H. Steklis, S. Harnad, & Jane Lancaster (Eds.), *Origins and evolution of language and speech*. Vol. 280. New York: Annals of the New York Academy of Sciences, 1976b.

chapter 10

Language Relevant Object- and Color-Naming Tasks

SUSAN M. ESSOCK

Brown University, and
Yerkes Regional Primate Research Center

TIMOTHY V. GILL

Yerkes Regional Primate Research Center, and
Georgia State University

DUANE M. RUMBAUGH

Georgia State University, and
Yerkes Regional Primate Research Center

When two people communicate, the fact that the speaker can direct the listener's attention to a specific object (the grapefruit, that tree, the cheapest used-car dealer) without having to point to the referenced object is of enormous value. The foundation for such an ability is the existence of a pool of names held in common by the speaker and the receiver. But two people need more than a common vocabulary in order to communicate with each other. It is also necessary that the receiver be able to use the information given by the speaker to direct his or her own attention to a likely environmental referent. The receiver must then be able to abstract information about that referent for use in conjunction with the information in the speaker's comment. For example, A may ask B, "What's that pink thing?" In order for B to answer, most of A's words, especially "pink" must be in B's vocabulary. In addition, B must be able to scan the environment for something pink and, when a possibility is located, must be able mentally and verbally to code information about it. B's response might be, "That's a jellyfish." B has then conveyed information to A about a referent that B

193

was able to single out because B and A share a common vocabulary and because B possesses the attentional skill necessary to locate the quest object and to extract from it the requested information. Of course, B's task would have been greatly simplified if A had said, "What's this?" and held up the jellyfish. This would have saved the step of extracting information from A's question to guide the search for the referent.

Clearly the ability to attach names to objects is fundamental to using language. When this phase of the study began in the early summer of 1974, Lana had acquired at least rudimentary naming skills (Gill & Rumbaugh, 1974). She had mastered the general concepts that things have names and that the name of an object is something different than the object itself. Once, for example, when an object she desired but did not yet know the name of was presented, she spontaneously made the following request: *? Tim give Lana name-of this* (Rumbaugh & Gill, 1975; Chapter 9, this volume). Impressed by Lana's apparent grasp of the function of names, we decided to explore her ability to use names more fully. To do so, we planned to present her with a task that would require her to make a visual search of objects and to answer specific questions as to their names and colors. We considered this a sophisticated task, and we recognized that we would first have to demonstrate the existence of the requisite common vocabulary before attempting to request information about a spatially removed referent via a linguistic code. The following set of experiments was designed to test for the existence of such skills.

METHOD

Subject

The subject, Lana, was $3\frac{3}{4}$ years old at the time testing began. Lana had been involved in the language-training situation for 20 months prior to the present study. Her previous training included extensive practice in giving the name or color of an object physically present or projected from a 35 mm slide (see Chapter 9). For the duration of the study (approximately 2 months) Lana's food intake was limited to the rewards received during training and testing with occasional supplements to meet her dietary needs.

Apparatus

The computer-controlled language-training facility has been described elsewhere (Rumbaugh, von Glasersfeld, Warner, Pisani, Gill, Brown & Bell

1973; Chapter 7, this volume). Briefly, this system enables Lana to control multiple aspects of each 24-hour day via a keyboard consisting of individual keys each of which represents a concept. Geometric patterns (lexigrams) are embossed on each key and as each key is depressed its pattern is displayed on a series of projectors located above the keyboard. A PDP-8 computer monitors each phrase to determine grammatical accuracy and, when a correct request for one of the various reinforcements is made, responds appropriately. The system also allows for conversation between humans and ape by projecting on a second series of projectors lexigrams corresponding to keys depressed on the operator's keyboard. A teletype records all that transpires. At the time the experiments described here took place, the summer of 1974, there were 75 keys on the keyboard. Unless otherwise noted, a cardboard screen hung on the door to the subject's room during testing periods and precluded visual contact between subject and experimenter.

EXPERIMENT I. COLOR VERSUS OBJECT NAMING OF PROJECTED PHOTOGRAPHS

Prior to the start of the studies reported here, Lana, as already outlined, had learned to name various objects and to give their colors. The first experiment addressed the question of whether she could view a projected slide of a familiar object and correctly respond to the questions, *? What name-of this* or *? What color of this.*

Procedure

Stimuli were 36 slides which were projected directly above Lana's keyboard (see Figure 1). Each slide was a familiar photograph of one of six possible objects on a white background, each of which had been spray painted one of six different colors. The six objects were: ball, bowl, box, can, cup, and shoe. The six colors were black, blue, orange, purple, red, and yellow. The projected image of the object varied between 4.5 and 13 inches in any given direction.

At the beginning of each trial, the experimenter would depress keys on his keyboard to ask the subject either *? What name-of this* or *? What color of this.* As the key for *this* was depressed, a slide was projected. Each daily session consisted of 36 trials, slides presented randomly with the restriction that each object and each color should appear once before any objects or colors could be repeated. Each day, 18 trials were given in the late morning

Figure 1. Lana at her keyboard.

and another 18 were given in mid-afternoon. Requests for *Name-of this* and for *Color of this* were randomized with the restrictions that each was requested 18 times in each session, and that neither was requested more than three times in a row. The sessions were paired (1&2; 3&4; 5&6), and within a pair of sessions the same slides appeared in the same order in both sessions, but in the second session of each pair the questions were always reversed. That is, if in Session 1, Lana had been asked *Color of this* for a given slide, the question accompanying that slide in Session 2 would be *Name-of this*. The order of slide presentation varied for each pair of sessions according to the restrictions already given. Thus at the end of 72 trials, both *Color of this* and *Name-of this* had been requested of each of the 36 slides. One of three different people served as experimenter, with only one person being present at any given time.

To answer the question, Lana first depressed the "period" key to erase the experimenter's question and then depressed the keys corresponding to her answer. If Lana's answer was correct, the experimenter depressed the *Yes* key, and a reinforcement (generally milk, juice, or a small piece of fruit) was delivered. If the subject made an error, either by answering the question incorrectly (i.e., calling a box red if it was blue) or by answering the inappropriate question (i.e., giving the color of an object when the object's name had been requested), the experimenter depressed the *No* key, and the trial was repeated until the correct response was made. The experimenter then typed *Yes*, but no food reward was given, and the next trial began.

A cardboard panel that hung on the door to Lana's chamber prevented visual contact between her and the experimenter. The experimenter could see no part of·Lana or her keyboard, and Lana's view of the experimenter was limited to the experimenter's legs and feet.

Results

As can be seen in Table 1, Lana's performance across sessions was quite variable. Overall, she gave a correct answer to the question *? What color of this* 83.2% of the time and answered *? What name-of this* correctly 76.1% of the time. A generous way to estimate what percentage of correct responses would be expected by chance alone (hence a conservative way of evaluating Lana's performance) would be to assume that Lana would always respond to the correct question using the correct sentence structure (either *color of this* or *name-of this*), but that she might guess as to which color or object key should be depressed. Since there would then be six possible keys to choose from when answering either question, the performance expected by chance alone would be about 16.7% correct. Lana's performance was

Table 1

EXPERIMENT I.COLOR VERSUS OBJECT NAMING OF PROJECTED
PHOTOGRAPHS[a]

Session	Color correct	Name correct
1	6/9 = 66.7%	7/9 = 77.8%
2	8/9 = 88.9%	6/9 = 66.7%
3	6/9 = 66.7%	5/9 = 55.6%
4	9/9 = 100.0%	8/9 = 88.9%
5	6/7 = 85.7%	9/11 = 81.7%
6	10/11 = 90.9%	6/7 = 85.7%
Mean	83.2%	76.1%

[a] Overall mean correct: 79.6%.

significantly above this figure, both when she was asked ? *What color of this* ($p < .001$, exact binomial) and when she was asked ? *What name-of this* ($p < .001$, exact binomial).

It is also clear that Lana was attentive to which question was being asked. Had she been guessing as to the appropriate response format (specifying either name or color), she should have used the correct format only about 50% of the time. In fact her answers were in the correct format 96.3% of the time.

EXPERIMENT II. COLOR NAMING OF NOVEL OBJECTS

Experiment I demonstrated that Lana could reliably give appropriate color responses when shown slides of familiar objects. Certainly we hoped, but could not be sure, that Lana's responses stemmed from a concept of color and not simply from a knowledge of which of the six "color" responses should be paired with which of the familiar objects. If Lana indeed had a concept of color, we reasoned, then she should be able to apply her color terms to describe unfamiliar objects. This is the task of Experiment II.

Procedure

Thirty-six novel junk objects measuring between $1\frac{1}{2}$ and 6 inches in any given direction were spray painted, if necessary, to conform to one of the six colors used in Experiment I. A session consisted of individual presentations of 18 of these objects selected randomly, with the restriction that each object appeared once before any object was repeated. At the beginning of each trial, the experimenter depressed the keys corresponding to *? What color of this.* With "this" the experimenter withdrew one of the junk objects from a box and held it under the cardboard screen in front of the glass door of Lana's room. Lana turned 60° to view the object and then turned back to her keyboard to answer. Reinforcement procedures for the six sessions of Experiment II were identical to those of Experiment I. Once again, the cardboard screen prevented visual contact between Lana and experimenter.

Results

Color naming of novel objects was a very easy task for Lana, and a summary of her performance can be found in Table 2. Again, a generous way to estimate chance performance would be to assume that Lana's responses would be limited to six color terms and that guessing or random responding should produce correct responses about $\frac{1}{6}$ or 16.7% of the time. Lana's performance was well above this figure ($p < .001$, normal approximation to the binomial); her mean percentage correct across sessions was 87.0%.

EXPERIMENT III. COLOR NAMING OF REQUESTED OBJECT WHEN SEVERAL OBJECTS ARE PRESENT

Up to this point, only one object had been present whenever Lana had been asked to give color or name responses. A more demanding task would involve asking similar questions with several objects present. Then, in order to answer correctly, Lana would have to do the following:

1. Read the question to determine what information was being requested about what object.

Table 2
EXPERIMENT II COLOR NAMING OF NOVEL OBJECTS

Session		Correct responses
1		15/18 = 83.3%
2		15/18 = 83.3%
3		14/18 = 77.8%
4		15/18 = 83.3%
5		17/18 = 94.4%
6		18/18 = 100.0%
	Mean	87.0%

2. Use the information extracted from the question to guide a visual search and isolate the desired object.
3. Examine the reference object to determine the requested information.
4. Code the requested information into Yerkish.
5. Depress the necessary keys to form the appropriate response.

Procedure

Part A—Three Objects Present

For this task, the actual objects photographed for the slides in Experiment I were presented three at a time to the subject in five blocks of 36 trials each, with 18 trials administered per session. Thus a given trial might begin with presentation of a blue box, a yellow bowl, and a red shoe. The subject was asked to give the color of a specific object present on that trial, for example, *? What color of this box.* Each object presented in any given trial was a different color and a different form from any other object present on that trial. Each of the six different types of objects (shoes, boxes, etc.) and each color was the target once before that object or color was presented as target again. The position of the target object was randomized with the restrictions that each position was correct no more than twice in a row. Each of the 36 objects was a nonrequested (incorrect) object twice in each block of 36 trials, and each object was a nonrequested object once before any object was a nonrequested object for a second time.

Testing was done with the door to Lana's room open so that she could come over to the door area and inspect the objects. The experimenter would draw an object to be used from a box and place it on a table immediately outside the subject's room (Figure 1). Objects were placed on the table one at a time in a predetermined order always beginning with the experimenter's left. When the objects were in place, the experimenter turned 90° to face the keyboard and typed, *? What color of this* followed by the name of an object. The experimenter then stared at the row of projectors immediately above his keyboard until Lana completed her answer. (Thus the experimenter could not see which keys Lana was about to press; therefore a possible source of inadvertent cuing such as feedback to Lana from facial expressions or small shifts in body position was avoided.) Lana depressed the key on her keyboard that corresponded to the name of the object requested (a procedure instituted to ensure that the subject was reading at least part of the question), erased the question, and typed her answer. Reinforcement procedures were the same as those in Experiments I and II.

Part B—Six Objects Present

Immediately after completion of Part A, the number of objects presented on each trial was increased from three to six. Objects appeared randomly with the restrictions that each trial contain one of each form and one of each color, that once a given form or color was the target that form or color was not the target again until each other form and color had been the target, and that each of the 36 objects was the target once. The 36 trials sufficient to fulfill these conditions were given in groups of six, twice a day, for three days.

Results

Part A

Responses to each question posed in this experiment contained two major sources of error yielding 72 chances to err per session. In order to gain reward, Lana had to use a correctly phrased response that both repeated the name of the object and gave its color (e.g., *Color of this shoe blue*). Table 3 shows that her performance was very consistent across sessions (averaging 78.9% correct) and that her major source of error was giving the incorrect color. For all "color" error trials, Lana gave the color for one of the two nonrequested objects present on those trials. Her performance was clearly above that expected by chance ($p < .001$, exact binomial).

Table 3
EXPERIMENT III COLOR NAMING GIVEN OBJECT NAME

Session		Correct name and color	Sentence correct except wrong color	Sentence correct except wrong name
		Part A—3 objects present		
1		27/36 = 75.0%	8/36	1/36
2		28/36 = 77.8%	8/36	1/36
3		29/36 = 80.6%	7/36	1/36
4		29/36 = 80.6%	7/36	2/36
5		29/36 = 80.6%	7/36	2/36
	Mean	78.9%		
		Part B—6 objects present		
6		12/12 = 100.0%	0/12	0/12
7		11/12 = 91.7%	1/12	0/12
8		9/12 = 75.0%	3/12	0/12
	Mean	88.9%		

Part B

Lana's performance *improved* when the number of objects was increased from three to six (averaging 88.9% correct). This improvement in performance coincided with a behavioral change on Lana's part. Once the experimenter had typed out the question and Lana had inspected the objects, she went to her keyboard and typed out the first part of her answer (e.g., *Color of this shoe*) as before; but when six objects were present, she then turned toward the objects once again before finishing the sentence. This second "inspection" of the objects was presumably a visual check that she imposed on herself when the task of remembering the correct object without a second look became more difficult.

EXPERIMENT IV. NAMING OF OBJECT REQUESTED BY COLOR WHEN SEVERAL OBJECTS ARE PRESENT

In Experiment III Lana demonstrated that she could give the color of a requested object when more than one object was present. Experiment IV was conceived as a parallel to see whether Lana could give the name of an object identified only by its color when more than one object was present.

Procedure

Part A—Three Objects Present

This experiment is analogous to Experiment IIIA, except that the object name was asked for by specifying the color of one of the objects present. The question posed to Lana went as follows, *? What name of this that's* _____, the blank being filled in by the color of one of the three objects present on that trial. The presentation procedure was the same as that of Experiment III except that only two sessions of 18 trials each were given. This allowed for each object to be present once in each color.

Part B—Six Objects Present

Again, this experiment is analogous to Experiment IIIB, except that the object's name was requested by stating the color of one of the six objects present in each trial. The 36 trials necessary to allow each form/color combination to be the correct item were presented in two sessions of 18 trials each.

Table 4
EXPERIMENT IV NAMING OF OBJECT REQUESTED BY COLOR WHEN SEVERAL OBJECTS
ARE PRESENT

Session		Correct name and color	Wrong color	Wrong name
		Part A—3 objects present		
1		16/18 = 88.9%	1/18	2/18
2		17/18 = 94.4%	2/18	1/18
	Mean	91.7%		
		Part B—6 objects present		
3		17/18 = 94.4%	0/18	1/18
4		17/18 = 94.4%	0/18	1/18
	Mean	94.4%		

Results

Lana also did well on this task (Table 4). Although there were twice as many chances to make major errors (giving incorrect color or name) as there were questions, Lana's overall percentage correct in Part A was about 92%, which is well above the level expected by chance alone ($p < .001$, exact binomial). Of the few errors Lana made, half consisted of giving an incorrect color. In Part B, Lana's performance again was not hindered when the task was made more difficult by increasing the number of objects present during each trial (Table 4, mean percentage correct: 94.4).

EXPERIMENT V. INTERMINGLED COLOR AND OBJECT NAMING QUESTIONS OF A REQUESTED OBJECT WITH SIX OBJECTS PRESENT

We next wondered how Lana would perform if the questions *? What color of this* and *? What name-of this* were intermixed. A high level of performance on such a task would indicate that she could both differentiate between what was requested and answer a specific question when a number of objects were present.

Procedure

In this experiment, the 36 objects were again presented to Lana in groups of 6 (one of each object with each color present) with either the question of Experiment II (? *What color of this* _____) or of Experiment IV (? *What name of this that's* _____) being posed. The question to be asked was selected randomly with the restrictions that not more than three questions of one type should be asked in a row and that within the 36 trials each question should be asked 18 times. A second series of 36 trials was then given using the same stimulus arrays, with the opposite questions being asked.

Results

Lana demonstrated the same high level of performance when the questions ? *What color of this* [object name] and ? *What name-of this that's* [color] were intermingled as when a series of each was asked separately (Table 5, overall about 92% correct). Clearly, she both noted what information was being requested and responded correctly even when several objects were present.

DISCUSSION

Lana's success on these tasks indicates that she can mentally manipulate abstract concepts that have been defined by means of an arbitrary code. Such manipulation is necessary if one is to scan a set of objects and mentally select one on the basis of a linguistically expressed criterion. Answering ? *What name of this that's blue* when several objects are present demands more than a vocabulary containing a particular set of words/lexigrams. A goal-directed visual search must be initiated that is based on information

Table 5
EXPERIMENT V INTERMINGLED COLOR- AND OBJECT-NAMING QUESTIONS OF A REQUESTED OBJECT WITH SIX OBJECTS PRESENT[a]

Session		Correct when color requested	Correct when object name requested
1		7/9 = 77.8%	9/9 = 100.0%
2		9/9 = 100.0%	8/9 = 88.9%
3		10/10 = 100.0%	8/8 = 100.0%
4		6/8 = 75.0%	8/10 = 80.0%
	Mean	88.2%	92.2%

[a] Overall mean correct: 92.2%.

deduced from the linguistically coded question. The result of this search must then be linguistically coded and expressed.

This would seem an impressive task for an only-very-recently-linguistic chimp, but we have no reason to believe that it was a particularly difficult one for Lana. Although her performance was generally less than 100% correct, she was always well above the figure that would be achieved by guessing. Moreover, we would speculate that most of Lana's errors stemmed from a wavering devotion to the task at hand since, typically, the first few trials of a session were error free.

We finished the set of experiments just described as they had been conceived, but we have since begun looking for tasks that would be more enjoyable for Lana. Also, we found that working for several brief periods each morning and afternoon appears to be more productive than the single longer session each morning and afternoon that was used in the set of experiments reported here. From their earliest reports, the Gardners stressed that they aimed to provide the most interesting environment possible to ensure that Washoe would have something to talk about (Gardner & Gardner, 1971). Our experiences emphatically support their intuition. The breath and depth of Lana's linguistic skills have been revealed more often in situations where the unexpected has spurred conversation. (See, for instance, those conversations reported in Chapters 9 and 12 of this volume.)

Formal testing such as that reported here appeared arduous for Lana. At times she whined or asked to be taken outside. Certainly the sessions were useful even though it is doubtful that Lana learned very much from them. (Her percentage correct was fairly constant across the sessions comprising any given experiment.) From them we gained certainty about what we suspected or hoped Lana could do. We now know that Lana can describe a given object in more than one way and can select her description according to the question posed; she can mentally transpose a linguistically phrased question into what is necessary for a visual search and once the requested information is obtained give it via a linguistic code; and she can identify her six training colors regardless of the shape or familiarity of the colored object. Rigorous testing gives comfort to the experimenters who must interpret the results. The experimenters learned that Lana had all these abilities. The tests held no surprises for her.

SUMMARY

1. Lana can reliably designate objects using either their colors or their names as a means of identification. In the course of doing this, she demon-

strated that she was both reading the question posed to her and responding differentially to the different question formats. Furthermore, when increasing the number of objects present increased the difficulty of the task, she introduced a review (a second visual scan) for her own benefit and at her own initiative.

2. In the tasks where one object had to be mentally selected from several others, Lana was able to single out objects on the basis of either name or color. That is, her language-relevant skills had given her a means of selective attention.

3. Lana did not confine the six color and six object names to the pool of 36 training objects which were used for the training and initial formal testing of the color and object name terms. In Experiment II she immediately transferred use of the color terms to describe novel junk objects that had been painted with the various training colors. (She has also frequently transferred use of the object names; see Chapter 9 of this volume.)

REFERENCES

Gardner, B. T., & Gardner, R. A. Two-way communications with an infant chimpanzee. In A. Schrier & F. Stollnitz (Eds.), *Behavior of nonhuman primates.* Vol. 4. New York: Academic Press, 1971.

Gill, T. V., & Rumbaugh, D. M. Mastery of naming skills by a chimpanzee. *Journal of Human Evolution*, 1974, *3*, 483–492.

Rumbaugh, D. M., & Gill, T. V. Language and the acquisition of language-type skills by a chimpanzee (*Pan*). In K. Salzinger (Ed.), *Psychology in Progress.* Vol. 270. New York: New York Academy of Sciences, 1976.

Rumbaugh, D. M., von Glasersfeld, E. C., Warner, H., Pisani, P., Gill, T. V., Brown, J. V., & Bell, C. L. A computer-controlled language training system for investigating the language skills of young apes. *Behavior Research Methods and Instrumentation*, 1973, *5*, 385–392.

chapter 11

Color Perception and Color Classification

SUSAN M. ESSOCK

Brown University, and
Yerkes Regional Primate Research Center

This chapter describes a set of experiments designed to investigate Lana's color perception. The work began in the summer of 1974, when Lana had already acquired color terms for eight specific training colors: red, orange, yellow, green, blue, purple, black, and white (Chapter 10, this volume). The investigation to be described here was initiated primarily to see how consistent Lana would be in her use of color terms and to see how she would assign color names to colors other than her training colors. In addition, the study asked whether Lana's division of color space through use of her color terms would be influenced more by her own perception of color space or by the particular training colors that were used to teach her the color terms.

In natural languages, color terms, when found, serve as conceptual codes that describe variations in hue. Such color-naming systems are not arbitrarily derived; rather, the opponent-process underpinnings of hue perception apparently provide for the evolution of color terms based on physiological contingencies (for reviews see Hurvich & Jameson, 1974; Bornstein, 1973). Berlin and Kay (1969) have amply documented the striking similarities that characterize the semantic development of color terms in widely varying societies. Their survey of 98 languages showed four progressive stages in the evolution of color terms: In Stage I terms exist for describing black and white or for coding the brightness dimension by some other means. In Stage II, a color term for red is added. In Stage III, terms for green, yellow, and blue are added; and in Stage IV, terms are added for one or more of the purple, pink, brown, and orange categories. Thus a Stage I culture such as the Dani of New Guinea possesses "color" terms that refer only to brightness. English is a language of a Stage IV culture because it contains terms for brightness, for all of the primary colors, and for additional, monolexonic color terms (e.g., "purple" rather than "reddish-blue"). Berlin and Kay (1969) suggest that experiential (or, to use their term, *social–technological*) factors determine the stage of a given culture. This developmental emphasis is in contrast to but not in conflict with a physiologically based theory of hue perception. The very fact that populations with enormous cultural differences have evolved terms with the same few referents suggests that experience serves to force the creation of labels for those sensations which similar bodies are built to perceive most easily. Certainly, an extreme environmentalist viewpoint, which states that experience alone shapes perception—a view typified by Sapir–Whorf hypothesis (Whorf, 1956) or the emphasis of Brown and Lenneberg (1954)—is incompatible with physiologically based theories. Although once popular, strict environmentalist theories of color perception have been experimentally refuted (Bornstein, 1973; Bornstein, Kessen, & Weiskopf, 1976; Heider, 1972).

An interpretation incorporating both environmental and physiological influences on language suggests that when a culture evolves to the degree that color terms emerge, the color terms will refer to those areas of color space which are perceptually the most salient. Support for this notion comes from Bornstein's (1973) correlational study, which suggests that when the morphology of the visual system of a population is altered, the color terms of that population can be expected to change. Bornstein argues that the color systems of cultures near the Equator frequently have a single color term for what in English is coded by the two color terms blue and green. He argues that the two categories are collapsed into a single term (which sometimes also includes what in English is called black), because of the relative abundance of yellow macular or intraocular pigment in the visual systems of people who live near the Equator. This pigment serves to decrease sensitivity to the blue end of the spectrum, and hence the color systems of these cultures are characterized by "collapsed" color terms at the short-wavelength end of the spectrum. A human then, given the necessary visual apparatus, the necessary linguistic environment, and the requisite cognitive capacity, will develop an arbitrary conceptual code which serves reliably to denote nonarbitrary portions of color space. The study to be reported here asked if a chimpanzee would do the same.

All available evidence suggests that a chimpanzee's visual apparatus provides color vision that is perceptually extremely similar to that of normal humans. Behavioral tests have shown the following similarities between the two: The chimpanzee can discriminate between similar hues as well as a human in the blue–green region of the spectrum and nearly if not equally as well in the red and yellow regions (Grether, 1940a); those hues which are complementary for a human will also combine to make white for a chimpanzee; the chimpanzee requires the same proportion of complementary colors as a human for the mix to match white (Grether, 1940b), and finally the range of the visual spectrum of the chimpanzee is at least as extensive as that of humans (Grether, 1940c). For a more comprehensive review of what is known about the chimpanzee visual system, see Riesen (1970). Although physiological evidence concerning the chimpanzee visual system is scant, there is excellent evidence to suggest that cells in the lateral geniculate nucleus of the rhesus monkey respond in opponent fashion ("on" versus "off") to code either red or green, blue or yellow, or brightness (DeValois, Abramov, & Jacobs, 1966). Since behavioral evidence also suggests that rhesus color perception is quite similar to human color perception (De-Valois, 1965), and since chimpanzee color perception is also very similar to rhesus and human color perception, we can in all likelihood assume that the physiology of hominoid (ape and human) color vision is very similar to that of rhesus color vision. This implies that the morphology of Lana, an anthropoid ape, is such that her visual apparatus is the functional equivalent of that of a normal human.

In humans the coupling of such a visual system with an adequate linguistic environment yields an individual with conceptual color codes. For the purpose of the argument here, let us assume that the visual apparatus and the linguistic environment are the only necessary conditions for the development of color codes in those beings with cognitive skills sufficient for the assimilation of such codes. It follows that if Lana does indeed possess such cognitive skills, then following the coupling of her adequate morphology with a sufficiently linguistic environment, she should show evidence of possessing conceptual color codes. That is, Lana should use her color terms as a means of describing variations in hue; she should be consistent in her use of color terms; her color-naming responses should form a discrete distribution along the hue continuum, and her color responses should be relatively invariant despite changes in brightness or saturation. Also, no more than two color names should ever compete as the label for a particular sample. Conversely, the demonstration of such codes would imply that the environment that produced them was a suitably conceptual/ linguistic one for fostering the emergence of abstract codes in an ape.

If Lana's training with eight specific color terms applied to eight specific colors was sufficient to allow her both to develop a concept of color and to express this concept in an arbitrary code, then her color-naming responses should resemble those of people in Stage IV of the Berlin and Kay model. If, on the other hand, training on eight specific color terms taught her only the appropriate responses to those eight stimulus colors, then the terms should not serve as conceptual codes, and her color-naming responses to various stimulus colors should reflect only stimulus generalization from her training colors. In particular, a training color should lie near the center of an area of color space called by that color term, and Lana's color-naming accuracy and consistency should break down for stimuli perceptually distant from her training stimuli.

EXPERIMENT I

The purpose of the first experiment was to determine how Lana assigned her color terms to various portions of color space and to compare her responses to chips of maximum saturation for a given hue and brightness both to those responses of human observers tested under the same conditions and to the cross-cultural data of Berlin and Kay (1969).

Method

Subjects

Lana was 4 years old and had been in the language training program for about 2 years when this study began (Rumbaugh, von Glasersfeld, Warner, Pisani, Gill, Brown, & Bell, 1973; Gill & Rumbaugh, 1974; Chapter 4 of this volume). Her past experience included pairing eight arbitrary symbols (simple geometric shapes such as a circle, rectangle, or parallel horizontal lines, all of which were white figures on a black background) with eight specific training colors (red, orange, yellow, green, blue, purple, black, and white; see Chapters 9 and 10 this volume).

Three female Yerkes employees also served as subjects.

Apparatus

The computer-controlled language-training facility has been described elsewhere (Rumbaugh et al., 1973; Chapters 5–7 of this volume).

The experiment was conducted in Lana's room, a 7 foot × 7 foot × 7 foot cube, which was illuminated with a mixture of G.E. Cool White and Warm White florescent bulbs and some daylight. The stimuli were all color chips from the 1969 loose-leaf edition of the *Munsell Book of Color*. These chips all fell between Munsell values 3–8 and Munsell chroma 6–12 for each of the 40 hues in the book. In the Munsell terminology, the word *value* denotes brightness, and the word *chroma* denotes saturation. The Munsell notation system specifies a color by its hue designation (a number and one or more letters) and a value/chroma fraction to designate brightness and saturation, as in the expression 10PB4/6 in which 10PB stands for a particular shade of purple–blue.

All chips were matte finish, $\frac{5}{8}$ inch × $\frac{7}{8}$ inch, and were attached to the pages of the Munsell book. Chips were exposed using gray cardboard masks (approximate Munsell notation N7/0) which either revealed only one color chip at a time or which covered all chips except those falling between Munsell values 3–8 and chromas 6–12.

Procedure

When testing Lana, the experimenter and subject sat about 1 foot apart on a small bench directly in front of Lana's keyboard. The experimenter exposed one color chip at a time, and Lana made a single lexigram color response, pushing the key for either red, orange, yellow, green, blue, or purple. (All keys were active; Lana herself limited her responses to those keys.) After exposing a color chip, the experimenter stared at the row of projectors until Lana made her response. All responses were immediately reinforced; the experimenter gave Lana a small bit of fruit or an M&M candy. Lana then erased her response by depressing the "period" key, and the next trial began.

At the beginning of each session, those pages of the *Munsell Book of Color* containing the color chips that most nearly matched Lana's training colors were sorted out and shuffled. These pages were presented one at a time covered by the gray cardboard mask, which revealed any chips falling between Munsell values 3–8 and chromas 6–12. This series of training colors was given twice for a total of 12 responses. In this way Lana had the opportunity to depress each of her color keys for a reward at the beginning of each session. Following presentation of the training colors, the set of all chips of a given value and chroma were shown as a series. At the end of one series the experimenter, following a predetermined random order, selected stimuli of a different value and chroma for the next series. Before testing began stimuli within a series were "randomized" by shuffling the pages on which they appeared. The number of trials in a series varied depending on how many hues were present for a given value and chroma. Since the number of Munsell color chips decreases greatly at high value or high chroma levels (see Figure 2 for exact numbers), four additional "dummy" colors were randomly selected and included in any series in which there were fewer than four chips in the series, and when these were neighboring hues. Several series could be run per half hour session. The sessions continued until each color chip had been shown three times for a total of 1071 responses.

The human observers were tested in another room which was also illuminated by the same mixture of light sources. Before testing, the experimenter showed the observers the Munsell chips most closely approximating Lana's training colors and asked that these chips be used as the standards for the only allowable color responses: red, orange, yellow, green, blue, or purple. All three observers were tested simultaneously, and each recorded her own response. The humans were shown only the color chips of maximum saturation for a given hue and brightness value. The chips were shown to them in random order, and testing was completed in a single 1½-hour session.

Results

This task seemed to be very enjoyable for Lana. She frequently hooted with apparent pleasure when the experimenter entered the room carrying the pages from the Munsell book (the experimenter alone rarely produced such a response), and she voluntarily stayed at the keyboard for as long as testing continued. She responded very rapidly. Twenty trials averaged about 4 minutes, and this period included the time necessary for her to consume her reward. Yet for all of her speed, she remained very accurate and consistent in naming the various areas of color space.

When using the Munsell color chips, it is convenient to think of color space as being roughly cylindrical. All achromatic colors (colors having zero hue and therefore having zero chroma/saturation also) lie along the central vertical axis of the color solid and are arranged by increasing brightness. A line traveling out from the central core in a straight line perpendicular to the central axis passes through colors that are constant in hue and in value/brightness, but that increase steadily in saturation. Colors of various hues and brightnesses but of equal saturation define a cylinder with all points equidistant from the achromatic core. Horizontal slices through the cylinder produce the set of all hues of equal brightness. The charts in Figure 1 give Lana's color responses for six such slices. They yield six brightness levels (Munsell values 3/, 4/, 5/, 6/, 7/, 8/) and show color responses for all 40 hues at increasing levels of saturation (Munsell chromas /6, /8, /10, /12). Color responses coded with a single capital letter indicate that Lana gave the same color response all three times when that particular point in color space appeared as the stimulus. Groups of three small letters show the individual color responses Lana made to a chip when she made different responses to the same chip on different occasions.

In almost all instances two responses at most competed as possible labels for a given color chip, and when two responses did compete, these were almost always the names for spectrally adjacent hues. The only exceptions were instances of what will be called Lana's orange–green confusion. Since her early training, Lana has occasionally erred by interchanging the symbols for orange (an open circle) and for green (an open diamond). This confusion has diminished considerably but is still occasionally present (Figure 1). Since the overwhelming majority of her identifications for Munsell hues 7.5R–10YR were "orange" and for 7.5GY–10BG were "green," and since no single chip showed this irregularity more than once, it is unlikely that this error represents an actual confusion in color perception. It is much more likely that Lana is occasionally careless about differentiating between the lexigrams for orange and green. If the responses in question related to a particular area of color space or if the colors involved suggested some physiological deficit, then color mechanisms and not lexigram confusion might be suspect. But since the data do not favor a faulty color-perception interpretation, instances of this confusion will be ignored in the ensuing presentation of Lana's color perception data. The 9 inappropriate orange and green responses (out of a total of over 300 orange and green responses) will henceforth be treated like green and orange responses, respectively.

The "outer shell" of the Munsell color solid contains those chips of maximum saturation for a given hue and brightness value. Figure 2a shows Lana's responses to the outer-shell color chips displayed in the manner of the cross-cultural data of Berlin and Kay (1969). Areas where chips were called by a single color term are unshaded and will be referred to as central areas. Border areas are the portions of color space in which a chip was called by more than a single color term; for instance, the six color chips falling between the central area for the color name green and the central area for the color name blue were called green on some presentations and blue on others. All of Lana's training colors are most nearly matched by color chips on the outer shell, and these chips are cross hatched in Figure 2a. Notice that these chips do *not* always lie in the middle of the central area for that hue name as they should if Lana's color-naming responses were the result of generalization from her training colors. For example, the training color for red falls just on the red side of the red–orange border, and the training color for yellow is just on the yellow side of the orange–yellow border. Since each of the responses to a given chip was separated by an

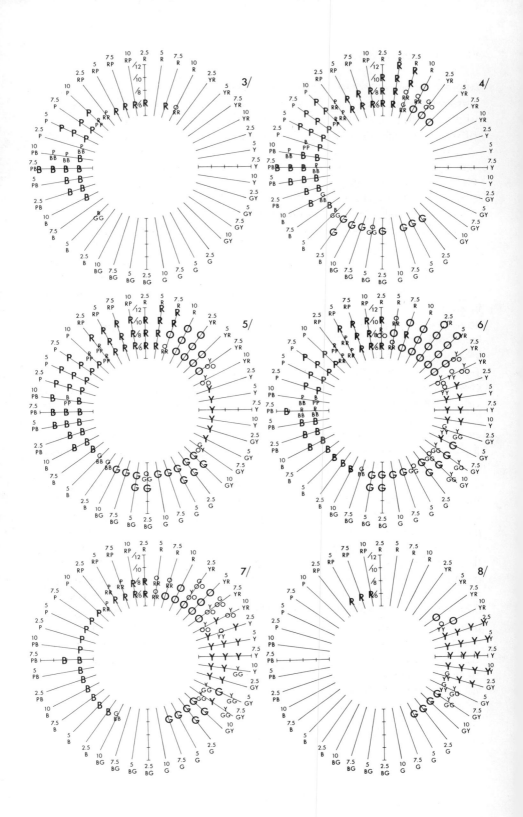

average of over 350 responses, it is extremely unlikely that Lana simply remembered that she had been reinforced for a given response in the past and made that response again. Rather, she appears to have her own notion of what key best describes a given color chip.

Lana's division of color space into clusters of color names can be compared to that of the human observers by contrasting Lana's data in Figure 2a with that of the humans in Figure 2b. The human data also show central and border areas that are very similar to Lana's responses at high brightness values (the upper rows of Figure 2a and 2b) but are less similar at lower brightness values. In responding to these darker colors, Lana was still consistently calling chips green whereas the humans in naming the same colors had already passed through the blue–green border area and were consistently calling chips blue. The human data appear somewhat less consistent than Lana's in that they have relatively larger border areas. But the humans were handicapped in that they were limited to using Lana's color terms; hence, they had to substitute alternative color terms for areas which we would normally call pink (such as the upper right-hand corner of the charts in Figure 2) or brown (such as the darker values of Munsell hues 5YR–2.5Y). Lana's data appear none the worse for the lack of these color terms; she consistently called red what we would call pink, and she called orange and yellow, respectively, those dark oranges and dark yellows that we would call brown.

As can be seen in any of the charts in Figure 1, Lana's names for a given hue appear to be very consistent across wide changes in the amount of the hue present (the chroma/saturation of the hue) for all brightness levels tested. The changes in color responses in the transition areas between one color name and another are not a function of saturation. In contrast to her consistency despite changes in saturation, Lana's responses suggest an *apparent* influence of changes in brightness: As a given hue was increased in brightness, its hue component appeared to shift toward the short-wavelength (blue) end of the spectrum (i.e., the shift is from red to orange and not from orange to red or a random mixture of orange and red). Such a shift cannot be accounted for simply by irregularities in the Munsell hue components because the corrected Munsell values (Newhall, Nickerson, & Judd, 1943) do not show any consistent shift in hue with increasing brightness. The shift more likely stems from the use of a light source in which all elements of the

Figure 1. Color naming responses for 40 hues at 4 saturation levels (Munsell chromas /6, /8, /10, /12) in six planes of constant brightness (Munsell values 3/, 4/, 5/, 6/, 7/, 8/). R = red, O = orange, Y = yellow, G = green, B = blue, P = purple. A single large letter indicates that all three responses were the color term that letter stands for. Groups of three smaller letters show the individual color responses made to a chip when responses to a chip varied on different occasions.

RED

PURPLE

BLUE

GREEN

G. G.

YELLOW

ORANGE

RED

10RP
7.5 RP
5RP
2.5 RP
10P
7.5 P
5P
2.5 P
10PB
7.5 PB
5PB
2.5 PB
10B
7.5 B
5B
2.5 B
10BG
7.5 BG
5BG
2.5 BG
10G
7.5 G
5G
2.5 G
10GY
7.5 GY
5GY
2.5 GY
10Y
7.5 Y
5Y
2.5 Y
10YR
7.5 YR
5YR
2.5 YR
10R
7.5 R
5R
2.5 R

(a)

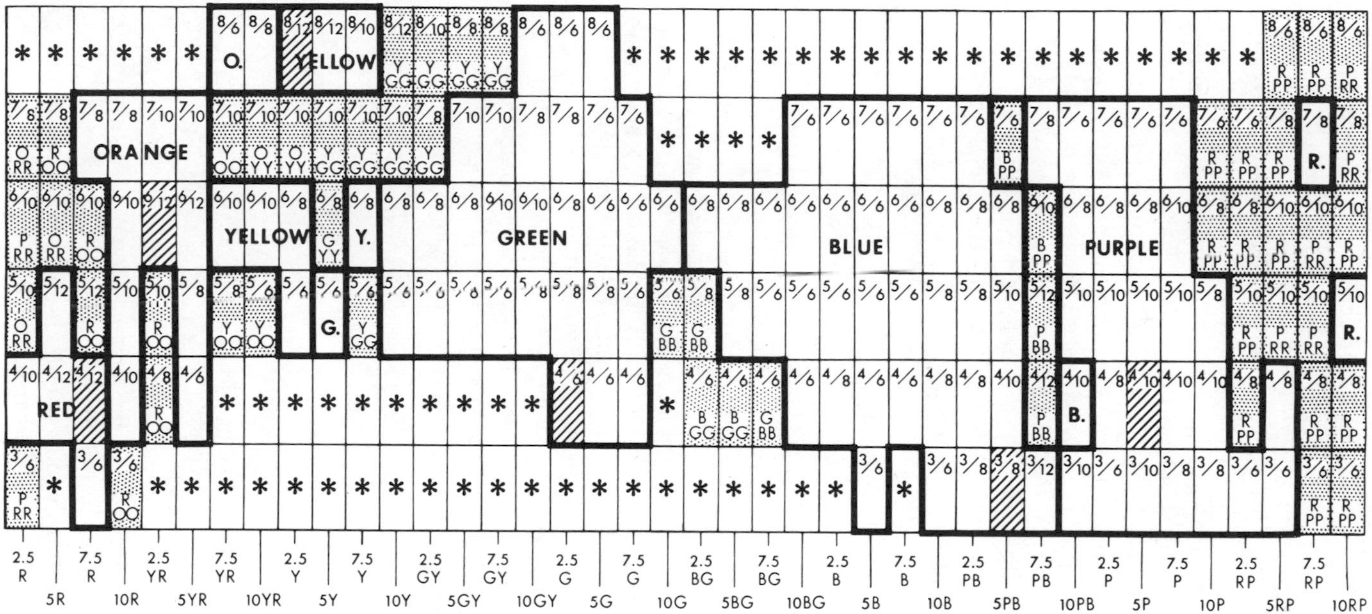

Figure 2. (a) Capital letters are the abbreviations for Lana's color responses to chips of maximum saturation for a given hue and brightness. Hue changes along the vertical axis and brightness increases along the horizontal axis. Individual rectangles represent individual color chips with maximum saturation value noted. Response abbreviations are given in the order in which they were obtained. An asterisk indicates that the *Munsell Book of Color* (1969 Edition) does not contain a chip of that particular hue at that brightness level. Cross hatched rectangles indicate training colors. Check marks indicate color samples used in Experiment II. (b) The same data for human observers.

217

visual spectrum were not equally represented. Any irregularities introduced by nonlinearities in the illuminant would be expected to increase with increasing brightness in a regular fashion and could produce an apparent regular hue shift with increasing brightness. The regularity of the shift strongly implicates the unfortunate lighting conditions as the cause, although it may also be that lines of constant hue as defined by the human visual system (the calibration source for the Munsell system) are not precisely lines of constant hue to the chimpanzee. Nor is the apparent hue shift a demonstration of the Bezold–Brücke effect (where increasing the brightness of a chromatic light source causes the light to appear increasingly like blue or yellow), since the Munsell system takes the Bezold–Brücke hue shift into account by spacing their slips using perceptual, and not physical, units.

EXPERIMENT II

Previous experiments (Heider, 1971, 1972) have demonstrated that "focal colors," those colors which are the best examples of a given color term, are more accurately recognized and matched than are nonfocal colors. This is true both in cultures that have color terms in their language and in those that do not (Heider, 1972), a finding that dealt a severe blow to the causal interpretations of the influence of language on cognition found in earlier studies. The second experiment examined whether Lana would show recognition differences between those colors that were in the central and those that were in the border areas of the color areas defined by Experiment I (Figure 2a). It was predicted that colors from the middle of the central areas would act like focal colors and would be more easily remembered by Lana than would colors from the border areas between areas of consistent color names.

Method

Subject

The subject, Lana, was 5 years old at the time of testing.

Apparatus

The experiment took place in the subject's room with the subject and the experimenter sitting on the bench described in Experiment I. The stimuli were three sets of matte-finish color samples ordered from the Munsell Color Company. The first set corresponded to the color samples most closely approximating Lana's training colors (red = 7.5R4/12, orange = 2.5YR6/12,

yellow = 2.5Y8/12, green = 2.5G4/6, blue = 5PB3/8, purple = 5P4/10).
The remaining two sets were composed of selected color samples that fell in
the center of the central areas of Experiment I plus selected samples that fell
in the border areas between areas of consistent color names in Experiment I.
These colors are marked with a check in Figure 2a. Where Lana's responding had been so consistent that central areas met without intermediate
border areas, a color from the outer portion of the central area was selected
as the border sample (Figure 2a, sample 10PB7/6). The samples within a set
were all of the same Munsell value (Munsell value 7 for the light set and
Munsell value 5 for the dark set). This assured that all samples were approximately equally bright so that no one stimulus would stand out from the
others on the basis of brightness alone. Standard 3-inch × 5-inch color
samples were cut into two 2.5-inch × 3-inch rectangles and encased in
clear plastic. The samples could be easily mounted and rearranged on a gray
(approximate Munsell notation N7/0) board. Half-inch squares of Velcro
fabric were used to secure the back of the color sample to various positions
on the board.

Procedure

Pretraining consisted of teaching Lana to match-to-sample using the
backs of three pairs from different decks of playing cards. Specifically, her
task was to point first to a sample card and then to that card which matched
the sample in a row of three alternatives. After each correct response she
was rewarded and the experimenter then rearranged the cards. After about 1
hour of training time, her performance was correct over 75% of the time.
Next she was required to point to a sample card held on one side of a 4-inch
× 9-inch board, after which the experimenter turned the board over revealing three different cards, and Lana was required to point to the card that
matched the sample. She transferred easily to this task, and training with the
Munsell colors then began.

In the next session Lana was required to match-to-sample using the
eight Munsell samples that most nearly matched her training colors. The
eight samples were shuffled and laid out on one side of the gray board in two
rows of three samples each and one row of two samples with a .5-inch space
between samples, and an identical set of eight samples was shuffled and
placed in a pile next to the experimenter. The experimenter selected the top
sample from the pile, pressed it to the middle of the other side of the board,
and held the single-sample side of the board about a foot away from Lana.
When Lana touched the sample, the experimenter turned the board over,
and Lana touched a color sample in the array. If correct, she was rewarded
with a small piece of fruit or an M&M candy; if not, the experimenter said
"No" and the next trial began. After each of the eight color samples had

served as the stimulus sample, the array of eight was reshuffled and the process was repeated. The series was repeated four times, and then testing began in the next session.

Testing

Testing consisted of presentation of series of the six central and six border color samples either of Munsell value 5 or of Munsell value 7, with one set of 12 different colors used per session. Within a series, the testing procedure was like that at the end of pretraining: The stimuli were shuffled and dealt out in a 3 × 4 array on one side of the gray board. Then the 12 samples were shuffled and presented one at a time by fastening one sample at a time to the reverse side of the stimulus board. Lana touched the sample, the board was turned, and she touched one of the samples in the array. This procedure was continued until each set of 12 colors had been presented 6 times.

Results

For the dark stimulus group, Lana correctly matched central colors 29 times out of 36 presentations, and she correctly matched border colors on 24 out of 36 presentations. For the light stimulus group, she was correct for central colors 21 out of 36 times and for border colors 20 out of 36 times. Although the results are in the predicted direction, they fail to reach significance (analysis of variance, no significant effect for stimulus location, brightness, or trials at the .05 rejection level).

DISCUSSION

In a sense, the LANA Project is a cross-cultural study that also happens to cross family lines (*Hominidae* to *Pongidae*). The data gathered from Lana may be a function of her physiology as a chimpanzee, of her experiences in the Lana project, or some combination of the two. Clearly, either source may be enormously influential. Lana can both interact with humans via the linguistic-type communication she has acquired from her special training (as, for example, when she requested, *? you give apple which-is orange* when an orange was brought into view), and she can communicate like any other chimpanzee (as by hooting when she spies a preferred food).

Lana has demonstrated that she does possess sufficient cognitive capabilities to assimilate and adopt arbitrary codes, and that she uses these codes to describe her world as she sees it. Three separate aspects of Experiment I support this conclusion. First, Lana's assignment of color names to various areas of color-space did *not* produce areas identified by a given color term surrounding the training color for that term with random responding at areas perceptually distant from the training colors. We would expect such a result if her responses represented simple stimulus generalization (with accompanying response generalization) from her training colors. In reality, however, her responses formed well-defined areas identified by the various color terms, and the locations where her training colors fell did not often correspond to the center of the areas called by the various color terms. Her training colors for red and orange fell near the edge of their respective central areas, indicating that her training color for red was nearly orange to her, as was her training color for yellow (Figure 2a). The human data strongly support her opinion (Figure 2b), providing further evidence that the color perception of humans is very similar to that of chimpanzees and that the color space for each is naturally divisible into nonarbitrary areas of perceived similarities (reddish areas, bluish areas, etc.).

Second, Lana's great regularity in giving consistent color names to central and border hues regardless of great changes in brightness or saturation suggests that her color names are codes for hue attributes and not just names for specific physical stimuli. Particularly impressive is her reliable differentiation between yellows and oranges at low saturation and brightness levels (Figure 1c); these stimuli are all what we would call brown.

The third type of evidence supporting Lana's use of her color terms as conceptual codes comes from the observation that only two color names ever competed as a response for a given color chip, and that these color names were always the names for spectrally adjacent hues. This finding indicates that a border color received different responses on different presentations because the chip *looked* two colors (a greenish blue or a reddish orange, for example) and not because it was an unfamiliar color and she was guessing among one of six possible alternatives.

Interpretation of the lack of a difference in border versus central color recognition in Experiment II should be held in abeyance. Such differences are expected when highly saturated colors are used (Heider, 1972) but not for desaturated colors (Burnham & Clark, 1955). The stimuli used in Experiment II were at maximum saturation for the color chips of the 1969 edition of the *Munsell Book of Color,* but the outer-shell stimuli (those of maximum saturation for a given hue and brightness) vary from one edition of the Munsell book to another, and all of Heider's (1972) stimuli were more highly saturated than those used here. Also, the prediction of differences in recognition of central versus border colors rests on the assumption that the center of Lana's central areas should be focal colors (the best examples of a given color term). This assumption is probably close to true since the maps of Lana's central areas do resemble the focal areas of Berlin and Kay's (1969)

Stage IV populations. Berlin and Kay asked their subjects to look at an array of colors and to pick the best example of a given color term. Now that evidence exists that Lana does code colors into perceptual units, her focal colors can be determined following the Berlin and Kay method.

Munsell color samples provide a convenient way to investigate color perception without requiring elaborate optical systems, which frequently can provide hues over only limited brightness and saturation ranges. But the Munsell stimuli only approximate the Munsell ideal of precisely specifying colors along dimensions consisting of psychologically equally spaced units. A Munsell renotation system has been devised so that the redefined loci of constant hue, brightness, and saturation more nearly approximate the ideal (Newhall, Nickerson, & Judd, 1955), but claims of equal hue, saturation, or brightness can be met only when the proper illuminant is used. The proper illuminant is CIE illuminant C, which is cheaply approximated by use of G.E. Daylight fluorescent bulbs but *not* by the use of the G.E. Warm White or Cool White bulbs used here. Since the conclusions of this study rest on the relative aspects of color—color name changes with changes in hue, brightness, or saturation—and not on absolute estimates of hue, brightness, or saturation, the stimuli and illuminant used here were sufficient for the purpose of this study. And since the humans were tested under the same lighting conditions, it is also reasonable to compare their data with Lana's data. Fortunately, Lana's new quarters (she moved in January, 1976) have improved lighting conditions, which should allow for a finer evaluation of her color perception.

Many interesting chimpanzee color-perception questions still remain. For instance, if Lana were limited to only the color terms blue, yellow, red, and green, would she expand the central areas for these four primary colors to incorporate the areas for orange and purple? Humans do this (Boynton & Gordon, 1965; Sternheim & Boynton, 1966), indicating that we use some color terms (e.g., orange, purple, pink, brown) out of convenience even though they do not describe primary sensations. Does Lana see purple and orange as being composed, or as primary colors?

The present study rests on the data of only one subject because only one subject is currently available. As new subjects are brought into the project, it will be interesting to observe how their central and border areas overlap with Lana's if they are given the same training colors. Likewise it will be interesting to see what their division of color space will look like if they are given training colors that fall within Lana's central areas but are relatively distant from her training colors (e.g., a greenish yellow rather than an orangish yellow). The divisions of color space should be very similar irrespective of the exact location of the training colors if the chimpanzees' training gives them a means of coding areas that are perceptually most salient prior to any language-like training, as is the case with humans (Heider, 1972). Even a small group of such chimpanzees, when compared to a group of nonlinguistically trained chimpanzees, could provide a rich source of data on the relative contributions to perception of experience, cognitive skills, and physiology.

IMPLICATIONS AND CONCLUSIONS

Data from a single subject should certainly be interpreted with caution. The presence of categorical perception in chimpanzees can be inferred with greater certainty only after research with additional subjects trained with different training colors has been carried out, and only after evidence of differential response latencies between central and border areas has been found. Such studies are planned. Still, the present findings are sufficient to conclude that Lana does possess sufficient cognitive capabilities to assimilate arbitrary codes, and that she uses these codes to describe her world as she sees it.

REFERENCES

Berlin, B., & Kay, P. *Basic color terms: Their universality and evolution.* Berkeley: University of California Press, 1969.

Bornstein, M. H. Color vision and color naming. *Psychological Bulletin,* 1973, *80,* 257–285.

Bornstein, M. H., Kessen, W., & Weiskopf, S. The categories of hue in infancy. *Science,* 1976, *191,* 201–202.

Boynton, R. M., & Gordon, J. Bezold–Brücke hue shift measured by a color-naming technique. *Journal of the Optical Society of America,* 1965, *55,* 78–86.

Brown, R. W., & Lenneberg, E. A study in language and cognition. *Journal of Abnormal and Social Psychology,* 1954, *49,* 454–462.

Burnham, R. W., & Clark, J. R. A test of hue memory. *Journal of Applied Psychology,* 1955, *39,* 164–172.

DeValois, R. L. Behavioral and electrophysiological studies of primate vision. In W. D. Neff (Ed.), *Contributions to sensory psychology* (Vol. 1). New York: Academic Press, 1965.

DeValois, R. L., Abramov, I., & Jacobs, G. H. Analysis of response patterns of LGN cells. *Journal of the Optical Society of America,* 1966, *56,* 966–977.

Gill, T. V., & Rumbaugh, D. M. Mastery of naming skills by a chimpanzee. *Journal of Human Evolution,* 1974, *3,* 483–492.

Grether, W. F. Chimpanzee color vision. I. Hue discrimination at three spectral points. *Journal of Comparative and Physiological Psychology,* 1940, *29,* 167–177. (a)

Grether, W. F. Chimpanzee color vision. II. Color mixture proportions. *Journal of Comparative and Physiological Psychology,* 1940, *29,* 179–186. (b)

Grether, W. F. Chimpanzee color vision. III. Spectral limits. *Journal of Comparative and Physiological Psychology,* 1940, *29,* 187–192. (c)

Heider, E. R. "Focal" color areas and the development of color names. *Developmental Psychology,* 1971, *4,* 447–455.

Heider, E. R. Universals in color naming and memory. *Journal of Experimental Psychology,* 1972, *93,* 10–20.

Hurvich, L., & Jameson, D. Opponent processes as a model of neural organization. *American Psychologist,* 1974, *29,* 88–102.

Newhall, S., Nickerson, D., & Judd, D. Final report of the O. S. A. Subcommittee on the spacing of Munsell colors. *Journal of the Optical Society of America,* 1943, *33,* 385–418.

Riesen, A. H. Chimpanzee visual perception. In G. Bourne (Ed.), *The chimpanzee* (Vol. 2). Basel/New York: Karger, 1970.

Rumbaugh, D. M., von Glasersfeld, E. C., Warner, H., Pisani, P., Gill, T., Brown, J. V., & Bell, C. L. A computer-controlled language training system for investigating the language skills of young apes. *Behavior Research Methods and Instrumentation,* 1973, *5,* 385–392.

Sternheim, O. E., & Boynton, R. M. Uniqueness of perceived hues investigated with a continuous judgement technique. *Journal of Experimental Psychology,* 1966, *72,* 770–776.

Whorf, B. *Language, thought, and reality.* Cambridge: M.I.T. Press, 1956.

chapter **12**

Conversations with Lana

TIMOTHY V. GILL

*Yerkes Regional Primate Research Center, and
Georgia State University*

One of the major functions of language is the exchange of information between individuals. This exchange takes place in what is normally called the conversation in which "(1) there must be a linguistic-type of exchange between two beings, (2) there must be novelty in at least one of the communications transmitted by each of the two beings, and (3) the topic or subject of the exchange must remain relatively organized and constant across time [Rumbaugh & Gill, 1976]."

Typical outcomes of a conversation include the exchange of information and/or the obtaining of a goal by one (or both) of the individuals involved. The initiator of a conversation presumably starts the conversation with some goal in mind, and, likewise, the recipient of that information is also presumed to have a goal when in turn responding to the initiator. Within a conversation, the goal(s) must be known by both parties. To the extent that one member lacks such knowledge, the conversation will persist on a route directed at establishing knowledge of the goal in the naive individual. When this is accomplished, the direction of the conversation can shift to obtaining the goal.

Another possible impediment in establishing a conversation is a lack of concurrence between the individuals involved concerning the meanings of the words being used. "Meaning" here refers to agreements about what the signs (words) being used represent, since words are actually referents for the private symbols of the individual (Rumbaugh & Gill, 1976). Only when concurrence as to both meaning and goal has been obtained among all members of a conversation can the conversation proceed with maximal ease and speed toward attainment of the desired goal by the initiating member of the conversation.

During a conversation, irrelevant information, or information that does not pertain to the subject at hand, is normally discarded, at least temporarily. Central to the question of relevance is the motivational state of the individual receiving the information. For example, a person entering a bar to buy a drink would probably disregard an attempt by another person to engage him in a discussion of the economy before he had obtained his drink, but he might be keenly attentive if asked what kind of drink he wanted. Drink in hand, however, he might well warm to the topic of economics. If it is relevant, then, novel information is attended to and utilized in a conversation to the extent that it facilitates obtaining the desired goal.

Research aimed at understanding the parameters of conversation per se has received little attention in the past. McNeill in 1970 and McCarthy in 1954 wrote excellent reviews of language development, but neither dealt with the role of conversation. Conversations have been studied extensively in linguistic research, but usually with the sole purpose of understanding topics relating to syntax and, more recently, semantics. Pease and Arnold (1973), using a modified version of Miller and Selfridge's (1950) "approximations to English" dialogue, generated dialogues of utterances and investigated the plausibility of the dialogues relative to each other. This research represented an attempt to assess the role of contextual constraints in conversation, and did not concern itself with the role of connected discourse in the communication of wants and needs. Yet conversation is primarily a goal-oriented, problem-solving activity. In a problem situation the individual will generally be forced to rely on past experience, but frequently will also be forced to reason, combining past experiences in a new way so that the problem at hand can be solved. Only if reasoning is present can the highest form of linguistic exchange, the conversation, take place.

Lana, the subject involved in the present experiment, had been in her linguistic-type environment for approximately 2 years when the experiments began. During these 2 years, Lana had been partner with me in a number of linguistic exchanges that can be called conversations; each was directed toward solving a particular problem that confronted Lana. On one occasion, for example, she wanted an orange but did not have the word in her vocabulary (see Chapter 9, this volume; also Rumbaugh & Gill, 1975). When I refused to accept her substitution of the word *this* for "orange," she modified the name of a fruit which was in her vocabulary (apple) and asked for the *apple which-is orange* (color). (At the time she made this statement, Lana had the names for a number of other edible items as well as seven other color terms in her vocabulary.) At a later date she asked for the same object by describing its position relative to a bowl: *? You give this in bowl.*

All of these conversations had two features in common: They were aimed at solving a particular problem Lana was experiencing and they were impromptu. No prearranged procedures were utilized to determine the conditions necessary to initiate a conversation between Lana and the experimenter or to identify possible sources of confusion that might arise in such a conversation. I knew from experience, of course, that if I had something Lana desired, a conversation would be likely to ensue. The course of that conversation, however, and the degree to which changing conditions might modify it were unknown.

The study to be reported here was undertaken specifically to explore some of the parameters of conversation. Specifically, I planned to introduce into Lana's daily routine a series of misrepresentations of truth and other problem situations that would enable Lana to show the extent of her ability to deal with problems that interfere with the attainment of desired goals.

In addition, because the conversation is a central form of linguistic communication, a second aim of the study was to discover whether or not Lana actually possessed the ability to converse. To what extent can a chimpanzee with no natural language system of its own learn an artificial language and use it in conversational problem solving? To the degree that evidence of these skills could be found in Lana, support would be given for the thesis that humans are not alone in their potential to communicate linguistically.

EXPERIMENT I

Method

Subject

Lana, the subject of this experiment, was 4.5 years old at the time of testing. She had been involved in the language-training situation for approximately 2 years when testing began, and had become totally dependent on her linguistic capabilities for all of her nourishment and for any other stimulation that she might desire (e.g., movies, music, or companionship).

Apparatus

The apparatus (including the keyboards and the language) has been described in detail in Chapters 5 and 7.

Procedure See Figure 1 for a schematic of the procedure.

Part A: Enticement. Three alternative methods were used to entice Lana into conversation:

1. The experimenter (Tim) would enter the area adjacent to Lana's room (the anteroom) where his keyboard was located and ask Lana the following question: *? Lana want what drink.*
2. The experimenter would enter the anteroom with either a food or a drink with which Lana was acquainted and hold it in front of her glass door where she could readily see it.
3. The experimenter would enter the anteroom and ask Lana the following question: *? Lana want what eat.*

Only one of these three alternatives was used during a given session. Sessions were held twice daily at the normal feeding times (9:30 a.m. and 4:30 p.m.) for 16 days. The order of presenting the alternatives was randomized with the restriction that each alternative be offered at least 10 times within the 16-day period.

These three alternatives were chosen because they were the normal means whereby Lana and the experimenter engaged in conversation. The information was familiar to both parties, and presumably one of the goals of the exchange was also known by both. Both Lana and I knew Lana's goal was to obtain her ration of food. Of course my goal was usually quite different from Lana's; I was interested in obtaining a novel communication from Lana.

Although the second alternative, holding familiar food or drink within Lana's view, had already provided the occasion for a number of remarkable exchanges with Lana, only the first and third alternatives had been utilized extensively with her, and they, in fact, constituted integral parts of her daily routine. Normally Lana was asked *? Lana want what drink* only in the morning when she obtained her usual serving of milk and likewise was asked *? Lana want what eat* only at other times during the day, usually in late afternoon when she received her daily ration of Monkey Chow. Through the subsequent presentation of each of these three alternatives at random it was hoped that the degree to which a normal daily routine could be utilized as an experimental paradigm could be determined. It was expected that when Lana's goal and the question or situation corresponded to each other,

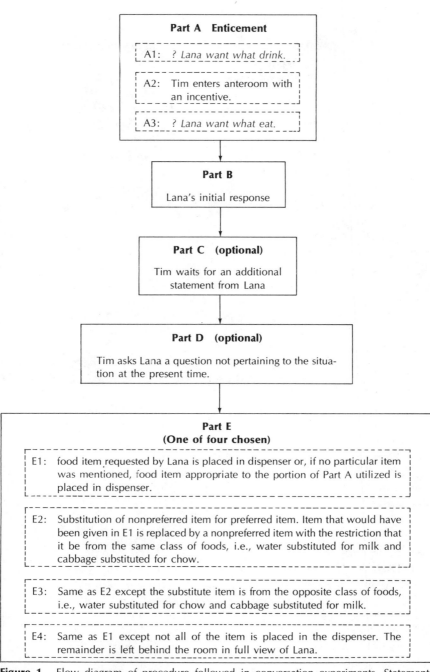

Figure 1. Flow diagram of procedure followed in conversation experiments. Statements enclosed by dashed lines indicate alternative forms of the same part of the experiment. Only one was utilized in any one session. Parts indicated as optional appeared in half of the test sessions. When absent, the experiment flowed on to the next part immediately.

the ensuing conversation would be relatively brief. When they differed (e.g., if she were asked if she wanted to eat when it was morning and normally the time for milk), a more prolonged conversation was predicted.

Part B: Lana's Initial Response. This part involved only Lana's initial response to one of the three conditions presented to her in Part A. This was of course the most crucial part, for if a conversation was to take place at all, Lana had to make an initial response to the question or situation presented to her. There was no doubt that simply eliciting an initial response from Lana when the circumstances involved food or drink would not be a problem, because she is always ready to eat or drink. However, several questions concerning the nature of her initial response remained to be answered.

One question was whether Lana's initial response would be directly related to the immediate question or situation or to the goal toward which she was oriented. For example, Lana normally drinks milk in the morning. To what extent might she differentiate between the two questions used in Parts A-1 and A-3? Given the question *? Lana want what eat* in the morning, would she respond *Lana want eat chow* or *Lana want drink milk?* Conversely, if presented with milk or alternative 1 in the afternoon, would she simply ask that it be given to her, or would the milk stimulus serve to motivate her to ask for Monkey Chow, her normal afternoon food? Another question was whether Lana would confine her answer to the situation at hand, i.e., eating or drinking, or whether she would respond by depressing keys at random from among the 90 active keys on her keyboard.

Part C. This part called for me to pause after Lana's initial response *until* she had typed out an additional message to me. Part C was included only in half of the sessions: When it was omitted, the experiment moved directly from Part B to Part D. Thus, after having been asked either of the two questions in Part A and having responded appropriately with *Lana want eat/drink* (item) *period,* Lana would normally proceed in Part C to ask that the item in question be placed in the food dispenser so that she could obtain it by asking the machine for it. For example, after responding *Lana want drink milk period,* Lana would then ask *? You put milk in machine period* to which the experimenter would respond *Yes period* and place milk in the dispenser. Lana would then obtain the milk by repeatedly requesting *Please machine give milk period.* With each request she received several ounces of milk. Part C, then, allowed Lana to request that a specific item be placed in a vending device or be given to her. The omission of this part afforded her no such choice.

Part D. This part was also omitted in half of the test sessions. When utilized, it involved two responses on the part of the experimenter and one from Lana. My first response was to answer *Yes* either to whatever Lana had responded with in Part C (if it was utilized) or to Lana's initial response in

Part B. I then followed my affirmative response by asking Lana one of two types of questions. Regardless of type, the questions were all such that an affirmative answer to any of them would lead to interference with Lana's obtaining her goal. The first type of question concerned the occurrence of an event controlled by the computer. For example, after responding *Yes* to Lana's request that milk be put in the machine (Part C), I would ask a question such as ? *Lana want machine make window open.* Should Lana answer *Yes* to this question, I would instruct the computer to open the window, a procedure that would "tie up" the computer for 2.5 minutes. (At the time of this study the computer was "dedicated" to doing one thing at a time: That is, it would hold the window open for as long as it was programmed to and during that time would do nothing else. Apparently Lana was aware of this fact since she would often request that the window be opened when she became frustrated with a particular task that the experimenter was working on with her, and thus she herself would "tie up" the computer. When caused unintentionally, however, such a delay would indeed be unfortunate for a chimpanzee who depends on a computer for her food.) The other type of question concerned my moving to someplace other than the anteroom. For example, I might ask ? *Lana want Tim move into room.* If answered affirmatively, this question would keep me from placing the desired food in the dispenser since I would enter Lana's room instead. When utilized, these two types of questions were presented in a random order with the restriction that each would appear in half of the scheduled sessions. Thus, whenever Lana discerned what was being asked of her and answered appropriately, her goal of obtaining food would be at least 2.5 minutes closer.

Part E. The fifth and final phase, involving systematic manipulation of the course of conversation, contained four alternatives. The first alternative (E-1) involved placing in Lana's food dispenser the item that had been referred to in the preceding parts of the session. If Lana had not mentioned a particular item, either the item normal to that time of day (milk in the morning, chow in the afternoon) or the item appropriate to the question being asked (chow for ? *Lana want what eat* and milk for ? *Lana want what drink*) was placed in the food dispenser. In this alternative, then, milk and monkey chow were the only two items possible unless a particular item had been mentioned by Lana.

The second alternative (E-2) was to substitute an item for the one that would have been given in E-1, with the restriction that the item substituted had to be of the same class. Water was used as a substitute for any liquid, and cabbage was substituted for all solid foods. Lana would consume both of these substitutes, but, unlike milk and chow, they were not among her favorites.

The third alternative (E-3) was analogous to the second, except that the restriction called for the substitute to be taken from the opposite class of ingestibles. Thus water was substituted for any solid food, and cabbage was substituted for any liquid.

The fourth alternative (E-4) was a modification of the first alternative. The item requested or called for was put in the dispenser, but not all of it was made available for Lana to consume. The remainder was placed in full view of Lana behind her room in the general area of the vending devices.

It was predicted that when E-1 was the alternative for a given session and Part A had not called for any manipulations, Lana would be fully satisfied, since her normal routine would have been maintained. For example, if she were asked if she wanted to drink in the morning and subsequently obtained all of her milk, then it was predicted that the conversation with the experimenter would cease, and communication with the computer would begin. If Part A called for a manipulation and Part E-1 was to follow later, then the conversation should be longer since Lana's normal routine would be disrupted.

The second and third alternatives were, in fact, deliberate prevarications on my part, at least when Parts C and D were included in the session. That is, if Lana asked for milk to be put in her dispenser (Part C) and I responded *Yes period* (Part D), but then substituted water or cabbage for milk, then I had lied to her. Both of these alternatives were expected to prolong the conversation because they would frustrate Lana's attempt to obtain her original goal.

It was predicted that the final alternative would satisfy Lana at least for the moment, but that the conversation would persist, being interrupted only during the time necessary for Lana to consume that portion of the food initially given to her. After the initial ration was consumed, Lana would see the remainder, and the original conversation would resume with Lana's request that *more* be put in the dispenser (which would, of course, be done).

After completion of Part E, the final phase of the session took place. This phase involved no predetermined manipulations. Rather, it consisted of open and free-flowing conversation, the subject of which was determined at the end of Part E. The goal in this part was to respond initially to a question/statement/request by Lana in a manner that would re-engage Lana in a conversation. For example, after Lana had been lied to in Part E-2, perhaps the conversation would concern that event, or perhaps Lana would re-engage the experimenter in a conversation concerning what had just occurred and/or her original goal. To say that I had no idea how Lana would respond in this final phase, particularly on occasions after she had been lied to, is not an understatement. It was predicted, however, that she would be noticeably upset when a change as in Parts E-2 and E-3 was made.

Results

Part A: Enticement, and
Part B: Lana's Initial Response

It was predicted that Lana would discern the differences between the questions asked of her and answer them accordingly. It was not known, however, how she would do this. Dividing the overall experiment into two sections, one consisting of those questions or situations appropriate to the time of day and the other consisting of the inappropriate questions, revealed no significant differences between the mean number of exchanges or the mean duration of the sessions. (Exchanges here refers to a statement/ question by Lana or me followed by an appropriate response to that question/statement by the recipient of it. The duration of the session refers to the total time in the session in minutes excluding any time spent consuming food.)

Part A, of course, is not meaningful without a consideration of Part B, Lana's initial response. Taken together, these two parts indicate Lana's ability to read the question posed to her and to decide upon a course of action. In all instances in which the question or situation was appropriate to the time of day, Lana's initial response was correct, and in 9 of the 11 sessions starting with inappropriate questions, she was again very accurate. Her responses to these inappropriate questions were of major importance because these responses held the greatest promise for revealing her linguistic abilities. In three of the first four occasions when she was asked an inappropriate question, Lana answered the question appropriately with a response which suited it; e.g., if asked *? Lana want what eat* in the morning, she responded *Lana want eat bread period.* As already mentioned, Lana normally drinks milk and has no solid food in the morning. Upon being asked an inappropriate question, on these occasions, however, she correctly answered the question posed to her with an appropriate response. In six of the seven remaining sessions in which inappropriate questions were asked, Lana modified the question each time. In four of these sessions she simply negated the idea of performing the inappropriate action suggested to her by the experimenter. For example:

TIM: *? Lana want what drink.* (Part A, in the afternoon, her normal time for solid food.)
LANA: *No Lana want drink.*

In two of the other sessions, her responses to the inappropriate questions can be taken as declarations of her real wish. For example:

TIM: *? Lana want what eat.* (Part A, in the morning, her normal time for
         liquids.)
LANA: *Lana want drink.*

or alternatively,

TIM: *? Lana want what drink.* (Part A, in the afternoon, her normal time
         for solid food.)
LANA: *Lana want drink* (pause) *eat chow.* (She corrected herself in mid-
         sentence after pausing for several seconds.)

Both error responses were probably a result of Lana not attending to the
question posed. For example:

TIM: *? Lana want what drink.* (Part A, in the afternoon, her normal time
         for solid food.)
LANA: *Lana want drink chow in machine.*

Here she started off correctly *(Lana want drink)* but completed the sentence
with an inappropriate object (chow is not to be drunk).

Part C

This portion of the experiment provided an opportunity for Lana to
request that a specific item be placed in the vending device either so that she
could consume it (when Part B was used to answer one of the two questions
that could be asked in Part A) or as a restatement of Part B when Part B had
been used to request that the item shown to her be placed in the vending
device. Lana correctly utilized this opportunity 14 of the 16 times it occurred
(88% right). An error was defined as a response that did not follow logically
from the preceding statement made by her. The two errors she made are of
interest here because in conjunction with her request in Part B they indicate
a desire for her normal food.

TIM: *? Lana want what eat.* (Part A, in the morning.)
LANA: *Lana want eat bread.* (Part B, appropriate to Part A.)
LANA: *? You put milk in machine.* (Part C, inappropriate to Part B re-
         sponse.)

Likewise:

TIM: *? Lana want what drink.* (Part A, in the afternoon.)
LANA: *Lana want drink juice.* (Part B, appropriate to Part A.)

LANA: *? You put chow in machine.* (Part C, inappropriate to her response
         in Part B.)

These two "errors" occurred in the third and fourth instances of the C
condition after which point Lana employed the following strategy: (see
Figure 2 for a schematic.)

   1. Given Part A-1 or A-3 normal to the time of day, Part B was used to
answer the question, and Part C was used to ask that the particular item
mentioned in her response in Part B be placed in the machine. For example:

   TIM: *? Lana want what drink.* (Part A, in the morning.)
   LANA: *Lana want drink milk.* (Part B, appropriate to Part A.)
   LANA: *? You put milk in machine.* (Part C, appropriate to her response in
           Part B.)

   2. Given Part A-2 (food present, no question), Part B was used to ask

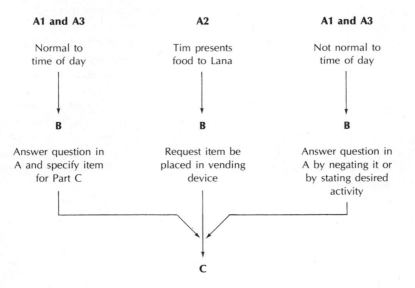

Request item be placed in vending device:

? You put (item) *in machine.*

Figure 2.   Possible paths Lana could take to arrive at same statement in Part C. What is said by
Lana in Part B is determined by the conditions prevailing in Part A. Statement in Part C can
therefore be repetitive (middle route), partially repetitive (left branch, where "item" had been
mentioned in B), or novel (right branch, where B was used to negate A or state desired activity).

that the item present be placed in the machine, and Part C was a repetition of the response in Part B. For example:

TIM: (Stands in front of Lana's door, holding a bowl of Monkey Chow.)
LANA: *? You put chow in machine.* (Part B, appropriate to the situation.)
LANA: *? You put chow in machine.* (Part C)

(Perhaps the repetition was made by Lana to make sure I saw what she responded with in Part B.)

3. Given A-1 or A-3 inappropriate to the time of day, Part B was used to correct the situation established by Part A (by negating the question posed or by stating her own desire), and Part C was used as a request that the normal item be placed in the vending device.

Part D: Asking a Question of Lana Not Directly Related to the Situation at Hand

This part served to explore Lana's capacity to discriminate between the questions being asked of her and also the factors related to engaging her attention. Five different questions were used in all, and these questions took one of two forms: *? Lana want machine make* (event) or *? Lana want Tim move* (location). The possible events were *music* and *window open,* and the possible locations were *out-of-room, into room,* and *behind room.* Half the questions were of the first type and half of the second type. The answer to any of these questions should have been *No.* An affirmative answer to questions of the first type "tied up" the computer, and an affirmative answer to questions of the second type resulted in the experimenter's doing something other than placing Lana's food in the vending device. Lana was correct seven out of eight times in responding to questions of the first type and only four out of eight times in responding to questions of the second type. All of her incorrect responses to questions of the second type were confined to questions involving the directional preposition *out-of.*

Part E: Food Manipulation

Devising a means to analyze conversations is obviously a complex problem; however, an analysis in terms of what was predicted beforehand was feasible. The major manipulation of this experiment was confined to Part E in which procedure dictated that either the normal feeding pattern for the time of day or for the question asked be adhered to (Parts E-1 and E-4) or a substitution be made (Parts E-2 and E-3).

Since conversations are goal-directed activities, it was predicted that once Lana had obtained the desired item the conversation with the experimenter would end, and Lana would begin addressing the computer in order to obtain the food that was loaded into the vending machine. Because this sequence of events occurred in a straightforward manner in Parts E-1 and E-4, the probability that an extended conversation would take place in these parts was assumed to be low. Conversely, since the attainment of the presumably desired item is interfered with in Parts E-2 and E-3, the probability that an extended conversation would take place in either of these parts was assumed to be high.

Accordingly, the conversations were divided into two groups: those with a relatively low probability of being extended (Parts E-1 and E-4, the low-probability groups) and those with a relatively high probability of being extended (Parts E-2 and E-3, the high-probability groups). Two measures of extension were used: duration in minutes and number of exchanges. The initial statement/question in an exchange could be in the form of a problem situation (e.g., me entering the room with a desired item) or a question directed to Lana through the language system (e.g., ? *Lana want what eat*). The answer was always through the language system (e.g., ? *You put chow in machine*, if I had entered the room with a bowl of Monkey Chow). In calculating the duration of the session, time spent actively obtaining the normal food was included, but time spent by Lana to consume food was not. When conditions C and/or D were included, the duration of the session was necessarily longer; however, since these conditions were balanced across both the high- and low-probability groups, the additional time required to complete these parts was constant.

The results of this analysis are given in Table 1. Tests of significance between the means of the low- and high-probability sessions revealed significant differences in both duration of conversation and number of exchanges ($p < .01$). As would be predicted, a significant correlation was found between duration and number of exchanges ($r = .94$, $p < .01$).

It is also possible to construct a ratio of number of exchanges to

Table 1

MEAN DURATION, MEAN NUMBER OF EXCHANGES, RANGES, AND STANDARD DE-VIATIONS FOR THE LOW- AND HIGH-PROBABILITY SESSIONS

	Low		High	
	Duration (min)	Exchanges	Duration (min)	Exchanges
Mean	3.0	3.38	12.56	12
Range	1–14	1–11	3–32	2–39
SD	1.8	2.85	8.12	11.07
Number of sessions	16		16	

duration in minutes to obtain a measure of constancy of exchange rate across the two types of sessions. For the overall experiment the ratios were 1.13 exchanges per minute for the low-probability sessions and 1.00 exchanges per minute for the high-probability sessions.

Visual inspection of the data revealed that Lana appeared to be taking considerably longer to obtain her goal toward the end of the experiments than she had at the beginning. It was therefore decided to divide the experiment into two sections, one containing the first 16 sessions and the other the remaining 16 sessions. The results are given in Table 2.

Tests of significance between first-half and last-half scores revealed that in the high-probability sessions the mean number of exchanges was significantly greater ($p < .01$) in the second half of the experiment than in the first. In addition, the mean duration in the high-probability sessions increased from the first to the second half of the study, although this difference fell just short of significance ($.05 < p < .06$). Likewise, the ratio of exchanges/duration increased from the first to the second half in both the low- and high-probability groups, indicating that an increased amount of information was being exchanged within a constant amount of time.

Within each half of the experiment, the differences between the high and low groups with respect to mean duration and mean number of exchanges were significant at the .05 level, except for the difference in the mean number of exchanges in the first half of study (3.0 exchanges and 6.13 exchanges for the low and high groups, respectively).

By dividing the conversations into low- and high-probability groups on the basis of reward conditions, it was possible to predict the duration of the conversation. That is, when Lana was given a reward different from the normal or from what she had requested, the conversation should have been prolonged until the desired item was obtained. In all but one session, the conversation, did, in fact, persist until the normal or desired item was ob-

Table 2

MEAN DURATIONS, MEAN NUMBER OF EXCHANGES, AND RATES OF EXCHANGE PER MINUTE FOR THE FIRST AND SECOND HALVES OF EXPERIMENT I

	Mean duration	Mean no. exchanges	Rate/minute	Number of sessions
First Half				
Low	3.88	3.00	.77	8
High	9.13	6.13	.67	8
Second Half				
Low	2.13	3.75	1.76	8
High	16.00	17.88	1.12	8

tained. Under these conditions Lana could obtain the normal or desired item in only one way: She had to tell me that she knew a switch had been made. I could easily tell through facial expressions and the state of piloerection when Lana was upset. During the experiment, however, Lana could communicate her desire that the contents of the vending devices be changed only through her keyboard. Not until the last session in which a switch was made (cabbage for chow) did Lana stop short of obtaining her desired incentive. She ate a few bites of cabbage (by requesting *Please machine give piece of cabbage period*), then stopped working altogether and refused to answer any questions from me for over an hour.

In all five instances in which water was substituted for the normal or requested item, Lana requested that the water be removed. For example, in the first session in which water was substituted for chow, Lana responded as follows: *? You move water out-of machine.* I responded *Yes* and removed the water. Lana then continued with *? You put chow in machine,* to which I responded *Yes,* and the conversation ended. (This time chow was put into the machine.) Lana's request that the water be removed was novel; she had not been trained to ask that things be removed from various locations, and her only previous use of *out-of* had been in relation to moving herself *out-of* her room. On three occasions she had also asked that cabbage be removed from the machine; however, she had chosen to eat the cabbage on the other occasions rather than prolong the conversation. (Perhaps eating the cabbage was preferable to haggling with me over its presence.) The fifth time cabbage was placed in the machine, Lana responded to the question: *? What in machine* with *Tim put cabbage in machine,* a statement she was to repeat in a later conversation under similar conditions. In both sessions, this statement was followed by a request that the cabbage be removed from the vending device.

An important point to be made here is that in *every* instance in which a substitution was made, Lana acknowledged that fact. As the following statements will demonstrate, her acknowledgments did not always take the same form, but each one reflected her awareness of the presence of one item not normal to the time of day or the question asked by me:

1. *Please machine give piece of cabbage.* (6 sessions. A request for the item substituted from the machine.)

2. *? You move water out-of machine.* (5 sessions. A request that the substituted item be removed.)

3. *Tim put cabbage in machine.* (2 sessions. A statement of the obvious.)

4. *No chow in machine.*   (1 session. Another state-
                                                ment of the obvious.)

5. *No juice. Water in milk.*   (1 session. A statement
                                                that water had been
                                                placed in the milk dis-
                                                penser.)

6. *? You move cabbage out-of machine.*   (3 sessions. A request that
                                                the substituted item be
                                                removed.)

7. *? You move machine out-of room.*   (1 session. A request
                                                made after water had
                                                been placed in the
                                                "machine.")

In some instances Lana made two "awareness" statements in the same session.

In all sessions in which all of the normal item was loaded into the vending device in the course of a conversation, the conversation with the experimenter ended and Lana shifted to addressing the computer for that item. When only part of the item was loaded into the vending device (E-4), the conversation was always reestablished for one final exchange: *? You put more* (item) *in machine.*

EXPERIMENT II

Method

Subject and Apparatus

Lana was again the subject. The apparatus was identical except for the addition of an opaque screen on Lana's door, which prevented Lana and me from seeing each other. Thus all communication was through the language-training system.

Procedure

The first 16 sessions of Experiment I were repeated after 1 month, with the same procedures being followed.

Results

Analyses identical to those performed in Experiment I were made, and the results of the second experiment were not significantly different from those of the first. In the low-probability sessions, the mean duration was 4.25 minutes, and the mean number of exchanges was 6.0. In the high-probability sessions, the mean duration was 10.0 minutes, and the mean number of exchanges was 8.75. Lana again recognized the presence of an undesired food, asked that it be removed, and persisted in the conversation until the desired food was obtained. She did this on all but one occasion when she apparently decided to drink the water placed in the dispenser by repeatedly saying *Please machine give milk.* (Saying *Please machine give water* would have emptied the water dispenser and not the milk dispenser in which the water had been placed.)

GENERAL DISCUSSION

One of the most interesting developments to come out of this study was Lana's change in strategy during the first half of Experiment I. Lana initially responded to questions that were inappropriate to the time of day by going along with them; that is, if she were asked whether she wanted to eat in the morning, she would request food, and if she were asked whether she wanted to drink in the afternoon, she would request a drink. She then stopped complying in such situations and began stating that she did not want to do what was being asked of her. It is interesting that this change did not occur until after she had had positive results from her two requests that the water be removed from the machine. Perhaps her success with these two requests for the removal of an unwanted item gave her a feeling of greater control over the situation. Until the time of these experiments, nobody had ever "lied" to Lana or played tricks on her within the confines of her language system. Consequently, the potential of her language system to counteract the undesirable acts of others may not have been known to her, and several trials may have been needed in order for her to discover it. In any event, she eventually learned that it was possible not to agree with me, and, more importantly, to control my actions.

With respect to Part C, Lana did use the opportunity to ask that specific items be placed in the vending device. Her two errors in this part both followed occasions when inappropriate questions had been asked of her. In both cases she had answered the questions correctly in Part B but in Part C switched back to the food item normal to the time of day. Lana had probably asked for milk in the morning and chow in the afternoon hundreds of times before the experiment, and it was no great surprise that she did so "incorrectly" on two occasions during this experiment.

Part D of the experiment demonstrated that Lana was able to respond to an irrelevant question and answer it correctly. In so doing, Lana did not simply respond with *No* to the question being asked her but always para-phrased part of it as in the following exchanges:

TIM: *? Lana want machine make window open.*
LANA: *No open window.*
TIM: *? Lana want Tim move behind room.*
LANA: *No Tim move behind room.*

In interpreting the data, a problem does arise in determining what the operation *out-of* meant to Lana. She had previously used this preposition in requesting that she be taken out-of-doors, e.g., *? You carry Lana out-of room.* She also used it within this experiment in a novel sense to request that undesirable foods be removed from the vending devices, e.g., *? You move water out-of machine.* Perhaps, without my realizing it, Lana had broadened the meaning of the preposition *out-of.* This explanation is quite plausi-ble in view of an earlier extension Lana had made with the lexigram *be-hind.*

To reach the vending devices, the experimenter had to leave the keyboard area anteroom and go to another "room." Previously, the preposi-tion *behind* had been reserved for this purpose, and Lana had come to use this preposition to request that some action be taken in connection with the vending devices, as in the following examples: *? You move behind room,* or *? You move chow* (or some other item) *behind room.* Possibly in answering the questions in Part D of this experiment, Lana was equating *out-of* with *behind.* Over many trials, Lana persisted in answering *Yes* when asked whether the experimenter should move *out-of* the room and even invented a novel form herself during the experiments: *? You move Tim out-of room.* This statement was made by Lana a number of times, always after she had been frustrated for a long time and after other attempts to obtain her desired food had failed. Whenever she made this statement, I would comply, and leave the anteroom but would stand outside the main room and not go to the area of the vending devices. This infuriated Lana, as evidenced by increased screaming, and she then had to ask me to move back into the room before any other question could be answered. Still she persisted in using *out-of* in this manner. Apparently her understanding of *out-of* was broader than my understanding of the term, and she was using it to refer to moving "behind the room" and loading food or drink into the vending devices. Only after considerable duress and a large number of "errors" did she finally answer *No* to the question, perhaps because she had at last understood what I meant by the lexigram *out-of.* It is unfortunate that I did not realize earlier what Lana meant by it.

Another point to consider is the difference between the summary mea-sures of the first and second halves of Experiment I. These measures were compared after a visual inspection of the summary data for Experiment I indicated that Lana was apparently beginning to tire of having frustrating interactions with me. As was indicated in the results section, there was a significant increase in the number of exchanges made under the high-probability conditions over the number made in the low-probability condition, and the increase in the duration of the conversations approached significance also. In looking at the printed records of the conversations, however, it became obvious that the increased "information" that was passed was of a repetitive and persistent nature. That is, in the second half of the experiment, instead of using the novel forms that she had invented during the first half to cope with undesirable food items that had been placed in her vending devices, Lana simply persisted in asking for the food item normal to the time of day. Only after she had made persistent requests for the normal food would she acknowledge the presence of the undesirable food item and ask that it be removed or, if it were cabbage, eat it. During these periods of perseverance, Lana asked for the desired item in many different ways. For example, on Day 12 of the experiment when, according to plan, water was placed in the milk dispenser, Lana formulated requests for milk in 10 different ways: *? You put milk in machine; ? You give cup of milk; ? You give milk to Lana; ? You give cup to Lana; ? You move behind room* (to where the dispensers are); *? You put more milk in machine* (after being told, *Milk in machine); ? You put milk behind room; ? You give milk in machine; ? You move milk in machine; ? You move milk behind room.* The first six of these statements and the last one are all grammatically correct, and all are directed toward getting Lana her milk. The time involved in making these statements was 20 minutes, or 63% of the total session. During the remaining 5 minutes of the conversation, Lana correctly acknowledged that water was in the dispenser, asked that it be removed, and then proceeded to ask for milk in the normal manner *(? You put milk in machine)* one final time. The point is that the conversations tended to become extended in the second half of the study because Lana apparently became weary of the treatment she was receiving. The results from Experiment II support this possibility; after a month's "vacation" from the routine, Lana responded at rates comparable to those of the first half of the study in both number and duration of exchanges even with a screen blocking her view of the experimenter.

On Day 6 of the experiments, in the conversation quoted below, Lana spontaneously used an important grammatical form which she had never been taught: The experimenter had just placed cabbage in the vending device after Lana had requested juice and had answered *Yes* to her request.

LANA: *Please machine give piece of cabbage.* (twice)   [4:42 p.m.]
   TIM: *? What in machine.*

LANA: *Tim drink.*   [4:43 p.m.]
  TIM: *? What in machine.*
LANA: *Tim swing.* (This was probably a typing error.)
  TIM: *? What in machine.*
LANA: *Tim put cabbage in machine.*   [4:44 p.m.]
        ? Tim put juice in machine.

Lana had not learned the past tense; however, the sentence *Tim put cabbage in machine* clearly implies that she meant to use it, for that sentence describes what I had indeed just done. Previously she had used the verb "put" only as an approximate equivalent for "will you put" in requests that items be given to her. In this instance she was describing an event that had occurred in the past. She later used this same form once again to describe a past event, only this time, four high-probability sessions intervened between the event and her use of this form. Lana's suggested use of the past tense is important, for it implies that a concept of the past is cognitively present in her. Perhaps in the future linguistic markers for tense can be employed with her in order to investigate her perception of time.

Another point of interest is Lana's use of the negative to both describe and cope with the situation at hand. For example, after I had placed cabbage in the vending device, Lana asked *? You put chow in machine,* to which I responded *Yes.* This exchange was repeated five times. After the fifth time, Lana asked *? Chow in machine,* to which I again responded *Yes.* Lana was in no way willing to agree with this statement, for she immediately responded with *No chow in machine,* which was indeed true; she had taken the initiative and formed a negation that described accurately the situation. She then responded in a similar fashion five additional times after repeatedly being "lied" to.

As mentioned earlier, the increase in the variety of Lana's sentences may have been due to her sense of increasing control and probably also to an increasing awareness of the possibilities afforded her through the use of her language system. Her use of negation tends to support this idea, as do her requests for the removal of unwanted items from the vending devices. The novel sentences generated by Lana are the best evidence of Lana's awareness of the world around her:

1.   LANA: *No open window.* (This was given after Lana had been asked whether the window should be opened. Normally Yerkish grammar calls for *window open;* however, Lana modified the normal form.)
2.   LANA: *? You move water* (or *cabbage) out-of machine.* (As mentioned previously, this statement had obvious instrumental value.)
3.   LANA: *No open.* (Given in the same situation as the first response.)

4. LANA: *No music.* (Again, the same situation as in the first response, except that the topic was music instead of the window.)
5. LANA: *No Lana want more.* (Given by Lana when asked if she wanted any more cabbage to be put in the vending device after she had already consumed a considerable portion. Normally, more is used as follows: *? You put more* (item) *in machine.*)
6. LANA: *Tim put cabbage in machine.* (Past tense, as described earlier.)
7. LANA: *No chow in machine.* (Water had been placed in the milk dispenser, and the chow Lana had requested had not been placed in the chow dispenser.)
8. LANA: *No chow in machine.* (Denial of a condition, as described earlier.)

Still other examples of Lana's awareness of the world about her could be given, one of which clearly demonstrates her use of the language system to understand her environment: I had placed water in the milk dispenser and later had asked Lana the following question: *? What name-of this that's in machine.* Lana replied, *Please machine give milk,* which would give her a small amount of whatever was in the milk dispenser, and after tasting the water replied: *Water name-of this.* After being asked the name of what was in the vending device, Lana requested that the machine give her some of whatever it was and then proceeded to give me the name of it.

A final point concerns the overall direction that the conversations took. In all but a few cases, Lana and I remained locked in conversation until Lana had obtained what she desired, the food normal to that time of day. When conditions called for no manipulation of reward conditions, the conversations were quite short, about 3 minutes long. When conditions called for alternatives to be placed into the vending devices, the conversations persisted for a longer period of time, as long as necessary for Lana to obtain the desired food. Some of the problems within the high-probability conversations were of a semantic nature such as the problem of *out-of.* As mentioned in the introduction, these are the kinds of problems that must be overcome before the actual goal of a conversation can be obtained. Lana tried to overcome these problems through the novel and productive use of her language system—and usually succeeded.

In conclusion, it can be said that through systematic manipulation of variables relevant to the world of the chimpanzee, it is possible to obtain conversations that are coherent and goal-directed. Lana persistently solved "problems" presented to her and usually did so through her language system. She made many novel and productive statements probably as a direct outgrowth of the experiments themselves. In these experiments, Lana clearly demonstrated that she is operating in a domain once held exclusive to man, that of language.

REFERENCES

McCarthy, D. Language development in children. In L. Carmichael (Ed.), *Manual of child psychology*. New York: Wiley, 1954.

McNeill, D. The development of language. In P. H. Mussen (Ed.), *Carmichael's manual of child psychology*. New York: Wiley, 1970.

Miller, G. A., & Selfridge, J. A. Verbal context and the recall of meaningful material. *American Journal of Psychology*, 1950, *63*, 176–185.

Pease, K., & Arnold, P. Approximations to dialogue. *American Journal of Psychology*, 1973, *86*, 769–776.

Rumbaugh, D. M., & Gill, T. V. Language, apes, and the apple which-is orange, please. In S. Kondo, M. Kawai, A. Ehara, & S. Kawamura (Eds.), *Proceedings from the symposia of the fifth congress of the international primatological society*. Tokyo: Japan Science Press, 1975.

Rumbaugh, D. M., & Gill, T. V. Language and the acquisition of language-type skills by a chimpanzee *(Pan)*. In K. Salzinger (Ed.), *Psychology in progress: An interim report*. Vol. 270. New York: The New York Academy of Sciences, 1976. Pp. 90–123.

chapter 13

Acquisition and Use of Mathematical Skills by a Linguistic Chimpanzee

GWENDOLYN B. DOOLEY AND TIMOTHY V. GILL

Georgia State University, and
Yerkes Regional Primate Research Center

Eric Lenneberg (1971) and Lenneberg and Long (1974) believe that man's mathematical abilities are derived from the same foundation as those used for language. Lenneberg (1971) emphasized that, "the basis for mathematical constructs seems to be contained in the basis for language constructs . . . for every mathematical notion there is a homologous one in the sphere of language, the former always being more restricted and well defined than the latter [p. 1]." Although knowing language is not the same as knowing mathematics, both have much in common. Numbers correspond to names in language, function or relational words in language parallel the symbols for mathematical operations (+, =, ∩, ⊂), and concatenations of words are the equivalent of mathematical phrases (1 + 5, Set A ∩ Set B). All the basic notions at the foundation of numbers and mathematical operations are derivations from language and linguistic operations.

Virtually every aspect of both language and mathematics is *relational*, with the relations in mathematics being more precisely determinable. Names of objects and "content words" imply not only a name but a physical

247

reference base. For example, kinship terms like *aunt, brother,* and *grand-mother* name a particular person and imply both the physical person referent and the kinship relationship denoted. Adjectives such as *tall* and *dark* can only be understood in regard to a reference base (Lenneberg & Long, 1974).

Numbers, like the "content words" of language, have both names and involve relations. Numerals are the names for conceptualized quantities. Every number represents many possible relational compositions: $3 = 1 + 4 - 2$ or $3 = 251 - 248$, and every arithmetic phrase can be replaced by one number. The particular number that a mathematical composition denotes has been precisely determined by a knowledge of the ordinal and cardinal values involved and by the type of operation performed. Thus mathematical relations are more precisely mapped than linguistic relations.

Lenneberg's (1971) and Lenneberg and Long's (1974) ideas of mathematics serving to map language on a very precise level are suggestive of Piaget's concept of logico-mathematical knowledge. Piaget believes that logico-mathematical knowledge (the knowledge of states, relations between states and/or actions, and the effects of actions on states) underlies the development of language, dreaming, and playing, as well as mathematical abilities. He hypothesizes that numerical or arithmetic knowledge requires a definite learning period with the process involving a relational form of learning (Piaget, 1971). As a child begins to handle objects, especially sets of items, he makes a connection item by item between two or more series of objects; this is one-to-one correspondence. The child then discovers that the numerical sum of each collection remains constant even though the components of each configuration are altered. This process of inclusion, seriation, and one-to-one correspondence generates cardinal numbers as well as the ordinal value relationships inherent in numbers. By a series of logico-mathematical experiences, a child constructs numbers and their relationships from operations performed on the objects by himself, and not from some characteristic inherent within the objects themselves, such as weight, volume, or shape (Piaget, 1971).

The type of logico-mathematical conceptualization which Piaget proposes took millennia to evolve from a common *hominoid* ability to form concepts based on concrete referents and relationships between objects and/or self (Campbell, 1974). At some point in *hominid* evolution, man's ancestors began communicating about events in their lives. It seems likely that names and actions were the backbone of early language. It also appears probable that these hominids were capable of some type of numeric decision as in judging more food versus less food. A herd of killed deer supplies a larger quantity of meat than does a single animal, and a handful of tubers provides a greater amount of food than a few grains of wheat. Perhaps the initial notions of more and less were built from such basic concepts. Later a numbering system was developed as a way of relating precise quantities to environmental objects and animates. At least as early as 30,000 years ago, man began storing numerical information as scratches on bone, on notched tally sticks, and with knotted cords, and by 2000 B.C., he was making arithmetic and trigonometric computations on clay tablets (Claiborne, 1974).

Previous studies with nonhuman primates have shown that some number and/or mathematical relationships can be learned by at least rhesus macaques and chimpanzees. In 1956, Hicks conducted a well-controlled experiment in which eight rhesus macaques learned to respond to "three-ness" significantly above chance when extraneous cues of color, form, size, and spatial arrangement were varied. Rohles and Devine (1966, 1967) found that an adolescent female chimpanzee could discriminate numerical "middleness" with 75% accuracy with as many as 17 objects placed over wells in a form board. The authors could not determine the exact process by which the middleness discriminations were made, but they suggested that primitive counting might have been involved.

Ferster (1966) and Ferster and Hammer (1966) studied the abilities of two chimpanzees in the use of binary codes for the numbers 1–7. The chimpanzees required about 500,000 trials in order to match 1 to 7 objects to the number of objects in the sample, with 95% accuracy. An additional 170,000 trials were necessary for them to be able to "write" or type out the correct binary number code for the 1 to 7 objects presented across trials on a random basis (Ferster, 1966).

In the 1950s, the Hayes's chimpanzee, Viki, was tested on visual number matching (Hayes & Nissen, 1971). On a matching-to-sample task in visual number matching, cards with dots in various sizes and configurations were presented across trials, with 10 particular ratios of numbers (1:4, 3:6, 2:4, 4:6, 3:5, 1:2, 2:3, 3:4, 4:5, 5:6) composing the test pairs. These ratios involved a difference between terms of 1, 2, or 3 units. Both the 3.5-year-old Viki and children aged 3.5 to 5 years old were tested. Hayes and Nissen (1971) reported that Viki's skills were equivalent to that of the precounting children, who were 3.5 to 4 years old; both Viki and these children made more consistent errors as the matched numbers became too similar (2:3, 4:5) or too large in number (4:6, 5:6). Hayes and Nissen (1971) suggested that the ability to handle numbers might be similar to the phylogenetic language skill differences existing between man and chimpanzee.

The language project experiments have demonstrated that at least chimpanzees among the nonhuman primates possess language-type abilities (Fouts, 1974; Gardner & Gardner, 1971; Premack, 1971; Rumbaugh & Gill, 1976). Studies by Hicks (1956), Ferster (1966), Ferster and Hammer (1966),

Hayes and Nissen (1971), and Rohles and Devine (1966, 1967) suggested that rhesus macaques and especially chimpanzees possess the ability to learn concepts that are similar to those formed by precounting children. If the basis for mathematical constructs is indeed the same as that for linguistic constructs, it would seem logical that chimpanzees capable of rudimentary language operations should also be capable of rudimentary mathematical operations.

Presumably Lana would have developed premathematical concepts on her own to distinguish "more" versus "less" amounts of items in her environment. A premathematical concept is defined as the nontutored ability to make judgments concerning continuous and noncontinuous (discrete) quantities; specific computations entailing counting are not necessarily involved in quantity determination. A premathematical experiment could determine Lana's ability to make repeated consummatory responses to the greater quantity when she was simultaneously presented with "more" food as compared with "less" food.

A mathematical concept is defined as a numerical concept of discrete quantity, i.e., the discrimination of numbers of discrete (noncontinuous) units is required, this being distinct from discrimination of mass or volume. The development of the numerical concept of discrete quantity would include the recognition of number in an absolute or cardinal sense and the recognition of the ordinal interrelationships among individual numbers. The transition from the basic premathematical ability to one involving numerical/mathematical skills could be explored by teaching Lana to discriminate and then to label discrete quantities of "more" and "less" when continuous quantity dimensions were constantly varied.

The ability of a chimpanzee to learn the numerical/mathematical concepts of "more" and "less," when variables such as surface area or mass are controlled for, could be taken as further support for the thesis that the differences between human and chimpanzee cognition is one of degree and not kind.

EXPERIMENT 1A: ABILITY TO SELECT THE GREATER QUANTITY WITH FRUIT LOOP RATIOS 1:2–4:5

Method

Subject

Lana, aged 5 at the time of this experiment, was the subject for this premathematical experiment. Previously Lana had had 2.5 years of extensive linguistic training in such concepts as naming, color identification, cross-modal naming, and identification in terms of *same* or different (*no same*) (Rumbaugh & Gill, 1976), and specification of the environmental relationships *in, on, under,* and *behind* that existed between two objects or an object and a person (Rumbaugh & Gill, 1976; Stahlke, 1976).

Apparatus

Unbroken Fruit Loop cereal pieces were used as incentives as well as the stimuli to be discriminated. These cereals were placed on two thin, square boards which measured 30.48 cm on each side. A row of 10 black dots placed 2.54 cm apart down the middle of the black wooden boards allowed for even placement of the cereal bits. The row of cereal bits was placed horizontally in front of Lana. The two black boards rested on a short wooden table between the experimenter (Gwendolyn Dooley) and Lana, who always faced her. All testing occurred in Lana's room.

Procedure

Fifteen ratios of the cereal bits, composed by pairing the numbers 1 through 5 only once (1:1, 1:2, 1:3, 1:4, 1:5, 2:2, 2:3, 2:4, 2:5, 3:3, 3:4, 3:5, 4:4, 4:5, 5:5), were presented to Lana. The control ratios (1:1, 2:2, 3:3, 4:4, 5:5) were included to determine if Lana had a side preference. Only one ratio was presented during any one trial with one portion of the ratio being presented on the left board and the other on the right board. The right–left position of the larger ratio portion and the order of presentation of the 15 different ratios were all randomly determined prior to testing.

Lana was allowed to observe the placement of the incentives on the boards; placement always occurred from her right to left across both boards. Since differences in numbers of cereal bits occurred within most ratios (1:2, 2:4, 3:5, etc.), time for placement of the two ratio portions on their assigned boards was equalized. Once placement was complete, the investigator held or touched hands with Lana over the boards for 5 sec prior to allowing a choice so that if Lana desired, she could glance several times at both amounts of incentives. After the hands were dropped, Lana quickly made a choice either by raking the cereal bits toward her, by picking them up with her lips directly from the board, or by picking up each bit and placing it individually in her mouth. Whenever Lana had removed all the cereal bits from her selected board, the cereal pieces from the other board were removed by the investigator, and a new problem was presented.

Two sessions of the 15 ratios were conducted each day for 20 days. Within each session, all 15 ratios were presented in a randomized order. Each ratio was presented 40 times during the experiment.

Results

The null hypothesis in Experiment 1 was that Lana had no preference for the larger number of cereal bits. This meant that either A or B in an A:B ratio would have been selected 50% of the time, excluding a preference for one board over the other. If the null hypothesis was rejected for the 10 ratios of unequal terms, then Lana could be said to have a preference for the larger amount of cereal bits. It was hypothesized that the larger portion in the ratios with a larger proportionate difference (1:4, 1:5, 2:5) would be selected with a greater frequency than the larger portion in the ratios with smaller proportionate differences (1:2, 2:3, 3:4, 4:5).

Table 1 shows the portion of times the larger amount was chosen for the uneven ratios. Lana's mean proportion of correct responses in selecting the larger amount of Fruit Loop bits was .94 for the uneven ratios. Since Lana was well above chance even for her least proportionally correct responses, the null hypothesis was rejected. As also hypothesized, the larger term in the ratios with larger proportionate differences (1:5, 2:5, etc.) was more often correctly selected. The larger term in the ratios with small proportionate differences (1:2, 3:5, etc.) was more likely to be confused with the smaller ratio term, especially for the ratios of a difference of 1 between terms, and for the ratios which were composed of the largest terms. For the control ratios, Lana responded to the right side at a mean .54 proportion of the time although a slight right side preference occurred for the ratio 1:1. That Lana chose almost equally between sides when presented with even, control ratios and that she selected the larger number of cereal bits for the uneven ratios, regardless of side, demonstrated her quite accurate premathematical ability to distinguish between two quantities.

EXPERIMENT 1B: ABILITY TO SELECT THE GREATER QUANTITY WITH FRUIT LOOP RATIOS 1:2–9:10

Method

Procedure

Fifty-five ratios of whole bits of Fruit Loop cereal were composed by pairing the numbers 1 through 10 only once (1:1, 1:2, . . . , 10:10). Control ratios used were 1:1, 2:2, 3:3, . . . , 10:10 and were included to determine if Lana had a side preference. Except for the ratios presented, the

Table 1

PROPORTION OF CORRECT RESPONSES IN SELECTING THE LARGER TERM
IN UNEVEN RATIOS, OR IN SELECTING THE RIGHT SIDE FOR EVEN RATIOS

1:1 (.68)				
1:2 (.95)	2:2 (.52)			
1:3 (1.00)	2:3 (.82)	3:3 (.45)		
1:4 (.98)	2:4 (1.00)	3:4 (.82)	4:4 (.52)	
1:5 (1.00)	2:5 (1.00)	3:5 (.98)	4:5 (.80)	5:5 (.52)

procedure was essentially the same as in Experiment 1. The set of 55 ratios was presented each day for 20 days.

Results

Table 2 shows the proportions of times the larger amount was selected for the uneven ratios, beginning at the second diagonal from the top and continuing down the diagonals in the table. The top diagonal shows the proportion of times the right side was chosen for those control ratios of equal terms. Lana's mean proportion right side preference for the control ratios was .59, which was close to chance level, showing only a slight right preference. Lana's mean proportion of correct responses to the uneven ratios was .94. The first null hypothesis for Experiment 2 can be rejected; Lana chose the larger term in the uneven ratios at a much greater than chance level. Lana had the most difficulty in correctly selecting the larger term in ratios with an absolute difference of 1 between the two terms of the ratio; she ranged from .60 to .95 with a mean proportion of .77 in correctly choosing the larger term in such cases (see the second diagonal from the top in Table 2). For the ratios 1:1 to 4:10 (the nonshaded region of Table 2), the larger term in the ratios with a difference between terms greater than 1 was correctly selected each of the 20 times the ratio was presented.

Owing to the larger quantities involved in the second set of ratios from 5:5 to 10:10 (the shaded region of Table 2), the difference between terms in any ratio was less likely to be consistently discriminated and the larger term less likely to be selected when compared to the first set of data (nonshaded region of Table 2). Subitization, a process in which a breakdown occurs in the ability to discriminate quantities correctly without precisely counting them (Kaufman, Lord, Reese, & Volkman, 1949), could account for the second set of data including more responses to the smaller ratio amount. The mean proportion of correct responses for the uneven ratios in the shaded region of Table 2 was .86. The ratios of a difference of 1 in the second diagonal from the top in the shaded region range from .60 to .85 whereas in the first set (nonshaded region of Table 2) they range from .65 to .95. In the

Table 2

PROPORTION OF CORRECT RESPONSES IN EXPERIMENT

A. *Ratios Tested*

1:1									
1:2	2:2								
1:3	2:3	3:3							
1:4	2:4	3:4	4:4						
1:5	2:5	3:5	4:5	5:5					
1:6	2:6	3:6	4:6	5:6	6:6				
1:7	2:7	3:7	4:7	5:7	6:7	7:7			
1:8	2:8	3:8	4:8	5:8	6:8	7:8	8:8		
1:9	2:9	3:9	4:9	5:9	6:9	7:9	8:9	9:9	
1:10	2:10	3:10	4:10	5:10	6:10	7:10	8:10	9:10	10:10

B. *Proportion of Correct Responses in Selecting the Larger Term in Uneven Ratios in A or in Selecting the Right Side for Even Ratios in A*

.50									
.95	.60								
1.00	.90	.55							
1.00	1.00	.90	.60						
1.00	1.00	1.00	.65	.65					
1.00	1.00	1.00	1.00	.60	.80				
1.00	1.00	1.00	1.00	.95	.85	.65			
1.00	1.00	1.00	1.00	.95	.80	.60	.70		
1.00	1.00	1.00	1.00	1.00	1.00	.85	.80	.45	
1.00	1.00	1.00	1.00	1.00	1.00	1.00	.85	.70	.40

third diagonal, no incorrect choices were made for the first set of ratios (possibly a practice effect due to Experiment 1), but in the second ratio set (shaded region of Table 2) for the same diagonal, the proportion of correct choices was lower, ranging from .80 to .95. The larger term in the ratios 5:9, 5:10, 6:9, 6:10, and 7:10 was always correctly selected for the larger amount.

DISCUSSION

Without being tutored in recognizing larger quantities of discrete items, Lana demonstrated in these experiments that she possessed the skill to determine the greater quantity of Fruit Loop pieces presented to her. As with humans (Hayes & Nissen, 1971), Lana found it harder to discriminate the larger quantity when a difference of 1 and sometimes 2 existed between the two quantities presented and when the two amounts involved 5 or more numbers of cereal bits. Lana appeared to make responses based on number although mass, surface area, etc., could not be definitely excluded.

EXPERIMENT 2: MATHEMATICAL ABILITY TO DISTINGUISH "MORE" AND "LESS" IN TERMS OF RELATIVE NUMBER

Method

This study entailed Lana's ability to master *more* and *less* labeling. Lana's prior experience or knowledge of *more* only extended to requesting that additional quantities of food or liquids be given to her or placed in her vending devices (Rumbaugh & Gill, 1976). Although *less* was placed on her keyboard prior to this experiment, she had little or no concept of the meaning of *less* since no training had been conducted with this lexigram.

Apparatus

To train the mathematical skill of labeling discrete numbers of items in regard to *more* or *less,* many washers of various sizes were randomly presented to Lana on the same two ratio boards as used in the previous experiments. A large, vertical, wooden, black board presented the pertinent questions in Lana's lexigrams: *? What more* or *? What less.* The lexigrams were constructed from cardboard facsimiles of Lana's keyboard lexigrams, and were placed within flat Plexiglas squares and attached by double-faced adhesive near the top of the vertical board. The answer lexigrams of *more* and *less* were similarly constructed and placed at the lower middle right of the question board for Lana's selection.

Procedure

Training

The gradual process of training extended over 7 months. Lana was required to learn several relationships:

1. Which answer lexigram was the correct response for the question presented (*more* or *less*).
2. Which quantity of washers in the 10 different ratios was the correct answer to be labeled with the appropriate answer lexigram:

   a. *More* was the possible answer to the quantities 2, 3, 4, and 5;

more was never the correct answer for 1. In terms of set theory,
more = {2, 3, 4, 5}.

b. Less was the possible answer to the quantities 1, 2, 3, and 4; less
was never the correct answer for 5. In terms of set theory, less =
{1, 2, 3, 4}.

c. More or less were the possible answers for the quantities 2, 3,
and 4 (more ∩ less = {2, 3, 4}) depending on: (1) which
question was posed, and (2) what quantity (other ratio term) these
numbers were paired with on a particular trial.

3. That number (and not the extraneous variables of mass, surface area,
etc.) was the only consistently rewarded cue.

From such complex interrelations, Lana was required to learn the task of
relative more and less number-labeling of discrete numbers of variable sizes
of washers.

During the experiment, Lana sat facing the experimenter, with the
boards on the floor between Lana and the experimenter and with the
question and answer board situated to Lana's right. A trial began with the
placement of the washers from Lana's right to left across the two boards
according to a randomized list of ratios. The larger term in the ratios 1:2,
1:3, 1:4, 1:5, 2:3, 2:4, 2:5, 3:4, 3:5, 4:5 was also randomized. Lana was
required to sequence her responses as follows: pointing to the question,
selecting the appropriate answer lexigram, correctly labeling the amount
referred to in the question, and tapping each washer placed along the line
on the labeled board. When she executed the correct responses in the
required sequence she received a food reward.

The basic task of training involved teaching Lana the sequence with
more until she was 85% correct within a session; the same procedure was
then followed for teaching less. Some problems occurred when Lana was
initially required to answer both questions within a session. Retraining was
finally instituted in which she was required to work with more until she was
85% correct within a session of 40 trials with two sessions presented daily.
Then less was trained to the same criterion. Eventually the number of
sessions required to achieve criterion decreased until she was able to meet
criterion within a single session.

Next, within-session presentation of the questions was initiated in
which blocks of more and less questions were asked. A 70% criterion was
instituted for the within-session training under the assumption that frequent
concept switching would aid the differentiation of the more and less concepts. Once a session with just one concept shift was mastered to the 70%
criterion then a session with three concept shifts was presented. Within-
session concept switching was quickly mastered to the point that Lana could

shift concept labeling after five consecutive trials of either *more* or *less* to the new 70% criterion. The lowered criterion for this last phase of training helped ensure that Lana did not overlearn the task to the point that testing would be meaningless.

Testing

At this point, testing began with randomly presented ratios in blocks of 10 ratios and with randomly presented questions with the restriction that not more than three consecutive trials of the same question could occur. Right–left placement of the larger term in each ratio was also randomly determined. Two 50-trial test sessions were presented.

A control test of another 50 trials was presented to determine if Lana was cuing on the amount of time, as such, that it took to prepare the varying numbers of washers on the ratio boards. A large cardboard box was placed over the ratio boards during washer placement, with the time spent in placing the washers under the right and left sides of the box equalized. As an added control, the question was not completed until after washer placement so that Lana had no way of knowing if *more* or *less* would be asked until immediately before the box was removed.

A second control test of 50 trials was conducted by Tim Gill, who had not previously trained Lana on this task. This test was to check against unconscious cuing by Gwendolyn Dooley.

Results

After 7 months of training involving 3025 trials with *more* and 3520 trials with *less,* Lana was ready for testing of her mathematical abilities. Over the 100 test trials, Lana was 89% correct in answering the presented questions. During the first test session she was 90% correct, and over the 50 trials in the second session, she was 88% correct. She was 90% correct on overall labeling with *more* and 88% correct in labeling with *less.* As could be expected from the findings with the first tests, Lana had difficulty in distinguishing the ratio amounts with a difference of 1 between terms. The hardest ratios for her to distinguish between the component amounts were with 3:5 and 4:5; she was only 60% correct in appropriately labeling the terms involved in these ratios, whereas she was either 90% or 100% correct in labeling the terms in the remaining ratio pairs.

The two control tests upheld the findings of the last test. On the test controlling for placement time, she scored 80% correct in answering the questions posed to her in random order. When Tim Gill tested Lana, she scored 74% correct over the 50 test trials, which was still well above chance.

DISCUSSION

As of summer, 1976, Lana has demonstrated her competence in answering *more* and *less* questions directed toward discrete numbers of variable sizes of washers. Since surface area and mass were randomly varied in the selection of the washers on any trial, Lana was only consistently rewarded for correctly labeling number. Lana's high test performance at the 89% level also suggested that number was the cue to which she was responding, especially as her errors occurred on the ratios with large numbers of washers or on the ratios with very similar component portions.

The results from the two control tests further suggested that Lana was making her responses based on number of washers. The control test for placement time of the washers excluded this variable since Lana continued to respond at the high level of 80% correct. The score on the control test conducted by Tim Gill was above chance performance and suggested that differential cuing by Gwendolyn Dooley was not a factor in her original test score. Lana had previously fluctuated 15% correct (or more) during training sessions depending on her different moods. The decreased score of 74% obtained in this control test was attributed to Lana's playful attitude toward the task when she had a substitute teacher; perhaps the chimpanzee was testing Tim Gill to see if he knew the task as well as the usual math teacher. A relational numerical/mathematical concept based on number is indicated from these control tests.

Future mathematical research with Lana includes teaching her the names of precise numbers and the ordinal relationships involved among the numbers 1–10. It is conceivable that mental number manipulation in terms of summing (addition) might already be in Lana's repertoire of mathematical skills. If it is not, it is probable that such operations as addition, subtraction, intersection, etc., can be taught to her since these operations have their correlates in environmental actions and linguistic operations. Since Lana is also a language project chimpanzee, it may be possible to delimit the meanings involved in the linguistic operations of *and* and *or* (which Lana does not presently have lexigrams for) by the mathematical operations of addition and intersection.

Rumbaugh, Gill, and von Glasersfeld mused in 1973 at the start of Lana's linguistic training that: "if successful completion of the valid sentence starts is viewed as analogous to typewriting, it can be said that Lana both reads and writes. Alas, we have no evidence of her ability for the third 'R', arithmetic [p. 733]." In 1976, the Lana Language Project is beginning to obtain evidence for Lana's mathematical abilities, and it appears that at the very least Lana chimpanzee possessed premathematical skills adapted for survival-related, consummatory responses prior to any formal mathematical training in labeling with *more* and *less*. Probably due to that ability, Lana was subsequently able to learn the complex relationships between the *more* and *less* questions posed her, the selection of the correct answer lexigram, and the appropriate labeling of the correct amount in the ratio presented where sometimes a specific number (i.e., 3) was correct and sometimes incorrect depending on which term of the ratio it was presented along with (i.e., 1:3 or 3:5) as well as whether the question being asked was for "more" or "less." That Lana was able to learn the *more—less* distinction involved in this mathematical—linguistic task was due to her nontutored, premathematical abilities as well as her linguistic training in labeling and in spatially relating objects in her environment.

REFERENCES

Campbell, B. G. *Human evolution* (2nd ed.). Chicago: Aldine, 1974.

Claiborne, R. *The birth of writing*. New York: Time-Life Books, 1974.

Ferster, C. B. Arithmetic behavior in chimpanzees. *Scientific American*, May 1966, *210*, 98–106.

Ferster, C. B., & Hammer, C. E. Synthesizing the components of arithmetic behavior. In W. K. Honig (Ed.), *Operant behavior*. New York: Meredith, 1966.

Fouts, R. S. Language: Origins, definitions, and chimpanzees. *Journal of Human Evolution*, 1974, *3*(6), 475–482.

Gardner, B. T., & Gardner, R. A. Two-way communication with an infant chimpanzee. In A. M. Schrier & F. Stollnitz (Eds.), *Behavior of nonhuman primates*, Vol. 4. New York: Academic Press, 1971.

Hayes, K. J., & Nissen, C. H. Higher mental functions of a home-raised chimpanzee. In A. M. Schrier & F. Stollnitz (Eds.), *Behavior of nonhuman primates*, Vol. 4. New York: Academic Press, 1971.

Hicks, L. H. An analysis of number-concept formation in the rhesus monkey. *Journal of Comparative and Physiological Psychology*, 1956, *49*, 212–218.

Kaufman, E. L., Lord, M. W., Reese, T. W., & Volkman, J. The discrimination of visual number. *American Journal of Psychology*, 1949, *62*, 498–525.

Lenneberg, E. H. Of language knowledge, apes, and brains. *Journal of Psycholinguistic Research*, 1971, *1*(1), 1–29.

Lenneberg, E. H., & Long, B. S. Language development. In J. A. Swets & L. L. Elliot (Eds.), *Psychology and the handicapped child*. Washington, D. C.: U. S. Government Printing Office, 1974.

Piaget, J. *Biology and knowledge*. Chicago: University of Chicago Press, 1971.

Premack, D. On the assessment of language competence in the chimpanzee. In A. M. Schrier &

F. Stollnitz (Eds.), *Behavior of nonhuman primates*, Vol. 4. New York: Academic Press, 1971.

Rohles, F. N., & Devine, J. V. Chimpanzee performance on a problem involving the concept of middleness. *Animal Behavior*, 1966, *14*(1), 159–162.

Rohles, F. H., & Devine, J. V. Further studies of the middleness concept with the chimpanzee. *Animal Behavior*, 1967, *15*(1), 107–112.

Rumbaugh, D. M., Gill, T. V., & von Glasersfeld, E. C. Reading and sentence completion by a chimpanzee (*Pan*). *Science*, 1973, *182*, 731–733.

Rumbaugh, D. M., & Gill, T. V. Language and the acquisition of language-type skills by a chimpanzee (*Pan*). In K. Salzinger (Ed.), *Psychology in progress: An interim report* (Vol. 270). New York: Annals of the New York Academy of Sciences, 1976.

Stahlke, H. F. W. The acquisition and use of relational terms in a primate language analogue. Unpublished manuscript, Georgia State University, 1976.

PART IV

Projects for
the Future

chapter 14

The Conversation Board

HAROLD WARNER, CHARLES L. BELL, AND JOSEPHINE V. BROWN

Yerkes Regional Primate Research Center and
Georgia State University

INTRODUCTION

The studies in language formation described in detail in previous chapters of this book depended solely upon a stationary, computer-controlled instrumentation environment. There was no opportunity for a subject to acquire language training in a different normal environment or situation away from this stationary facility. Studies in language formation now being pursued by us at the Georgia Retardation Center with mentally retarded children, and simultaneously, studies with chimpanzees at the Yerkes Primate Center have been employing similar stationary computer-controlled language teaching facilities. It was during reflection upon the restrictions involved in working with stationary facilities only that Harold Warner conceived the idea for a conversation board (CB), a technique that, it is believed, will enhance language formation and help evaluate teaching methods in both the children and the great apes.

General Description

A CB weighing approximately 14 pounds less the power supply, and completely portable when powered by batteries, has been designed and developed. Measuring $22\frac{5}{8}$ inches long and $16\frac{1}{4}$ inches wide on the keyboard surface and 8 inches deep, it is equipped with a two-unit keyboard having a total capacity of 112 words and a visual display for sentences of up to 10 words in length (see Figure 1). Through self-contained logic circuitry the keyboard integrates with the visual display in a manner somewhat similar to that contained in the stationary computer-controlled facilities presently in use. Binary encoded outputs indicating which keys are being depressed can be made available for possible magnetic tape recording and later playback into the computer data storage. When conversing in an area where building power mains are available, a plug-in cable can be used. Thus, employing the CB, the child or animal and the experimenter can proceed to desirable areas in and around the Georgia Retardation Center or the Yerkes Primate Center and converse together.

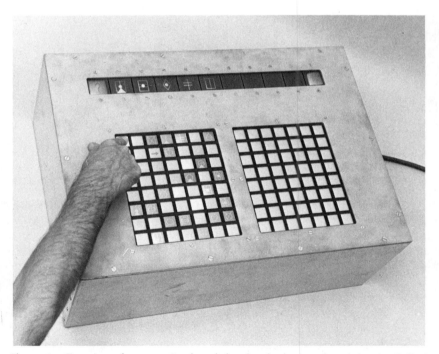

Figure 1. Top view of conversation board showing the keyboard, and the visual display.

Need for the Device

Although, during initial and intermediate language training of subjects, the CB has been designed to serve chiefly as a language training adjunct, it may prove valuable as a device for conversation between subject and experimenter or perhaps even between one subject and another after elementary and intermediate language training with the stationary facility. Thus, a portable device has been made available which operates much like the stationary computer-controlled facility, but allows conversation almost anywhere at the discretion of the experimenter. Certainly, it should permit the acquisition of new vocabulary related to these different environments.

In attempting further to delineate the manner in which the CB might serve in these language studies, we posed the following questions: Will the use of this device make for generalization of the Yerkish language as taught in the computer-controlled facility? In other words, will the employment of this device free the language from being merely a means to communicate with or through a stationary machine, to becoming a language for general communication in any situation? Can the CB, after being employed with the experimenter's vocal support in environments where important events (to the subject) are taking place, perhaps encourage the child to utilize vocal expression at times when the device with its keyboard is not available? In adding names of objects to the child's vocabulary, will the CB permit a better grasp of the variety of situations to which the objects can be related or in which the objects can be employed? Will it affect the rate of learning to name? Finally, will the CB make the social aspects of language become important or at least hasten the process?

A CONVERSATION BOARD SYSTEM

The Keyboard

The keyboard for the conversation board is substantially different from the unit described in Chapter 7 of this volume (see page 145). As shown in Figure 1, it consists of two units procured from Industrial Electronic Engineers, Inc. of Van Nuys, California, mounted into the console face along with the visual display. Lexigrams, denoting words, are applied to the face of the keys by inserting lexigram transparencies into a transparent vinyl carrier sheet affixed over the keys. The active portion of each key consists of a conductive metal intersect. Pressure on the lexigram surface completes the circuit in the intersect and by means of strobing and coincidence circuitry, the particular row and column of the depressed key, and subsequently, the key itself, are identified. Relays are not employed with these keyboards; solid-state circuitry is used throughout.

The circuit that encodes the particular key-signal into a 12-bit code word is a diode matrix similar to the unit referred to in Chapter 7 (see page 146). The difference between the two is physical rather than electrical. In the CB, each Yerkish word is contained in a physically separate diode circuit-unit, which can be plugged into any one of 112 sockets; thus any key can produce a signal for any plugged-in Yerkish word. In the diode matrix, referred to in Chapter 7, the diodes are wired integrally and thus a patch panel is required to change Yerkish words, or their location, on the keyboard.

Visually, the lexigram on the face of the key has been designed to be legible in dim light or in bright daylight, whether or not the back illumination in the key has been activated. It will be necessary to change the lexigram on the face of the key at frequent intervals since vocabulary will vary with the different situations within which the CB will be employed. This is easily accomplished by removing the keyboard-unit cover, extracting the vinyl carrier sheet and inserting the new lexigrams.

Although the keyboards are rugged enough to withstand greater than normal abuse, the presence of an experimenter or attendant whenever the CB is used makes it unnecessary for the unit to be as rugged as the keyboards exposed directly to the subject in the stationary computer-controlled environment.

Visual Display

This display consists of a single row of ten of the size 010 projectors as described in Chapter 7 (page 147). During operation of the CB, both parties in the conversation use the same row of projectors. For example, after the subject has keyed a sentence into the visual display, the experimenter depresses the period key, which erases the sentence. The experimenter then keys his reply into the visual display. The subject can then again use the period key, erasing the experimenter's entry, and so continue the conversation. As before, when the subject keys a sentence on the keyboard, the projectors display each lexigram from left to right in the sequence in which they were keyed. Circuits for controlling the sequencing of these projectors are likewise similar to those described in Chapter 7 (page 148), and are contained on a circuit board that we have dubbed the "Isthmus." It is so named because it is a relatively small block of circuitry that mediates between the large number of lexigram keys and a large number of projector lamps. The Isthmus is not required to address two different banks of projectors, since only one bank is used in the conversation board. On the other hand, the Isthmus circuitry must generate the clock, shift, and reset pulses, which in the stationary unit are furnished by the computer.

Power Supplies

Two sources of power can be used for the CB. When the device is to be used outside, away from building electricity, a battery power supply is available. This supply will operate the CB for approximately 2 hours. It weighs 16 pounds and can be carried by the experimenter in a shoulder-sling or backpack. In order to permit rapid battery replacement, an identical battery may be maintained "on-charge" by a battery charger connected to the building mains. Although the battery is a wet-cell type, it is of a gel-composition sealed against leakage. Thus, there is normally no danger of corrosive effluents.

When the CB is employed indoors, a separate power supply connected to the building mains is used. It is essentially a battery eliminator consisting of a transformer, rectifier, and voltage regulator circuit. Its output-cable plugs directly into the battery input connector in the CB. This source of power can supply the CB indefinitely.

THE CONVERSATION BOARD SYSTEM OPERATION

In the following discussion we will integrate all of the components described in the previous section into the complete conversation board logic system by describing in detail the overall operation of the device. During this discussion, the reader should refer to the system block diagram in Figure 2 and to descriptions of individual component operation in the previous section.

When the lexigram surface of one of the keys in the keyboard (A) is depressed, strobing circuitry designed into the keyboard produces an output denoting the row and column of the particular key. In the keyboard decoding circuits (B), coincidence circuits determine from the row and column information the particular key which has been depressed and deliver a specific pulsed signal over one of 112 lines to the keyboard illumination control (C) and to the diode-coding matrix (D). The keyboard illumination control circuits cause the key that has been depressed to be illuminated,

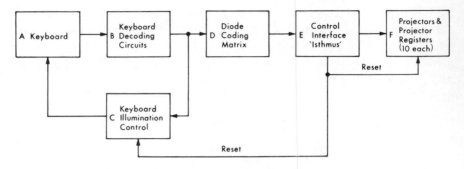

Figure 2.   Conversation-board system block diagram.

furnishing feedback information to the subject. The diode-coding matrix encodes the pulsed signal into a 12-bit code-word, which is applied over 12 lines to the control interface, the Isthmus (E). Here, several very important functions take place with respect to control of the visual display. The first incoming data-word permits the Isthmus to generate a shift pulse, which serves to arm the output to the first of the projector registers (F). A closely following clock pulse, also generated in the Isthmus, loads the data-word into the armed projector-register and the lexigram appears on the screen of the projector. When a second key is depressed at the keyboard (A), the action is identical in circuit blocks B, C, and D. However, in the Isthmus, the second data-word causes the generation of a shift-pulse that now arms the output to the second projector register, and the subsequent clock-pulse loads the second data-word into the second projector register, while allowing the first data-word to remain in the first projector register. Thus, projectors 1 and 2 (F) show the first and second lexigrams, respectively. Additional lexigram-key depressions allow the remaining projectors to be loaded in the same manner. When the sentence is completed as indicated by the depression of the period-key, the Isthmus generates a reset pulse, which clears its own shift register, the keyboard illumination control registers, and the projector registers; thus, the projectors and the keyboard become dark.

PROCEDURES FOR EMPLOYING THE CB AS
A LANGUAGE LEARNING TOOL

By dividing a subject's training time between different proportions of computer-assisted training and CB training, we should be able to determine the potential effectiveness of the CB as a training device. Following preliminary mastery of basic Yerkish phrases, subjects will be matched on the basis of their performance thus far, and divided into two or three groups. The first group will continue with computer-assisted training only. The second group will switch entirely to CB training. A third group, if a sufficient number of subjects is available, will spend half its training time with the computer and half with the CB. The absolute amount of training time for subjects in the three groups will be equal; only the ratio of computer to CB training time will vary across groups. Such a division should let us estimate the value of multisituational training (as provided by the CB) at various stages in training. We will also be able to determine if CB training alone is sufficient to foster the same amount of language usage as is manifest in the computer-only or computer + CB groups. Since the CB is completely portable and could be manufactured on a large scale, it should be regarded as a potential means of communication between retardates, or between retardates and others inside or outside institutions. The success of the second group should indicate the potential for extrainstitutional CB use or for general use within the institution. The following subsections give examples of testing procedures that should serve to estimate the comparative effectiveness of the CB and computer-assisted training in the acquisition, use, and generalization of language.

Object Naming and Preposition Use

Fundamental to language usage is the concept of naming, that is, that names serve as symbols for objects, and yet are differentiated from them (see Chapters 8, 9, and 10). A great variety of naming situations may provide the best climate for the emergence of the necessary abstraction that a name is a symbolic representation of an object and that all objects have names. Access to a CB would enable an experimenter and a subject to explore their environment on "naming trips," employing both Yerkish and vocal English, thus possibly optimizing the potential for emergence of these abstractions. When presented with previously unseen objects that belong to already-trained classes of objects (e.g., bowls, cups, balls), subjects with at least partial CB training may be more likely to identify these new objects correctly than would the subject whose training was solely through the computer-assisted facility.

As the subject continues to master new names, prepositions such as "into," "over," and "behind" can be introduced. Vocal English or Yerkish + vocal English commands will be used with the CB for testing mastery and for determining whether the groups differ in their acquisition of preposition usage. Will any differences be in the same direction as seen during initial object-naming acquisition? It may be that the asymptotic performance level of the groups after extended training will be about the same, and that only speed of acquisition may vary across groups. Or, the training methods may truly provide reliably different levels of mastery across groups. If there are differences between groups, such differences may be reversible after additional training in deficient areas. If any combination of either computer or CB or both proves successful, then the method of choice for future research can be that which is most convenient for a particular research or training program.

Generalization of Language Use

Maximum benefits will be gained by the retarded children in this project only if they acquire language skills that can be used apart from the specific situations in which language training occurs. Since lack of learning transfer or generalization is a common problem when training retardates, it is hoped that the CB will facilitate transfer from a computer-dominated training environment to the computerless world. Even for subjects from whom vocal speech will never be expected, perhaps vocal articulation will be understood and responded to outside as well as inside the experimental situation. Here we might expect the CB users to excel most over the computer-only subjects, because the shift can be accomplished most naturally from the CB and its symbol plus the attendant's speech to the vocal communication of the outside world. As subjects become proficient with the use of Yerkish, the projector illumination of the computer or the CB can be gradually faded away until only the attendant's voice and progressively more ambiguous finger pointing remains. Reese (personal communication, 1975) has successfully used similar fading techniques to give retardates multisituational counting skills. This procedure would allow for a gradual shift from Yerkish questions or commands to spoken English. Ongoing testing of the ability of subjects in each of the three groups to respond to verbal commands will serve to evaluate the relative advantage of computer-assisted or CB training, or the combination of both.

Social Aspects of Language

We hope that the CB communication will serve as a reinforcer in such a way that it will foster language usage in many different situations. Turning off Lana's keyboard, thus depriving her of her language, is the most effective means we have found thus far to punish undesirable behavior. Our experience with Lana would lead us to believe that the CB would also be highly desirable as measured by preference tests. An increase in preference for the

CB over time should indicate an increase in the subject's preference for communication via the route provided by the CB. There is no reason to assume that this desire for communication potential should change as the illumination of the CB projectors is gradually faded away in favor of the vocal. Certainly the extracommunication aspects of Lana's keyboard had little reinforcing value, for she was rarely at her keyboard unless she was pushing keys, and the vast majority of her key presses resulted in correct Yerkish phrases. Thus the CB should provide a means to take advantage of the desire for communication potential so that the gap from language facility in the computer environment to language facility in the subject's regular environment can be bridged.

chapter 15

Implications of the Yerkes Technology for Mentally Retarded Human Subjects

DOROTHY A. PARKEL, ROYCE A. WHITE, AND HAROLD WARNER

Georgia Retardation Center and Yerkes Regional Primate Research Center

The success of the Yerkes team with Lana has sparked numerous inquiries from clinicians in the field of mental retardation and from families of nonverbal retarded people. Similar interest has been shown in the implications of other projects in which primate subjects have been trained in human-like communication skills (Carrier, 1974). Currently, there are several well-known and promising language intervention programs being developed with this population (Graham, 1976), but the Yerkes system seems to us to offer unique advantages in trying to reach a group of people usually overlooked for existing programs—persons labeled severely or profoundly retarded who have no functional expressive language. Thus, we are undertaking a study to evaluate the Yerkes technology as a basis for language training of retarded human subjects. Adopting the system developed with Lana is prompted not by the remarkable communication behavior demonstrated in a nonhuman species, but by those features of the Yerkes technology which address known or suspected learning deficits in the retarded. Since this project is just getting underway, we can only speculate about the import of the Yerkes system for our target population.

SELECTION OF THE TARGET POPULATION

Persons labeled severely or profoundly retarded pose educational and training problems that are little researched by specialists in the field. Procedures for language training that could reach a population heretofore largely uninvestigated and often regarded as unlikely to benefit from available programs would be of considerable significance to the study of retardation as a whole. Since less expensive language-intervention programs have already been shown to work with higher-level subjects, success with this population could justify the expense of computer mediation.

Our initial sample consists of persons whose expressive language consists of less than 10 long-exhibited, barely intelligible, single words. This is an upper limit, since we are also including persons who have not demonstrated any attempt at intelligible utterances. To profit from such a program, subjects must have an adequate attention span for a workable training schedule (at least 10 minutes). They must also demonstrate sufficient maturity for language acquisition; a Cattell MA estimate between 15 and 18 months was set as a lower limit, since expressive language skills have begun to emerge in normal children by this developmental level. The minimal receptive skills include the ability to follow at least two one-step commands, such as, "sit down," and the ability to identify at least four common items when named. Since we did not want to expend undue effort in training subjects to discriminate the lexigrams, we chose subjects who were able to learn, with fading and prompting, a two-choice discrimination task involving two-element lexigrams, then transfer to a new problem in which fading and prompting were not supplied.

SUMMARY OF RELEVANT LITERATURE

Since little research on cognitive or prelinguistic skills is done on retarded samples of this developmental level, we are forced to make inferences from studies of higher-level retarded groups, and since many extensive reviews are available elsewhere, ours is brief.

As is well-documented in the literature on operant conditioning, it is necessary to break learning tasks for retardates into small units, and to provide small increments of change from one level of mastery to the next (Thompson & Grabowski, 1972). Their need for assistance in focusing attention on task-relevant stimuli is clear in the literature on discrimination learning (Zeaman & House, 1963) and incidental learning (Ross, 1970). Their problem in handling multiple cues are demonstrated in discrimination learning (Ullman & Routh, 1971; Zeaman & House, 1963) and matching tasks (Olson, 1971; Ullman, 1974). Difficulties of transfer have been shown in discrimination learning (Kaufman & Prehm, 1966) and memory studies (Borkowski & Wanschura, 1974). Problems of short-term memory and information overload have been demonstrated in both paired-associate and serial learning tasks (Baumeister & Kellas, 1971; Ellis, 1970; Scott & Scott, 1968); a major explanation for these problems deals with deficits in organizational strategies (Brown, 1974; Spitz, 1966). Research based on such theories suggests that retarded subjects are less likely than normals to operate on incoming information through rehearsal and perhaps through abstracting or selecting out potentially useful characteristics; it also suggests that they use few strategies to reduce information to more manageable units. Finally, motivational problems, which are particularly prevalent in institutional populations, are suggested as a significant deterrent to performance (Zigler, 1973). In short, retardates seem to need highly structured assistance in developing information stores and skill repertories that can be efficiently called up and applied. Furthermore, they require explicit aid in expanding the use of known skills extensively and appropriately. The dependence of these skills on a verbal system is central to our concern in this undertaking.

SPECULATIONS ON THE TECHNOLOGICAL
ADVANTAGES OF THE SYSTEM

There are numerous features of the Yerkes technology that might facilitate the acquisition of a symbol system by nonverbal retarded people. In the laboratory setting necessary for the computer, the stimulus field can be limited, thus aiding the focus of attention. Also, the possibilities for incorrect responses are minimized. The computer-controlled system can deliver immediate feedback and reinforcement, and can provide a structure in which the consequences of various behaviors are consistent and predictable, thereby presenting more stable models than those encountered in the everyday environment. For people with short-term memory problems and problems in organizing incoming information, it is important to have sufficient structure within which to internalize action–consequence models.

With this system, the experimenter can easily pace the subject's responding, that is, reduce the tendency toward impulsive responding so often encountered in the performance of such subjects on extremely difficult tasks (Lowry & Ross, 1975). In addition, the novelty of the communication device seems to aid some subjects initially by motivating and eliciting appropriate attention-orienting responses. The potential of a computerized system to provide extended practice is obvious. Also, the data-gathering capacity of the system provides for the continuing evaluation and feedback necessary to tailor the program to individual subject needs.

This technology may also make it possible to reduce the level of cognitive strain involved in this highly complex undertaking. Although we hope that this system will serve as a bridge in the development of spoken language, the first objective is to assist the subjects in internalizing a manageable symbol system. In the early stages of the program, the only output response required of the subject is to depress the appropriately labeled key, a far less complex response than that required in most first-learned communication systems. Anyone who has tried to speak a foreign language that uses sounds not contained in his own will readily recognize the complexity of vocalization. The motor requirements of sign language are also extremely complex; nonetheless, as an early substitute for spoken communication, sign language has been found to facilitate language acquisition in higher-level subjects (Bricker, 1972). Even manual manipulation of cardboard or plastic symbols is time-consuming and motorically complicated compared with the single button-press required for each unit of response using a computer. Minimizing the attention necessary for output could allow greater attention for the cognitive tasks, which are essentially the same as those required in normal communication: discrimination of the input elements, recogntion of their referents or functions, comprehension of intention, evaluation of response requirements and selection of appropriate output elements. In essence, a computer-based method breaks the task into two sequential steps: (a) acquisition of an internal coding system that will serve to cue both internal and external responses, and (b) acquisition of appropriate motor responses necessary for vocal communication. The latter task will be deferred until competence is developed in the former. Although the task requires associating auditory signals and visual symbols, it requires less sensory integration of output feedback, since the subject does not have to match his own spoken output with the models provided by the experimenter, a task that would require attention both to remembered auditory patterns and to the manipulation of the vocal apparatus.

A further advantage of this system involves the use of multimodal input. First, this increases the probability of engaging a potentially functional system, that is, one in which decoding and encoding can be mastered by the subject. It also provides specific training in associating two modalities. Although multimodal input requires attention to two systems—auditory and visual—the visual stimuli are more clearly perceptible as individual units; thus the visual support may help the subject delimit the boundaries of auditory stimuli (a task that is difficult for anyone—consider, for instance, the problem of discerning the beginnings and endings of words in a rapidly spoken string of words in an unfamiliar language). Using visual symbols also makes it possible to prolong exposure to the linguistic stimuli; auditory stimuli are transient by nature and their exposure can be prolonged only through repetition. It is possible that visual information is more easily sorted out in the natural environment, since it can be more readily correlated with information gained through other modalities, such as touch and movement. This may well be the primary modality for such subjects, in which case, operating mainly in a visual medium should reduce the stress of integrating input and output signals. Therefore, this modality may serve more readily to internalize a system of information that is both abstract and arbitrary.

Finally, if the failure of language acquisition in the population we are investigating occurs because of the excessive difficulty of speech or because of the difficulty of accurately associating auditory symbols and their environmental referents in natural settings, then this technology might at least aid in the internalization of a coding system which could first serve as a substitute system and eventually as a bridge to a more normal communication system. Even if intelligible approximations of a normal output system cannot be mastered by subjects of this level, a substitute system would at least serve to expand the possibilities of researching cognitive problems in people so severely retarded. Until this study no extensive research has been done on language acquisition in retardates of this functional level.

MODIFICATIONS OF THE SYSTEM

The Yerkes computer system was moved to the Georgia Retardation Center virtually intact and a new expanded one was installed for continued work with Lana. Certain features of the system, however, have been modified to facilitate work with our population. Although the same lexigrams used with Lana are used with these subjects, word reassignments have been made. The vocabulary considered appropriate for this population is somewhat different from that used with Lana, and is based on diary studies of language acquisition of normal children (Bloom, 1970; Nelson, 1973; Schlesinger, 1971) and on clinical data in speech pathology of retarded children (Holland, 1975). In addition, the data on discrimination-learning problems in retarded subjects indicate that careful attention should be given to the selection of lexigrams. Flat, abstract stimuli are difficult for this population (Zeaman & House, 1963); thus an attempt has been made to provide maximum discriminability among the lexigrams in each word class. Pilot work with our subjects indicates that redundant color cues facilitate discrimination between classes.

A second change involves the display of the experimenter's communication to the subject. As with Lana, the display appears in projectors immediately above those for the subject's communication; in addition it remains on display while the subject selects the lexigrams for his own communication. This is done to alleviate difficulties associated with short-term memory and attentional problems.

It was also decided that the degree of precision required in Lana's performance is not necessarily desirable for our subjects, since motivation, a well-known problem in an institutionalized population, would not be improved if performance expectations were too high. Also, it can be inferred from studies on normal language acquisition that interpretability, not syntactic precision, is usually the prime factor in parents' acceptance of communication attempts by their very young children (Brown, Cazden, & Bellugi, 1967). Thus, the experimenter can override the computer's evaluation and deliver reinforcement on the basis of the correspondence between the communication content and contextual cues.

In order to facilitate transfer from Yerkish symbols to spoken English, the experimenter pronounces the English word associated with the lexigram on the key as it is depressed either by himself or by the subject, except when reading skills are being tested.

Finally, in addition to a system for projecting slides, movies are made of the subjects engaging in the actions they are being taught in the laboratory. This makes it possible not merely to depict actions more realistically, but also to slow them down and isolate movements in order to focus attention on specific attributes of actions. This is considered especially important in view of the difficulty that retarded subjects show in learning actions words (Stephens & Komechack, 1968).

OVERVIEW OF THE PROGRAM PLANS

Our initial study involves two approaches, one based on the procedures used with Lana, a second based on patterns of language acquisition found in normal children. Both programs involve a conversational format in which the experimenter asks questions, gives instructions, and provides commentary in the form of feedback. The experimenter's communications provide the primary multiword or sentence-like models for subjects in the second program and additional models for subjects in the first program. They also provide the linguistic context within which the subject's truncated communications are to be interpreted.

Training Method I

This approach involves training in the use of stock sentences into which a variety of objects, actions, agents, and modifiers can be substituted. Five general forms have been chosen, each governing a different communication function: requesting, naming, describing action, designating possession, and describing objects. The first sentence, *Please Experimenter give popcorn period* has been taught to one pilot subject using procedures similar to those used with Lana. First, the subject was taught to respond with *popcorn*; next, *Popcorn period*; then *Please popcorn period*. Next he was required to insert the action, *give*, and finally the experimenter's name. After the first 7 weeks of training, the subject was able to request five edibles with this sentence. His ability to identify these items was verified through a second sentence structure (the naming sentence), which he learned to use within a single session. After 14 additional weeks he can name 13 other objects. He also makes occasional spontaneous attempts to utter the words while pressing the keys. Eventually he will be taught to substitute other actions and then other agents.

Vocabulary expansion will be accomplished through the naming sentence, so that a variety of object names will be known by the time the pilot subject is introduced to new communication functions. A wide variety of substitutions will be taught in each sentence in order to provide maximum generality of each communication structure. All sentences will be extremely short during initial training, the longest consisting of no more than four words in addition to the period. After the subject gains proficiency with these sentences, it will be possible to expand by extending these sentences, by adding new sentence forms, and by teaching transformations.

Training Method II

Because Method I places a rather heavy output burden on the subject, a second approach has been designed, to be tested with another group of subjects of the same functional level. This approach involves teaching the same communication functions as with Method I and building toward the same sentence structures. In this approach, however, subjects are first taught to communicate with single words, then to construct two-word, and, later, longer, rule-governed strings. At the single-word stage, each word functions as a complete communication, its meaning, or the subject's intent, being inferred from the context as with normal children. New words are introduced in a single, unambigious context; then in order to maximize the usefulness of his vocabulary, the subject is taught to respond with that word to a new set of cues to obtain a somewhat different outcome. Since this procedure minimizes, in the earliest stages, the amount of output required in order to obtain a particular outcome, it should facilitate early acquisition of a variety of linguistic functions. After 17 weeks of training one subject has mastered 40 words and can respond to the experimenter's instruction to touch each object, which requires the subject to read the lexigrams communicated by the experimenter.

After five functions have been taught using single-word communications, the subject will be exposed to a new set of cues and new requirements to perform. These are designed to optimize his chances of producing intelligible two-word communications by forcing him to make deductions about the stimuli and link these with words he already knows. For example, an oddity problem could be given involving a red hat, a red box, and a blue box. The red box would be baited with a primary reinforcer and the subject asked to indicate which object he wants. In order to receive the baited box, he would be required to reply, *Red box*. If he said only *Red*, he would be given the red hat; if only *Box*, he would be given the blue box.

The linguistic context of the experimenter's communications will be manipulated so that in the early stages, when single-word communications are being taught, they will be highly specific and in later communications will become more and more general, necessitating greater specificity by the subject in order to obtain a desired outcome. Greater specificity will include not only longer word strings involving designation of actors, actions and objects, but also more complex structures including modifiers and prepositions.

Conclusion

All learning tasks involve developing internal representations for configurations of stimuli that can be accessed for later use. This process can be facilitated by externally provided codes (e.g., words) that delimit specific configurations. Conceived in this way, words can be seen to accomplish the following: to draw attention to the set of stimuli; to link elements of the set into wholes, thereby stabilizing the set; and to provide cues for retrieval of the elements discriminated and coded earlier. Since the symbol system must function as a primary cuing device, it must be internalized along with experiential stimuli and organized so as to facilitate retrieval and internal operations. One goal of the project is the study of the characteristics of the system of codes (i.e., the language) and the patterns of symbol use which demonstrate the nature and roles of the mechanisms involved. A more immediate goal, however, is to evaluate the strategies and technological features available in this training system.

It may be found that one training approach (probably the second) functions better for lower-level subjects, whereas the other is more useful with higher-level subjects. If a subject is capable of developing only single-word communications, it would seem more useful to teach him a wide variety of communication functions and a useful core vocabulary for doing so. Although Method II has the advantage of teaching a wider variety of communication functions in the earliest stage, Method I may facilitate higher linguistic accuracy. Method I provides a complete model of each communication structure, which, although initially not completely comprehensible to the subject, should become differentiated as substitutions are made in each word position. Method I may provide a stronger basis for learning to use multiword communication forms in a fashion that will be intelligible to the recipients of the communication, since it may be easier with this form of training for the subject to develop response chains using words that have no physically perceptible referents and whose linguistic function is to relate words which do refer to specific objects, actions, or attributes. Method I, however, not only places a heavy output requirement on the subject; it also requires considerably more processing in order to associate the individual communication elements with their referents, since, in Method I, elements will have to be abstracted from the sentence arrays in which they are learned.

It should be easier for the subject trained with Method II to develop a clear understanding of the meanings or referents of individual words that he will later use as components of more explicit and complex communication structures. The development of linguistic performance skills is limited by both output competence and perceptual development—one cannot develop reliable internal representations of entities that he cannot perceive in a stable manner. Consideration must be given to the development of processes for differentiating environmental stimuli and for organizing them in ways that facilitate first the recognition of existence; second, the conceptualization of defining properties; and, third, the comprehension of temporal and spatial relations among items. Performance tasks that exceed the ability of the subjects to handle these processes will be mastered either not at all or merely in rote fashion, and thus not be fully functional or completely under the subject's control. Thus a manageable program must break the learning tasks into sequences of experiences which provide explicit focus of attention on the referents or on the linguistic functions of words. Training Method II is addressed to these considerations.

Although some may feel that the sequence of mastery manifest by normal children provides the better model for such a program, it can be argued that these subjects are not normal, and have failed to profit from the experiences that facilitate language acquisition not only in children of normal intelligence but also in retarded children who function at a higher level than these subjects; thus, it seems worthwhile to try an approach that is different but that has been found to work with a subject of another species. On the other hand, it can be argued that the stages of linguistic mastery exhibited by normal children reflect the development of cognitive competence; thus, performance tasks should be structured so that processing complexities are introduced in manageable increments; since we do not yet understand the cognitive bases underlying the acquisition of linguistic skills, the pattern of emergence of linguistic performance skills in normal children should be taken as the model, on the assumption that the cognitive bases for these skills develop in terms of increasing difficulty and complexity. Which approach will in the long run facilitate the greatest intelligibility and linguistic productivity, however, must be determined empirically.

REFERENCES

Baumeister, A. A., & Kellas, G. Process variables in paired-associate learning of retardates. In N. R. Ellis (Ed.) *International review of research in mental retardation*, Vol. 5. New York: Academic Press, 1971.

Bloom, L. *Language development: Form and function in emerging grammars.* Cambridge, Massachusetts: MIT Press, 1970.

Borkowski, J. G., & Wanschura, P. B. Mediational processes in the retarded. In N. R. Ellis (Ed.), *International review of research in mental retardation*, Vol. 7. New York: Academic Press, 1974.

Bricker, D. Imitative sign training as a facilitator of word–object association with low-functioning children. *American Journal of Mental Deficiency*, 1972, 76, 509–516.

Brown, A. L. The role of strategic behavior in retardate memory. In N. R. Ellis (Ed.), *International review of research in mental retardation*, Vol. 7. New York: Academic Press, 1974.

Brown, R., Cazden, C. G., & Bellugi, U. The Child's Grammar from 1 to 11. Paper presented at 1967 Minnesota Symposium on Child Psychology, Minneapolis, 1967.

Carrier, J. K., Jr. Nonspeech noun usage training with severely and profoundly retarded children. *Journal of Speech and Hearing Research*, 1974, 17, 510–517.

Ellis, N. R. Memory processes in retardates and normals. In N. R. Ellis (Ed.), *International review of research in mental retardation*, Vol. 4. New York: Academic Press, 1970.

Graham, L. W. Language programming and intervention. In L. L. Lloyd (Ed.), *Communication assessment and intervention strategies*. Baltimore: University Park Press, 1976.

Holland, A. L. Language therapy for children: Some thoughts on context and content. *Journal of Speech and Hearing Disorders*, 1975, 40, 514–523.

Kaufman, M. E.,& Prehm, H. J. A review of research on learning sets and transfer of training in mental defectives. In N. R. Ellis (Ed.), *International review of research in mental retardation*, Vol. 2. New York: Academic Press, 1966.

Lowry, P. W., & Ross, L. E. Severely retarded children as impulsive responders: Improved performance with response delay. *American Journal of Mental Deficiency*, 1975, 80, 133–138.

Nelson, K. Structure and strategy in learning to talk. *Monographs of the Society for Research in Child Development*, 1973, 38 (1–2, Serial No. 149).

Olson, D. R. Information-processing limitations of mentally retarded children. *American Journal of Mental Deficiency*, 1971, *75*, 478–486.

Ross, D. The relationship between intentional learning, incidental learning and type of reward in preschool, educable mental retardates. *Child Development*, 1970, *41*, 1151–1158.

Schlesinger, I. M. Production of utterances and language acquisition. In D. I. Slobin (Ed.), *The ontogenesis of grammar: A theoretical symposium*. New York: Academic Press, 1971.

Scott, K. G., & Scott, M. S. Research and theory in short-term memory. In N. R. Ellis (Ed.), *International review of research in mental retardation*, Vol. 3. New York: Academic Press, 1968.

Spitz, H. H. The role of input organization in the learning and memory of mental retardates. In N. R. Ellis (Ed.), *International review of research in mental retardation*, Vol. 2. New York: Academic Press, 1966.

Stephens, W. E., & Komechack, M. Concept learning in mentally retarded subjects using three types of verbal labels. *Psychonomic Science*, 1968, *13*, 231–232.

Thompson, T., & Grabowski, J. *Behavior modification of the mentally retarded*. New York: Oxford University Press, 1972.

Ullman, D. G. Breadth of attention and retention in mentally retarded and intellectually average children. *American Journal of Mental Deficiency*, 1974, *78*, 640–648.

Ullman, D. G., & Routh, D. K. Discrimination learning in mentally retarded and non-retarded children as a function of the number of relevant dimensions. *American Journal of Mental Deficiency*, 1971, *76*, 176–180.

Zeaman, D., & House, B. J. The role of attention in retardate discrimination learning. In N. R. Ellis (Ed.), *Handbook of mental deficiency*. New York: McGraw-Hill, 1963.

Zigler, E. The retarded child as a whole person. In D. K. Routh (Ed.), *The experimental psychology of mental retardation*. Chicago: Aldine, 1973.

PART V

Language and Communication: A Perspective

chapter 16

Communication, Language, and Lana: A Perspective

E. SUE SAVAGE AND DUANE M. RUMBAUGH

Georgia State University, and
Yerkes Regional Primate Research Center

INTRODUCTION

The LANA Project was initiated with a twofold purpose in mind: first to determine whether or not chimpanzees could acquire and use complex grammatical linguistic skills, and second, to find out if modern technology and computer science might be advantageously employed to aid in the acquisition and maintenance of such skills. Although other projects had dealt with the first question (Gardner & Gardner, 1971; Premack, 1971), it was felt that since language learning was such a complex cumulative process, neither its acquisition nor its use could be thoroughly understood or demonstrated without a complete record of all exchanges between man and ape.

It has become apparent that not only can modern technology and computer science be successfully wedded to aid chimpanzees in the acquisition of language skills, but the system, now that it has been developed, can also be used with alinguistic human beings (Parkel, White, & Warner, Chapter 15, this volume). As so often seems to be the case, the latter question, which is basically a technical one, has proved to be much easier to answer than the first one, whose nature is fundamentally theoretical. Prior to the success of the Gardners' project, there had been little concern or disagreement about the nature and definition of language. Language was that which man did, and one presumed that if animals could talk, they would do so in a fashion similar to man. However, they could not, and a species-oriented definition of language was perfectly acceptable. When the chimpanzee language projects began to demonstrate that apes were capable of something that appeared to be suspiciously language-like, the species-oriented definition had to be cast aside, and the search for a structural and/or functional definition of language, which would differentiate language from all other types of communication, began.

It is now apparent that a final decision as to whether Lana (or any chimpanzee) does or does not have language cannot be made until a better understanding of the requisites for, and processes of, language is reached. This is a difficult task since, in order to define those properties which are unique to linguistic exchanges, it is necessary to consider communicative processes in general. The apparent gap between the nonverbal communication systems of all nonhuman primates and language has long been regarded as an enigma and, consequently, often led to the premature conclusion that the two types of communication systems (verbal and nonverbal) are two independent, although compatible, systems (Lancaster, 1975). Although this conclusion is flattering to our own species, it is not acceptable within an evolutionary framework. For a communicative system as complex and pervasive as language to have suddenly appeared with a complicated grammar and unique internal structure, completely independent of the former highly elaborate and effective nonverbal communicative mode, would be something of an evolutionary heresy. Yet, the link between the communication systems of all the other primates and that of man has, to date, remained unclear, and its existence repeatedly questioned. It is to this issue that the chimpanzee language projects must address themselves.

To place the LANA Project (and the other chimpanzee language studies) in proper perspective, the findings should be related to primate nonverbal skills, on the one hand, and to human linguistic skills, on the other hand. We must look to see what an animal who does not typically acquire language, when given some language skills, can tell us about the relationship which exists between these two forms of communication. Just as Lana, herself, has learned to span the gulf which, until now, had separated nonverbal from verbal creatures, so must we, by careful study, try to understand the nature and implications of this bridge she has structured.

This final chapter is a preliminary attempt to evaluate and reassess some widely held ideas regarding nonhuman primate communication in general. This reassessment is based upon much that Lana has taught us, but also upon the many things that other primates have demonstrated that they can do. Previous definitions and classification systems of primate nonverbal communication are considered and found lacking in any sort of framework that differentiates communicative processes of the rather advanced primates, such as chimpanzees and gorillas, from those of lower primates.

Communication is, in our opinion, more than patterns, signs, signals or symbols; it is also a functional process in which information is transmitted back and forth between two or more individuals.[1] Previous analyses of nonhuman primate communication are reviewed and found to concentrate upon the sequencing and patterning of various signals as opposed to the semantics of the transmission. A new approach is presented which eschews the set of all social signals as being the base of communication and which emphasizes instead information transmission. It is hoped that this view will enable common questions to be asked and answered, of both linguistic and alinguistic communicative interchanges. For it is only through such an approach that similarities in the processing and structuring of the maze of communicative stimuli can be revealed between the linguistic and the nonverbal communication systems. Ways in which studies of chimpanzee language acquisition can, and have, helped to illuminate the cognitive encoding and decoding processes that must also occur in many complex nonverbal chimpanzee-like communicative exchanges are discussed in conclusion, and the implications of such studies for future research are considered.

DEFINITIONS OF COMMUNICATION

To date, *communication* is a term that has been used to cover a broad range of phenomena, encompassing innate releasing mechanisms, language, and a great deal in between. Hockett (1960) defined communication as an act by which one individual "triggered" the behavior of another ("triggering" in this sense implies that the energy expended during the output of a communicative pattern is unrelated to the energy of the response). Altmann (1967) later attempted to make this definition somewhat more concise by stating that communication can be said to have occurred when "the behavior of one individual affects the behavior of the other [p. 326]." Although this definition is widely accepted by the majority of researchers dealing with animal communication, it suffers from what is at once both its greatest strength and weakness: its generality. As stated, it encompasses even reflexive, nondirected acts such as yawning, blinking, sneez-

---

[1]The term *information* is used here in the general sense of "knowledge acquired in any manner" (Webster's), and not in the specific sense of information theory.

ing, etc., when such acts alter the response pattern of any individual who happens to react to their occurrence. Such a definition also obfuscates differing levels of complexity of the communicative process because viewing communication as reducible to altered probabilities of the set of all social behaviors enables little to be said other than that two or more acts tend to be ordered or conditionally dependent in time and/or space. This definition does not deal with the question of how an animal initially selects, from a wide range of behaviors, the precise pattern or set of patterns that it does to instigate a particular type of communicative interchange (grooming, play, copulation, etc.), nor does it address the question of how the recipient selectively interprets and attends to one pattern (or one set of patterns) from among the influx of numerous simultaneous environmental happenings. Cognitive encoding and decoding processes are not viewed as structuring communication in other than a sequential sense, and neither the initiator nor the recipient is viewed as "monitoring" the effect of his communicative patterns for the purpose of appropriately altering his behaviors when that which he is trying to communicate is not successfully transmitted.

CATEGORICAL SCHEMATA AND
SEQUENTIAL ANALYSES

Present attempts to classify or organize the varieties of communicative acts also suffer from the fact that they do not reflect any kind of phylogenetic ordering that would allow some communicative processes to be judged as relatively advanced in contrast to others. They have concentrated upon (1) physical attributes of the communicative act, such as the channel of transmission, intensity, or frequency (Scott, 1968); (2) sets of abstract properties (e.g., discrete or graded, openness, or displacement) that can be judged as either present or absent during any given communicative event (Hockett & Altmann, 1968); and (3) the basic functions or needs served by the communicative interchange (e.g., emotive, cooperative, identification, or social play) (Sebeok, 1965; Smith, 1969). None of these classification systems lends itself to any sort of hierarchical ordering that would correspond closely with the increasing elaboration found in the primate central nervous system. In fact, it is frequently pointed out that any connection between increasing cortical elaboration and complexity of communication systems is a tenuous one, as the number of nonverbal communicative display elements varies within a relatively narrow range (15–45) and is not closely correlated with degree of encephalization (Smith, 1969; Chevalier-Skolnikoff, 1974).

Thus, animal communication, as presently studied, is theoretically limited on two counts: (1) Functionally, it deals with the sequencing of display behaviors while emphasizing that neither the behaviors themselves nor their messages are similar to language; and (2) structurally, it offers categorical schemata that provide for a set of determinations to be made regarding various aspects of communicative acts, but no hierarchical structuring of types of communication is provided for after such determinations have been made. For example, whereas one communicative system may be judged to incorporate "broadcast transmission," "auditory channel," "rapid fading" and "interchangeability," there is no way to compare its level of complexity to a system that is judged to incorporate "discreteness," "semanticity," and "specialization."

Our approach differs from the traditional one in that we maintain that all communicative processes, in order to be understood, must be seen as contextually bound, rule-structured interchanges between two or more participants. To determine whether or not communication is occurring and, if so, what kind of communication it is, one needs to know more than that the likelihood of a particular event is increased or decreased by events which preceded it. It is also necessary to know the goal of the communication and the rules governing the exchange.

Altered probability distributions demonstrate only that the exchange of behavioral patterns between individuals is not entirely random, and that some patterned sequences can be detected during such an exchange. The reduction in uncertainty that a stochastic analysis provides should be recognized as being basically a measure of the observer's ability to predict the sequencing of those behavioral events which he has selected as "units." To the extent that his "units" correspond with those of the animal, the analysis may also reflect the animal's ability to predict another's behavior, but in no sense does it measure or even deal with the semantics of the transmission or the knowledge that the recipient has acquired via the sequenced exchange of signals. That it may seem to do so is a function of the choice of an information theory approach which equates "information" with the predictability of behavioral chains.[2] Such approaches presume that the set of all behavioral events (i.e., the ethogram) is equal to the total uncertainty in the situation. If the size of the initial set of behaviors can be reduced by half by knowing that a particular behavior has occurred, then the occurrence of that behavior is said to have provided one "bit" of "information" since the total uncertainty in the situation is, by definition, the same as the ethogram of all communicative events. These approaches make the basic assumption that communication is merely a complex exchange of these, and only these, behavioral units.

The difficulties inherent in these approaches can, perhaps, best be

[2]"Information" in this sense refers a specific usage as defined within information theory where one bit of information is said to be that amount of information which reduces the set of all possible choices by one-half. In this sense, it is strictly a unit of measurement.

illustrated by drawing an analogy with language. If we were to take as our base the set of all English words without regard for their semantic component, then the total initial uncertainty in any English linguistic interchange would be equal to the set of all English words. This means that by knowing a given word, for example, "into," we can attempt to determine whether or not some words are more likely to follow "into" than others. Indeed, such is the case, and lengthy lists of words that tend to co-occur in sequence have been devised within the sub-discipline of verbal learning. However, one would not presume that, by identifying sets of words that tended to occur in sequence, anything was learned about the knowledge or facts exchanged in a given communication, especially if the semantic component of the words were initially undefined. Indeed, taking the set of all words as our base would be seen as an error, since the words themselves are merely vehicles of transmission. There is nothing about the set of all words which we want to delimit with a sentence like: *He put the red block in the box on the table.* In such a case, it is a set of environmental facts, what did he put and where did he put it, that we wish to communicate. The exact words and their sequences are, within relatively broad limits, irrelevant to the facts to be transmitted. We could say, for example, *Into the open rectangle sitting on the flat-topped piece of furniture, the male placed a rouge-colored chunk of wood.* This sentence is perhaps less efficient, but nevertheless transmits the same facts with quite different words arranged in a completely different sequence.

COMMUNICATION AS RULE-GOVERNED EXCHANGES

While it may not be as obvious, the same sort of situation prevails with primate nonverbal communication systems. If conditional probability determinations are to be at all useful, we must first accurately define, for any given situation, what "real" information or facts are to be transmitted and then proceed to determine how communicative signals serve to transmit those facts. If we continue to equate the set of all signals with the total uncertainty that the signals themselves are intended to reduce, we shall learn very little about the true nature of primate communication and the analysis will be simply an intellectual exercise of expertise.

In contrast to viewing communication as merely a set of social behaviors and/or signals with associated conditional probabilities, we propose that it be viewed as a rule-governed, goal-oriented informational exchange between two or more participants. The rules governing the exchange are presumed to be commonly understood by all participants and to specify (1) which communicative events are to be attended to, (2) the order in which they are to be attended to, and (3) the way in which the informational content is to be extracted when two or more events co-occur. For an example of how this approach begins with a different base than does a stochastic analysis, let us take an example in which two chimpanzees are observed sitting near one another and one is holding two objects while the other chimpanzee is holding none. Let the situation be further circumscribed in that (if a bit of anthropomorphism may be permitted for the purpose of example) the first chimpanzee (A) wants one of the objects held by the second chimpanzee (B). The sequencing of communicative events using a sequential analysis approach would look something like:

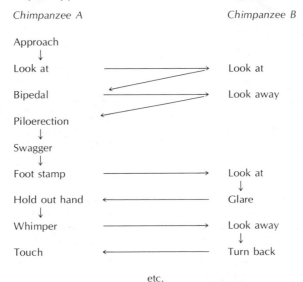

Chimpanzee A   Chimpanzee B

Approach
  ↓
Look at   ——————————→   Look at

Bipedal   ←——————————→   Look away

Piloerection
  ↓
Swagger
  ↓
Foot stamp   ——————————→   Look at
                                  ↓
Hold out hand ←——————————   Glare
  ↓
Whimper   ——————————→   Look away
                                  ↓
Touch   ←——————————   Turn back

etc.

With many such exchanges, patterns would begin to emerge and statements of the likelihood of occurrence could be constructed. For example, we might find that if we knew a "hold out hand" had just occurred, then a "low whimper" had a 60% chance of occurring next, and touch had a 25% chance. Together these two patterns would thus account for 85% of the events that followed "hold out hand." The sort of information that the chimpanzees transmitted about themselves, i.e., the objects they wanted, the context, etc., would not be considered.

The assessment of the same situation from a rule-governed, goal-directed approach would be quite different. Elements to be considered in terms of the informational content of the situation would be as follows:

Information to be transmitted by Chimpanzee A
1. He recognizes that the two objects held by B or on the ground next

to B are, indeed, in the possession of B (i.e., that B controls access to those objects and consequently will react to behaviors of others which are directed toward the objects)
2. He wants an object, as opposed to a gesture of reassurance, a bit of food, etc.
3. Which of the two objects it is that he wants
4. What kinds of behaviors might be engaged in to get that object

Information to be transmitted by Chimpanzee B
1. That the objects he holds, or which are nearby, are in his exclusive control
2. Whether or not control of an object might be relinquished
3. What he would require in order to relinquish control of an object
4. What kinds of behaviors might be engaged in to sustain exclusive access to the object

At any point during the communicative interchange, the information base could alter for a variety of reasons: A third individual might approach, another preferred object might be found lying around, a distracting fight could break out nearby, etc. The important point, however, is that while various complex patterns must be employed to transmit information of the above sort, the patterns themselves are not synonymous with that information.

A communicative analysis at such a level would attempt to determine how each of the enumerated "pieces of information" was transmitted. This would include the behavioral patterns employed and, if any, the referents of those patterns (thus, the referent of a "hold out hand" gesture would be the object toward which the hand was extended). It would also try to determine whether or not there were only rules for the juxtaposition of different signal patterns or for the juxtaposition of signal patterns and contextual referents.

Because this approach deals with the semantic or factual components of information transmitted in a given situation, it can be used to compare linguistic and nonlinguistic communication, as well as different types of each. For purposes of experimental investigation, the parameters of that which is to be communicated may be determined in advance (the situation in which one chimpanzee has two objects and another has none is, for example, relatively simple to contrive and control) and the manner of transmission may be studied across species and across communicative modes. However, unless *what* is communicated is separated from *how* it is communicated, such cross-species comparisons contain seriously confounded measures of both the means (or behaviors) of communication and the goal of the communication.

The example given (in which one chimpanzee wants a particular object held by another) does not delineate the way in which the factual information to be transmitted by the animal is to be arrived at. Such a determination is essential, though, if a rule-governed approach to communication is to be feasible. The goal of the communication must be determined in an arbitrary, nonsubjective, clearly definable manner. Admittedly, this is, at present, often difficult, and procedures providing for such determinations need to be developed. The chimpanzee language projects provide a valuable starting point for the development of such techniques because they offer a setting in which (1) a goal can be easily structured, (2) one of the communicating parties (the human experimenter) can intentionally vary his responses to indicate that the information, as transmitted, was not understood, thereby creating a situation in which that information must be rearranged and retransmitted, and (3) it becomes possible to allow a chimpanzee to translate or clarify, through the use of lexigrams, the information which it conveys nonverbally. Many of Tim's conversations with Lana (Gill, Chapter 12, this volume) are indicative of the feasibility of the approach, although they were not initiated with that in mind. The basic format of such conversations is as follows: Tim establishes, by observing Lana's nonverbal cues, combined with an extensive knowledge of her past behavior, that she would like a particular object, event, or food item. He then requests that she use her keyboard to ask for what he knows she would like. Through the keyboard, he intentionally indicates that he does not understand partial or indirect messages and he asks that she expand upon or alter her communication. She often does so, using novel combinations in an attempt to convey to Tim what she wants. It is important to note that Tim is able to "produce" these conversations because he has determined the information content to be transferred in advance of the linguistic exchange, and that this determination is often made at the nonverbal level.

COGNITIVE STRUCTURES AND COMMUNICATION

Implicit in this view is the assumption that nonverbal and verbal communications do not, as is so often presumed, represent discontiguous processes. Both are dependent, instead, upon similar complex coding and decoding cognitive processes and, to the extent that these processes are comparable between species, the abilities of different species to exchange various types of information will also be similar. Cognitive styles of perceiving and ordering the world are a combined function of an organism's innate neurological equipment and his sensory–motor interactions with his environmental surroundings.

Piaget (1952, 1972) has demonstrated in considerable detail how the human infant, through sensory–motor interaction with his environmental surroundings, comes to construct cognitive schemata and maps of the world. These schemata, in turn, affect the structuring of his perception of reality and become the logical lattices (displacement, associativity, reversibility, object permanence, etc.) which undergrid language. Language, therefore, is a public, external, commonly agreed upon productive system that maps the conceptual schemata that are themselves structured through sensory–motor interaction of the organism with the environment.

Nonhuman primate infants display many of the sensory–motor schemata described for human infants (Hughes & Redshaw, 1973, 1974) and, to the degree that they have the cognitive capacity to perform the operations of assimilation and accommodation commensurate with the human infant, their cognitive schemata should resemble those of human infants. Similarities in cognitive schemata across primates, especially between ape and man, should enable them to process the information entailed in complex communicative interchanges in a similar fashion, regardless of whether or not the mode of transmission is linguistic. The cognitive schemata involved in the exchange of information at a nonverbal level should be identical with those used to exchange the same information linguistically. This is not to say that the nonverbal communication system is to be equated with, or can handle, all the information that the linguistic system can; it cannot. However, this does imply that there is a great deal of overlap between the two systems and, when they exchange similar types of information, it is reasonable to presume that, at least in closely related species such as ape and man, similar cognitive schemata undergird the exchange, regardless of its transmission mode. It is through the comparative study of the structure and rules inherent in such cognitive schemata that we shall find the requisites for, and the deep grammar of, basic linguistic processes.

Numerous conceptual skills (more–less, same–different, if–then, etc.) previously believed to be strictly linguistic, have already been displayed by Lana and other language-trained chimpanzees. These chimpanzees are capable of demonstrating such abstract relational skills because the concepts are already a part of the way in which they have cognitively structured their world. The report of Lana's acquisition of "more–less" (Dooley & Gill, Chapter 13, this volume), clearly demonstrates this point. Lana was shown to be able to discriminate accurately "more and less" prior to any training. She then learned to attach abstract labels to these concepts and to make judgments based first upon one aspect and then upon another of the "more–less" relationship. Although this training may be viewed as sharpening and clarifying her perception of "more and less," it cannot be viewed as producing the original concept. Thus it appears that the chimpanzee language projects are basically efforts to build a formal or public linguistic bridge between man and ape. The ape possesses covert cognitive processes prerequisite to linguistic behavior, but lacks sufficient intelligence to formulate and concatenate, rapidly and spontaneously, unlimited arbitrary symbols that represent its percept of the world.

It is, perhaps, at this point appropriate to raise the question of why the verbal and nonverbal systems have, to date, been considered to be independent by students of either system (Altmann, 1968; Ekman, 1972; Lancaster, 1975; Werner & Kaplan, 1963). The answer, we believe, is threefold. First, man tends to be very egocentric and, thus, finds it self-satisfying to view language as a unique form of communication. Second, the "units" of primate nonverbal communication (but not necessarily the system governing their use) tend to have a heavy genetic component when contrasted with the arbitrary words characteristic of language. Third, models such as those of Piaget (1952), which describe the cognitive–linguistic development of the human child and which emphasize that language merely maps underlying conceptual skills, tend to limit their frame of reference to the human being. In so doing, many of their examples and descriptions deal with infant–object situations. Principles such as associativity and reversibility are developed mainly through observations of infant–object interaction patterns. Because nonhuman primate infants initially spend the majority of their time clinging to their mothers and most of their interactions with their surroundings are socially oriented as opposed to object oriented, these concepts have been viewed as difficult to apply to nonhuman primate behavior. There is no reason to presume, however, that much of what an infant can learn through interacting with objects cannot also be learned by interacting with other individuals in a complex social setting. Certainly, object permanence, if–then relationships, associativity, interchangeability, etc., can be acquired through social interaction, and this type of interaction may, in fact, be the prepotent setting in which to learn such concepts.

CLASSIFICATION OF COMMUNICATIVE ACTS

If we accept the ideas that similar species come to structure their cognitive worlds in common fashions through sensory–motor actions, that it is this cognitive structure which underlies their communicative processes, and that to understand these structures, or the processes themselves, we must look at communication from a semantic, rule-governed perspective; one question still remains. How did arbitrary word symbols, concatenated according to a complex grammatical system, arise from the interchange of nonverbal, heavily genetically prescribed, facial expressions, postures, vocalizations, etc? To answer this question, we must look at the nonverbal communicative system not in terms of channel, activity, discreteness, or any other such characteristics. Rather, we must develop a categorical schema that allows classification of communicative acts according to their increasing ability to separate, in both time and/or space, representations of events from events per se. However, to do so is not without some terminological drawbacks, since the words, symbol, signal, sign, etc., have repeatedly been used in such a variety of fashions as to make further distinctions between them a matter of additional confusion rather than clarification. But this ability (to separate events from their representations) is the fundamental element of language and it is the elaboration of this skill that gives language the power to create and shape a multitude of miniworlds within the minds of speaker and listener.

Level 1—Physiological Attributes

Important sources of information, though not communicative acts per se, are the more or less enduring characteristics associated with age, sex, and physiological states of animals. The natal coat of the infant, the distinguishing dimensions of sexual dimorphism, the elaborated canines of most males, and the estrous swellings of the females of some species, etc., all define important aspects of the nature of the animal and, consequently, are indicative of how it might be expected to respond in certain contexts. These physiological attributes cannot be said to be communicative events, since they are not really actions or events at all, but merely states of affairs. There is no separation in time between the physiological state and its representation. The information that these physiological states avail to the receiver is not the result of active communicative processes on the part of the initiator; rather it is due to the selective attention, interpretation, and inferences made by the receiver. Thus, at this level, communication, to use the term loosely, is not a two-way process; it is simply a function of the conclusions drawn by the perceiver. Other important sources of information, none of which are behavioral, include, among other things, the attributes of things and events of the physical world and the characteristics of vegetation, the states of the fruit which it bears, and the proximity of vegetation to one who might be searching for refuge. While neither the physical environment nor vegetation communicate their attributes through specific acts, the fact that they are what they are avails important information to the receiver because of his ability to organize and process such stimuli.

Level 2—Social Interchange and Parameters of Expression

At the next level, we move from states of affairs to discrete behavioral events, and it becomes important to draw a distinction between general social behavior and those specific behaviors which serve as communicative acts. All behavior holds the potential of affording important information to those observers who are able to draw the proper inferences, but that does not make all behavior tantamount to communication. For example, a bite might convey information regarding the initiator's emotional state or attitude, but it is not necessarily a communicative act. The *function* of a "communicative act" is the transmission of content information to others; it is important to distinguish between the action itself and its function. A "communicative act" cannot logically be the informational content that it transmits or the term is without meaning. Although this may seem overly obvious, many studies of primate "communication" focus primarily upon behaviors such as biting, grooming, playing, slapping, and chasing. Although such behaviors might, on occasion, serve to signal or to transmit information essentially apart from the acts themselves, they more often simply communicate that which they are.

However, associated with most social behaviors are parameters of expression, which include obvious things, like the intensity, frequency, duration and speed of the act, along with more subtle components, such as muscle tension and pauses. Using these parameters of expression, the individual conveys his mood and affect regarding the behavior patterns that are being exchanged and, through interindividual sequenced exchanges of similar behavior patterns (playslap, playbite, grab, pull on, etc.), all participants appear to coordinate their behaviors and bring their movements and physiological arousal states into synchrony (Smith, 1976; McGinnis, 1972). The exchange of complex social patterns such as play, reproduction and grooming, requires that the independent behavior of all participants be mutually coordinated and appropriately sequenced. This necessitates a constant monitoring system that can adjust both the patterning and intensity of entire sets of behaviors in order to accommodate reciprocal interchanges, such as occur during play or copulation. Thus, if one animal is engaging in rough, rapid play movements and another in slow, gentle play patterns, the interchange will be uneven and irregularly sequenced and probably will be quickly terminated.

These parameters of expression are often referred to as part of the animal communication system and, indeed, they do convey important aspects of its internal motivation. They are, however, also the event itself and, while a rough playslap may convey something quite distinct from a gentle one, both are behavioral, but not necessarily communicative events. It is in this area, that of the interindividual exchange of social behavior, that the traditional sort of stochastic analysis should prove most fruitful, since it is here that interindividual relationships are structured and, thus, the sequencing of social behaviors should vary with the type of social relationship.

Level 3—Elaborated Social Patterns

At the next level, we find communicative acts that are tied, in time and space, to the event, but that are not the event themselves. These are the first true communicative acts, and, through elaboration, alteration, or ritualization, serve to draw attention to the event and/or particular aspects of that event which they represent. An example would be the charging, slapping, drumming displays of the chimpanzee. These patterns are often closely correlated with attack, but the attack is typically a somewhat ritualized exercise consisting of hitting or stamping on the recipient. No real damage is generally done, but the display itself appears fierce. The communicative components (hunched shoulders, piloerection, glaring face, foot stamping, etc.) all may occur in an actual attack, but in a display they are disproportionately emphasized and separated, in contrast to other more serious components, like biting or slamming to the ground.

Level 4—Incipient Acts

At this level of separation between an event and representation, we encounter incipient acts, and the first type of communication in which an event begins to become detached in time from that which it represents. Incipient acts are defined as movements, expressions, etc., which are reduced or abbreviated versions of the events they represent. They are no longer actually connected to the event, but are small anticipatory portions of it and serve to suggest the events to others when generated. Social patterns such as "round mouth threat" (incipient licking motion), "head bob" (incipient attack motion), and "crouching" (incipient fleeing motion), would fall into this category. Some of these actions are probably strongly genetically predetermined; others, perhaps not at all.

Most incipient acts occur within a limited range of contextual situations. Thus, play signals are not seen during grooming bouts and lip begging is not seen during displays or threats. However, within the general context, an incipient act can be used in a wider variety of ways than a ritualized-event-linked act. Thus, a playface given while holding a leafy branch and moving away from another can be used to initiate a keep-away chase game. A playface given with vocal laughter and head-covering can be used as a signal to continue tickling. The fact that such signals can be combined and

recombined in various ways, and that environmental cues are also employed (e.g., holding a leafy branch), indicate that similar deductive processes must be occurring between sender and receiver, or else information
could not be adequately transmitted. Shaking of the branch draws attention
to the object, moving away is an incipient "being chased motion" and the
playface defines the motivational state of the sender. Such combined
signals transmit an invitation to a specific game because complementary
deductive inferences regarding their meaning are made by both participants
within the communicative exchange.

Level 5—Iconic Gestures

The next level of separation between an event and the communicative
signal representing that event is that of iconic gesturing. At this level, the
representation can become completely detached in time from the event
itself. With iconic gestures, the communicative signal is now no longer even
an abbreviated portion of the original event, but is, rather, a facsimile of that
event. Occasionally this distinction is blurred at a morphological level
because iconic gestures and incipient acts may appear similar. However,
only iconic gestures can be used to indicate what the recipient of the signal
should do. For example, a "come" gesture, made by moving the hand
toward the body (McGinnis, 1972) is not an incipient approach movement
by the signaler, but rather a facsimile of the movement the initiator wishes
the recipient to make.

Iconic gesturing is observed frequently in man, and can be used to
transfer complex information between individuals of differing linguistic and
cultural backgrounds (Hewes, Chapter 1, this volume). It has also been
reported for both wild and captive chimpanzees (van Lawick-Goodall,
1968; Savage & Bakeman, 1976). Because iconic gestures are facsimiles of
events, they occur in a much broader range of contexts than incipient
signals. For example, the open extended palm, an iconic begging gesture,
can be used to ask for food when animals are eating, for objects in the
possession of another, for another to approach and play, approach and
groom, etc. They are not, however, independent of context; their appropriate interpretation is almost completely dependent upon the manner in
which each gesture is incorporated into a given context. Furthermore, the
greater the variety of situations in which a given signal can be used, the
more flexible the communication system becomes. Yet, increasing flexibility
necessitates an increasingly complex encoding and decoding process and, if
only particular contextual cues are to be considered as opposed to others
that are present but irrelevant, then markers to indicate which are the
relevant cues must also be employed.

As context-dependent coding of nonverbal information through the coordinated use of elaborated social patterns, incipient acts, and iconic gestures becomes more complex, both because increasing numbers of signals occur simultaneously and because they come to be used in a wide variety of differing contexts, the number of possible interpretations that can be made in any particular communicative setting also increases. It is difficult to see how information could be adequately transmitted in a situation where there are elaborated social patterns, incipient acts, iconic gestures, and contextual cues combined in a communicative interchange, unless there is some set of common rules whereby the salient features of any given situation are selected, combined, and interpreted in a similar fashion by all members of the species. Such rules could only be based on the inferential logic inherent in the situation and in the compatible cognitive capacities of signaler and recipient.

Level 6—Arbitrary Signs

The final level of separation between an event and the communicative representation of that event is that of the arbitrary representations (e.g., words, lexigrams). At this level, there is no necessary spatial or temporal connection whatsoever between the event and the arbitrary representation which stands for that event. Furthermore, unlike iconic gestures, arbitrary representations can be applied to abstract properties and concepts that are impossible to depict iconically. For example, a particular shape, such as triangular or circular, can be iconically represented, yet how can one represent the concept of "shape" itself with an iconic gesture? Only an arbitrary representation will suffice. This property allows arbitrary representations, when concatenated in numbers, to themselves become the context, the syntax, for their own expression. Contexts can be represented by them and, thus, the final separation of a communicative event and its representation is accomplished. Now communication no longer needs to take place in a context so that use can be made of the cues present therein. The context itself can be portrayed by, and becomes, the interrelationship of arbitrary signs; language is born.

The juxtaposition and sequencing of these arbitrary representations is, of course, not done randomly, but according to predefined rules that are agreed upon by all members of a common linguistic community. Yet whereas these rules may, at first, seem to vary from one language to another, there appear to be some basic commonalities among all human languages, and it is probably these basic structural–perceptual commonalities that allow individuals from different linguistic backgrounds to communicate rather adequately by making heavy use of the contextual surroundings (holding up or pointing to the objects of discussion) and iconic gestures. This type of communication is possible because of similar interpretive processes on the part of both individuals. For example, if A points to the bat, then to the ball, then swings the bat and holds it toward B, B can *infer* that *he* is being asked to do something to the *ball* with the *bat*, even though the linguistic grammatical translations of such actions might be very different in both languages. These common inferential or deductive-logical processes are suggestive of the deep structure of Chomskyian (1968) grammar; that is, the phrase markers that contain all of the information relevant to the semantic interpretation of a sentence.

SUMMARY AND CONCLUSIONS

It is clear that the central requisite to communication is interpretation. Without it, communicative acts would be merely random stimuli impinging upon sense modalities. The demands placed upon the receiver for accurate interpretation vary as some positive function of the complexity of the nervous system. In the more primitive life forms, where one finds both a high degree of selective attention and a restriction of possible responses, there is also a relatively straightforward series of events that intervene between the reception of a communication and the determination of a response. On the other hand, those forms with the more highly elaborated central nervous systems will bring to bear inferences both upon the interpretation of the communication and the formulation of an appropriate response. In short, complex nervous systems enhance behavioral plasticity.

To us, another interesting possibility is that with the evolution of complex nervous systems, the signals of animals come to serve more than just as information sources from which conspecifics might benefit. The signals come *to direct* the receivers to events from which other important information, not inherent in the initial communication, may be obtained. Once obtained, that information needs processing in a manner so that probability estimations emanating from inference can provide the foundations for adaptive responses. Thus, very rich social behavior, as with chimpanzees in the field, can be provided for, despite the absence of a formal language system, as used by man. The suggestion is that the chimpanzee's rich social behavior is possible because the chimpanzee is able to draw accurate inferences on the basis of information obtained by having its attention directed by signals to the important dynamics of each event, despite the fact that its signal system is relatively simple. Were the chimpanzee to have a public and formal language system, it would, of course, be able to do what man does—engage in the mutual and formal exchange of information, not necessarily dictated by the event of the moment, and engage mutually in assessments for the determination of appropriate responses, appropriate to other times and places.

However, the public and formal language systems are contingent upon more than primitive signal systems and the ability to draw inferences. Language requires the ability for two or more beings to be able to agree upon the meaning of a new signal or a new word that is to be added to the communication system. To do so requires an intellectual capacity of a high order, considerably higher than that of the chimpanzee. To be able to add new words or new signals would seemingly provide the base from which inevitably would emerge the abilities to concatenate word or signal order so as to modulate meaning through syntax.

In conclusion, our perspective regarding communication and language, which has been significantly shaped by Lana and other linguistically trained chimpanzees, includes the following:

1. Nonverbal and verbal communicative processes do overlap.
2. Both processes rely upon a similar cognitive base and, up to a certain point of complexity, either process can be used interchangeably.
3. The cognitive base that undergirds both verbal and nonverbal communication arises out of sensory–motor interaction with the animate and inanimate surroundings.
4. The grammar of sensory–motor interaction comes to serve as the basic structure or rule base for communicative interchange, both linguistic and nonverbal.
5. Neither process can be adequately understood if viewed merely as a series of chained sequential responses.
6. Experimental analysis of either verbal or nonverbal communication must deal with the semantics of the transmission and not with the set of all behavioral acts or the set of all words.
7. The evolution of the verbal system out of the nonverbal system can be seen in the distancing of event and representation of event which is found as communicative units move from elaborated social patterns to incipient acts to iconic gestures to arbitrary representations.

Given this perspective, what kinds of defensible deductions can presently be drawn from the chimpanzee language projects? Although chimpanzee language studies are still very new and the skills demonstrated by Washoe, Sarah, and Lana need to be more throughly studied and compared, it nevertheless seems fair to state that there are certain findings common to all of the ape language projects to date (see Rumbaugh, 1977, for review of these projects).

1. Apes are relatively facile in the learning of arbitrary representations (i.e., Ameslan signs, lexigrams, words). Their initial slow progress develops

into a skill that frequently allows for word meaning to be learned in a single presentation. Although their readiness both to learn and to use arbitrary representations can no longer be questioned, this is not to conclude that the meanings of words for apes are the same as those for man. They are sufficiently similar to permit interpretable conversations between the two species, but it is highly improbable that their meanings are identical to our own. In any event, ape linguistic abilities are still far below the level that would be required for an inter-species discussion of semantic nuances.

2. Apes spontaneously string word units (signs, lexigrams) together. Additionally, they can learn prescribed grammatical rules for ordering these strings, thereby demonstrating at least elementary syntactical ability.

3. Apes are able, without specific training, to extend their use of both words and ordering rules beyond the specific context in which these skills were acquired. Without this ability, the ape language projects would be little more than interesting demonstrations of rote learning, i.e., mastery of immutable response chains.

4. Apes have at least limited ability to use those labels which they have learned to produce new terms by combining two or more familiar ones. These new terms seem to reflect the salient characteristics of what they name. Examples of such label production include Lana's calling a Fanta orange drink *Coke which-is orange*, (Rumbaugh & Gill, Chapter 9, this volume), Washoe's signing "water bird" when asked to name a duck, and Lucy's calling a radish "cry hurt food" (Fouts, 1974).

Are these statements tantamount to ascertaining that chimpanzees are, indeed, using language? This is now a matter of choosing those aspects of human language which man wishes to emphasize. Chimpanzees do not employ the vocal modality linguistically, they do not spontaneously acquire language, they have not yet used embedded clauses, they have not yet mastered tenses, etc. These skills may or may not be acquired in the future, but the commonalities between human and chimpanzee language-linked cognitive processes remain and their implications are clear. Language as a form of communication is not totally unique. It is based upon cognitive processes that have emerged through the course of evolution and are common to both nonverbal and verbal exchanges. The chimpanzee language projects allow us to state that neither the public production of language nor the cognitive prerequisites for this production are uniquely human. For a completely unique trait, we shall have to look elsewhere.

PROJECTIONS OF APE LANGUAGE PROJECTS

The chimpanzee has already caused man to reassess himself in ways that a decade ago were not even contemplated. Where will the chimpanzee projects go in the future? What is their potential and what are their limitations? Such predictions inevitably entail an inherent risk, for scientific foresight in this field is notoriously incorrect. That risk notwithstanding, we offer the following prognostications.

First, the projects will continue to define the apes' abilities for a variety of additional linguistic functions. Quite likely, they will master the simple uses of the future and past tenses, as well as a host of other skills. As the apes master these linguistic functions, it can be anticipated that there will be considerable impact upon thought relative to how training programs might be devised for assisting, when necessary, the learning of language by the child and the brain-damaged adult.

Second, it seems inevitable that the nature and definition of language will be further influenced by the accretion of new knowledge regarding the apes' abilities for various linguistic functions and their appropriate use. Language in relation to intelligence and complex learning skills will receive considerable attention. The use of language skills in the solving of problems will be an important area of study that will include ape subjects.

Third, there is the hope that the apes might be cultivated as animal models so as to permit research into the parameters of initial language learning processes which, to date, are precluded by the ethical constraints we place upon the use of the human child in research programs. We cannot, of course, deny children the experiences of everyday life that might be germane to the emergence of initial linguistic skills. To be able to do so with the apes holds the promise of our gaining a better appreciation of the interface between cognition, social attachment processes, intelligence, and language learning. The use of chimpanzees as animal models could permit critical research regarding the determination of those conditions which must prevail lest no learning of language in a normal sense will ensue. That knowledge should be invaluable to efforts designed to facilitate language learning in the mentally retarded child.

Limitations of the ape projects are, perhaps, more difficult to define and to project. There are certain ones, however, that should be anticipated. It does not seem likely that the spontaneous processes of normal language mastery by normal children will be clarified by ape language work. Furthermore, it seems unlikely that man and ape will have protracted, in-depth conversations relative to various topics chosen by whim. The ape is not man. Its circumscribed intelligence relative to man's will certainly delimit its abilities to engage in heavy linguistic discourse.

To leave this section on a positive note and to be somewhat venturesome, we do not rule out the possibility that someday language-trained apes will accompany man to the field to facilitate field research and the interpretation of the apes' signal systems. If so, the ensuing problems of credits and coauthoring of reports by man and his ape colleagues will just have to be resolved, if not otherwise frankly enjoyed!

A FINAL PERSPECTIVE

The ape language projects have grown out of the evolutionary perspective of comparative psychology and the methods of experimental psychology. Were it not for the basic research of these areas, the excitement spawned by Projects Washoe, Sarah, and Lana might have eluded us.

The ape language projects have taken place, however, and are continuing into the indefinite future. How shall they affect our views of ourselves and our relationship to the world?

Clearly, the projects serve to narrow the gap between man and ape. Although the curtain for the opening of communication between man and ape is being drawn still in total silence, the linguistic exchanges that have and will continue to transpire will serve to underscore the close biological relationship between the two and man's being as a natural life form in a natural world. The projects neither diminish nor demean man; neither do they serve to elevate (or to demote) the ape to human status. Man and ape are both distinctive and unique. They shall remain thus, but perhaps even so, they will gain a mutual understanding as to who each is in relation to the other.

Man has never lacked in egocentricity. He has suffered from the obsession of needing to be different and somehow apart from the natural order. Some continue to search for the distinguishing characteristics which will set man apart from the beast, despite the fact that no one ever confuses man's mirror-reflected images with those of the apes. Neither tool-using skills (van Lawick-Goodall, 1970) nor language serves qualitatively to separate man and beast any more. What does? Let us offer a possible point of differentiation to those who feel the need for at least one.

Man is surely distinct among primates in that he, and he alone, both formalizes and legalizes his social order and his social codes. He is able to do so, of course, because of his facility for language. And with that facility, he defines and predicts for his own kind what will likely happen should each part of the code be breached.

Otherwise, through language man has served his ends, both for good and for bad. Through it, he has been able to make long-term predictions in relation to events that took place eons ago. Perhaps, in the appreciation of the passage of time in that perspective, he alone has become sensitive to his individual demise and, to compensate therefore, has worked apace to collapse the living of an eternity into the brief span of a single lifetime.

BIBLIOGRAPHY

Altmann, S. A. The structure of primate social communication. In S. A. Altmann (Ed.), *Social communication among primates*. Chicago: University of Chicago Press, 1967.

Altmann, S. A. Primates. In T. A. Sebeok (Ed.), *Animal communication: Techniques of study and results of research.* Bloomington, Indiana: Indiana University Press, 1968.

Chevalier-Skolnikoff, S. The ontogeny of communication in the stumptail macaque (*Macaca arctoides*). In *Contributions to primatology,* Vol. II. Basel: S. Karger, 1974.

Chomsky, N. *Language and mind.* New York: Harcourt, Brace, Jovanovich, 1968.

Ekman, P. Universals and cultural differences in facial expression of emotion. In J. K. Cole (Ed.), *Nebraska symposium on motivation.* Lincoln, Nebraska: University of Nebraska Press, 1972.

Fouts, R. S. Acquisition and testing of gestural signs in four young chimpanzees. *Science,* 1973, *180,* 978–980.

Fouts, R. S. Language: Origins, definition and chimpanzees. *Journal of Human Evolution,* 1974, *3,* 475–482.

Fox, M. J., & Skolnick, B. P. Language in education: Problems and prospects in research and training. A Ford Foundation Report, New York, 1975.

Furness, W. H. *Proceedings from the American Philosophical Society,* 1916, *55,* 281.

Gallup, G. G., Jr. Chimpanzees: Self-recognition. *Science,* 1969, *167,* 86–87.

Gardner, B. T., & Gardner, R. A. Two-way communications with an infant chimpanzee. In A. M. Schrier & F. Stollnitz (Eds.), *Behavior of nonhuman primates,* Vol. 4. New York: Academic Press, 1971.

Gardner, B. T., & Gardner, R. A. Evidence for sentence consitutents in the early utterances of child and chimpanzee. *Journal of Experimental Psychology: General,* 1975, *104,* 244–267. (a)

Gardner, R. A., & Gardner, B. T. Teaching sign language to a chimpanzee. *Science,* 1969, *165,* 664–672.

Gardner, R. A., & Gardner, B. T. Early signs of language in child and chimpanzee. *Science,* 1975, *187,* 752–753. (b)

Gill, T. V., & Rumbaugh, D. M. Mastery of naming skills by a chimpanzee. *Journal of Human Evolution,* 1974, *3,* 483–492.

Hockett, C. F. Logical considerations in the study of animal communication. In W. E. Lanyon & W. N. Tavolga (Eds.), *Animal sounds and animal communication.* Washington, D. C.: American Institute of Biological Sciences, 1960.

Hockett, C. F., & Altmann, S. A. A note on design features. In T. A. Sebeok (Ed.), *Animal communication: Techniques of study and results of research.* Bloomington, Indiana: Indiana University Press, 1968.

Hughes, J., & Redshaw, M. The psychological development of two infant gorilla: A preliminary report. *Animal Report of the New Jersey Wildlife Preservation Trust,* 1973, *10,* 34–36.

Hughes, J., & Redshaw, M. Cognitive, manipulative and social skills in gorilla. *Annual Report of the New Jersey Wildlife Preservation Trust,* 1974, *11,* 53–60.

Lancaster, J. B. *Primate behavior and the emergence of human culture.* New York: Holt, Rinehart & Winston, 1975.

McGinnis, P. K. Patterns of sexual behavior in a community of free-living chimpanzees. Unpublished doctoral dissertation, Darwin College, 1972.

Menzel, E. W., & Johnson, M. C. Communication and cognitive organization in humans and other animals. Paper presented at the New York Academy of Sciences, New York, September 1975.

Miller, N. E. Extensions of liberalized S–R theory. In S. Koch (Ed.), *Psychology: A study of a science.* Vol. 2: *General systematic formulations, learning, and special processes.* New York: McGraw-Hill, 1959.

Moore, T. E. Introduction. In T. E. Moore (Ed.), *Cognitive development and the acquisition of language.* New York: Academic Press, 1973.

Nottebohm, F. The origins of vocal learning. *The American Naturalist,* 1972, *106,* 116–140.

Osgood, C. E. A behavioristic analysis of perception and language as cognitive phenomena. *Contemporary approaches to cognition: A symposium held at the University of Colorado.* Cambridge, Massachusetts: Harvard University Press, 1957.

Parker, C. H. The antecedents of man the manipulator. *Journal of Human Evolution,* 1974, *3,* 493–500.

Patterson, F. The gestures of a gorilla: Language acquisition in another pongoid species. In D. Hamburg, J. Goodall, & R. E. McCown (Eds.), *Perspectives on human evolution,* Vol. 5. Menlo Park: Benjamin, in press.

Piaget, J. *The origins of intelligence in children.* New York: International Universities Press, 1952.

Piaget, J. Operational structures of intelligence and organic controls. In A. G. Karczmer and J. C. Eccks (Eds.) *Brain and human behavior.* New York: Springer-Verlag, 1972.

Premack, D. On the assessment of language competence in the chimpanzee. In A. M. Schrier & F. Stollnitz (Eds.), *Behavior of nonhuman primates: Modern research trends,* Vol. 4. New York: Academic Press, 1971.

Rumbaugh, D. M. Language behavior. In A. M. Schrier (Ed.), *Behavioral primatology: Advances in research,* Vol. 1. Hillsdale, New Jersey: Lawrence Erlbaum Associates, 1977.

Savage, E. S., & Bakeman, R. Sexual morphism and behavior in *Pan paniscus.* Paper presented at the 6th International Congress on Primatology, Cambridge, September 1976.

Scott, W. J. Message-meaning analysis. In T. A. Sebeok (Ed.), *Animal communication: Techniques of study and results of research.* Bloomington: Indiana University Press, 1968.

Sebeok, T. A. Animal communication: A communication network for language as applied to signaling behavior in animals. *Science,* 1965, *147, 1006–1014.*

Smith, E. O. Unpublished doctoral dissertation, University of Ohio, 1976.

Smith, W. J. Messages of vertebrate communication. *Science, 165,* 1969, 145–150.

Terrace, H., & Bever, T. *What might be learned from studying language in a chimpanzee.* Paper presented at the Conference on Origins and Evolution of Language and Speech, New York, September 1975.

Toulmin, S. Brain and language: A commentary. *Synthese,* 1971, *22,* 369–395.

van Lawick-Goodall, J. The behavior of free-living chimpanzees in the Gombe Stream Reserve. *Animal Behavior Monographs,* 1968, *1,* 161–311.

van Lawick-Goodall, J. Tool-using in primates and other vertebrates. *Advances in the Study of Behavior,* 1970, *3,* 195–249.

von Glasersfeld, E. C. The Yerkish language for nonhuman primates. *American Journal of Computational Linguistics,* 1975, Microfiche 12.

Warner, H., Bell, C. L., Rumbaugh, D. M., & Gill, T. V. Computer-controlled teaching instrumentation for linguistic studies with great apes. *IEEE Transactions on Computers,* 1976, *C-25,* 38–43.

Warren, J. M. Possibly unique characteristics of learning by primates. *Journal of Human Evolution,* 1974, *3,* 445–454.

Wechsler, D. Intelligence defined and undefined: A relativistic appraisal. *American Psychologist,* 1975, *30,* 135–139.

Werner, H., & Kaplan, B. *Symbol formation: An organismic-developmental approach to language and the expression of thought.* New York: John Wiley & Sons, 1963.

Wickelgren, W. Memory. In J. A. Swets & L. L. Elliot (Eds.), *Psychology and the handicapped child.* Washington, D. C.: U.S. Government Printing Office, 1974.

Witner, L. *Psychological Clinic,* 1909, *3,* 179–205.

Yeni-Komshian, G. H., & Benson, D. A. Anatomical study of cerebral asymmetry in the temporal lobe of humans, chimpanzees and rhesus monkeys. *Science,* 1976, *192,* 387–389.

Chronological Bibliography of LANA Project Publications

Rumbaugh, D. M., von Glasersfeld, E. C., Gill, T. V., Warner, H., Pisani, P., Brown, J. V., & Bell, C. L. A computer-controlled language training system for investigating the language skills of young apes. *Behavioral Research Methods and Instrumentation*, 1973, *5*, 385–392.

Rumbaugh, D. M., von Glasersfeld, E. C., Warner, H., Pisani, P., Gill, T. V., Brown, J. V., & Bell, C. L. Exploring the language skills of Lana chimpanzee. *International Journal of Symbology*, 1973, *4*, 1–9.

Rumbaugh, D. M., Gill, T. V., & von Glasersfeld, E. C. Reading and sentence completion by a chimpanzee (*Pan*). *Science*, 1973, *182*, 731–733.

Rumbaugh, D. M., Gill, T. V., and von Glasersfeld, E. C. A rejoinder to language in man, monkeys, and machine. *Science*, 1974, *185*, 871–872.

Rumbaugh, D. M., von Glasersfeld, E. C., Warner, H., Pisani, P., and Gill, T. V. Lana (chimpanzee) learning language: A progress report. *Brain and Language*, 1974, *1*, 205–212.

Gill, T. V., & Rumbaugh, D. M. Mastery of naming skills by a chimpanzee. *Journal of Human Evolution*, 1974, *3*, 483–492.

von Glasersfeld, E. Signs, communication, and language. *Journal of Human Evolution*, 1974, *3*, 465–474.

von Glasersfeld, E. The Yerkish language for non-human primates. *American Journal of Computational Linguistics*, 1974, *1*, microfiche 12.

Rumbaugh, D. M., Gill, T. V., Language, apes, and the apple which-is orange, please. In S.

Kondo, M. Kawai, A. Ehara, & S. Kawamura (Eds.), *Proceedings from the Symposia of the Fifth Congress of the International Primatological Society.* Tokyo: Japan Science Press, 1975. Pp. 247–257.

Rumbaugh, D. M., Gill, T. V., von Glasersfeld, E. C., Warner, H., & Pisani, P. Conversations with a chimpanzee in a computer-controlled environment. *Biological Psychiatry*, 1975, *10*, 627–641.

Rumbaugh, D. M., von Glasersfeld, E. C., Gill, T. V., Warner, H., Pisani, P., Brown, J., & Bell, C. L. The language skills of a young chimpanzee in a computer-controlled training situation. In Russell H. Tuttle (Ed.), *Socioecology and psychology of primates.* The Hague: Mouton, 1975, Pp. 391–401.

Warner, H., Bell C. L., Rumbaugh, D. M., & Gill, T. V. Computer-controlled teaching instrumentation for linguistic studies with great apes. *IEEE Transactions on Computers*, 1976, *25*, 38–43.

Rumbaugh, D. M., & Gill, T. V. Language and the acquisition of language-type skills by a chimpanzee *(Pan).* In K. Salzinger (Ed.), *Psychology in progress, 270.* New York: Annals of the New York Academy of Science, 1976.

von Glasersfeld, E. The development of language as purposive behavior. In H. Steklis, S. Harnad, & Jane Lancaster (Eds.), *Origins and evolution of language and speech, 280.* New York: Annals of the New York Academy of Sciences, 1976.

Rumbaugh, D. M., & Gill, T. V. Lana's mastery of language skills. In H. Steklis, S. Harnad, & Jane Lancaster (Eds.), *Origins and evolution of language and speech, 280.* New York: Annals of the New York Academy of Sciences, 1976.

Rumbaugh, D. M. Language behavior of apes. In A. M. Schrier (Ed.), *Behavioral primatology: Advances in research and theory.* Hillsdale, New Jersey: Lawrence Erlbaum Associates, Inc., 1977.

Rumbaugh, D. M., & Gill, T. V. Language and language-type communication: Studies with a chimpanzee. In M. Lewis & L. Rosenblum (Eds.), *Communication and language: The origins of behavior,* Vol. 5. New York, Wiley, 1977.

A
B 7
C 8
D 9
E 0
F 1
G 2
H 3
I 4
J 5